Managing Acquisitions

Managing
Acquisitions

Creating Value Through
Corporate Renewal

Philippe C. Haspeslagh
David B. Jemison

THE FREE PRESS
A Division of Macmillan, Inc.
NEW YORK

Collier Macmillan Canada
TORONTO

Maxwell Macmillan International
NEW YORK   OXFORD   SINGAPORE   SYDNEY

The Free Press
A Division of Macmillan, Inc.
866 Third Avenue, New York, N.Y. 10022

Collier Macmillan Canada, Inc.
1200 Eglinton Avenue East
Suite 200
Don Mills, Ontario M3C 3N1

Printed in the United States of America

printing number

1 2 3 4 5 6 7 8 9 10

Library of Congress Cataloging-in-Publication Data

Haspeslagh, Philippe C.
　　Managing acquisitions: creating value through corporate renewal /
Philippe C. Haspeslagh, David B. Jemison.
　　　　p.　　cm.
　　Includes bibliographical references and index.
　　ISBN 0–02–914165–6
　　1. Organizational change—Management.　2. Consolidation and merger
of corporations—Management.　3. Corporate reorganizations—
Management.　　I. Jemison, David B.　　II. Title.
HD58.8.H377　　1991
658.1′6—dc20　　　　　　　　　　　　　　　　　　　　90–45945
　　　　　　　　　　　　　　　　　　　　　　　　　　　CIP

Contents

Preface

THE WORLD OF THE MODERN CORPORATION IS being transformed by mergers and acquisitions. As they continue, acquisitions are at the center of controversy among managers, public policy makers, and academics about their purpose, motives, contributions, and impact on society. Yet despite all this attention, we know very little about what makes acquisitions succeed or fail.

This book is about developing a better understanding of how to make mergers and acquisitions work. The primary message from our research is that managers can improve their success with acquisitions by developing a better understanding of the decision-making and integration processes and by developing the organizational capacity to adopt a strategic perspective on acquisitions.

We propose an expanded perspective on acquisitions that puts strategic, financial, and organizational considerations into the context of the decision-making and integration processes through which they are developed and by which their success or failure is determined.

This book itself is the result of a merger between the research of two authors, one on each side of the Atlantic, who had set out to better understand the factors associated with successful and unsuccessful acquisitive strategies. Combined it represents eight collective years of research involving more than 300 interviews in 20 firms.

Jemison conducted two distinct studies on acquisitions. In a first study carried out in 1983–1984, in collaboration with Sim Sitkin, broad, cross-sectional interviews were used to develop an understanding of the acquisition decision process and of the problems involved. Initial field research was conducted in the United States, Great Britain, and France among experienced acquisitive companies and their advisory firms (e.g., investment banks, consulting firms, auditors, attorneys) to learn about the factors that contributed to acquisition success and failure. Many of the basic insights of the process perspective and identification of problems in the acquisition decision-making process were developed from this study.

Next, Jemison explored the integration process in depth in another clinical field study of seven acquisitions and mergers among twelve firms, for which the field work took place in 1984–1985. These acquisitions were chosen to better understand what happened in related business acquisitions when firms had to transfer skills, knowledge, resources, and ways of managing to improve their relative competitive positions. This study led to an overall model of the integration process and insights into the integration problems that managers encounter as they try to improve their competitive position by transferring capabilities between acquired and acquiring firms.

Research for Philippe Haspeslagh's project on acquisitive renewal strategies was conducted from 1985 to 1989 in the context of INSEAD's Management of Technology and Innovation program. It involved three phases. The first phase, from 1985 to 1987, was a detailed investigation of both the acquisition decision-making and integration processes in a structured sample of acquisitions within three large companies in the broadly defined chemical sector: ICI, British Petroleum, and an American firm disguised as "Unichem." In these companies a matched sample was identified of both highly successful and unsuccessful acquisitions in each of three categories: acquisitions in a core business, acquisitions related to a core business, and acquisitions into completely new areas.

The acquisition decision and integration processes were longitudinally traced in detail in eleven acquisition cases. A structured comparison between successful and unsuccessful integration processes of different types led to a contingent framework of acquisition integration approaches, for which the respective metaphors of absorption, preservation, and symbiosis were selected. These integration approaches were juxtaposed with the integration process problems identified by Jemison to identify ways to address these problems.

During 1987–1988, in a second phase of the project, this integration framework was tested and refined through a similar investigation of three more acquisitions in a fourth chemical company, the German BASF AG. A comparison of the acquisition decision-making practices of all four of these experienced acquirers led to the insights in how to overcome decision-making problems such as those identified by Jemison and Sitkin and how to manage the acquisition decision process.

In a third phase of the INSEAD project during 1988–1989, Haspeslagh examined the acquisitions of a number of firms in other industries in a field study. This research was focused on how the corporate-level approach to acquisitions had evolved inside firms that had used acquisitions to assemble leading positions in rapidly restructuring industries. This continuing work on such "strategic assemblers" as the Swedish Electrolux in white goods or the Finnish Valmet in paper machinery is directed at identifying the strategic and organizational challenges beyond acquisition management and the linkage between acquisitive development and multinational competitiveness.

In total we studied in-depth acquisitions in ten countries: the United States, Great Britain, France, Italy, Germany, Japan, Switzerland, Sweden, Finland, and the Netherlands, ranging in size from $3 million to $1 billion. (See Appendix A for a detailed description of our research method and the firms we studied.)

Like any merger, the integration process in writing this book took longer than expected, involved a lot of time and energy, and required attention to detail. As is often the case, it was greatly fostered by the extent to which both sides in the merger shared an overriding interest, in our case the importance of pursuing research questions from a general management perspective. As in any merger, neither all the problems nor all of the benefits of the integration were fully foreseen at the time of the decision to collaborate. Indeed, like many of the acquisitions we studied, the process of collaboration forced us to refine and sharpen our insights in a way that we would have been unable to do independently.

A number of people have contributed to our quest to better understand how acquisitions work. While the support of each is appreciated, several of them deserve special mention.

Philippe Haspeslagh owes tremendously in his development as an educator in this area to Dominique Heau, who in 1981 founded with him INSEAD's Strategic Issues in Mergers and Acquisitions program (SIMA), and with whom some of his early acquisition cases were written. The clarity of Dominique's critique on an earlier draft of our manuscript was a tall order to live up to.

To Alison Farquhar, his research associate on the project during 1986–1988, Haspeslagh owes a special credit. Not only was she widely involved in the interviewing process, but her intellectual rigor, critical mind, and common sense were equally invaluable in the analysis process. She cowrote a first paper on the contingent framework for integration, as well as several teaching cases on the basis of the research material including the "Francoplast" series; "ICI: The Beatrice Acquisition"; and "BASF: The Inmont Acquisition."

Other research assistants who provided important assistance to Haspeslagh with parts of the study include Roselle Bruce-Jardine for work on BP Nutrition, Sarah Williams on "The European Hydrocarbon Company," and Chris Taubmann and Dana Hyde, who are currently assisting to extend this work in the insurance and banking sectors.

David Jemison is particularly grateful for the collaboration of Sim Sitkin during the early phase of his research stream. Sim is an ideal colleague—intellectually curious, energetic, and scrupulously disciplined in his pursuit of questions at the intersection of managerial practice and management theory. Sim was involved in the development of the early work and ideas about the importance of the acquisition decision-making process and how this may have affected acquisition outcomes. This collaboration resulted in the publication of papers in the *Academy of Management Review* and *Harvard Business Review* that launched the study of the process perspective on acquisitions.

It is always particularly pleasant to be able to work with colleagues with complementary interests, particularly if they share your values; Philippe Haspeslagh thanks his INSEAD colleagues Yves Doz and Sumantra Ghoshal. With Yves he has made a joint examination of the complementarity between internal venturing and acquisitive development in the context of the "European Hydrocarbon Company." And with Sumantra Ghoshal, he was able to explore the transition from acquisitive development to ongoing multinational management in the context of Electrolux.

We appreciate the assistance of Kim Williams in helping develop Appendix B and Vincent Cellard, who helped develop Appendix C.

The ideas in this book evolved as they were tested on our colleagues and on practicing executives in different settings including the academic journal review process, presentations at professional society meetings, management development programs, and with management teams in individual firms. Several colleagues and friends were especially helpful in the development of our ideas. Yves Doz, George Foster, Sumantra Ghoshal, Martine Van den Poel, and Steve Wheelwright provided continuing and lasting encouragement for us to pursue these questions. Our thanks for critical review and questioning of the ideas also go to the experienced managers in INSEAD's SIMA program with whom both of us have been able to interact extensively.

Major projects such as this are not possible without financial support to visit research sites; to have time to write in an academic schedule; and to travel to collaborate and write together. For their help in securing financial support, as well as their encouragement, we would like to thank Deans Bob Witt at Texas; Bob Jaedicke and Chuck Holloway at Stanford; and Philippe Naert and Claude Rameau at INSEAD; as well as the Japan-American Foundation and INSEAD's Management of Technology and Innovation (MTI) program.

We owe special debt to the executives who gave us their time and access to their firms. The rich access to the basic data from which our insights were developed would not have been possible without the support and interest of these executives in the research. Moreover their candor; their willingness to share insights with us; their willingness to participate in multiple, lengthy interviews; and their help in finding a particular colleague who could give us insights into an important question paved the way for our work. A few of these executives appear in the book because we selected their acquisition to illustrate our ideas. Our thanks go equally to the many executives who do not appear in name for reasons of confidentiality, redundancy, or space. They may recognize themselves in some of the incidents we describe or in the lessons we drew from some of the cases that were illustrated in detail.

During the process by which our insights were developed and the book was written, a number of colleagues gave us detailed, critical feedback on academic papers, chapters in various stages of completion, or the entire manuscript. In addition to those already mentioned we greatly benefited from the insightful comments of Ana Adaniya, David Bastien, Norm Berg, Bob Choplin, Karel Cool, Syd Finkelstein, Jim Fredrickson, Armando Gallegos, Don Hambrick, John Kimberly, Tom Lenz, Michael Lubatkin, Amy Pablo, Mal Salter, Mark Shanley, and Harbir Singh. While their insights and critique sharpened our thinking and improved our logic, we bear full responsibility for the book, its arguments, errors, and omissions.

We owe a great deal to our families. They endured many weeks of travel for data gathering, many more weeks of inattention because we had to "work on the book," and more than a little frustration when we often decided that we weren't quite yet finished. Their love and support make life worthwhile. It is to Martine, Frederik, and Sophie and to Kelley, Zack, and Emily that our respective efforts are dedicated.

Fontainebleau, France
Austin, Texas
June 1990

PHILIPPE C. HASPESLAGH
DAVID B. JEMISON

Acquisitions and Value Creation

1

Mastering the Acquisition Process

The Key to Value Creation

ACQUISITIONS HAVE a unique potential to transform firms and to contribute to corporate renewal. They can help a firm renew its market positions at a speed not achievable through internal development. They can provide an ability to gain all the benefits from combining assets and sharing capabilities in a way not obtainable through partnerships. More profoundly, however, acquisitions can bring into a company capabilities the organization finds hard to develop, or they can provide the opportunity to leverage existing capabilities into much more significant positions.

The aim of this book is to help unshackle the potential of mergers and acquisitions by providing a perspective that differs from the prevailing financial, or even strategic, views.[1] Our primary message is that key differences between acquisition success and failure lie in understanding and better managing the *processes* by which acquisition decisions are made and by which they are integrated.

Our arguments are directed to managers, executives, and directors of firms whose acquisitions are driven by strategic, not simply financial, motives for corporate renewal. They also address the interests of scholars concerned with how strategic factors, organizational factors, and performance interact in acquisitions.

3

THE ACQUISITIVE PHENOMENON

In the past, acquisitions tended to come in distinct waves, but in the eighties acquisitions became an increasingly broad-based phenomenon as firms renewed their competitive positions, as industry after industry went through its own wave of restructuring, and as acquisition activity spread across the globe.[2] Although it is too early to tell to whether the current level of acquisitive activity will continue or is just another wave, its composition is more varied and its nature more international than those of earlier waves.

In the United States, acquisition transactions in excess of $35 million increased from $186.4 billion in 1985 to $234.1 billion in 1989.[3] Of these totals, acquisitions by European firms accounted for $28.8 billion, or 12.3 percent, compared with $4.5 billion in 1985, a figure that represented 2.4 percent then. Recently Japanese firms have begun to make acquisitions in the United States, moving from $126.5 million in 1985 to $7 billion in 1989, which is still only 3 percent of all acquisition transactions. Notwithstanding the publicity received by hostile takeovers during the period, the number of hostile bids in the United States was relatively small. During the period 1985–1989 there were only 114 such hostile takeover contests with a purchase price of more than $50 million. Of these, only thirty-eight were ultimately acquired.[4]

In Europe, acquisition activity has not traditionally been as intense as it has been in the United States. Only Great Britain has an American-style market for corporate control. Yet with $87.1 billion of recorded acquisitions in 1989, European acquisition activity had increased eightfold since 1985, a figure that might be underestimated, given the less complete reporting of transactions involving privately held firms. In terms of value, cross-border acquisitions had risen from 13 percent in 1985 to 36 percent in 1989, as the move to an integrated Europe gathered steam toward a unified market in 1992.[5] Strong regional differences persisted, born out of different traditions and regulatory contexts.[6]

In the meantime, Japan, which historically had known acquisitions mainly as an orderly rescue for troubled firms, was warming up to acquisitive development. The number of acquisitions involving Japanese companies increased from 289 in 1985 to 660 in 1989. Of this 1989 total, only fifteen were acquisitions by foreign companies in Japan.[7]

In sum, going into the nineties, the acquisition phenomenon appeared increasingly broad based, fragmented, and global. Yet the issue of making acquisitions work has been relatively ignored by the academic literature, as well as by the media coverage of large takeovers. Ironically, while the public's attention has been turned to raiders, hostile take-overs, and financial acquisitions, the great preponderance of acquisitions in the United States and the United Kingdom, and almost all the activity in Continental Europe and Japan, has been strategic, generally amicable, and among firms and management groups who have neither sought nor encouraged publicity.[8] Public attention is focused on the wrong issues for understandable reasons. After all, hostile takeovers by rapacious acquirers make far more interesting stories than friendly divisional acquisitions that contribute to the patient renewal of a firm's capabilities and competitive position.

THE DEBATE ABOUT ACQUISITIONS

Acquisitions have engendered an important debate among managers, public policy makers, and academics about their effects on, and importance to, economic welfare. Most of the academic research on acquisitions focuses on the financial impact of acquisition transactions, logical prescriptions for screening acquisition candidates, or the effect of acquisitions on the people or communities involved. While these issues are clearly complex, there is common agreement that from the perspective of the acquiring company, many acquisitions fail to accomplish their purpose. But the factors associated with these disappointing acquisition experiences are not addressed. We suggest that a focus on the pre-acquisition decision making and the post-acquisition integration processes will lead to new insights into how acquisitions can be used more effectively for strategic renewal.

PROBLEMS IN ACQUISITION DECISION MAKING

The problems frequently presented by pre-acquisition decision making are not self-evident. Whatever the pressures for time and secrecy that surround acquisition decisions, companies and managers do not make such decisions lightly, and they expend substantial resources to make the best decision possible. Yet they readily acknowledge frustrations with the process, as illustrated by this manager, whose acquisition we studied:

> The speed with which things took place was mind-boggling. If
> we had done that sort of quickie analysis for a capital expendi-

ture decision, the board's audit committee would have been down around our ears in a minute.

Chief financial officer of an acquiring firm

In an environment often characterized by real or perceived pressures for speed and secrecy, many managers and specialists engage not only in a process of analysis and evaluation, but also in a process of internal selling and negotiation, the outcome of which is not only an agreement to bid a certain price, but also a much more complex view of how the acquisition will be justified. As our research has revealed, despite all formal analysis and due process, the quality of that justification is often wanting, as acknowledged by another manager we interviewed:

> A big justification for the merger was to cross-sell to each other's customers. But we made money in such different ways [fee for service versus interest income] that . . . nobody spoke the same language. Ultimately, we discovered that the fundamental characteristics of our customer bases were quite different and there wasn't nearly as much overlap as we had originally thought or hoped for.
>
> Senior executive of an acquiring bank

THE PROBLEMS OF INTEGRATION

Decision-making problems are only a part of the story. Even if an acquisition opportunity is sound, the expected synergies have to be realized during the integration phase. Here, too, the contrast in experiences is stark. Consider the following comments from firms that were less experienced in acquisitions:

> The chairman and president brought the top 10 people from both firms together and told us that we had a lot of potential if we could merge product lines and use each other's systems. They then told us that although there would be some start-up costs, they were confident that synergies would more than outweigh these and that we shouldn't have a performance dip. After they left the room, the two sides sat staring at each other, wondering why we were there and how we were going to make it work.
>
> Executive from an acquired financial services firm

> We were cast adrift . . . there was no support for us within the parent firm and nobody understood what we were. This was OK

until the managers sent by the parent arrived with no instructions about what to do except make money.

Manager in a finance company acquired by a bank

The lack of direction that comes through in these remarks contrasts
sharply with the sense of purpose that stands out in comments by
experienced acquirers:

We knew from day one that they had to retain their entrepreneurial, market-oriented culture and be run at arm's length. Yet
at the same time, we had to find ways to get the synergy.

Manager in ICI after the Beatrice Chemicals acquisition

When we make an acquisition, we adopt a centralized approach
from the outset. We have a definite plan worked out when we
go in, and there is virtually no need for extended discussions.

Manager in Electrolux after acquiring Zanussi

A lot of the success [with the integration] stemmed from the
[negotiation of a] policy statement. The statement itself went
into the drawer and never came out again. Its importance was
that through protracted negotiations over every clause, each
side came to understand the primary concerns of the other, and
most importantly that trust and commitment was built up.

Managing Director, British Petroleum's Nutrition business

Why do some companies seem to handle acquisition decisions well
when others do not? Why are some able to provide direction to integration efforts where others fail? In this book we describe the process
by which value is created by firms, explore the ways in which acquisitions can contribute to value creation, and then address solutions to
problems that management teams encounter when they use acquisitions
as part of their overall corporate renewal strategies. Understanding this
process of value creation, however, will require a shift in conception of
the firm from a focus on immediate financial outcomes or current
product-market positions to the capabilities that underlie these positions
or financial results in the long term.

KEY CHALLENGES IN MANAGING ACQUISITIONS

Our research has identified four common challenges in managing acquisitions:

- Ensuring that acquisitions support the firm's overall corporate renewal strategy.
- Developing a pre-acquisition decision-making process that will allow consideration of the "right" acquisitions and that will develop for any particular acquisition a meaningful justification, given limited information and the need for speed and secrecy.
- Managing the post-acquisition integration process to create the value hoped for when the acquisition was conceived.
- Fostering both acquisition-specific and broader organizational learning from the exposure to the acquisition

The variety and range of issues involved in strategic acquisitions are quite broad, as illustrated by the following example.

Strategic Acquisitions: The Case of BASF

For senior managers in BASF, one of Germany's diversified chemical giants, the spring of 1985 was a fascinating time. The *Vorstand*, as the management committee of German companies is called, was considering three different acquisition opportunities in the United States. The combined value of these acquisitions was $1.3 billion, which would significantly shift the geographic and business portfolio of the group.

One involved a bid for Inmont, the U.S. paint manufacturer. The acquisition would bring capabilities to project BASF's Paints division into one of the top three positions in the automotive paints sector, which was becoming increasingly concentrated and global (PPG and Du Pont were the other leading companies). At the same time, however, Inmont's printing ink businesses would present a considerable organizational challenge in an area where BASF was present but had had, until now, limited ambitions. The auction of Inmont involved many of BASF's traditional competitors, including ICI and Akzo.

Akzo, considered one of the most eager candidate buyers for Inmont, was at the same time the prospective seller in a second acquisition decision BASF was facing: the purchase of American Enka's fiber business. The logic here was quite straightforward: Enka's Fibres business strengthened BASF's vertically integrated position in the U.S.-fibers market and provided captive use for the company's American caprolactam facilities.

The third acquisition, a bid for Celanese Corporation's advanced composites businesses, was quite different. Whereas current applications of advanced composites were mainly in aerospace and military and civilian aviation, future applications foreseen for this industry were vast. These composites would provide high-performance substitutes for higher-volume automotive components and other applications. Despite its early position, Celanese had decided it could not wait for the payoffs from its investment to come. BASF, like other bidders, had to decide whether it was willing to pay a big premium for the opportunity to make the future investments required to develop the capabilities it would need to remain a key player in this emerging industry.

These three acquisitions illustrate the interwoven nature of strategic acquisition and divestiture activity among firms, not only in the chemical industry, but in a vast array of fields ranging from power equipment to consumer goods to financial services to publishing to transportation. Above all, they illustrate how the over-publicized deal-making aspect is only the tip of the iceberg in terms of the challenges faced by managers who make strategic acquisitions.

CHALLENGE #1: CONSISTENCY WITH STRATEGY

Acquisitions are strategic decisions that can both reinforce and change a firm's direction. But ensuring that acquisition decisions are consistent with strategy is difficult, no matter how clear top management is about its current strategy or how disciplined a strategic planning process a company has. Individual acquisition opportunities call a firm's strategy into question almost as often as they fit with it. When should acquisition opportunities that fall outside the scope of the strategy be discarded, and when should they be embraced as a new potential thrust for the firm? Each of the three BASF acquisitions is an example of this ambiguous relationship between acquisitions and strategy:

• The Enka acquisition was fairly straightforward as a logical way of implementing the company's well-defined strategy of building a strong vertically integrated position in the United States.

• The Inmont acquisition opportunity, on the other hand, did not fit with the recently approved strategy for the Paints Division. The company had already tried to penetrate the U.S. automotive paints market on a much smaller scale through Glasurit America Inc. But in absence of a realistic chance to acquire significant market share, since then the division manager had received approval for a more modest European strategy. Now, with Inmont as a possibility, the board encouraged him not only to analyze Inmont, but also redefine a new divisional strategy including a much higher use of the group's cash flow.

• The Celanese acquisition, on the other hand, was in an area where the group did not yet have significant resources, apart from its considerable R&D competence. It represented a business where detailed strategic plans would seem mere fictions, given the uncertainties involved. Ultimately the decision would have to be based on the managers' trust in their vision for this field of advanced composites and their willingness to invest in the experience and capabilities they would need to become a player in that industry. It is a commitment that BASF, along with some other companies like Hoechst, ICI, and British Petroleum, has been willing to make, while other firms have stayed out or sold their businesses because they could not justify their activities in advanced composites on a classic net present value basis.

Most of the managers we interviewed were searching for an appropriate balance between opportunism and planning in acquisitions and the extent to which acquisition strategies could be pinned down specifically enough for financial valuation. They were often at pains to reconcile their confidence in the strategic logic of an acquisition and its demonstrable discounted cash-flow numbers. The need to manage the complex relationships among a firm's strategy, the uncertainties associated with its acquisitions, and the pressure for results is one of the themes of this book.

Challenge #2: Quality of Acquisition Decision Making

Many of the managers we observed did not pause to consider how their decision-making process affected either their decision or the acquisition outcome itself. Somehow the justification process inside the company, involving many managers and specialists from inside and outside the firm, often seemed to turn into a sparring match between the acquisition champion and other managers. The champion was out to sell the idea, while the other managers, each from their own perspectives, were erecting hurdles to clear. The resulting justification might have been clear in terms of the financial numbers that supported the price, but strategic and organizational considerations were by no means clarified to the same extent.

Some companies, even with limited time, were able to consider a complex acquisition and develop an understanding and a common view both of the benefits to be expected and the costs. These firms tended to have as much discussion about the risks involved and how to manage them as about how the benefits would be created. They were also able to consider the organizational requirements and consequences of the acquisition. In contrast, other firms spent as much time and money as their counterparts and involved just as many people, but their efforts resulted in shallow acquisition justifications into which different groups of managers could read their own priorities.

Making acquisition decisions is never easy—there are always uncertainties. Another challenge we explore in this book is how a firm can discipline itself to develop meaningful acquisition justifications despite the uncertainties, pressures, and limitations inherent in the acquisition decision-making process.

Challenge #3: Capability to Integrate

Many acquisitions look great on paper. Yet no matter how attractive the opportunity, value is not created until after the acquisition, when capabilities are transferred and people from both organizations collaborate to create the expected benefits or to discover others. This collaboration relies on the will and ability of managers in both organizations to work together toward a new strategic task. All too often, firms forgo the benefits of an acquisition by insisting on compliance with a predetermined path or, to the contrary, by avoiding changes in the acquired company that would minimize resistance and disruption. The key to integration is to obtain the participation of the people involved without compromising the strategic task.

Our research found that acquisition integration involves several challenges: adapting pre-acquisition views to embrace reality, an ability to create the atmosphere necessary for capability transfer, the leadership to provide a common vision, and careful management of the interactions between the organizations. However, because there are many purposes for acquisitions, there is no one best way to integrate. Later we will consider how integration takes place, how it can be better managed, and how it varies under different circumstances.

Challenge #4: Capacity for Learning

The acquisitions we examined gave executives unique opportunities to learn (which were sometimes expensive) as they moved their firms into situations outside their regular strategic, organizational, and cultural contexts. One type of learning opportunity was acquisition-specific.

This learning related to how to handle acquisitions and which acquisitions to avoid. In some firms an explicit effort was made and mechanisms were created to derive such learning systematically from each acquisition. In others, by contrast, business managers were left to learn from their own experience, or hasty generalizations were drawn after limited exposure to what had actually happened. Thus, companies often wrote off costly acquisition failures without learning from them.

At a broader level, acquisitions gave companies an opportunity to develop new insights into their own strategic direction and to learn how to adapt their own organizational approach. We were struck by the extent to which acquisitions could be at the root of major strategic and organizational adaptation in the acquiring organization. Some firms were hardly altered by the acquisitions they made; in others, acquisitions led to major changes in the rest of the firm.

A PROCESS PERSPECTIVE

A common thread running through each of these challenges is the role of the acquisition process itself. For every acquisition we studied, the decision-making and integration processes had a substantial impact on the source of ideas, the quality of the justification, the integration approach, and the results (see Figure 1-1).

Adopting a process perspective shifts the focus from an acquisition's results to the drivers that cause these results: the transfer of capabilities that will lead to competitive advantage. In the process perspective, acquisitions are not independent, one-off deals. Instead, they are a means to the end of corporate renewal. The transaction itself does not bring the expected benefits; instead, actions and activities of the managers after the agreement determine the results.

This process perspective presents a clear contrast to the conventional view of acquisitions advocated by some managers and scholars.[9] In the conventional view, acquisitions are seen as individual deals in

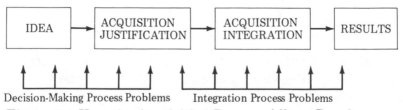

Figure 1-1 How the Acquisition Process Affects Results

which price is paramount. The conventional view also sees acquisition decision making as a sequential, segmented process in which the key elements are financial valuation and the pre-acquisition analysis of strategic fit. In addition, it presumes that the value of an acquisition can be understood and predicted accurately at the time of the agreement. (Figure 1-2 presents the elements of the conventional view.) In contrast, the process perspective emphasizes the role that acquisition decision making plays in helping a management team understand how value will be created, not just how to assign a financial value to a firm. We suggest that while pre-acquisition analysis of strategic fit and organizational fit are important, they indicate only the value-creating potential of an acquisition and the anticipated implementation difficulties.

Our research found that the acquisition decision-making and integration processes present separate and unique problems and opportunities. At the same time, they are interactive and the issues that arise during these processes require that they be considered together. In contrast, practitioners of the conventional view often delegate post-acquisition decision making and integration to managers who were excluded from the pre-acquisition decision process for reasons of secrecy, time availability, or lack of status. They tend to presume that integration problems can be addressed either by keeping the people happy or by getting rid of them.

We are not suggesting that there is one universal approach to dealing with acquisitions. Although it is tempting to develop a standard approach to deal with all acquisitions, important differences exist among them. Our research has led to a contingency-based approach to managing acquisitions that (1) considers the strategic task that needs to be accomplished in any acquisition, and the integration needs this implies, yet (2) is conscious of the organizational requirements for autonomy, when they are central to achieving the acquisition purpose.

The problems firms experience with acquisitions are not always due

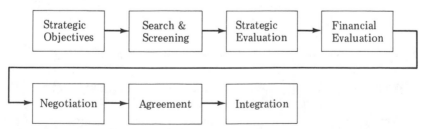

Figure 1-2 **Conventional View of Acquisitions**

to individuals or to a lack of insight into what should be done. Instead, they are embedded in the organizational processes by which managers tackle those issues (see again Figure 1-1). In most firms the decision-making approaches through which acquisitions are examined and the organizational repertoires used to integrate them were not developed for making decisions about acquisitions in the first place. Acquisitions are a severe test of a firm's organizational capabilities, one on which many firms do not achieve a passing grade.

OVERVIEW OF THE BOOK

The book comprises five parts, each of which addresses several basic questions about acquisitions, acquisition decision making, and acquisition integration. Figure 1-3 presents the major themes and conclusions around which our arguments are developed.

Chapter 2 completes the first part of the book, "Acquisitions and Value Creation." Chapter 2, which is more conceptual than the other chapters, provides an overall foundation for the arguments we make about value creation and anchors the logic of our argument in theory. We believe that most readers will find this theory interesting and useful as a way to frame their thinking. Readers who prefer to go directly to managerial issues can move to the rest of the book and can refer back to Chapter 2 as they read. The questions addressed in Chapter 2 are:

- How should managers view value creation?
- How do acquisitions relate to strategy?
- How do acquisitions create value?

The second part, "Acquisition Decision Making" focuses on issues and problems in the acquisition decision-making process and addresses these questions:

- How and why are acquisition decisions different from other invest-ment decisions? (Chapter 3)
- What are the elements of a sound acquisition justification? (Chap-ter 3)
- What are the key problems in the acquisition decision-making pro-cess? How do they affect the acquisition outcome? (Chapter 4)
- How do differences in a company's resource allocation style affect its ability to make acquisition decisions? (Chapter 4)

Figure 1-3 **Major Themes and Conclusions**

1. To understand the contribution that acquisitions can make to a firm requires a shift in focus from acquisitions per se to an acquisitive strategy for renewal.

2. The essential element in managing an acquisitive strategy is understanding the acquisition process:

   - All value creation takes place after the acquisition; hence the critical importance of the quality of the post-merger integration process.

   - The pre-acquisition decision-making process presents a variety of problems that affect not only the firm's ability to understand the value-creating potential of an acquisition, but also its ability to achieve successful post-acquisition integration.

3. At the most fundamental level, acquisitions create value when they enhance the strategic capabilities of the combined firms, thereby improving either the acquired or acquiring firm's competitive position, which in turn will produce financial operating results.

4. The success of a particular acquisition depends on the managers' ability to reconcile the need for strategic interdependence between the two firms that is required to transfer strategic capabilities and the need for organizational autonomy of the acquired firm that is required to preserve the acquired strategic capabilities.

5. The balance of these two factors determines the appropriate integration approach. Three approaches can be distinguished that involve different processes and lead to different outcomes: absorption, where the two organizations become one; preservation, which implies safeguarding the cultural identity of the acquired firm; and symbiosis, which represents a mutual mutual adaptation and amalgamation of the organizations.

6. A firm's ability to manage these integration approaches depends on the way in which the interactions between the two firms are managed over time and hence on its ability to manage the interface between the firms.

7. Although it differs by integration approach, the management of these interactions is a two-phased process. The first phase sets the stage for integration and creates the appropriate atmosphere within which capability transfer can take place. The second stage brings about the actual capability transfer that will improve competitive advantage and lead to value creation.

8. For value creation to be realized, integration must be seen as an evolutionary process of adaptation, rather than as a completely predictable, planned activity.

9. Individual acquisitions provide opportunities for firms to learn about both the renewal strategy being pursued and the company's overall organizational capabilities.

10. Beyond integration, acquisitive firms face an administrative reorientation in moving from a mode of assembling a series of acquisitions to managing an integrated network of operations.

- What alternatives do firms have to organize for acquisition decision making in general, and for individual acquisitions in particular? (Chapter 5)
- How do experienced acquirers organize for acquisition decision making? (Chapter 5)

The third part, "Integration: The Source of Value Creation," develops our conceptualization of the integration process. It addresses such questions as:

- What happens during acquisition integration? (Chapter 6)
- What are the key elements in creating an atmosphere where capability transfer can take place? (Chapter 6)
- What are the key problems in integration that affect value creation? (Chapter 7)
- Which integration approaches correspond to which situations? (Chapter 8)
- What are the key factors in each of these integration approaches? (Chapters 8 and 9)

The fourth part, "Managing the Integration Process," illustrates the managerial lessons identified in our integration research, exploring questions such as:

- How do managers create the appropriate atmosphere after the acquisition? (Chapter 10)
- What should be done and in what order? (Chapter 10)
- How can value be created in different types of acquisitions by:
  - absorbing the other firm? (Chapter 11)
  - preserving what you bought? (Chapter 12)
  - amalgamating the two organizations? (Chapter 13)

The final part, "Linking Acquisitions Back to Strategy," summarizes the issues covered in this book and places them in the perspective of the strategic activities that come before and after the acquisition process:

- What is involved in defining a corporate-level acquisition strategy? (Chapter 14)
- What capabilities are required to manage the acquisition process? (Chapter 14)
- How can companies better learn from acquisitions? (Chapter 14)
- What challenges lie beyond successful acquisitions? (Chapter 15)

A CALL FOR CAUTION AND AN ENCOURAGEMENT

Our perspective on acquisitions places strategic, financial, and organizational considerations in the context of decision-making and integration processes through which they are developed and by which their success or failure is determined. In this light, we hope that this book will serve as both a call for caution and an encouragement. Caution is required, because making successful acquisitions is much more complex than managers assume before they begin. Behind the financial aspects of the deal lurk complex strategic questions and even more challenging organizational tasks. Encouragement is warranted because the payoffs may be high for management teams who can learn from their own experience and from the experience of others about how to better manage the acquisition process.

2

A Capabilities-Based View of Value Creation

INTRODUCTION

THE RAPID INCREASE of acquisitive activity in all countries with market economies has heightened the debate among managers, academics, politicians, and regulators about acquisition activity, the roles of different players, the various motives for acquisitions, and the benefits they produce. Opinions on many of these topics are strongly held, but by no means universally accepted.[1] The crux of the arguments may lie in the difficulty in reconciling the clear benefits of an active market for corporate control, as enjoyed by countries like the United States and the United Kingdom, with the strategic investment behavior exhibited by firms in countries like Germany and Japan.

Most of this debate has focused on whether or not acquisitions lead to value creation. This has led to the neglect of equally important questions for managers and acquisitive firms: "How is value created in firms and how do acquisitions themselves contribute to value creation?" This chapter provides the conceptual foundation for our arguments by outlining an expanded view of how value creation takes place in firms and the role of acquisitions in that process. Subsequent chapters address solutions to problems that management teams encounter as they use acquisitions as part of their overall corporate development strategies.

In this chapter we explore the concept of value creation from different viewpoints. We then contrast value creation with value capture and

18

show how firms can create value by transferring and applying strategic capabilities that lead to competitive advantage. Finally, we discuss the different ways in which acquisitions can contribute to value creation.

PERSPECTIVES ON CORPORATE VALUE

The concept of corporate value has different meanings for different constituents of the firm. Before examining corporate value from a managerial perspective, we will briefly review the question of what value is from two other perspectives: the capital markets view and a broader stakeholders perspective.

CAPITAL MARKETS VIEW OF VALUE CREATION

The surge in acquisition activity worldwide and the rise of contested takeovers have highlighted the need to understand the criteria by which acquisitions should be judged. The capital markets perspective on this question asserts that the merits of an acquisition should be judged in terms of the immediate value created for the shareholders.[2] This view has attracted widespread support because its logic is derived from the tenets of the capitalist economic system in general and from the efficient markets hypothesis of financial economics in particular.[3] This view suggests that the market value of a firm's stock price reflects an unbiased estimate of all publicly available information about the firm's future cash flows and their related risks.

A natural extension of this view is that any acquisition that causes an immediate increase in market value (after adjustment for normal market fluctuations) is good, and one that causes an immediate decrease in market value is bad. Using this perspective, financial economists have concluded, after extensive research, that acquisitions on the average do not create value for shareholders of the acquiring firm. The same studies, however, reveal that, on the average, a significant premium accrues to the acquired firm's shareholders.[4]

In the aggregate the capital markets perspective argues that the entire economy benefits from the asset reallocation that results from acquisitions. In this market for corporate control, new owners pay a premium for a firm's shares and install different management.[5] The line of reasoning is that the new group of owners has been able to pay more for the firm because they believe the assets can be more productively utilized under the stewardship of management they choose. Former owners of the firm receive a premium for their shares and then reinvest the proceeds. When this premium plus the net change (positive or negative) in the value of the acquiring firm's shareholders' wealth is positive, acquisitions represent an overall creation of wealth, and the welfare of society is increased because assets have been allocated to more productive uses.[6]

While the capital markets perspective encourges a view of the firm that emphasizes optimal societal resource allocation, its relevance for managers is limited. In this view the firm is merely a bundle of assets; value is created when an acquisition either increases the income stream of those assets or decreases the variability.[7] But it does not address the *way* in which the income stream is created; it says only that it can be changed by reallocating the firm's portfolio among different sets of asserts. Thus the source of firm performance remains unexplained and seems to result from rather mysterious activities that take place in a black box.

The capital markets perspective is elegant in its simplicity and important because of the number of managers and academics who subscribe to it. Perhaps its most salutary contribution is that it reminds us to put value creation ahead of managerial motives. Yet, because it focuses on the entire economy and not a firm, it provides little guidance for action-oriented managers who want to understand how they can create value in a particular situation.[8] Managers and scholars need to understand more about the ways in which firms create value and the role of acquisitions in that value-creation process, topics central to the purpose of this book.[9]

OTHER CONSTITUENTS' VIEWS

In a broader sense, a firm's value can also be seen from the perspective of several groups other than shareholders, each of whom considers the value or worth of the firm differently, e.g. employees, communities, customers, suppliers.[10] Employees value a firm for many reasons including employment, pride of association, and a means of achieving personal goals. Communities value firms for the benefits they provide, through employment, taxes, the types of people they attract to the area, and the involvement of the firms' employees in the life of the community. Customers find value in a firm's ability to meet their needs for products and services. Suppliers value relationships with firms not only because they are outlets for goods and services but also because they provide valuable market information.

Even in the United States, where the capital markets view is prevalent, a constituents' view of acquisitions is far from theoretical. When the Norton Corporation, Worcester, Massachusetts' largest employer, with a tradition of community involvement, faced a takeover bid from the British conglomerate BTR, a public outcry was heard. It was feared that BTR would move jobs away and end the community service role that Norton had sustained for over fifty years. After repeated public and corporate protests, as well as hurried state legislation, BTR withdrew its bid. BTR's bid was replaced by one from a French firm. Saint-Gobain not only offered a higher price for the firm's shares, but also guaranteed to keep plants, jobs, and community involvement intact for at least the next five years.[11]

The view that managers' decisions should be guided by obligations broader than maximizing shareholder value is not as strongly held in countries with active markets for corporate control. Yet in some countries such as Japan, it has the same legitimacy that the capital markets view has in the United States and Great Britain. In other countries an amalgam of the two exists. In Germany, Switzerland, and Holland, for example, management is expected to balance stockholders' interests with those of other stakeholders when solving problems.[12] But, beyond suggesting the need to include more interests in decision making, the stakeholders' perspective does not provide much guidance for managers seeking to create value.

A Managerial Perspective on Value Creation

Most managers strike a middle ground between these two perspectives. The executives we interviewed were uncomfortable with the premise that the real measure of performance was either the immediate stock market reaction to their firm's acquisitions or broad stakeholder support. These managers believed that the investments they were making (many of which were acquisitions) were consistent with their strategic vision for the firm and would add to the firm's capabilities and long-term competitive position. Both financial results and the ability to serve the needs of all its stakeholders were expected to flow from these commitments. The managers' confidence in their decisions did not result from hubris as much as from their best judgment, based on an understanding of the strategic, technological, and market opportunities facing their firm and their vision of how they would compete in the future. They could support this confidence with precise financial projections for some acquisitions. But for others they would have been hard pressed to clarify and quantify precisely the linkage between their acquisition decision and positive changes in their firm's income stream. Although they used discounted cash flow analysis as one way to evaluate acquisitions, these managers had confidence in "a strategic premium" that reflected their judgment of the long-term benefits of an acquisition, rather than estimates of cash flows.

Clear differences existed across national boundaries in the extent to which managers' judgments in these matters were linked to the immediate reaction of capital markets. The divergence in resulting investment behavior was most striking in some "industries of the future" such as advanced composite materials or ceramic materials. In such situations, up-front investment in leading technology segments (in this case military and civilian aerospace) were expected to bear fruit only over time in terms of bigger markets such as automotive applications. In these industries, the German, Swiss, Japanese, and some of the British companies that we studied were all committing themselves not only to acquisitions, but also to major subsequent investments. In contrast, many of the American firms were either selling or waiting out the industry evolution.[13]

Firms we studied held very different views of what they should focus on to accomplish the corporate purpose. Some management groups emphasized realizing financial results, others conquering market positions, and others building up corporate capabilities. All managers interviewed agreed that financial performance was the long-term yardstick, but managers in some firms shared a much more complex and multidimensional view of how to balance an acquisition's short-term financial performance with long-term strategic needs.

VALUE CAPTURE VERSUS VALUE CREATION

The current debate about shareholder value masks the fact that there are two fundamentally different ways of improving shareholder wealth with acquisitions.[14] One, *value capture*, involves shifting value from previous shareholders or other stakeholders to the acquiring firm's shareholders. Value capture tends to be a one-time event, largely related to the transaction itself. The other way, *value creation*, is a long-term phenomenon that results from managerial action and interactions between the firms. It embodies the outcome of what many people refer to as synergy. In our conception, synergy occurs when capabilities transferred between firms improve a firm's competitive position and consequently its performance. Value creation implies a different concept of the firm.

How Is Value Created?

We believe that the most managerially relevant view of the value-creation process is to see a firm as a set of capabilities (embodied in an organizational framework) which, when applied in the marketplace, can create and sustain elements of competitive advantage for the firm.[15] These elements of competitive advantage produce operating results for the firm (with an associated risk profile) and create value for its shareholders. Figure 2-1 outlines the dynamics in this process.

The advantage to both managers and researchers of this capabilities-based perspective over the financial assets perspective is that it segments the value-creation process and allows careful consideration of each of the steps involved.

This perspective also contrasts with the traditional notion of strategy in which firms strive to achieve a distinctive competence, something they can do uniquely better than other firms that will give them a unique and lasting competitive advantage.[16] In the competitive situations facing most firms, it is illusory to expect that a single dimension will provide a decisive competitive advantage or, even if it did, to expect it to be sustainable.[17] In this capabilities-based perspective that we suggest, a firm's competitive advantage results from the application of a wide range of capabilities and, in particular, of a set of core capabilities, which can be defined as those capabilities central to competitive advantage, that (1) incorporate an integrated set of managerial and technological skills, (2) are hard to acquire other than through experience, (3) contribute significantly to perceived customer benefits, and (4) can be widely applied within the company's business domain.[18] But markets are sufficiently varied to provide room for different competitors with different capability profiles to coexist.[19] Thus the only real distinctive competence is in the ability to mobilize an organization to form new combinations of capabilities continually and to renew them.[20]

Conceptualizing a firm's competitive position as the result of a set of

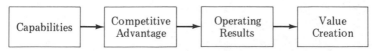

Figure 2-1 **A Capabilities-Based Perspective on Value Creation**

core capabilities leads to new insights. For example, the competitiveness of a firm like Canon, which competes in four broad product-markets (cameras, copiers, office equipment, and professional optics), can be better understood by regarding the company as a portfolio of capabilities, not businesses. These exist both upstream (quality manufacturing of small equipment, value engineering, and leading-edge technology in microelectronics, optics, and new materials) and downstream (mass merchandising, a dealer network, and a brand franchise).[21] A clear understanding of which capabilities are central to a firm's competitive success (and which are secondary) makes it possible to develop a corporate strategy for renewing such capabilities and a clearer picture of the options open to the firm. It is also central, as we shall argue, to developing an acquisitive strategy that will create value.

RENEWING A FIRM'S CAPABILITIES

Competition and other environmental changes naturally erode a firm's competitive advantages. Faced with a constant need to *renew* its competitive position, the firm seeks to add new capabilities or to change the product-markets where its existing capabilities are applied. These choices are not independent. Entry into new product-markets, which may be driven by the desire to exploit existing capabilities, usually brings with it the need for complementary new capabilities to compete effectively. Entry itself may add other new capabilities that can be deployed in one's existing product-markets or become the basis for further product-market diversification.

In this interactive process it is essential that the strategist keep the focus on which capabilities are core, i.e., central to competitive advantage in the companies' business domain, and which are secondary. That judgment is idiosyncratic, as every firm competes differently and has a unique set of capabilities.

One impediment to focusing strategic reflection on a firm's capabilities is that it is generally much easier to observe the renewal and change of the firm's businesses, products, or markets than the renewal of its capabilities. Yet the renewal of capabilities is central to long-term competitive strength. Firms compete on the basis of their relative ability to renew and deploy capabilities as much as they do on their ability to extract profits from product-markets.

This capabilities-based perspective of the firm also allows general managers to consider a variety of options for strategic renewal, including acquisitions, internal development, and joint ventures. The key is to focus on how the relative merits of each option contribute to the needed capabilities. However, because of the purpose of this book, we will focus our attention on how managers can use acquisitions effectively as a form of renewal, rather than on the trade-offs among these options. We will return to such corporate strategy choices in our concluding chapter.

How Is Value Captured?

While the focus of this book is value creation, we must address value capture briefly because of its popularity among some groups of managers and scholars. In fact, value capture embodies most directly the prevailing views of the capital markets perspective we discussed above. Many acquisitions are driven by the desire to capture value by transferring it from one set of stakeholders to shareholders or managers of the acquiring firm. These transactions usually involve either corporate restructuring (by individual raiders or by acquisitive firms) or leveraged buy-outs. Value is captured by a variety of one-time, transaction-oriented means, including acquiring undervalued assets, tax benefits, increasing debt, and asset stripping. The seller, future owners, the government, and existing creditors are the common sources of such captured value.

Value can be captured from the *seller* by identifying and acquiring firms whose market prices may be undervalued. For example, Charlie Bluhdorn stated that his motive in creating Gulf & Western was his confidence in his ability to spot undervalued asserts. Similarly, Boone Pickens's view at Mesa Petroleum is that he understands the oil business well enough to bid for the undervalued assets of firms like Gulf. The fact that the firm that first spotted the undervaluation does not always end up as the acquiring firm, does not mean that value capture did not take place. The discount at which the shares of a conglomerate or closed-end mutual fund sell is another example of undervaluation that can be released by simple breakup. Value capture from firms with undervalued assets is most commonly associated with multibusiness companies whose value is difficult for the stock market to assess or whose corporate managers do not pursue value-maximizing strategies. Even single-business firms may provide opportunities for value capture from the seller if some of their assets, e.g., buildings and other real estate, are not related to the cash-generating potential of the firm.

Value can also be captured *from future owners*, the shareholders of firms to whom a buyer intends to resell a portion of an acquired business. For example, a substantial part of the gains made by acquirers of conglomerate firms has been based on their ability to keep for themselves during negotiations a significant portion of the synergies that the industrial companies to which they resell individual businesses expected to achieve.

Hanson Trust, for example, acquired SCM in 1985 for $930 million. By the end of 1988 it had sold of SCM companies and assets for $1249.6 million, but it still owned Smith Corona, SCM Chemicals, and SCM Metals. It repeated this performance with the Imperial group, which it acquired in 1986 for $2.5 billion. After selling off Imperial assets for $2.247 billion by the end of 1988, it ended up owning Imperial Tobacco and a number of smaller businesses for a net price of $253 million. Again, in its 1987 acquisition of Kaiser Cement for $250 million, Hanson disposed of assets for $284.3 million and kept Kaiser's Northern California cement business for essentially no cost.[22]

The government is a favorite source of value capture for acquiring firms because they can take advantage of complexities and subtleties in the tax laws. Quite often, acquiring firms are able to reap substantial savings or reductions of tax liabilities through judicious application of tax loss carryforwards from the target firm, tax treatment of goodwill, or other special tax treatment of acquisitions.[23] In leveraged acquisitions the new owners also realize a transfer of value through an effective reduction in the cost of capital based on the tax deductibility of interest.

Finally, there may be some opportunities to transfer value to shareholders of the acquiring firm from the acquired firm's *existing creditors*.[24] One way is to increase the risk level of previous lenders by maintaining their old debt while significantly increasing post-acquisition indebtedness, especially through the use of so-called high-yield junk-bond financing. For example, when Campeau Corporation of Canada acquired Federated Department Stores in the United States in 1988, the market value of Federated's bonds fell by 17 percent because of the debt financing used by Campeau to complete the acquisition. In turnaround acquisitions, the acquisition may also provide a one-time opportunity to renegotiate downward the higher-risk debt of firms by providing guarantees that at least a portion of it will be repaid.

A firm's ability to *capture* value through acquisitions rests largely on the skills of a small but highly experienced cadre of legal and financial experts and operating managers with well-developed expertise in analysis and deal making. Above all, this ability rests on their judgment, their comfort with risk taking, and their ability to commit increasing sums of money to ever-larger takeovers that can contribute appreciably to the growing base of the firm.

Managers who are interested in value creation need to put the activity of value-capturing financial entrepreneurs in the proper perspective. Value capture is not a sufficient motive for strategic acquirers. Although the benefits of value capture can be very substantial for a particular acquisition opportunity, a solitary focus on value capture masks the need to focus on the managerially based process of true value creation. By the same token, we believe that strategic acquirers should also take full advantage of the opportunities to capture value in their acquisitions.

Through the acquisition of multibusiness firms in particular, a management team can gain access to individual business units that are of strategic interest to them for value creation and then capture value by reselling the rest, often paying less than it would have expected for the business of interest. For example, because ICI was willing to acquire all of Stauffer Chemical for $1.9 billion and then to resell part of these business activities to Akzo and Rhône-Poulenc, it was able to gain access to the agrochemical division it wanted at a net cost of less than $800 million.

Few firms are able to capture and create value in the same acquisition. Doing so requires both the quick decision making of the financial entrepreneur and the strategic view of the patient organization builder. Because our interest is on strategic acquisitions, we will concentrate in this book on value creation.

STRATEGIC ACQUISITIONS IN A CAPABILITIES-BASED PERSPECTIVE

Although they share the underlying motivation of value creation, the acquisitions we call "strategic" differ by the type of capability they transfer, their relation to corporate strategy, and their contribution to business strategy.[25] Each of these distinctions emphasizes a dimension important in our capabilities-based perspective, and each has consequences for the nature of the acquisition decision-making process and for the challenges in the integration process. The remainder of this chapter develops these three ways to distinguish among strategic acquisitions.

Our first classification addresses the differences in the type of capability transfer that underlies value creation in acquisitions. Our second classification distinguishes among acquisitions in terms of how they relate to corporate strategy. Finally, some acquisitions may be a small ingredient in an internal development strategy, while others actually represent the business strategy. Thus our third set of considerations focuses on what the acquisition contributes to implementing a particular business strategy.

ACQUISITIONS AND THE TYPE OF CAPABILITY TRANSFER

Acquisitions create value when the competitive advantage of one firm is improved through the transfer of strategic capabilities. To develop a practical understanding of how value creation will occur we must examine the specifics of what the exact source of capability transfer (in other words, of synergy) will be. Economists and business researchers have each developed categorization schemes and a language to look at the benefits flowing from acquisitions. Economists tend to focus on market power and cross-subsidization (neither of which they favor because of their anticompetitive nature), and economies of scale or scope, both of which they do like.[26] Management researchers have discussed a vast array of "synergies" typically related to different business functions: marketing synergies, manufacturing synergies, etc.[27]

Neither categorization corresponds well with the nature of the managerial task required for achieving synergies. The economist's notion of economies of scope, for example, may cover such disparate activities as incorporating a newly acquired company in one's planning and control system in such a way that operating units are little affected by their counterparts in the other organization, to cross-selling of products through each other's sales forces, which will require a great deal of coordination between both operating units. Popular managerial categories such as marketing synergies, on the other hand, cover anything from sales force rationalization to improved brand management, which represent very different sources of benefits and imply very different organizational tasks.

Our research suggests that four different categories of acquisition benefits can be distinguished. Each presents very different integration challenges: operational resource sharing, functional skill transfer, general management skill transfer, and combination benefits.[28] The first three involve strategic capability transfer and will be a primary focus of our book. The fourth, combination benefits, refers to a number of advantages that are present in many acquisitions but do not require capability transfer. Many acquisitions involve all four types of benefits, but we will discuss them individually for the sake of clarity.

Combination benefits accruing from some acquisitions do not involve formal capability transfer. For example, market power and increased purchasing power come from the leverage that size itself allows over customers, suppliers, distribution channels, and smaller competitors.[29] Financial resources may be shared, leading to lower financing costs or greater financing capability. Greater stability may be achieved through diversity.[30] Even reputation may be enhanced; as the increase in size and stature resulting from the merger that created Dai-Ichi Kangyo Bank enabled it to attract more top-quality university graduates and improve its overall management capabilities.

These combinations benefits have one aspect in common—they do not require a managerial process to transfer capabilities between the organizations. While they play a major role in some acquisitions, combination benefits are not at the heart of value creation in truly strategic acquisitions. It is in the three categories of resource sharing and the transfer of functional and general management skills that capability transfer takes place in value-creating acquisitions.

Resource sharing involves the combination and rationalization of some of the operating assets of both firms. Such rationalization can take place in one or more functions and leads to cost improvements that stem from economies of scale or scope. Economies of scale result when the combined unit volume allows the firm to operate at a lower unit cost. Economies of scope come about when the joint use of an asset results in a lower overall cost than the firms had when they operated independently. Sharing distribution channels and sales forces is a goal of acquirers seeking economies of scope. A major reason for the acquisition of Charles Schwab by Bank of America was to cross-sell each firm's products into the other's markets. Using the other firm's channels for related products would share the cost of establishing and maintaining customer relationships. Gaining the benefits from economies of scope sometimes requires eliminating duplication. For example, many of the benefits of Seagram's strategy of acquiring other brands like the French cognac Martell lie in the eliminating sales force duplication.

Even intangible assets such as brands can be shared. For example, when Black and Decker acquired General Electric's small home appliance business, they planned to lever their own brand's reputation in power hand tools onto the former GE products.

Although the economics of resource sharing seem straightforward, in practice the combination of operating resources brings with it a "cost of compromise." The overall economic benefits of resource sharing need to be balanced against any loss of effectiveness in their use. When Esselte acquired Dymo, for example, there was a clear opportunity for resource sharing by combining Esselte's stationery supplies sales force with the sales force for Dymo's well-known embossing tool, as their products overlapped almost completely at the store level. Against the economic benefits gained by creating a single sales force, the firm had to weigh the differences in the sales skills required for the two products. Esselte's products, which were low margined, required primarily order-taking and pricing. Dymo's were high margined and required merchandising and demonstration.[31] In practice, the potential for resource sharing often has to be traded off against the next source of benefits: the possibility for skill transfer.

Functional skill transfer creates value when one firm improves its capabilities by bringing in, from another firm, functional skills that can help it to be more competitive. Examples included advanced manufacturing process skills in the merger of two manufacturing firms, detailed knowledge of a distribution channel in the merger of two consumer goods firms, or cutting-edge research in financial theory used to develop new products in mergers between brokerage firms. The common denominator among these is that one firm improves its competitive position by learning from another through the transfer of functional skills.

The very factors that make capabilities strategic makes value creation through skill transfer difficult. Skills are typically embedded in the activities, habits, and automatic responses of key people throughout the organization.[32] The less replicable the skill, the more difficult it is to imitate and the more effective it can be as a competitive weapon. In addition, the most valuable skills are often organizational routines for performing particular activities. These routines are learned over time, often by trial and error; their performance often becomes automatic when a particular situation occurs.

This embeddedness creates problems for skill transfer in acquisitions because to benefit from a new skill, the firm must be able to apply it in its new context. In Chapter 6 we will discuss how such capability transfer takes place. In particular we will describe how an understanding of the context and an atmosphere that can promote capability transfer are developed and we will explore problems in the integration process that prevent the creation of such an atmosphere.

General management skill transfer occurs when one firm can make another more competitive by improving the range or depth of its general management skills. These capabilities range from the broad skills needed in setting corporate direction and leadership to more analytically oriented skills and systems, such as those needed for strategic planning, financial planning, control, or human resource management. For example, the Saga Corporation had developed general management skills in operating an institutional food services company. But its traditional markets in cafeteria management had stopped growing. To continue its growth, Saga targeted a series of small, high-potential restaurant chains. Its strategic logic was to enhance the growth of these chains by providing them with the benefit of Saga's general management skills.

The acquiring firm can also improve its own general management capabilities through acquisitions. For example, Esselte's acquisition of Dymo served another purpose besides providing a strong sales network. The Swedish stationery manufacturer had already made a series of loosely connected acquisitions in the stationery supplies field in Europe and had left each with its own systems intact. Another reason was that Dymo could bring management discipline and worldwide systems to these earlier, smaller acquisitions.

Sometimes firms make acquisitions to acquire good managers from other firms. This has occurred among building societies in Great Britain.[33] Because the building society industry had operated for many years with a highly protected, near-monopoly on making loans for home ownership, few individual societies had developed any general management talent in depth. In 1981 the Conservative government changed the rules of competition in the U.K. financial services industry. Building societies found themselves competing with banks and other financial institutions for deposits and home loan customers. This increased competition required general management talent that was more attuned to a competitive environment and different from that available in most societies. Several building society managers we interviewed conceded that a prime motive behind some of the mergers that had taken place had been a desire to acquire capable chief executives from other societies. Because of loyalty to their current society, they would not agree to become chief executive of another society unless the two were merged.

Every value-creating acquisition presents a potential mixture of the foregoing types of capability transfer. The important question, as we shall discuss later, is which of these types a firm's management will choose to focus on. These decisions will depend in part on the strategic motivation behind the acquisition; its relation to corporate strategy forms the basis for our next distinction among acquisitions.

ACQUISITIONS AND CORPORATE RENEWAL

Our second categorization distinguishes acquisitions in terms of their contribution to corporate-level strategy. From a corporate perspective, acquisitions have to be seen in light of their relation to maintaining or changing the balance between the firm's existing domain and the renewal of its capabilities. Each company operates within a "domain" that encompasses the set of businesses within which it is competitive, the capabilities that underlie them, with which its top management is familiar, and to which its corporate organization is suited.[34]

Acquisitions can contribute to the corporate renewal process in three ways: they can deepen the firm's presence in an existing domain; they can broaden that domain in terms of products, markets, or capabilities; or they can bring the company into entirely new areas. In other words, acquisition can be domain strengthening, domain extending, or domain exploring. Each of these types of acquisitions is fairly distinct, and, as we shall discuss later, they have different implications for how to approach the decision-making process as well as the integration process.

Domain Strengthening. Domain-strengthening acquisitions augment or renew the capabilities underlying a firm's competitive position in an existing business domain.[35] They correspond to firms' proactive or defensive reactions to the industry restructuring process.[36]

Although the essence of a domain-strengthening acquisition is the desire to defend or fortify a company's business domain, some variation obviously exists within this category. The most straightforward is a completely horizontal acquisition of a competitor with the same products in the same markets, for example, the French tire manufacturer Michelin's acquisition of the number two French manufacturer, Kleber-Colomb, to prevent it from falling into the hands of Goodyear. National consolidations in the airline industry are another example of domain-strengthening acquisitions made to achieve economies of scope and scale. The desire of airlines to dominate a hub airport, to gain market share on a set of key routes, to spread fixed costs of corporate staff over a large volume, and to consolidate reservations systems so as to increase demand for their planes drives much of this activity.

Sometimes the overlap between the firms is less complete because they are selling different products to the same market. This was the case of Stauffer Chemical's Agrochemical business, which was retained by ICI's Agrochemicals division. Although the two companies were selling to the same regions in the United States, they had product ranges for different crops of the same farmers. Similarly, the merger of Hughes Tool Company and Baker International, two oil industry supply firms, brought Hughes's market position and reputation in drill bits together with Baker's reputation and expertise in oil field equipment to consolidate efforts in a severely distressed industry.

A third variant, often seen in the context of globalization are acquisitions of competitors with similar or overlapping products who cover different geographic markets. An example is the purchase of the American paint manufacturer Inmont by BASF, which gave the German company an important share of Detroit's big three, all-important in the global automotive paints business. Another example is the regional expansion of such U.S. bank holding companies as NCNB, Wachovia, and BancOne.

Beyond the real forces driving driving domain-strengthening acquisitions, there is a lemming effect as the "urge to merge" spills over into areas where the economic benefits are less clear. Managers should be cautious in judging domain overlap with a potential partner. A common error is to focus more on the similarities than on the differences between the firms. For example, Louis Vuitton and Moët-Hennessey merged their luxury products firms in 1987 but soon discovered that their managerial concepts of luxury products were very different.

Domain Extension. Domain-extending acquisitions apply the firm's existing capabilities in new, adjacent businesses or bring new capabilities into the firm to apply in its existing businesses. The combined firms share the challenge of relating what is a new capability for one to what is a new business opportunity for the other.

Habitat's acquisition of Mothercare in the U.K. is a good example of an acquisition to apply a firm's existing capabilities in new product-market domains. Habitat, the U.K. furniture designer and retailer, had built its success on the ability to translate attractive, fashionable designs into reasonably priced home furnishings. Mothercare, a chain of retail shops that catered to expectant and new mothers, was well respected for its operating abilities. But because its maternity and baby clothing and accessories were perceived as dowdy and plain, it was beginning to lose fashion-conscious customers. Sir Terence Conran, Habitat's founder, transferred its design flair and fashion-conscious merchandising capability to Mothercare's product lines, stores, and catalogs, and Mothercare's sales and profitability both increased.

In an example of acquisitions intended to *add* capabilities, Computer Associates International became the largest independent software firm in the industry by making a series of acquisitions of software houses. Each of these acquisitions provided a new type of programming capability that contributed to Computer Associates International's ability to achieve its strategy of becoming a full-line software provider.[37]

Firms can also extend their capabilities by acquiring existing businesses. For example, the American automobile firms Ford and Chrysler bought free-standing financial service firms to augment their existing in-house financing arms. These moves have positioned them well for the future as the financial services industry deregulates. They also give the auto firms the ability to enhance their product offerings with coordinated financing packages and enable them to capture the profits from auto financing that formerly went to lenders. Ford's purchase of First Nationwide Savings is an interesting example of synergy in financial services. The savings arm is now able to match its shorter-term deposits with auto loan repayments rather than home mortgages, thus reducing the firm's interest rate risk on fixed-rate, long-term mortgages.

Domain Exploration. Domain-exploring acquisitions involve moves into new businesses that at the same time require new capability bases. These types of acquisitions are frequently driven by managerial motives such as the desire to use cash or to reduce risk. Contrary to managerial wisdom, value is not being created by risk reduction itself. Indeed, modern financial theory has shown that an investor can easily diversify his or her portfolio and thus achieve the same sort of systematic risk reduction as a conglomerate.[38]

Domain-exploring acquisitions can create value in two ways. In the first case the motive is a long-term concern about the core business. Here acquisitions may be a way to bring new capabilities or businesses into the firm that might at some point be relevant to existing businesses but cannot yet be incorporated in their current logic. An example of acquisitions that bring learning to a core domain was Ciba-Geigy's move into the consumer goods industry through a number of small acquisitions in the United States and Europe, particularly its acquisition of Airwick.[39] Although Airwick was divested in a subsequent portfolio restructuring, it did expose the Swiss pharmaceuticals and chemicals group to the culture and values of consumer marketing at a time when its core pharmaceuticals business was not ready to adopt the marketing culture needed to tackle the over-the-counter consumer market in that business.

Value can also be created by applying a firm's general management skills to foster a more rapid development or more disciplined management in unrelated acquired businesses without direct relevance to the core business. In such cases the host structure set up by the acquiring firm, over the acquisition performs a role akin to that of the corporate and group levels in a conglomerate. A domain exploration acquisition we will discuss extensively in Chapter 12 is British Petroleum's acquisition of Hendrix, a Dutch animal feed company, which BP nurtured into a Europe-wide nutrition business.

In some firms domain exploration involves acquiring a series of companies in a single new area and then clustering them to form a new business domain. One example is Lafarge New Materials, a new division set up by the French Lafarge Corporation, a leading cement manufacturer. The division has acquired a large number of small family firms clustered in three areas—facade surface materials, building material chemicals, and refractory products. These firms were only indirectly related to Lafarge's core businesses and to each other. But they could share a common management approach provided by the divisional umbrella.

Most often, however, the objective of domain exploration is to lever the industry-specific learning and the credibility from successful initial small acquisitions into a broader commitment to the acquisition and development of a more significant position in that industry. The early acquisitions by British Petroleum in the animal feed industry led not only to the nurturing of those companies but also to other acquisitions, including that of Purina Mills in the United States, which have made BP Nutrition the world's largest supplier in this industry.

ACQUISITIONS AND BUSINESS STRATEGY

A third useful distinction relates to an acquisition's contribution to a specific business strategy. We distinguish three broad types here: acquiring a specific capability, acquiring a platform, or acquiring an existing business position.[40] Our research has focused on the latter two, which, especially in the context of domain extension or exploration, present significantly different challenges to management.

Acquiring a Capability. Sometimes a firm will use a rifle-shot approach to acquire a specific capability it needs to implement a business strategy. We referred earlier to the software firm Computer Associates, which built a business by acquiring very small software houses, each specializing in a single type of system software programming. By pulling all the firms together, the firm acquired a broad-based capability to meet customers' evolving system software requirements.

Acquiring a Platform. We characterize acquisitions as platforms if they may have been viable before being acquired, but clearly will not be as part of the acquiring firm unless it commits to significant further investment. In that sense they represent a commitment to an investment strategy that far exceeds the initial purchase price.

British Petroleum's entry in advanced composite materials is a platform acquisition. When BP, after unsuccessful efforts in its central research lab, wanted to enter the advanced composite business, it first bought the small and relatively troubled British firm, Bristol Composites. After investing substantial resources in Bristol's turnaround and development, the sponsors of this investment, BP Ventures, used the know-how and credibility derived from this first investment to acquire Hitco, one of the leading U.S. firms in this area.

Acquiring a Business Position. In acquisitions that involve an existing business position, the acquisition itself almost implements the strategy. Nestlé's acquisition of Carnation in the United States is a case in point, as are Ford's purchase of First Nationwide Savings and Habitat's purchase of Mothercare.

These three categories represent different management challenges, both in pre-acquisition decision making and in integration. Whether a firm should have an internal development strategy, augmented with some acquired capabilities, or base an acquisitive strategy on acquisition of a platform or the direct pursuit of an existing business position becomes an important choice.[41] This choice should be informed by a clear understanding of differences in how these acquisitions would be integrated and contribute to value creation, issues that we address in Parts III and IV.

SUMMARY

This chapter proposed an overall perspective on how acquisitions can contribute to value creation which managers can relate to their own unique circumstances. We set aside financial engineering acquisitions that concentrate on value capture and focused on the vast majority of strategic acquisitions that are intended to create value. From a managerial perspective we argued that value is created after the acquisition and it is the product of managerial action over time. It requires an outlook focused on the underlying capabilities that allow a firm to establish a competitive advantage that leads to financial performance.

This capabilities-based perspective provides the conceptual basis for examining the strategic role of acquisitions and distinguishing among different types of acquisitions. Focusing on the capabilities that underlie competitive advantage and on the capability transfer that is expected to flow from an acquisition allows managers to link the desired results (an improvement in competitive advantage) with the processes through which these results are achieved over time (the activities and interactions involved in capability transfer). These activities involve the challenges not only of acquiring these capabilities, but also of preserving them, transferring them to the appropriate setting, and applying them in expectation of improved competitive advantage.

These challenges lie at the heart of making acquisitions work and they should not be underestimated. The acquired capabilities and the contexts from which they come and to which they will be applied are rooted in the organizational and cultural context of the acquiring and acquired firms. The nature and difficulty of these integration challenges depend on the factors we have outlined in this chapter, namely:

- How does the acquisition relate to the company's business domain?
- What does the potential acquisition contribute to the firm's strategy?
- What is the type of the strategic capability to be transferred?

Understanding these issues is at the heart of developing an adequate acquisition justification during the acquisition decision-making process and of being able to begin the integration process afterwards.

II

Managing the Acquisition Decision Process

The disappointing outcome of acquisition decisions in otherwise well-run organizations does not result from the absence of analytical or technical skills. Plenty of well-intentioned managers who have excellent skills in strategic, financial, and organizational analysis and are supported by legions of the best professional advisers that fees can buy run into trouble with acquisitions. An acquisition may not reach its potential for several reasons. Value may not be created during the integration stage. Alternatively, the potential value that was expected simply may not have been there in the first place or it may have been bargained away.

A major conclusion of our research is that the acquisition decision-making process itself can substantially affect the acquisition outcome through its impact on the quality of acquisition ideas that are examined, on the quality of the acquisition justification that is developed in the firm, and because what happens or does not happen before the acquisition carries over into the integration phase. In this section we examine the acquisition decision process, the problems managers encounter as they make acquisition decisions, and the ways they have developed to cope with these problems. In Chapter 3 we examine the quality in acquisition decision making, and we analyze how acquisition decisions are similar, yet different, from other resource allocation decisions.

In Chapter 4 we examine the problems with acquisition decision making at two levels. One level is a series of process problems that naturally occur during the acquisition decision process. These include fragmented decision making, increasing momentum, ambiguous expectations, and multiple motives. The seriousness of acquisition problems is rooted in broader aspects of a company's resource allocation style. We examine the factors that determine whether a company's regular resource allocation process can handle acquisition decisions well or not.

Chapter 5 offers suggestions dealing with these problems at two levels: organizing for acquisition decision making in general and building organizational routines for considering individual acquisitions.

3

Understanding the Acquisition Decision-Making Process

INTRODUCTION

ACQUISITION DECISION MAKING IS often portrayed as a step-by-step analytical process that starts with acquisition objectives and passes through phases of systematic search and screening, strategic evaluation, financial evaluation, and negotiation. The outcome is meant to be an acquisition at a justifiable price.

In reality both the purpose and nature of acquisition decision making are far more complex than that. The purpose of acquisition decision making is not just to decide whether or not to acquire a firm or what price to pay. The outcome of the acquisition decision process is a much broader justification that incorporates many dimensions. The interactions and negotiations of many people, in different functions, and at different levels, leads to a "theory" of the acquisition in which price considerations are only one element. Existing first in the collective minds of the actors involved, that theory is typically crystallized into the formal justification dossier and invariably translated into precise financial performance expectations. We suggest that the quality of the acquisition justification or theory is closely related to acquisition performance (see Figure 3-1).

Although some consider it highly rational, the acquisition process is not neatly analytical and segmented. Acquisitions are resource allocation decisions. Like other resource allocation decisions, they involve the

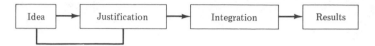

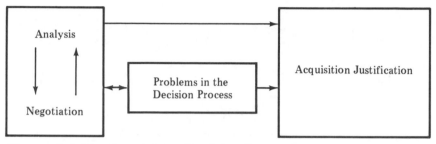

Figure 3-1 **The Acquisition Decision Process**

perception of an opportunity by a champion, its evaluation by many actors, and the building or withholding of a commitment to it. At the same time, acquisition decisions differ from ordinary investment decisions.

First we explore the nature of resource allocation decision processes and their relation to strategy in general. We acknowledge that acquisitions also pose unique challenges to managers for which their normal corporate routines may not be appropriate. Next we examine ways in which acquisitions are similar to, and different from, other resource allocation decisions and how companies adjust their practices to cope with these differences. In Chapter 4 we point out a series of problems that occur naturally as part of the acquisition decision process itself. These problems undercut the decision-making process in acquisitions.

Before developing these arguments, we will describe a research case that illustrates the acquisition decision process. This example is typical of many acquisitions in that it was relatively small, it was driven by the needs of the business, and it was made by a division of a large, diversified firm. Experienced readers may recognize and identify with the events as they unfold. For readers less familiar with a typical acquisition approval process, the case offers a good example of the pre-acquisition decision-making process during which firms develop the justification for an acquisition, the criteria used for decision making, the hurdles firms typically put in place, and the often counterproductive nature of such hurdles.

FRANCOPLAST[1]

Francoplast, a small ($12 million sales, $1 million acquisition price), family-owned French business specializing in plastic industrial pipes, was acquired by Eurochem, the $3 billion European subsidiary of Unichem, a $10 billion U.S. chemical firm, June 1983. The Francoplast acquisition was internally championed by two individuals from Eurochem's matrix organization: Arndt Wirtz, commercial director of Specialty Chemicals, and Stefan Wilcke, diversification manager for Resins and Intermediate Chemicals. After Francoplast was identified as a target, more than eleven months was spent in analysis and negotiation, which involved dozens of individuals at a variety of management levels in the firm.

Several events that made Francoplast an attractive acquisition candidate had begun long before Wirtz became aware of the company. At the corporate level, a broad strategic redirection of Unichem was being planned in response to a worldwide recession and overcapacity in the commodities business. As part of this redirection, a diversification strategy was launched to generate 50 percent of corporate earnings from specialty businesses within five years.

Because Wirtz was responsible for specialty chemical sales in Europe, he perceived this strategy as encouragement for building new business areas, one of which was specialty pipes. Some specialty pipes were already imported from the United States (plastic-lined metal pipe), and Eurochem's sales of epoxy resins suggested there was a rapidly growing market for a glass fiber-reinforced pipe. Market studies commissioned by Wirtz confirmed his decision to make entry into the pipe business one of his 1982 objectives. Although internal development was possible in theory, in practice, Wirtz felt that neither Eurochem nor Unichem had enough experience in this area. He thought it would be difficult to build the needed competitive capabilities from scratch internally. Even though there were a number of large ($500 million) and medium-sized ($100 million) firms in specialty pipes, Wirtz did not believe that Eurochem would agree at this stage to such a large-scale de novo entry, so he began to search for a smaller acquisition on which further growth could be built.

An initial opportunity was identified, but the target company had already reached advanced stages of negotiation with another firm. The decision deadline was approaching too rapidly for Wirtz to get the commitment necessary, given the internal sign-off and review process expected at Eurochem. Back at square one, Wirtz teamed up with Stefan

Wilcke, who was newly appointed as diversification manager for Resins and Intermediate Chemicals, a position reporting to Eurochem's research director. Wilcke, who knew the manufacturing manager at Francoplast socially, thought that the company might be a good target. A market study already under way at Eurochem was extended to examine in more depth the size and growth of the specific segments for heating pipes that Francoplast was serving.

Wilcke made the first informal contact with Francoplast in mid-August and followed with a formal meeting in early September that included representatives from Eurochem's legal and controller departments. Wilcke, together with Wirtz, began to develop a justification to acquire Francoplast. In addition, several staff dependents were asked for their comment and concurrence.

In the meantime, Wilcke traveled extensively to Unichem's U.S. divisions related to the pipe business and built a view of how Unichem's technological capabilities might be transferred to Francoplast to develop a European pipe business. Wirtz secured the cooperation of Eurochem's country manager for France, who accompanied him to the negotiations and discussed staffing issues. In the meantime, other functional departments compiled data to build a dossier justifying the acquisition. These included the departments responsible for economic evaluation, manufacturing, R&D, and safety. The personnel department was asked for its advice about managers who might be available for assignment to the new subsidiary. After a team from the controller, tax, and auditing departments was sent in to verify Francoplast's financial statements, a series of downward adjustments were made in the presumed value of the firm.

In January 1983, Wilcke formally proposed to the executive committee of Eurochem that Francoplast be acquired. His 61-page proposal covered the pipe market, Eurochem's diversification strategy, Unichem pipe systems, the Francoplast acquisition, a commercial and business review, manufacturing, R&D, economic evaluation, legal issues, tax impact, and summary. A detailed seven-year sales forecast projected growth from $13.6 million in 1983 to $98.2 million in 1990 on the basis of the introduction of a number of new product lines. A detailed schedule of planned technology transfers to make these commercial developments possible was a key justification for this optimistic scenario.

The analytical groundwork was quite extensive, and each of the departments involved in the process had signed off after its concerns had been met. The French manager supported further investment in France; the R&D directed was interested in Francoplast as a site to experiment with filament-winding technology because of his long-standing interest in advanced composites. Several U.S. divisions were interested in Francoplast as an outlet for their resin and their pipes or as an application for their technology. Given that Francoplast was a small family business, Wilcke proposed that Francoplast become a free-standing unit within the Eurochem matrix organization. On the basis of the proposal itself and Wirtz's overall track record, the proposal was enthusiastically endorsed by Eurochem's executive committee and passed on for corporate board approval.

A few days later, Wirtz and Wilcke learned that Francoplast might have to face claims for faulty pipe installation. But because they had just secured the commitment of Eurochem senior management to the acquisition, they decided that they would deal with those issues themselves, and they submitted the proposal to the corporate board, where it was approved. In the meantime, as they awaited French government approval, they began to prepare the necessary investments and to recruit managers from within the Eurochem organization for Francoplast. The government approval arrived a few months later, and the transfer of ownership was formally signed on June 6, 1983.

ACQUISITIONS AND STRATEGY

This example illustrates the complicated relationship between strategy and opportunism present in acquisitions. Wirtz's interest in championing the development of a new business like pipes sprang from Unichem top management's vision of specialty chemicals development. His interest in the pipe business itself, however, came from the potential to apply Eurochem's capabilities to the market opportunities he perceived in this business.

These capabilities included a distribution system for plastic-lined pipe, a strong sales force to which he could have access, and resin technology. He limited his interest to acquiring a small company because of the organizational constraints he felt, rather than substantive discussions of what would be the most appropriate entry strategy in this business.

In practice, the relationship between acquisitions and formal strategy varies widely, and neither the stereotype of rampant opportunism or that of a carefully planned acquisition is very prevalent. Most acquisitions involve an interaction between a strategy that is clarified over time and the opportunistic consideration of acquisition possibilities.

A truly *planned* acquisition involves the systematic implementation of a well-defined strategy, resulting from the formal planning process or from a formal search or screening process. We did observe such formal acquisition programs in practice, especially in firms that had formally identified a "growth gap" or a major repositioning need, but they were less frequent than the prescriptions of strategy researchers indicate. In addition, they rarely led to acquisitions.

Other acquisitions, to the contrary, were truly *opportunistic*. Not only were they triggered by an opportunity, rather than any proactive search, but, more importantly, the justification process did not lead to the clarification of a sound strategy. Even after approval of the acquisition, no strategy had been mapped out to guide integration.

Most acquisitions, like Francoplast, fall somewhere between opportunism and planning. The acquisition idea may have been suggested and promoted as an opportunity in a situation in which some broad idea or direction, if not a specific strategy, was considered. Acquisitions differed, however, in whether they became truly strategic. By a *strategic* acquisition we mean one for which the justification process resulted not only in the approval of the acquisition, but also in the clarification of a strategy within which the acquisition could fit and on the basis of which the integration could be guided. In other words, opportunism at the outset is fine, as long as the final justification is sound. Of course, a tighter relationship between strategic thinking and the acquisition opportunities being considered is preferable. But it should be emphasized that most significant acquisitions, even when contemplated in the context of an existing strategy, bring opportunities and questions that are likely to require amendment or modification of the strategy.[2]

THE QUALITY OF ACQUISITION JUSTIFICATIONS

The Francoplast example illustrates the myriad of issues that must be considered when evaluating an acquisition.[3] It also shows how the outcome of such analysis is more than a decision as to the desirability of the acquisition and the price to be offered. What emerges from the decision-making process is a much broader set of considerations, a multifaceted view that reflects in the internal and external logic by which the acquisition and its price are justified.

In our research we have closely examined acquisition justifications by studying the formal dossiers that were used to sell acquisitions internally and interviewing the key players about their views at the time. On some dimensions these dossiers were very similar. They all contained a broad statement of the acquisition's purpose, as well as detailed financial projections of expected stand-alone and synergy-related cash flows. But there was a wide variation in the range and detail of issues covered and in the quality of reasoning presented in the dossiers. After analyzing the dossiers and internal arguments of successful and unsuccessful acquisitions, we suggest six dimensions or criteria for judging the soundness of an acquisition justification.[4] See Figure 3-2.

Quality of the Strategic Assessment. The quality of the strategic assessment is a key ingredient in an acquisition justification because it addresses the value-creating *potential* of the acquisition. This assessment considers in detail the contribution of the acquisition to the firm's strategy, as well as the impact of that strategy on the firm's competitive position. Although the potential contribution is addressed in some depth in most acquisition dossiers, the strategy's impact often receives less explicit attention. Problems occur when the acquisition analysis focuses only on the target company itself, or is static, or fails to focus on either the firms' relative competitive positions or future industry requirements.

In the Francoplast example there is no a priori reason to question either the Unichem corporate strategic logic of moving into specialty products or Wirtz's logic in seeking to build a specialty pipe business. Both were underlying reasons for the interest in Francoplast. Yet, despite all the money and effort devoted to market studies and abundant allusions to the strategy of building a pipe systems business, the Francoplast evaluation never really addressed what sort of contribution (other than getting the firm committed to the business) such a small platform would make to Unichem's strategy. Neither did it consider the

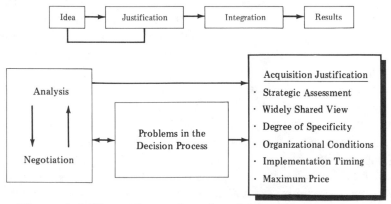

Figure 3-2 **Dimensions of an Acquisition Justification**

implications of building a vertically integrated pipe business for a manufacturer and seller of resins like Eurochem. Extensive consulting analyses focused on ascertaining the existence, size, and growth of various markets. Yet the relative cost position of competitors, the different value-added structure of various segments, and the desirability of entering through the district heating segment in a small way were never considered. All the risks and uncertainties in implementation were rationalized away.

The Francoplast example illustrates the blinders that every company's past success and history places on its managers.[5] In Unichem's traditionally successful commodity business, managers had to be certain about market size and market growth because investments in capacity were huge. But once the market's existence was understood, competitive manufacturing costs could be taken for granted. In the newer specialties business, these facts no longer applied and new questions had to be addressed.

The misorientation of analysis also shows how once an acquisition alternative has been identified, the analysis shifts from considering the type of acquisition candidate appropriate for a particular strategy to making sure that the details associated with the target identified are considered.[6] As a result, the fact that a particular company is considered often determines whether a market segment is entered, rather than whether that segment makes sense strategically.

Widely Shared View of Purpose. Although we observed variation in the soundness of strategic analysis, several factors combined to inject a good dose of "strategic thinking" in most of the acquisition dossiers we analyzed: the use of formal review processes, the popularity of strategic analysis concepts, the spread of analytical skills among managers, and the availability and use of consultants. Ironically, we often observed problems that arose not because strategic thinking was lacking but because too much of it was not well coordinated. In many situations, multiple, conflicting, strategic logics for an acquisition persisted, each espoused by different actors and grounded in its own self-interest and organizational agenda. Yet in the firms we studied, the degree to which a common strategic logic was shared by all key decision makers was a precondition for obtaining consensus for a single organizational approach to implementation.

In the Francoplast decision, at least three competing logics persisted. Francoplast could be seen as a platform for a pipe systems specialties business (Wirtz's view). At the same time, it could be seen in a vertical integration sense as both a captive outlet for resin or a competitor with Eurochem's own resin customers. For the R&D Department it represented an opportunity to experiment with new filament-winding technology in the context of their advanced composites interests.

The presence of multiple arguments for an acquisition is not by itself a problem. In fact, the sounder an acquisition opportunity is, the more numerous the dimensions of possible interaction may be.[7] The problem arises when there is no common understanding and agreement on which of the strategic logics will be the focus of the initial value-creation activities.

Specificity in Sources of Benefits and Problems. A common adherence to an overriding and sound strategic logic is one matter. The depth to which the justification delves into the sources of benefits and its clarity about potential problems is another. The acquisition justifications we analyzed differed widely in the degree to which sources of benefits were considered in detail and even more widely in the extent to which the attendant areas of risk or problems were addressed explicitly. In the Francoplast case, sources of synergies were identified very specifically on the R&D side, yet no questions were raised about the firm's ability to perform in other areas that would be critical if the forecasts were to be realized. The risks and uncertainties of implementation were not raised or rationalized away because of the sponsors' perceived need to sell the acquisition to top management.[8]

Regard for Organizational Conditions. Even if synergy expectations are considered precisely, they are often analyzed on the basis of cost structures or other technical parameters. In practice, however, the implementation of each of those synergies hinges on a number of organizational conditions, not the least of which is the availability of a responsible manager. Explicit regard for such organizational conditions is another key dimension in the quality of the acquisition justification. Although the notion of making Francoplast a freestanding business was incorporated in the acquisition justification, key questions about how to achieve the required independence for this very different business within Eurochem's organizational context and how to simultaneously create the necessary interfaces for technology transfer were never raised.

Timing of Implementation. Like organizational conditions, the timing of implementation is important. In the firms we studied, much of the pre-acquisition integration thinking was static. It projected the endpoint that was hoped for rather than the path to be followed to get there. A clear view of how to start, how fast to proceed, and how to get there is critical to successful integration. The only time-related issue addressed in the Francoplast acquisition was a calendar for transfer of the technological improvements upon which the strategic scenario rested. The expectations of building a highly profitable pipe business were based on the promise of a number of unproven technological developments. None of the relevant problems, risks, organizational conditions, or timing issues associated with this key assumption were considered during the analyses.

Maximum Price. The final component of an acquisition justification is the maximum, walk-away price one is willing to pay for the acquisition, which should be based on the expected value-creation potential and an assessment of its implementation chances. Company valuation will always be a subjective and imprecise exercise and should be recognized as such.[9] Moreover, the initial purchase price may quickly be matched and sometimes dwarfed by further investments in the business. This is, by definition, the case in platform acquisitions like Francoplast, where the initial price consideration of $1 million was immaterial compared with the investment requirements of a successful pipe business. In the larger business position acquisitions we examined as well, a doubling of the resources committed to the acquisition within three years was not uncommon.

Despite the imprecision of the financial valuation, it is important to translate the strategic and organizational assumptions embedded in the justification into a sensible financial valuation and to be committed to it as a walk-away price.[10] Particularly in bidding situations, the dynamics of the process, the fact that an acquisition has different values for different bidders, who may overestimate the uncertain benefits because of their desire to win the bid, results in a tendency to bargain away all potential benefits.[11] While many sins can be covered if a firm is truly a "bargain," the price of recovering from overpaying can be high. As Warren Buffett, chairman of Berkshire Hathaway, said in the firm's 1982 annual report:

> The market, like the Lord, helps those who help themselves. But, unlike the Lord, the market does not forgive those who know not what they do . . . a too high purchase price for the

stock of an excellent company can undo the effects of a subsequent decade of favorable business developments.[12]

The acquisition justification process is easily focused on financial valuation rather than strategic issues. But, unless the justification is built on the combination of a solid strategic assessment, a shared purpose, a specific examination of benefits and problems, a regard for organizational conditions, and attention to timing, the most mechanically elaborate financial case is merely a fiction.

ACQUISITIONS AS RESOURCE ALLOCATION DECISIONS

Acquisitions are both similar to and different from ordinary capital investment decisions. Like other resource commitment decisions, acquisitions seldom conform to the rational and comprehensive view that is embedded in investment theory. In such a rational view, a board-level or senior executive committee objectively selects investment proposals ranked on the basis of their expected return. In a more realistic view, investment decisions involve multiple actors, each of whom has a different perspective and agenda and engages in data-gathering, evaluation, selling, and negotiation activities. During this process the purpose, nature, and scope of the investment opportunity may shift, and a commitment may stall, reverse, or accelerate, depending on the way the process is managed and the whims of the decision makers.[13]

How Acquisitions Are Similar

The acquisition decision process and the general resource allocation process are similar. One useful stream of research has described two iterative stages in the process.[14] The first, more cognitive stage involves the perception, generation, and definition of the investment or acquisition opportunity. The second, more political stage involves building or witholding commitment to a point where managers feel comfortable allocating the resources or rejecting the project. In the Francoplast example, the first stage corresponded to the process in which Wirtz perceived the pipe systems business as a worthwhile opportunity, concluded that a small acquisition was needed, and ended up focusing on Francoplast, a French company in the heating segment. The second stage comprised the myriad of interactions in the evaluation and selling process whereby Wirtz and Wilcke accommodated concerns of different groups and thus secured corporate commitment to their acquisition idea.

In acquisitions made by divisions of large firms, as in other resource commitment decisions, the outcome of both stages is influenced more by the context created by the company's strategy, organizational practices, and culture than it is by substantive direct involvement by top management in the decision.[15] The vaguely encouraging strategic context of Unichem that called for a move into specialty chemicals gave Wirtz the impetus to move forward with a pipe systems project. At the same time, the absence of any prior strategic dialogue about this issue, and Wirtz's position in the organization, made him opt for a less visible small platform acquisition and ruled out the acquisition of one of the larger industry participants. Unichem's past success in a commodities business shaped the analysis and review process by emphasizing the technical feasibility of the project, rather than questioning the commercial and organizational requirements for success.

When firms evaluate investment opportunities for their existing businesses, these processes of opportunity identification, evaluation, and commitment building work well. Most firms have developed a standardized decision process and a discipline for capital appropriations that link project approval to strategic intentions, implementation risk, and available funding. This process is often nested within the firm's budget cycles and the strategic planning process. The outcomes of this iterative process of opportunity definition and commitment building are rather predictable resource allocation decisions. By changing the context in which a project is considered, top management can affect its relative desirability. Moreover, by influencing commitments early on in the process; by increasing or decreasing the scope of the project; or by slowing down or accelerating the project's progress, top management rarely ends up having to issue a formal rejection of a particular project.[16]

How Acquisitions Are Different

When firms consider acquisitions, a number of differences tend to interfere with the relatively smooth operation of the normal resource allocation process. They include:

- Their sporadic nature.
- Their dissimilarity from managers' regular experiences.

- Their opportunistic nature.
- The speed with which decisions must be made.
- The limited access to and processing of information.
- The indivisibility of the opportunity.
- Their inherent riskiness.

Sporadic Nature. Most firms or divisions of firms do not routinely make acquisitions. In Unichem, the new specialties strategy initiated an acquisition period in which Francoplast was one of the first experiences. Moreover, our research found that whatever the extent of experience at the broad corporate level, crucial aspects of the decision-making process devolve on individual managers like Wirtz and Wilcke who, like most managers, are not familiar with the intricacies of acquisition decision making, negotiation, and analysis. Thus, because of the sporadic nature of the process, managers must often make acquisition decisions with less and less insight into the possible results of those decisions than they expect when making routine resource allocation decisions. Because of this increased uncertainty, as we shall later discuss, mechanisms are needed to bring group-wide acquisition experience to the setting of each acquisition without taking responsibility for the acquisition away from line management.

Dissimilarity from Managers' Regular Experiences. Routine capital investment decisions typically take place within the context of the company's current strategy and they are carried out in an organizational context that is well understood. In contrast, acquisitions often imply a redefinition of the firm's strategy, and they always involve a second, entirely different organizational context—that of the company to be acquired. For example, the confidence of Unichem's managers in their sales and cost forecasts might have been justified if they had been making internal investments in the company's base chemicals businesses, for which the company had both manufacturing capability and marketing muscle. But to take these forecasts for granted in a new and unfamiliar business like pipes, as Wirtz and Wilcke did, is an entirely different matter. This wide-ranging difference between acquisitions that take place in familiar territory and others that bring into question the company's strategic and organizational routines also has to be dealt with in shaping the acquisition process.

Opportunity Driven. Acquisition decisions tend to be more opportunity driven than other corporate resource commitment proposals.

Wirtz's and Wilcke's quick fixation on Eurochem's first acquisition opportunity and then on Francoplast may not have represented a formal screening and approach of all candidates.[17] But it did represent an active, albeit superficial, scanning of industry opportunities that reflected the pressures from inside and outside the organization as well as the practical need to find a willing seller.

Wirtz may have become interested in Francoplast because he developed an objective of entering the pipe business. But Eurochem's actual entry into the heating segment occurred almost entirely as a result of his early focus on the Francoplast opportunity. As we shall later argue, the appropriateness of such opportunism depends on whether the strategic implications of such opportunities are clarified and found acceptable in the course of the decision-making process. The need both to appreciate and to balance the element of opportunism is fundamental in acquisitions.

Decision Speed. Unlike the Francoplast example, other acquisitions are often characterized by faster decision making than the long and iterative process that is typical of internal investments. The need for speedy decisions is based partly on the need to operate quickly in an economic climate with multiple bidders as soon as a firm is "in play."[18] In such circumstances, managers feel forced to collapse their decision-making process into a much shorter period than that used for ordinary capital appropriations. However, our research found that the pressures for speedy decisions are often self-imposed or result from tactics of the selling party, and they could be sidestepped or effectively dealt with.

Information Access and Information Processing. Information access and handling are much more constrained in acquisitions than in internal investment decisions. Critical information about the target firm's customers, technologies, market demand, finances, etc. is often proprietary; managers in target firms are not willing to share this information with potential acquirers, because it could be used against them if an agreement falls through. And the farther a potential acquisition candidate is from a manager's experience base, the less capable he or she will be of asking the right questions or searching for the right information.

Information is handled and analyzed differently in internal projects and acquisitions. Internal capital investment projects often require staffing coordination across the different business functions. In contrast, in acquisitions the sensitive nature of the information often limits participation in the decision-making process to senior-level managers and a few staff analysts. Operating managers who could better understand and interpret the data are frequently left out.[19]

Lumpiness. Internally developed investment projects typically undergo a series of iterations and revisions as their purpose is fine-tuned in light of the firm's strategy and associated resource constraints. The final decision may often be a far cry from what was originally envisioned, but it is typically more organizationally and strategically viable as a result of this fine-tuning. In contrast, an acquisition is often considered as a single take-it-or-leave-it decision about a bundle of assets that presents few possibilities to downsize, scale up, redefine, or otherwise modify the project *before* the firm is acquired. Making these changes afterward would create organizational turmoil. Thus, managers typically view acquisitions as one-time decisions that are less malleable than other resource allocation decisions they make.

Riskiness. These characteristics of acquisitions—their sporadic nature, their challenge to the existing strategy and organization, their opportunity-driven nature, the speed required for decisions, the limited access to and processing of information, and the lumpiness of the investment—combine to make acquisition decisions more risky than internal investments, both for the companies involved and for the executives who put their careers on the line.[20]

How Firms Compensate

Many firms have reacted to these characteristics of acquisitions by building a series of safeguards into their decision-making process. Typically they set lower approval limits for acquisitions or require top management approval of all acquisitions, no matter how small. They may impose higher hurdle rates than they set for internal investment to reflect the higher risk involved.[21] They may establish additional review and due process requirements in legal, financial, and environmental, and other areas. They may request more elaborate analysis and bring in outside specialists, such as consultants, lawyers and auditors.

Our research found that often these attempts to improve the justification merely add approval layers, higher hurdles, and additional bureaucratic hoops through which acquisition champions must jump. These additional requirements usually do not materially improve the quality of the decision. Instead, the acquisition dossier merely gets longer and more complex as each function adds its own approval requirements.

These additional hurdles may also shift the balance of the acquisition review toward the "hard" analysis of financial and legal aspects, and away from a consideration of the more subtle and emergent issues of integration, which are open to more ambiguous interpretations. For example, in the Francoplast case, lots of attention was paid to financial analysis, projections, and legal considerations. The question of how a freestanding business could or would operate in Eurochem's matrix structure was hardly raised. Moreover, how effectively the Francoplast personnel, who were accustomed to the decision-making environment in a small, family-controlled firm, would be able to work with seasoned, organizationally savvy Eurochem managers was not even considered. Yet our research shows that it is precisely these implementation and integration issues that determine value creation. Keeping in mind the need for specialist review and for later due diligence, we observed that these fragmented hurdles often failed to ensure that the acquisition was considered as a business proposition and that the justification to acquire was soundly developed. In Chapter 5 we will discuss ways that can help do just that, but first we need to examine in more depth the problems acquisition decision makers have to overcome.

SUMMARY

The acquisition decision process, and the acquisition justification to which it leads, is the first big challenge in acquisition management. A sound justification can improve the odds that value creation will be possible, that the benefits will not be bargained away in advance, and that the potential benefits can actually be realized.

As a category of resource allocation decisions, acquisition decisions are particularly taxing, because of the unique characteristics that make them more risky than the internal investments around which the resource allocation process of most companies was designed and honed. As much as an appropriate maximum price, the quality of a justification was seen to depend on whether a strategic logic was sound; how widely this logic was shared by key decision makers; if it was translated into a specific examination of both benefits and problems; and whether the organizational requirements and timing for implementation had been considered. In the next chapter we will look at how the decision-making process itself creates problems in developing the right sort of justification.

4

Problems in Acquisition Decision Making

INTRODUCTION

IN THE FIRST PHASE of our research we asked a variety of managers and their advisers why acquisitions did not meet their expectations. Many said that their disappointing results had occurred despite their efforts to follow classical prescriptions for acquisition analysis and integration.[1] As we probed more deeply about the reasons for success and failure, we found that aspects of the acquisition process itself intervened. Even when managers recognized the importance of analyzing strategic and organizational fit, they were prevented from understanding these factors by a series of problems inherent in the process of analyzing, negotiating with, and acquiring the other firm.

The process-related problems that they experienced did not stem from excessive opportunism or lack of scrutiny of the opportunity. If anything, the myth of an acquisition deal originated and committed to on the golf course is just that, a myth. The acquisitions we studied, at the corporate divisional levels, involved many analyses by a wide array of managers, specialists, and external professionals.[2] Within the constraints of time and secrecy, these groups of people engaged in what they considered an appropriate process to arrive at a decision about the potential of the acquisition. Yet, because of the way the decision-making process was managed, their good intentions were often in vain. The acquisition justifications developed sometimes lacked the depth and richness that were needed to understand how the acquisitions would create value. This chapter first discusses these process problems in detail and then explores how the quality of a firm's resource allocation process can contribute to, or address, the problems.

PROCESS PROBLEMS IN ACQUISITION DECISION MAKING[3]

Our research points to four problems inherent in the decision-making process that substantially limit a firm's ability to develop a good justification for an acquisition (see Figure 4-1):

- *Fragmented perspectives* of many specialists during analysis and decision making.
- *Increasing momentum* to consummate the transaction.
- *Ambiguous expectations* about key aspects of the acquisition between both sides in the negotiation.
- *Multiple motives* among acquiring managers.

FRAGMENTED PERSPECTIVES

Acquisition decision making often requires the support of many technical specialists who end up working in isolation from one another and making judgments and recommendations without coordination. This del-

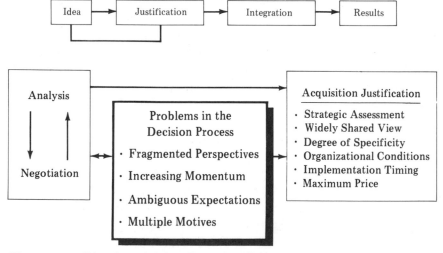

Figure 4-1 The Acquisition Decision Process

egation to specialists results in an emphasis on quantification of financial estimates instead of broader strategic and organizational considerations. Such fragmented decision making severely limits the firm's ability to develop the sort of rich justification needed to give the acquisition adequate consideration.

Every acquisition requires a variety of highly technical analyses, for example, financial valuation, product-market analysis, tax issues, antitrust considerations, pension fund liability, safety standards, etc. In large, complex transactions the phenomenon of fragmentation is exponential, because dozens of separate entities subject to different legal requirements, antitrust considerations, and accounting practices may be involved. Most firms, and certainly most divisions in firms, do not maintain an in-house staff of specialists on these topics because it would be too expensive to develop and keep specialists with such highly technical analytical capabilities on the payroll. As a result, these issues are often subcontracted out to outside advisers such as investment bankers, consultants, attorneys, accountants, and auditors, who are more familiar with the technicalities of a particular analysis. Even if the firm does have legions of qualified corporate staff, their role in the acquisition process is typically to represent and protect their function's (parochial) interests rather than to offer an overall viewpoint.

Because of these fragmented perspectives, it is often difficult for one manager or a group of managers to maintain a generalist's grasp of the transaction. Although most top executives recognize that an acquisitive strategy requires such a perspective, the problem of integrating a variety of overspecialized and fragmented views of the deal is quite common. As one CEO told us:

> During the negotiations, there were so many different people involved, it was hard to tell who was doing what, let alone how all their efforts would tie together.

Another CEO described how he assembled a team of more than 150 specialists, including investment bankers, consultants, attorneys, and accountants, as well as his corporate staff, within thirty hours to analyze a prospective acquisition. Few of these people had ever met or worked together before, and the entire process lasted only six days. Although extreme, this example highlights the problems generated when large teams of specialists with a narrow focus are thrown together to analyze a deal under intense time pressures. Under such conditions, people who have not worked closely together before or who do not share a common expertise, set of experiences, or vocabulary can communicate only the most standardized information quickly and effectively.[4]

Specialization is a characteristic of decision making in many organizational settings, to be sure. But in acquisitions the isolation of specialists makes it difficult to integrate their analyses. When large groups of specialists become involved in acquisitions, senior decision makers have increasing difficulty comparing and integrating the individual analyses. As a result, top managers often focus their attention on more easily and quickly communicated issues that can be quantified, rather than on the more subtle and qualitative concerns that surround broad issues of strategic fit, detailed questions of organizational fit, and the implications for value creation of different approaches to integration.

This tendency toward quantification occurs for several reasons. Many strategic fit issues are based on assumptions about volume, prices, and costs that lend themselves to standardized analytical approaches that assess markets, products, industries, or technologies. Although these techniques are used in good faith, the assessments they develop are only estimates. Too often these estimates become precise expectations because they are quantified and they reflect the stated purpose of the acquisition.

In contrast, issues of organizational fit or more abstract strategic considerations are less clear cut. Consultants and investment bankers cannot develop a model of organizational analysis for an acquisition candidate that they can apply from client to client as easily as they can develop models to value a company's securities or to assess the strategic attractiveness of a particular product-market.

Moreover, few channels of communication exist among the various groups of analysts, who perform their work in different time periods. They often work as if they were hermetically sealed off from each other. It is not uncommon to see a group of analysts developing the strategic argument in one room while another group in a different room is projecting a set of numbers on which the deal will be justified.

Although operating considerations are important in assessing the value of a target company, we found that line managers are often less influential than staff specialists or, in many cases, they take no part in pre-acquisition analysis. Furthermore, most of the staff specialists who are involved are operationally celibate in the companies' businesses. Similarly, the skills necessary to negotiate an acquisition differ from those required to run things afterwards. Consequently, specialists in negotiation and acquisition analysis may consider operating matters outside their area of responsibility and confine themselves to more familiar and easily analyzed financial issues.

Ego also plays a role here. Specialists, especially outsiders, tend to view issues of organizational fit not only as postponable but also as less prestigious and intrinsically less rewarding: One must work with many operating managers, not just CEOs, to assess organizational fit. Because resolution of these issues is not essential to completing the acquisition, they are postponed for others of lesser stature (or a lower hourly billable rate) to handle.

Investment bankers who must certify the appropriateness of the offering price in a fairness opinion to the firm's boards of directors are not called on to assess organizational fit; it simply isn't their brief. Moreover, issues of organizational fit are more subjective and therefore more open to challenge. Although they acknowledged the importance of qualitative issues in acquisition outcomes, the investment bankers we interviewed told us that they rely chiefly on calculations based on purely quantitative criteria that can be more easily defended if their opinion is challenged in court. But this specious accuracy seems futile when it is recognized how different assumptions can cause the range of prices represented by fairness opinions to vary widely.

INCREASING MOMENTUM

Momentum toward completing a deal often builds despite the additional decision-making hurdles put in place for acquisitions. The acquisition process is frequently described as having "a life of its own" characterized by alternating periods of waiting and frenetic activity. As the tension, pace, and involvement rise relentlessly, participants tend to feel unable to stop the acquisition process or even to slow its tempo. Usually described in vague, emotion-laden terms by those involved, this sense of inexorable momentum contrasts sharply with the traditional portrayal of acquisitions as carefully calculated strategic acts.

Momentum develops among all participants in the process—senior executives, middle managers, and outside advisers. Participants directly involved in the acquisition process often point to powerful forces beyond managerial control that accelerate the speed of transactions. Our research suggests that the forces that accelerate momentum in the acquisition process are stronger than those that can slow it down. The net result is an escalating desire to complete the process quickly and to "close the deal." Unchecked, this desire results in premature solutions, inadequate consideration of integration issues, and less likelihood of a successful outcome. As the chief financial officer of one company we studied said:

> The speed with which things took place was mind-boggling. If we had done that sort of quickie analysis for a capital expenditure decision, the board's audit committee would have been down around our ears in a minute.

How far such momentum can go is illustrated by the Francoplast acquisition discussed earlier. After they had committed themselves to European top management, the acquisition's sponsors, Wilcke and Wirtz, ignored the warnings about potentially serious quality claims that were received before final board approval was obtained and did nothing to halt the process.

Various forces help build momentum in the acquisition process. The predominant factors include increased personal commitment; secrecy and intense concentration; and outside advisers.

Increased Personal Commitment. Personal commitment to doing a deal, notwithstanding its relative merits, can be increased by several factors, including the time required, lack of experience, the participants' self-interest, individual career aspirations, and the firm's reward systems.

Acquisition analyses and negotiations frequently require a substantial, uninterrupted time commitment from participants. This investment of time can make the acquisition seem more important than it is and reduce executives' willingness to walk away from it. Moreover, the more managers identify with an acquisition, the less likely it is that they will be able to accept criticism that could either slow it down or drop it from consideration.

The CEO's lack of acquisition experience also can build commitment to completing the deal. CEO may feel pressure from both peers and subordinates to take on the role of the decisive risk-taking leader by personally overseeing an acquisition analysis and negotiation. Such pressures may be especially strong for CEOs who have never "done a deal." Because so many of their fellow CEOs have, they may feel they are among the uninitiated. This emphasis on personal image as a leader makes it increasingly difficult for an executive to walk away from a potential acquisition as the analysis and negotiation progress. Feeling that they have put their reputation for sound, decisive judgment on the line, some CEOs exhibit a classical case of escalating commitment, increasing their desire to complete the deal, in part to prove that their earlier judgments were correct.[5]

Pressures to conclude the acquisition occur at different levels and on both sides of the negotiating table. For managers in the acquiring company, the target may be a stepping-stone to enhance their own reputations. In the target firm, managers may be anxious to get out or, to the contrary, to gain access to the abundant resources of the parent that acquisition would place at their disposal.

A corporation's approach to acquisition analysis and its reward system may unintentionally reinforce the push to complete an acquisition at all costs. For example, the U.S. Tax Reform Act of 1985 eliminated the profitability of certain kinds of leasing operations. One major financial services firm was hit particularly hard by this law; about one-third of its revenue vanished at the stroke of President Reagan's pen. To compensate, a portion of the discretionary performance bonus of each of the heads of the firm's major divisions was made dependent on that manager making an acquisition to bring a new business to replace revenue lost from the change in the law.

These perverse incentives to do a deal are present in other forms as well. In many companies, for example, an acquisition task force or committee is used as the focal point for search, screening, and analysis. This group may think it has failed if an acquisition candidate is not found; to such a group the charge to look for suitable acquisition candidates becomes an open-ended hunting license. Moreover, task-force members may believe that negotiating an acquisition successfully will assure them of brighter career opportunities.

We believe that managers can never fully reduce (nor should they ever eliminate) the career uncertainty or opportunities associated with organizational assignments; these are one of the forces on which creativity is built. Senior executives should make sure that people involved in acquisitions do not believe that their career opportunities and rewards depend on whether a particular "deal" is made but on performance that is directed toward the firm's strategic needs.

Secrecy and Strain. Acquisition decision makers operate under conditions of secrecy and intense concentration. Once the possibility of a deal becomes known in a company, business as usual virtually ceases, and a period of uncertainty sets in for employees, shareholders, suppliers, customers, and competitors. To limit the impact of this uncertainty, the time provided for analysis is reduced as managers try to complete the arrangements before news is leaked that could cause internal or external disruptions or trigger a price run-up in the financial markets.

The personal and organizational stakes involved in an acquisition are greater and more uncertain than those most managers face in their day-to-day work. The strain everyone feels, together with the intense time pressures, compounds the desire to wrap things up. "It's torrid," said one investment banker. "We're at the limits of our physical and mental capacities."[6]

Outside Advisers. Many outside advisers, especially investment bankers, have a major interest in consummating a deal because they are compensated on a transaction basis. Because bankers' fees do not vary dramatically whether a deal takes three weeks or nine months to close, it is in their interest therefore, to conclude the process quickly. As a prominent investment banker told us:

> It's hard not to be affected by the fees. Look, it's margin times turnover. The margins [in mergers and acquisitions] are great and we need the turnover because the other two pieces of our business, corporate finance and [government bond] sales and trading both require risk capital and are under severe competitive pressures.

This situation creates a serious problem. Companies use these outside experts to provide objective, professional advice, yet these advisers face a conflict between representing their own interests and those of their clients.[7] As Felix Rohatyn of Lazard Frères put it,

> Fees are sometimes ten times as large as when a deal closes as when it doesn't, so you'd about have to be a saint not to be affected by the numbers involved . . . the level of fees has reached a point that . . . invites the suspicion that there's too much incentive to do a deal.[8]

Slowing the Process. The momentum in an acquisition process can be slowed down. Bernard Schwartz, chairman and CEO of Loral Electronics, told us, "Some of the deals I'm most proud of were killed during the process because they didn't meet our objectives." Internal approval processes, resistance of the target firm, regulatory obstacles, and managerial experience can operate to limit the rush to close a deal. But, on balance, our research suggests that these forces are often weaker than the forces that propel a deal to closure.

Even if the standard organizational approval process does slow down the decision, it does not diminish the momentum toward serious evaluation of the acquisition opportunity as a business prospect. Precisely because the acquisition puts so many specialized hurdles in their way, managers like Wirtz and Wilcke move quickly from an evaluative mode into a selling mode. Once in the selling mode, they rarely stop to reconsider their position, even when additional information brings some of their assumptions into question.

We should also recognize that acquisitions are often announced and then canceled. Despite the apparent strategic logic of the combination, other forces can come into play. For example, the merger of Ford-Europe and Fiat was called off because the parties could not agree on who would be in control. As Gianni Agnelli, chairman of Fiat SpA said,

> Ford is a very proud company; Fiat is a very proud company. When you come to the question of control and evaluation, we thought it was best to call it off.[9]

Another illustration of excessive momentum is the canceled merger between the Dutch AMRO bank and the Belgian Société Générale de Banque, after both sides had already purchased an equity stake in the other and had committed to pooling their international operations. The agreement to merge was rushed through partly because of the takeover pressure on Société Générale de Banque's parent. The undoing of the deal stemmed from the next factors—to which excessive momentum often leads—the fact that many key issues between and within the parties often remain unresolved.

Of course, it is not always possible or desirable to slow down the acquisition process. Once a potential candidate is identified, managers face the very real threat that another company could buy it. Indeed, moving quickly to acquire another firm is appropriate in many cases, and dealing with opportunistic acquisitions is a key ingredient of an acquisitive strategy. But such speed should not come at the expense of the quality of the acquisition justification.

For example, Percy Barnevik, architect of the 1987 merger between ASEA and Brown Boveri to form ABB, the world's largest heavy electrical business company, describes the need for secrecy as follows:

> We took a couple of months to complete the process . . . I can tell you that had we followed the normal American way, with a host of lawyers looking for skeletons in the closet, it would have taken years and the merger would never have come about. An

operation of this magnitude can only succeed because of a surprise effect. Had the project been known for months, we would
have failed. The unions, governments, and other interested parties would have easily intervened, slowed down the process, or
even halted it.[10]

AMBIGUOUS EXPECTATIONS

Agreeing to disagree by postponing consideration of contentious issues often helps conclude a deal. At some point in the negotiations,
when many issues have been resolved and momentum has built up on
both sides of the table, the temptation is great to reach an agreement
despite the knowledge that a number of issues will have to be resolved
later. These unresolved issues become part of the immediate legacy of
the operating managers, who then have to make the "deal" work. It is
clear that while such ambiguity may help to conclude a deal, when
carried to the integration phase, it can create substantial problems and
reduce the chances for successful integration.[11]

Both firms enter into negotiations with certain expectations about the
purpose of the acquisition, future performance levels, and the timing of
particular actions. Because there is great potential for disagreement on
these points during negotiations, managers often agree to disagree until
later, thus sustaining momentum and keeping the deal on track. Thus
ambiguity can serve both parties well. It provides maneuvering room in
negotiations and opportunities to save face in public announcements,
and it helps the parties find a common denominator for agreement on
seemingly intractable issues during the fast-paced process in which they
are involved.

Sooner or later, however, especially when the integration process
begins, the ambiguity that was essential to reaching an agreement ironically becomes a major source of difficulty and conflict. The parties must
eventually clarify the key parts of the agreement previously left ambiguous. Sometimes these ambiguities involve top managers themselves,
as important issues of post-merger responsibilities and power sharing
may be left unclarified. Sometimes these ambiguities involve more operational decisions, where clarification is often left to managers who
were not directly involved in the negotiations and whose personal interests favor maintaining the status quo. In other situations, they can
involve matters as important as who will be the chairman.

For example, when Banco de Bilbao and Banco de Vizcaya merged,
their respective chairmen, Señor Sanchez Asiain and Señor Toledo

were to preside as cochairmen of Spain's largest banking group. The unexpected death of Señor Toledo precipitated a major crisis. Banco de Vizcaya's former board members moved to replace Sēnor Toledo with one of their executives Sēnor Saenz, claiming that a four-year cochairmanship had been agreed on. The Banco de Bilbao side expected Sēnor Sanchez Asiain to remain as sole chairman. The confusion and irritation resulting from an apparent lack of clarity in the power-sharing arrangements between former top managements plunged the bank into an embarrassing power struggle until Spain's national bank used its influence to bring about a solution.[12]

When the same points of disagreement continue to arise after the agreement, relationships woven during the negotiation process, including fragile bonds of trust, may begin to unravel. As trust breaks down, both parent and subsidiary managers may overreact, which often sets off a cycle of escalating conflict and further distrust. To regain a sense of control over the situation, parent company executives may clamp down and impose rigorous or standardized performance expectations and milestones on the new subsidiary. These standards may be inappropriate for the special needs of the subsidiary's business. Yet, when performance expectations are not met (often predictably), parent firm managers may react as though their fears of weak or incompetent subsidiary management have been confirmed. In response, subsidiary managers typically defend their autonomy against all parent firms requests, which merely fuels the parent's preconceived need for increased control and intervention. The continuing cycle of escalating conflict may seem to confirm subsidiary managers' worst fears of a malevolent takeover.

A good example of the implementation problems ambiguity can create is General Motors' acquisition of Electronic Data Systems. One of the strategic reasons for the acquisition was to improve the automaker's ability to manage increasingly complex information flows and improve its information systems. To compensate for the different managerial incentive systems of the two firms, a new class of General Motors shares was created (Class E). These shares were intended to compensate EDS managers with stock options that reflected the performance of the EDS subsidiary. After the acquisition, when negotiating prices for EDS services in GM divisions, the GM financial controllers expected the work to be done at cost or a negotiated price in typical GM fashion in the driver's seat. Yet the merger agreement called for long-term, fixed-price contracts for EDS.[13] Apparently implementation of the transfer pricing policy had not been discussed in detail during the pre-acquisition negotiations. This ambiguity added to the subsequent hostility between the two groups of managers.

The implications of ambiguity are significant. We believe that ambiguity is useful—if not essential—to develop the internal and interfirm political coalitions necessary to reach agreement during the negotiation phase. Yet the same ambiguity that aids in negotiations can sow the seeds of later post-acquisition problems.

MULTIPLE MOTIVES

Ambiguities in talks across the bargaining table are not the only source of postmerger problems. A similar ambiguity often persists within the acquiring firm. We already noted that acquisitions are frequently driven by multiple motives in the minds of one or several actors. The Francoplast acquisition can be viewed from several perspectives: as a platform for pipe systems business, as a downstream outlet for resin sales, or as a laboratory for advanced composites manufacturing know-how.

The process of internal negotiation and championing often leads to the persistence rather than the clarification of these different motives. Managers faced with a multitude of hurdles overcome them by selling (slightly) different views of the acquisition to different stakeholders in the hope of winning their support. In many instances that we observed, the specific synergies listed in the acquisition justification represented implicit promises to one part of the organization that it would be allowed to pursue its own agenda with respect to the acquisition. In one case, a particularly zealous young manager had convinced his (American) company to make a small manufacturing acquisition in Europe. No fewer than four units in the parent organization felt that they had been "promised" that the business would be required to report to them: two U.S. product divisions to whose products the acquisition's activity related; the U.K. manufacturing organization, which was the company's only manufacturing base in Europe; and the continental European sales and service organization, in whose territory this would be a first manufacturing acquisition.

Thus the ambiguity that was especially useful for internal negotiations can return to haunt the management during the integration phase because these multiple justifications cannot all be addressed at once. The list of expected synergies often becomes the sum of all these expectations, which are largely incompatible. Before an acquisition, this addition was useful to help justify the acquisition premium and to gain broad commitment. After the agreement it becomes the basis for multiple claims on post-merger priorities and involvement. In Francoplast these multiple claims were at the heart of a post-acquisition situation in which the organizational choices implicit in developing a pipe business, selling resin, or bringing an experimental center on line were found to be radically different.

SUMMARY

These process-related problems do not stem from excessive opportunism or lack of scrutiny of acquisition opportunities. The acquisitions we studied, especially those at the divisional level, involved a good deal of analysis by a wide array of managers, specialists, and external professionals. Within the constraints of time and secrecy these groups of people engaged in what they considered an appropriate process to decide about the potential of the acquisition. Yet, because of the way the decision-making process was managed, their good intentions were often in vain.

The problems of fragmented decision making, escalating momentum, ambiguous expectations, and multiple motives played an important role in acquisition failure in a wide range of acquisitions that we studied. As we will discuss next, these problems are linked to more general characteristics of the firm's resource allocation processes.

QUALITY OF THE RESOURCE ALLOCATION PROCESS[14]

The critical role of these process problems was corroborated in another phase of this research. We traced in detail the acquisition process in a selected sample of fourteen successful and unsuccessful acquisitions in four large diversified firms, one American, one German, and two British (see Appendix A). These problems occurred repeatedly in the unsuccessful acquisitions, but were counterbalanced in successful situations by safeguards and changes in the decision-making process that kept them in check.

As we studied the complex and multilevel decision-making process in these acquisitions by interviewing participants and reviewing relevant documents, another dimension emerged. These problems, and their severity, could be traced back to more general characteristics of the firms' resource allocation process.[15] The resource allocation process appears to be much more robust and adaptable in some companies than others. In some firms the resource allocation process that is adequate for regular internal investment decisions tends to break down in the face of unusual or risky commitments such as acquisitions.

Our research found that such differences in resource allocation decision making affects the severity of problems experienced and the means by which they can be overcome, as we will discuss in the next chapter.

We identified five interactive dimensions that, taken together, typified a company's resource allocation style:

- Time horizon of managers.
- Managers' concept of how to compete.
- Substantive involvement of top management.
- Analytical versus political decision making.
- Consensual versus individualistic decisions.

Each of these factors is clearly rooted in the firm's own history, and also in the national environment within which its decision-making capability originated, as capital markets, labor markets, and general cultural characteristics exert their influence.[16] We will discuss each of these dimensions and then examine their consequences for companies' acquisition decision-making practices.

Time Horizon of Managers. The time horizon of top managers and its impact on decision making is a topic of much discussion.[17] One line of argument holds that capital market pressures in countries such as the United Kingdom and the United States impose shorter time horizons upon top managers than they might otherwise adopt. The argument is that top managers naturally have the long-term survival of their organization at heart, but capital market expectations clap a straightjacket on them from which their Japanese or even German colleagues are largely spared.[18]

Our research was conducted in companies that made strategic, not financial, acquisitions, and we observed important differences in the time horizon embedded in the acquisition decision-making process. Not surprisingly, American companies like Unichem and German companies like BASF were on opposite ends of this spectrum. The time horizon embodied in the decision making of British companies such as ICI or BP tended to vary across the middle.

The differences we refer to did not emerge from statements by top management. For example, in many instances top management of Unichem not only spoke, but also acted, with a clear, long-term perspective. Nor do the differences show up in formal hurdles like the discount rates applied to project evaluation. Formally, the investment approval system in Unichem applied the same sort of discount rates over the same time horizon as did European companies such as BASF or ICI or BP.

The differences that mattered were in the time horizon within which operating managers perceived they had to deliver performance in financial terms, and in their ability to differentiate that time horizon appropriately by type of acquisition. That perception did not flow as much from their reaction to substantive statements by top management as it did from other signals top management sent. For example, the messages conveyed by consistently negative reactions to acquisition opportunities that would dilute earnings in the short run or an impatience for financial results from acquisitions were clearly read by operating managers.

The experienced successful acquirers we studied were able to tolerate and encourage very different expectations about when to expect financial returns, depending on the strategic purposes of the acquisitions. They were as tough-minded about realizing the financial benefits of domain defense acquisitions quickly as they were flexible in providing excess resources for post-acquisition integration in more complex domain extension acquisitions.

Managers' Concept of How to Compete. The ways in which managers conceived of the basis of competition and the extent to which they shared (their own version of) the capabilities-based perspective we outlined in Chapter 2 affected the resource allocation process and materially differed among firms. We discussed in that chapter how ultimate financial performance flows from a competitive position in product-markets that is achieved by building and applying superior capabilities. Although many senior managers we interviewed espoused such a capabilities-based view in theory, we observed important differences in the way that operating managers in those same companies viewed the competitive game in which they were involved.

In some companies, the underlying concept of competition was one of long-term strength built on broad-based capabilities. For example, whenever managers at BASF discussed their acquisitions, this theme came through, whether they were discussing the need to understand and possess the fundamental chemistry base underlying a business like paints or the need to build a more integrated position in the United States to underpin each of the businesses, the focus was on the basic capabilities from which market position could be achieved or strengthened.

In ICI (often in similar, if not identical, businesses), capabilities were also considered, especially by the more technical managers. Most strategic considerations and discussions, however, seemed to emphasize the need to establish dominant market positions in the face of prevalent industry restructuring. Acquiring either scale or market share often seemed to be their first ambition; it was implicitly assumed that either would bring with it both needed strengths and economic results.

Such approaches contrasted with those of other companies, like Unichem, where operating managers perceived the need to frame all investments in terms of financial outcomes, and where scant attention was paid to capability building. Sometimes much attention is attached to framing the competitive game in terms of establishing market position— as in GE's stated dedication to establish a number one or number two position in each of its businesses, or to opt out. Often that dedication is nominal, however, and operating managers know full well that top management's support of such a strategy depends on fast financial results.

Substantive Involvement of Top Management. Top management wants and expects to be involved in acquisition decisions because of their strategic nature and the potential risks involved. But the larger and more diversified a company, the less top management can be involved in the substantive detail even of fairly large resource commitment decisions.

One way of coping with the resulting gap between managers with substantive knowledge of the business and those with formal power over resource allocation is for senior managers to rely on the track record of the sponsoring "general managers in the middle" to calibrate the reliability of the financial numbers that are presented.[19] Another way to remedy this lack of real-time detailed involvement in individual resource allocation decisions is to channel substantive discussion through a regular business planning review process.[20]

Yet, among the companies of similar size and complexity we studied, firms varied substantially in the degree to which top management was substantively involved in resource allocation decisions of a similar magnitude. At Unichem, the involvement of top management in the decision to acquire a pipe company was very limited. Even the strategic decision whether to enter the pipe business was largely left to Wirtz, the business champion. On the basis of his reading of the corporate signals,

Wirtz decided to go for a small platform only and that he would need to promise a superior financial and growth record.

In contrast, at other firms substantive involvement was extensive but fairly indirect and was largely embodied in the planning process. For example, in ICI a very active planning process was geared to assure that the corporate executive team would have the final say over a unit's choice of a business strategy. Once a strategy was agreed upon, however, group resources were, in principle, committed to projects in the context of the strategy, and its implementation was largely delegated to the business level. In British Petroleum the corporate planning function played a strong role not only in the approval of the business strategy during regular strategy reviews, but also by supporting or critiquing each individual acquisition decision.

At BASF the *Vorstand* (General Management Board) itself discussed every proposed business strategy in detail, often in the absence of the business unit manager whose business it was. In addition to this indirect substantive involvement, at least three executive committee members (those with oversight for the business, the country involved, and finance) steeped themselves in the substance of any acquisition or other serious resource commitment decision. Moreover, before a proposal was formally discussed by the *Vorstand*, the investment committee, consisting of senior staff members, scrutinized the dossier in much more detail than was customary in other firms we studied.

The extent of top management involvement in the substance of individual resource commitment decisions has clear implications for the political and risk-sharing aspects of such decisions, which we discuss next. If the discussion across organizational levels is truly substantive, a firm is more likely to develop an analytical tradition of examining all facts and sharing the risks for key decisions.

Analytical versus Political Decision Making. Another factor related to the corporate/business dialogue was the degree to which the basis for discussion and approval was factual merit rather than political influence. The resource allocation process always has analytical and political components, both of which are healthy ingredients in complex decision making. Yet the balance and nature of these two dimensions vary greatly across companies. At one end of the spectrum are companies that have essentially an "analytical" process, and at the other end are those with a "political" process.[21]

In an "analytical" process, support for a project as it moves from level to level in the organization is based largely on a presentation and discussion of facts in which information is expected to be condensed, but not skewed. The advocacy process may still be strong, but it operates at the level of inference and judgment, not by subverting the facts that are transmitted to higher levels.

In a "political" process, advocacy is exercised by editing and massaging data to filter out most indications of uncertainties and risks. Never a formal policy, this practice is condoned by top management which, in a sense, brings it about by its automatically negative reaction to projects that do reflect realistic uncertainties and risks. As a safeguard against the risks of this gaming process, top management frequently relies on the track record of the project champion.

In the course of our inquiry into acquisition decisions, we witnessed extreme differences in the process among companies. At BASF, resource commitment proposals were clearly expected to be factual, and nothing but factual. The right selling approach consisted of clarifying and summarizing all aspects, not just the benefits, but especially the possible risks and costs. Managers who put a project forward were confident that the decision on their project would weigh all factors on balance. This approach is in stark contrast to that used by companies in which a full discussion of project risks would quickly eliminate a proposal from consideration. In Unichem, for example, even after it became clear that claims might arise as a result of faulty installation of pipe systems, middle managers felt they needed to keep this fact from surfacing so the already approved acquisition would not be jeopardized. Instead of raising the issue, they absorbed the risk at their own level, betting their careers on the hope that somehow they would be able to manage the situation if claims were filed against Francoplast.

Where a company falls on this analytical versus political dimension is highly idiosyncratic and depends on its own administrative heritage.[22] We observed the same detached, analytical view and respect for the apparent "facts" in the decision making at ICI that we described in BASF. Yet in BP, which operated in adjacent, if not overlapping, business areas, and recruited managers from the same British schools, such as Imperial College and Oxford, the balance between analytical and political considerations was often closer to the political end of the spectrum.

Consensual versus Individualistic Decisions. Whether political positions take the upper hand over analytical arguments relates to the qualitative aspects of management's operation as a team, particularly to the extent to which the decision-making process depends on a single champion at each level. In *all* firms, the acquisition decision involved the consent of many individuals and the clear advocacy of a few. Yet strong differences existed in the extent to which responsibility for the outcome of the acquisition rested with a single individual or were collectively shared. For example, in Unichem, as in many classical American companies, one individual at each level clearly stood to gain the lion's share of the reward or the blame for a resource commitment. This fact is one clear consequence of the traditional American conception of a single, powerful general manager who is personally responsible for the consequences of his or her organization's performance.

In ICI, by contrast, *business-level* managers tended to stick their necks out more collectively vis-à-vis corporate. At the same time, corporate-level management was more consensual as well, as illustrated by the following comment from a senior corporate manager:

> Our senior executive team is not headed by a CEO. We have a Chairman, who is basically a *primus inter pares*, and who traditionally has been given a fairly short tenure, between three and five years. Each of the executive directors has both a business overseeing responsibility and a functional one. He is, however, not an advocate of the proposals of the businesses he oversees.

> Moreover, the role of our outside Board members is very active. No acquisition of over 20 million—for us not a big amount—will be approved without them getting seriously involved. This involvement does not always lead to a slowdown. As a matter of fact, in some cases their role has been more to accelerate and tell us to get on with it.

In BASF, with its classic German organization of top management in a *Vorstand* in which each member has functional, territorial, and business responsibility, the search for a collective opinion was parceled out not only at the level of the business or at the corporate level, but also largely across levels.

RESOURCE ALLOCATION STYLE AND QUALITY OF ACQUISITION JUSTIFICATIONS

Although the elements described above are only a part of the complex and subtle web of factors that determine the style of resource allocation, they are closely related to the presence or absence of the acquisition decision-making problems we discussed in Chapter 3 and to some of the post-acquisition integration problems we will discuss in Chapter 7.

On the basis of our study of these four firms and partial observations in a wide range of other firms, we suggest that the closer a company's resource allocation style was to the left or "limited" side in Figure 4-2, the more pervasive were the acquisition problems we discussed in the previous section. This is not to say that such companies cannot generally be successful. But the effectiveness of their resource allocation processes is limited to making more routine internal investments. In such companies the quality of acquisition justifications that we examined was frequently low. Their successful acquisitions were either less demanding ones that could be accomplished in a short time within the narrow strategic context of an existing business, or it was based on the combination of a skillful manager and fortuitous circumstances. The good acquisitions in such firms could not be considered a product of the way in which resources were allocated.

The resource allocation style corresponding to the right-hand side in Figure 4-2, which we call "robust," was much more adaptable than the "limited" style across a wide range of acquisition challenges and led to much richer acquisition justifications in terms of the variables we discussed in the previous chapter. A drawback frequently mentioned by the managers in such companies was the perceived slowness of decision. This slowness was partly compensated for by time gained through more thorough preparation of post-acquisition issues. Moreover, despite these internal assertions, we did not observe anything to corroborate this perceived slowness. To the contrary, management's

Factors	Limited	<------>	Robust
Managerial time horizon	short		long
Concept of competition	results		capabilities
Substantive involvement	low		high
Basis of decision making	political		analytical
Nature of decision making	singular		consensual

Figure 4-2 **Resource Allocation Styles**

substantive involvement observed in companies like BASF, made possible swift decision making when the situation demanded.

Companies with a robust resource allocation style needed few adjustments to handle acquisition decision making effectively, whereas those with a "limited" style often had problems. BASF achieved what were by our standards excellent acquisition justifications by adding a few features to its regular resource commitment process. A single individual within strategic planning was the contact person for all acquisition/divestment and joint-venture submissions to the *Vorstand*. The "financial investment" committee that reviewed all proposals both for approval to negotiate and for final recommendation had only a slightly different composition than the internal investment committee. In the case of acquisitions, the financial function played a more formal role, putting the financial case together on the basis of the scenarios provided by the business.

In many companies, a short time horizon, a financial results orientation, remoteness of top management, and a political process with clear individual champions are more or less a fact of organizational life. To get at the root of acquisition decision-making problems by addressing the general quality of resource allocation decisions may require a pervasive change in the company's corporate culture and demand strong corporate leadership: It is not a simple matter to change a corporate culture on any of the dimensions we discussed. Moreover, such changes might "go against the grain" of the company's national environment and the pressures flowing from its capital markets and labor markets.

In the face of such constraints, companies may want to differentiate the process by which they examine acquisitions from their ongoing investment decision process. In the next chapter we will turn to organizing for acquisition decision making.

SUMMARY

Every executive wants to make a sound judgment about potential acquisitions. Despite managers' best intentions, however, acquisitions often do not live up to their hopes. Our research found that a major reason for these disappointments and failures lies in a series of problems that occur naturally during the acquisition decision-making process. These problems include fragmented decision making, escalating momentum, multiple motives, and ambiguous expectations.

The severity of these problems was linked to the company's resource allocation style, which we described as ranging from limited to robust on a number of dimensions. The broader problems that tended to limit the effectiveness of a company's resource allocation style included: short time horizons, a financial results oriented perspective on competition, limited top management involvement in the substance of the decision, politics driving out facts, and a single champion approach to investment responsibility. Such problems, however, can be managed and dealt with effectively. Our next chapter presents suggestions based on the practice of firms that have effectively managed the acquisition decision-making process.

Managing Acquisition Decision Making

INTRODUCTION

WE HAVE POINTED OUT that the regular resource allocation processes in firms are often not well adapted to acquisition decisions. The traditional response has been to add more hurdles to these processes rather than to acknowledge and provide for the unique characteristics of acquisitions. This chapter discusses how firms can address the problems we described in Chapter 4. We will approach the issue at two levels: first, how to organize for acquisition decision making in general, creating a context in which acquisitions can be properly considered, and second, how to build the organizational routines needed to consider individual acquisitions within this context.[1]

Our discussion at both these levels is addressed to helping managers deal with four key tasks in acquisition decision making. The first is systematically to assure the quality of the acquisition justification. The second task is to combine such high-quality justifications with the real-world needs for speed and confidentiality. The third task is to be able to apply these ideas across a wide range of acquisition types, so that a firm's management capabilities can support a wide range of strategies. Finally, the fourth task is to foster learning and transfer of acquisition experience within the firm, so that every new acquisition benefits from the firm's accumulated experience and, in turn, contributes to the success of later ones.

IDENTIFYING THE NEED FOR A SEPARATE ACQUISITION PROCESS

The need for separate organizational mechanisms or routines to help a company deal with these tasks effectively and the nature of the mechanisms that are best adapted to a particular company depend upon a number of factors. The first, as we discussed earlier, is the overall resource allocation process. Firms should start by evaluating the robustness of their own process in terms of the dimensions we discussed in the previous chapter. Beyond this, for acquisitions, a firm must consider its needs on the basis of:

- The type of company it is.
- The general level of acquisition activity it foresees.
- The type and variety of acquisitions it will need to undertake.
- The prior acquisition experience of its managers.

The first distinction concerns whether the firm is diversified or essentially in a single business. In larger diversified firms, business-level management and corporate management have different roles, and internal staff may be available for specialized roles. In smaller, single-business firms, the same managers may assume all these roles while most professional help is hired outside. The problems faced, in addition to the process problems we discussed in the previous chapter, are likely to be of a more technical nature of knowing how to go about the variety of tasks to be performed.

It is also important to consider how much acquisition activity is foreseen for the firm. Firms expecting few acquisitions can rely on more outside talent or make secondary, less permanent assignments to internal experts. Companies that want to engage very actively in acquisitive development usually dedicate a cadre of in-house professionals to manage the process. Note that assigning permanent roles with respect to acquisition activity usually ensures that a firm will have more acquisitions. Whether or not this increased attention also improves acquisition quality depends on further considerations.

The decision about how to approach acquisition decision making also varies by type of acquisition. Here the most fundamental distinction is probably between corporate- and business-level acquisitions. This distinction does not allude to the sources of acquisition ideas. Rather it relates to which organizational level has the primary responsibility for developing the acquisition justification and the request for resource commitment. That decision, in turn, depends on corporate strategy considerations, particularly the relation of the acquisition opportunity to the existing business. Entering a new domain is, in principle, a corporate-level endeavor. Strengthening an existing domain, on the otherhand, is typically the province of the managers in that business. Domain extension decisions may be made at either the corporate or business level.

If a firm's acquisition activities consist of many similar acquisitions, a simple, specialized, and detailed repertoire may be most effective. In support of this repertoire the firm can develop a series of rules of thumb for the strategic, organizational, or financial assessment. In one company that was regularly buying factories in its mature core business, the complexity of the financial evaluation had been boiled down to two ratios: the price paid per ton of capacity, and whether the price remained under six times EBIT (earnings before interest and tax). These ratios were perfectly valid for acquisitions of production capacity because they reflected the fundamental economics of this particular business. But when the company began to diversify into faster-growth areas, these rules proved too simplistic and severely limited the range of opportunities the company could consider. In this case the managers lost sight of the simplifying assumptions on which their rules of thumb were based. If firms expect to be able to handle domain strengthening, domain extension, and domain prospection acquisitions, and to span the range from small platform acquisitions to mega-mergers, they need to develop a much more complex and sophisticated administrative repertoire, one in which a number of roles can be activated and adjusted.

The final factor on which the acquisition management approach, particularly corporate involvement in divisional acquisitions, depends is the prior acquisition experience of the managers involved. This experience is of two general types. One is general managerial experience in developing and selling an acquisition justification in the firm and dealing with the range of strategic and organizational challenges that an acquisition implies. The other is acquisition-specific experience. Acquisitions present the management team with a unique range of technical issues and even if business managers do not need to handle these issues themselves, they must be aware of them so they can call in the appropriate support in time.

Our discussion will focus on the most complex case: that of large diversified companies that frequently engage in acquisition activity, involving a wide range of acquisitions for whom their managers are not prepared by their prior experience.[2] Readers from smaller, less diverse organizations may find simpler ways of addressing the problems we raised. But by exploring the most complex circumstances we will offer

a number of approaches, many of which may be applied or easily trans-
posed to other situations.

We will first examine ways in which such large companies can organize themselves for acquisitions in general. Then we will examine ways
of dealing with specific acquisition opportunities. In the latter context
we will consider the ways in which business-level and corporate management interact in two situations: a regular divisional acquisition, and
the increasingly frequent multibusiness acquisition in which only a part
of the acquired company falls within the current domain of a division.

ORGANIZING FOR ACQUISITION DECISION MAKING

An overall corporate capability for making acquisitions involves two
components. The first ensures that acquisition decisions are raised and
examined in the context of the business strategy. This can be accomplished by anchoring the acquisition decision process firmly in the business planning process. The second component is a corporate-level
process in which each acquisition decision is considered thoroughly in
light of accumulated corporate experience.

ANCHORING ACQUISITION THINKING IN BUSINESS STRATEGY

Ideas for acquisitions come from many sources: senior executives,
corporate staff, business unit managers, and outside advisers. In larger
and more complex firms, divisional acquisitions are initiated by divisional
management as frequently as by top management, and implementation
requires the early involvement of divisional management. Consequently,
an important factor in effective acquisition decision making is a thought-
ful, careful link to the firm's regular business planning process. In our
research we observed that the companies that did not encourage the
consideration of acquisitions as strategic alternatives during the business planning process were frequently unprepared to contend adequately in public bids. Their decision-making process was slow because
they had no prior strategic context in which the opportunity could be
considered.

Benefits. Including acquisition considerations in the regular business
planning process brings a number of benefits. Some flow from a deeper
exploration of ways in which acquisitions can accelerate the accomplishment of a company's strategic mission in terms of business position and

the development of capabilities that could lead to competitive advantage. A natural outgrowth is the creation of a context for effective decision making when an acquisition opportunity presents itself.

Perhaps the most fundamental benefit of including acquisition scenarios in the business planning process is to encourage a broad consideration of alternatives. If acquisitions are considered in isolation, without a link to business planning, the range of corporate renewal opportunities that will be explored is severely constrained. A corporate renewal strategy calls for a judicious blend of different types of acquisitions, internal development, and partnership opportunities. Considering such alternatives in the context of a business planning process allows managers to judge the quality of opportunities that present themselves.

A third benefit of a tie-in with business planning is a better understanding of the nature of competition in the industry. Adding a reflection on acquisitive growth and acquisition scenarios and candidates to the regular planning process is likely to sharpen the industry and competitive analysis in the business plan. Such acquisition planning informs the strategic analysis process at the same time that it benefits from it. A fourth advantage of acquisition planning is more realism in integration. It forces the division or business unit of the organization in which the acquisition will reside to review much sooner the organizational and human resource considerations that will flow from an acquisition program.

Limits of Formal Search and Screening Efforts. Many companies that want to increase their acquisition activity have used formal acquisition screening and search efforts outside the context of the regular business planning process.[3] Such one-time efforts do bring some of the aforementioned benefits of the more organic approach we described. In particular, they help to clarify the acquisition objectives and to build commitment to making acquisitions. However, these end runs carry with them greater dangers. They are likely to introduce a more isolated analytical perspective and unnecessary momentum as pressure builds on those heading the screening project to come up with acquisition candidates that can get through the screen.

Moreover, the formal screening systems sometimes respond to "filling the gap." (See Figure 5-1.) When acquisition objectives are established with clear financial criteria in mind but less attention to strategic issues, a formal search and screening system can contribute to one of two errors. It can screen out opportunities that do not seem to meet the financial criteria but make sense strategically, or it may let through the

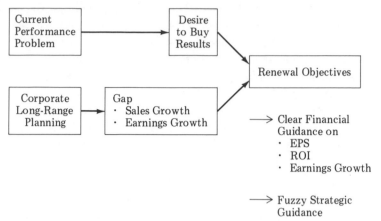

Figure 5-1 **Pressures Leading to Inappropriate Screening Criteria**

screen projects that meet the financial hurdles but are fuzzy on a strategic basis. Thus, such formal screening exercises do not bring the
wider benefits to ongoing business thinking that flow from considering
acquisitions in the context of regular business planning.

In sum, many firms can extend acquisition considerations into
business planning farther than they do now and the benefits can be
considerable. For example, Electrolux, the Swedish white goods manufacturer, closely links ongoing competitive analysis and acquisition
preparation. The company regularly draws up scenarios for acquisitions
of its competitors, projecting what a combination of the two would
represent in terms of market and organization. Such extensive incorporation of acquisitions in routine business planning does not conflict
with the inherently opportunistic nature of actual acquisition situations.
To the contrary, the benefits of such "homework" become apparent
when the firm is able to quickly appraise seemingly serendipitous opportunities.

Corporate-Level Acquisition Coordination

The need to bring coordination, thoroughness, and experience to the
acquisition process is leading many companies to establish a separate
corporate acquisition function. Such a function fulfills at least four roles
that are crucial to improving the acquisition process:

- Encouraging a proactive acquisition approach.
- Acting as a clearinghouse for acquisition leads and ideas.

- Fostering internal learning.
- Providing professional help in the acquisition process.

In some large companies this corporate acquisition function is handled by a full-time, formally established staff group with its own identity. In others a single individual draws on corporate resources when necessary. In other situations, typically smaller firms, a "second-hat" approach is used in which key corporate staff member(s) serve in a primary job and are seconded to a temporary acquisition role as needed. In many firms the brief of this function extends to the coordination of all external growth decisions including acquisitions, divestments, and joint ventures.

Some firms, of course, are wary of creating a separate corporate acquisition function, which is often seen, in the words of one manager, as "hijacking the acquisition decision away from line management." One CEO told us:

> In our firm we have a really decentralized approach. It is operating management that makes the investment decisions. We have enough staff in corporate finance and other functions to keep a check. Though I agree we should do something about our acquisition process, people surely would not like to have to deal with an acquisition team as yet another corporate staff unit.

The debate over the usefulness of a corporate acquisition function parallels in many ways the discussions that have raged over the usefulness of strategic planning staffs. A firm's strategic planners help clarify the strategic context at both the business and corporate levels, but they should not be allowed to grow beyond their educational and coordinating roles.[4] Equally, the role of a corporate acquisition function should be well understood. It is not to make acquisition decisions but instead to facilitate and support the process. Responsibility for the acquisition remains with line management. In the words of Electrolux's acquisition manager:

> I see my job as taking some of the workload off the CEO and Senior EVP. I would not dream of buying a company for which there is no line manager willing to stand up and say "I want this company." Operating managers must feel responsibility. For that they must be convinced it is the right strategy. They must be involved in the process. And there must be a smooth transition between my role and how they take on the situation.

The effectiveness of these corporate acquisition units, as we shall further discuss, depends not so much on their size, but on how they are staffed, where they report in the organization, how they are regarded by management, and, most of all, how they play their role.[5] It should be emphasized that they are a conduit and a catalyst, rather than a substitute for line authority.

The approach taken by ICI's acquisition corporate team illustrates these issues. The early eighties had been a difficult period for ICI, the British diversified chemical company. Overcapacity in Europe, an overvalued pound sterling, a heavy concentration on commodities, and a focus on U.K. business had created a crisis situation for ICI. In response, the board had turned to John Harvey-Jones, who in 1984 embarked on a major strategic and organizational overhaul in which acquisitions of different types were to play a major role.

This reorganization required managers to consider the strategic situations of existing businesses in conjunction with central initiatives directed at broad restructuring, the generation of new businesses, and the achievement of targeted acquisitions.[6] Because of its earlier mixed experience with acquisitions, ICI created a small corporate acquisition team as one means to support this strategic change. The subsequent functioning of this team illustrates each of the four roles corporate acquisition coordination plays and the issues involved in fulfilling them.

Encouraging a Proactive Acquisition Approach. Corporate management often finds itself reacting to acquisition leads from many sources. The opportunities they consider may already be "happening" or they may result more from an investment banker's creativity in imagining "plays" than from an internal, proactive reflection. It is difficult for operating units to change habits and "feed" corporate with acquisition ideas, when for years they have been constrained to internal development thinking. John Dewhurst, an ICI acquisition team member, and later its manager, described this role as follows:

> [the objective was] to become more proactive and to actually go out and seek acquisitions, having now the possibility to handle corporate, multi-business acquisitions rather than just divisional ones.

Encouraging business units to be proactive is important. Apart from the fact that divisional managers will not change years of internal development tradition without corporate prodding, our research suggests that most business-level managers refrain from considering acquisitions in which the opportunities that interest them are lumped with many other activities outside their purview.

The benefits of having a corporate acquisition function in such situations can be illustrated by ICI's purchase of Beatrice Chemicals and Stauffer Chemicals. Beatrice Chemicals was a company consisting of ten businesses, only three of which were of strong a priori interest to ICI. If ICI had not set up its corporate acquisitions team at the time of the Beatrice Chemicals sale, it is doubtful the two ICI divisions that were interested in these three Beatrice companies would have worked together to obtain a corporate commitment for a winning bid for the whole firm. Similarly, without this corporate function, ICI's agrochemicals division might not have pushed for the acquisition of Stauffer Chemicals, because two-thirds of Stauffer's businesses fell outside the division's interest. The agrochemicals managers were able to concentrate on the business of interest to them, while the acquisition team handled the resale of other parts to Akzo and Rhône-Poulenc.

The need for a proactive influence at the corporate level is even greater, of course, when one considers the issue of divestment.[7] As Electrolux's acquisition manager commented:

> Nobody likes to be sold. In divestments we often have to play a more pushing role. Sometimes we make the initial contacts and receive proposals from potential buyers without involving our business-level managers.

A basic fact about a corporate acquisition function is that it will generate acquisitions. The ICI team, for example, helped increase ICI's acquisition flow from less than ten per year in the early eighties to more than thirty per year after its inception. Although a firm does not need an acquisition volume of that magnitude to use a corporate acquisition team well, such a permanent function should be considered only if the company expects to enter a phase in which the normal acquisition activity must be accelerated or a specific acquisition program carried out while operating management has its hands full.

Acting as a Clearinghouse for Acquisition Leads. An entire industry of intermediaries and brokers exists whose sole mission is to conceive of acquisition ideas and to sell companies to anyone they can identify as possibly interested. It is not easy, however, for these intermediaries to guess or to learn what is of strategic interest to the varied businesses a company may be in. As a member of ICI's team said:

> Another reason [for the team] was to be a focal point, a postbox for all sorts of contacts, inside and outside the company. Outside bankers and deal makers need somebody to go to, and it is amazing how many propositions walk in when you provide them with a clear entry point. Our job, of course, was to filter out these propositions and relay back to the businesses those that were of interest.

Thus a corporate acquisition function can play a central role not only in keeping track of all leads; but also in fostering them from many sources.

Fostering Internal Learning. The third role is to foster internal learning beyond a single acquisition. Because acquisitions are complex and evolving, learning from them is largely a matter of experience. As we shall discuss in Chapter 14, learning occurs at the level of the individuals involved and at the level of the firm.[8] Unfortunately, in many large companies, individual managers tend to reinvent the wheel as they experience their first acquisition. Later acquisitions in which they are involved may be of a different type. If so, whatever was learned from the first may become misapplied with the second or third. In the words of ICI's John Dewhurst:

> Our acquisitions team is meant to accumulate internal learning so that lessons, good or bad, experienced in one area of the company would be used elsewhere.

Acquisition teams are not the only means of accumulating learning from acquisition experiences. Some companies have tried to codify some of that learning with a postmortem of the acquisition experience. Such postmortems can provide lasting insights if it is possible to understand the causes of success and failure. Effective postmortems ask whether the results were due to an individual, the corporate systems that influence managerial behavior, the competitive marketplace, or a combination of these factors.

British Petroleum, for example, has a longtime practice of such postmortems. BP's post-project appraisal unit operates with five people. Its proposed appraisals (about six per year) of both acquisitions and internal investments are approved by a board committee. Each project or acquisition is examined from conception to two years after completion through an interview process that results in a written appraisal submitted to a Board Committee for endorsement and communicated to the managers responsible for the project. A continually updated summary of major lessons learned is made available to management and staff involved with acquisition decisions throughout the company.[9] Other companies conduct postmortems by asking an outsider to write a case on an actual acquisition and discuss it with the actors involved, as well as other managers present.

In firms like BP, where postmortems are performed carefully and professionally, recurring problems are identified, as well as the factors that contribute to success. Some of the lessons regarding acquisitions that the unit has helped BP learn include the need for increased attention to local environmental health and safety regulation, refusal to be pressured into hasty acquisition deadlines, and acceptance of clear responsibility for integration.

Postmortems are far from a panacea, however. To begin with, few companies can politically accept a truthful reexamination of decisions that went awry if the original decision makers are still with the company. Even in firms that have the fortitude to conduct postmortems, it is not easy to review matters that go beyond the procedural or the situation-specific. Sometimes lessons put on paper lose some of the multidimensional appreciation of those who experienced them or even of those who audited them. The impact of diffusing such "lessons" to managers throughout the organization is, thus, not as great as hoped for. In sum, postmortems have the potential to influence learning and offer a surrogate for experience. But the learning benefits developed by a corporate acquisition function may offer more perspective, be based on a wider exposure to acquisitions, and allow more rapid application.

Providing Professional Help in the Acquisition Process. The most important role of the corporate acquisition function is applying its experience and professionalism to the acquisition process. Most companies with less acquisition experience acknowledge this role for an individual or an acquisition team but define the expertise that is brought to the acquisition process primarily in terms of specialized financial, legal, or negotiation skills. The need for experience in such technical areas is great indeed. Expertise needed in such areas ranges from detailed knowledge of the finer points of valuation to knowing how to negotiate fees with intermediaries.

We suggest, however, that a more important aspect of this role is ensuring the general quality of the acquisition process, including not only pre-acquisition consideration of integration issues, but also support for the early stages of post-merger integration. In the effective acquisition teams we observed, what was present above all was a generalist perspective and credibility throughout the organization, starting at the top. Their job was not to be the technical specialists, but to know when to ask for technical advice and bring it in if required.

ESTABLISHING A CORPORATE ACQUISITION FUNCTION

When establishing a corporate acquisition function, firms should consider its size, the sort of individuals who should compose it, and to whom it should report. For example, to annually handle more than thirty acquisitions, half as many divestitures, and a number of joint ventures (plus many that never reached completion), ICI used a team consisting of only four individuals. Each person was involved in several negotiations at a time and monitored a dozen "active" situations.

Many firms can operate with one or two individuals in this function. At Electrolux the sole corporate acquisition manager estimated that in a typical year he worked on 25 completed acquisitions, 7 or 8 divestitures, 10 acquisitions that did not go through, and evaluated 120 acquisition opportunities. The depth of the corporate acquisition function's involvement varies a great deal, depending on the experience of operating management and the nature of the opportunity.

Although some financial analysis capability and negotiation expertise is, of course, useful, setting the function up as a financial/legal group clearly restricts the role it can play and its usefulness in protecting the company from process problems. Instead of only basic technical skills, our research suggests that it is much more important to include someone with operating credibility within the acquiring firm. The function can be even more effective if it includes someone who has been part of an acquired firm and hence knows how the company operates after an acquisition.

Companies that set up their corporate acquisition functions with only the decision-making process in mind may limit their ability to focus attention on integration thinking before the fact. ICI is a typical example. The early ICI team was led by the former assistant treasurer. The three other members were an operating manager with international experience, an analyst from the pension fund, and a merchant banker on secondment to the company. Over time, however, the team acquired more of an operating profile, and its concerns shifted somewhat into consideration of the organizational issues.

Because a corporate acquisition function has a variety of roles to play, having it report directly to top management, as the ICI team did, seems a better solution than operating under the wings of the chief financial officer, as is sometimes the case. In other companies the corporate acquisition function does not formally report directly to the CEO but may be a subunit of the corporate planning and development department. This arrangement has the advantage of facilitating strategic coordination. It does require, however, an openness in the corporate office and the planning department itself.

In the day-to-day activity, the acquisition function must be free to deal with a host of internal and external constituencies but still have direct access to the top. Often the ability to gain the attention of top management quickly is important because obtaining a firm commitment quickly may be crucial to making an acquisition. At ICI, three board members were always on call in case an acquisition decision had to be discussed. If needed, the full board would convene on short notice.

Ultimately, except for the respect it earns from business unit managers, the only capital the corporate acquisition function has is the confidence top management has in it. As the corporate acquisition manager at Electrolux said:

> When the product line manager and I agree that the acquisition is OK and the price reasonable, it always has to be approved by the CEO. Of course, he feels more comfortable if I do.

A corporate acquisition function is a conduit, never a substitute for line authority.

Early Steps

The formation of a corporate acquisition function often runs against the grain of a company, both organizationally and politically. The new function vaults over traditional prerogatives, especially of the legal and financial functions, to determine its own involvement. Reactions from individual business units are typically mixed at the appearance of yet another staff unit that, they think, will take authority away from them. At ICI, for example, some business units were relieved to have a single point of contact at the center, because they no longer had to seek opinions from all corners. Others were reticent, wondering what these so-called experts in the center knew about their business. To them the team was only another component of bureaucracy. Other business units, though less commonly, acted as though nothing had changed.

Faced with such mixed responses, managers in the corporate acquisition function must be quick to clarify their role and to earn respect by helping the businesses. In the words of one ICI team member:

We went to visit every business, saw the Chief Executive, and explained our role. The first thing we said was: We are not here to rubber stamp, nor to be yet another hurdle that you have to get over. We see our role as being able to talk to you about possible acquisitions, and once we have jointly agreed that an acquisition is worth doing in strategic terms, in financial terms, and otherwise, to do our darndest to get that through the system, and approved by the Committee.

One important aspect of clarifying the function's role is to list broad criteria for acquisition activity so that the business can prescreen potential acquisitions and know what sort of questions they should be able to answer.[10] A prerequisite for being useful and earning the respect of businesses is to become thoroughly familiar with their business planning issues, not only through close contact with corporate planning, but also through regular discussions with the divisional managers and their business development people.

At the same time that they learn the business and strive for credibility, the team can set up a system for keeping track of every acquisition opportunity that comes into the company, from inside or outside. Thus every division notifies the corporate function whenever it is considering an acquisition, and an appropriate level of checking is set up for different stages. To track these opportunities at ICI, the acquisitions team assigned a code to each case in the computer database, ranging from 1, which is a possible acquisition that may someday be looked at seriously, to code 6, which represents acquisitions on which the team is currently taking action.

Once a system for tracking opportunities is established, a method of deciding which acquisitions to pursue further is needed. Often companies establish a *staged* process in which top management must give clearance before any contact or negotiation can be made with the acquisition target.

Establishing a Working Process

The real challenge for the corporate acquisition function is to establish a working process. In this process the interactions between the individual, team, or task force responsible for acquisitions and its clients—top management and business management, as well as support staff such as corporate planning, finance, and legal—become clear and cooperative.

The role of the corporate-level unit depends on a number of factors. One is the size of the opportunity. Whether a corporate acquisition team in a large firm should get involved in *all* acquisitions, regardless of their size, is a matter for discussion. Most acquisition teams we studied were involved in all acquisitions, though to widely differing degrees.

In ICI there was some disagreement about this at first. Executives who were slated to become members of the team felt that they did not have to be involved in acquisitions of less than £5 million and that the businesses should be given discretionary power over acquisitions up to that limit, just as they were with internal investment. The executive board overruled this notion on the grounds that any acquisition, however big or small, could entail significant risks, particularly environmental ones. Hence every acquisition in ICI goes through the process, although only those over £10 million need full board approval. Other companies are even stricter than ICI, demanding not only that the acquisition team be notified of and possibly involved in any deal, but also that a formal go-ahead be obtained on a preliminary dossier before any permission for outside or target contact is granted.

Although acquisition size is important in determining the corporate acquisition function's role, our research suggests that other factors are more salient. The interaction of the uniqueness of a particular acquisition opportunity and the acquisition experience of the business managers in question may be more important. If one division's strategy led the management team to buy a series of former distributors, they may have developed a know-how and useful rules of thumb for quickly and effectively making further acquisitions of this type. But this experience may not be relevant if they consider buying a competitor to gain access to its sales force. Involvement by the corporate acquisitions function may prevent such learning from being misapplied.[11]

Finally, the corporate acquisitions function must be able to monitor business acquisitions on the one hand and multibusiness and hence corporate opportunities on the other. We discuss these tasks later in this chapter.

ORGANIZING FOR A SPECIFIC ACQUISITION

Although the corporate acquisition function may provide critical inputs and act to guide and control the general approach to acquisitions, the quality of every business-level acquisition still depends on the way the business unit approaches it. While a business unit's strategy may have been presold to corporate thinking through the planning process, a business-level acquisition team or task force needs to be appointed as soon as an acquisition candidate is being considered.

The main role of the acquisition or task force is to organize and coordinate the actual investigation for the business manager. In addition, the task force is the relay for the learning transmitted by the corporate acquisition function, as well as the vehicle through which the division can build up its own learning and expertise.

Our research suggests that it is best to harness, whenever possible, the same group of business-level and functional managers each time an acquisition is considered, to ensure that they can apply their accumulated experience. It is important to clarify that they are, first and foremost, members of the task force, rather than representatives of their function. The task force should be led by an operating-oriented executive, who is, or who stands in for, the general manager of the business into which the acquisition will report.

The task force should include someone who may be asked to play a substantial management role after the acquisition. With such a manager on the task force integration issues are more likely to be given careful attention before the decision is made. In addition the acquiring firm is better able to retain the understanding, respect, and authority that build up during the often lengthy negotiating process. After the acquisition, the managers in the acquired firm often regard changes in contact points or the cast of characters as a violation of trust. Whether a representative of the corporate acquisition function plays a role on that task force or not depends on the situation. In any case, a corporate function should maintain a clear and continuous liaison with the ad hoc business-level acquisition task force.

MONITORING BUSINESS-LEVEL ACQUISITIONS

In the interest of consistency and control, some firms try to prescribe the process through which their business units should relate to the corporate acquisition team when they have an acquisition idea. Typically the approval process consists of following steps:

- Request for preliminary investigation.
- Detailed strategic evaluation.
- Request for permission to negotiate within approved range.
- Request for board approval of the negotiated outcome.

A formal request for preliminary investigation is the first step. Approval triggers the creation of an acquisition team and grants permission to seek preliminary contact. This procedure ensures early communication and also surfaces early in the process any corporate strategic or tactical issues that may impinge on the decision, especially on any existing contacts with the firm in question. A good example of this is the BASF acquisition discussed earlier. BASF's paints division was engaged in a competitive bid for Inmont against Akzo at the same time that the BASF fibres division was negotiating the purchase of American ENKA, an Akzo subsidiary. If the fibres division's negotiations had been completed earlier than the paint division's, the sale of ENKA would have added to the cash resources available to Akzo in its bid for Inmont.

If the acquisition possibility falls clearly within a well-articulated strategy, preliminary authorization may be granted without further discussion. But if the acquisition would bring the current strategy into question, the request provides an opportunity to raise strategic and tactical issues early in the process, so that acquisition investigation and strategy clarification can proceed in step.

The second step is a detailed strategic evaluation by the acquisition task force. The third step is a formal approval request by the line manager of the business that would be responsible for the acquisition. If the request is approved, permission is given to negotiate within a certain range of price and terms and conditions. The final step is a request for formal board approval of the negotiated outcome, subject to satisfactory outcome of further due diligence.

In all these activities the corporate acquisition function adjusts informally to the circumstances in any particular situation. The informal elements of the process are as important, if not more important, than the formal review component. The corporate group reviews and questions the formal proposal put forward by the business unit on the basis of the task force's work. Throughout the process the corporate team injects its experience, advice, and help through its membership on that task force or through regular contact with the managers interested in the acquisition candidate. As one acquisition manager commented: "The operating divisions really look upon us more as consultants who can help them."

Beyond the fabric of substantive involvement, ICI's corporate approach to monitoring a business-level acquisition points to the benefits of informality. The resolution of differences of judgment between the corporate acquisition unit and the business is a subtle process, which should not be carried out through the exchange of memos but through continuous contact and questioning. The corporate unit's task is to inject the right sort of questions into the process; the business task force, however, must come up with its answers. As John Dewhurst explained:

> Most of the time we get our differences out by asking questions during the process, often informally over the phone. In perhaps a third of the acquisitions we end up together deciding that we will not go ahead with the process. If the business people feel strongly about pushing ahead anyway, we have an intermediate stage where I can suggest that both of us go and first talk to the Director that nominally is in charge of this part of the portfolio.

The result is quite a bit of influence for the corporate acquisition function, though this influence is largely informal.[12] As Dewhurst continued:

> We have no authority in the sense of saying yes or no, but have developed a credibility and an expertise. They know what is going to happen if I say, "Let's go to your director." He will ask me why I don't like it. He may respond that he hears what I say, but still feels the Committee should look at it, or I may convince him. Normally, however, we tend to get an agreement between us and the business, whatever the issue, whether it is price, environmental issues, or others.

Although the businesses were becoming increasingly thorough in their proposals, Dewhurst felt that the ICI acquisition team was still needed:

> The people in the businesses are confident, professional. Typically people in the business development slots are managers who are going places. They may already have done two or three acquisitions. So they know, before they come in, 80% of the questions we will ask, and they have the answers, which is great because it saves a lot of time. Still they are in the business; they are caught up in the chase and can convince themselves too easily. You still need someone who stands back and can say "Yes, I can see it is in the company's interest to do that."

This description of the functioning of an effective approach to acquisition analysis illustrates how such a corporate function can help safeguard the process from the problems we discussed in the previous chapter. Indeed, by orchestrating the involvement of various players, by making sure external players contribute while keeping the driver's seat in-house, and by keeping the central focus on the business proposition, the corporate acquisition function eliminates the danger of fragmentation without standing in the way of a thorough analysis.

By their ability to question and their direct access to the top, the corporate unit members can regulate momentum throughout the process. Their control function is especially useful in the negotiating phase, because they are in the best position to represent broader corporate interests either to help "bridge the gap" when the business has stalled in its negotiations, or to keep a cool perspective when the business unit gets caught up in momentum. Most important, by ensuring that the right questions are raised and discussed between corporate and the business, they clarify ambiguous motives and provide more critical, in-depth consideration of the acquisition justification. They can achieve these objectives only if the answers are not theirs but those of the businesses' managers.

HANDLING MULTIBUSINESS ACQUISITIONS

Important as a corporate acquisition function may be for business-level acquisitions, its role becomes almost indispensable in handling the acquisition of multibusiness firms or major corporate bids. Increasingly, companies for sale tend to be in multiple businesses that may be of interest to several divisions of the same firm. There also may be large parts of the acquired company in which the interest is unclear or clearly absent. Such companies are often auctioned off as a whole by investment bankers. On the basis of a prospectus, the bankers set up a tight schedule of preliminary bidding, short-list leading candidates, and request one-time sealed bids based upon very limited access to information. In this environment, companies without a central acquisition capability may find that none of their businesses wants or can take on the challenge of bidding for the whole company. Consequently, they forgo an acquisition opportunity or acquire a later spinout at high prices from the first acquirer, who is often financially oriented.

An exclusive reliance on investment bankers to orchestrate a firm's approach to such a situation may provide the tactical judgment and technical expertise needed to clinch the deal and structure it properly. But such outside advisers do not provide the ability to harness the internal business judgment without which any winning bid may well be only a shot in the dark. It is in such bids that the professionalism and organization of the corporate acquisition function come to the fore.

In an environment of limited time and limited access to information, there is an even greater premium on acquisition experience as part of business planning, as well as on active scanning of external events so as to get an early lead. In the Beatrice acquisition, both happened to be the case for ICI.

ICI-Beatrice

In May 1984, when the Beatrice Company announced its intention to acquire Esmark, Rex Palmer, a senior manager in ICI's planning department, believed the company, which had been unsuccessfully approached two years earlier for its advanced material businesses, might have to sell off businesses to avoid too heavy a debt load.

After informal confirmation that Beatrice Chemicals might be sold, Palmer started to put together as much information as possible. A particular interest emerged in three of the ten businesses, Fiberite, and LNP (two advanced materials businesses), and Polyvinyl, a resin manufacturer of interest to ICI's Mond division. The other businesses appeared to be freestanding specialty chemicals businesses, generally attractive but without any particular prospects for synergy.

When Beatrice officially announced its intention to sell, Rex Palmer sent a first memo to the ICI executive directors. They agreed, along with more than three dozen other companies, to express interest. In September all of these companies received a classic prospectus prepared by Beatrice's investment bankers with business descriptions, financial statements, and a very positive discussion of prospects.

At such a time, the magnitude and time pressure of the job put a premium on having a corporate acquisitions function. On the basis of a written prospectus, its own internal information, and whatever fieldwork it wants to organize, a company is supposed to put in a preliminary offer that will put it in the range to be short-listed and gain access to the target. In the Beatrice example, bidders were given thirty days to make an offer for all of the ten Beatrice businesses. These bidders represented forty legal entities in eighteen countries, two-thirds of them in the United States.

On October 1, an ICI appraisal team of seven people was established for Beatrice, whose job was to coordinate the views of other parts in the company. Five days later a first appraisal was submitted to the executive committee, which gave its support within three days. On October

22 a paper supporting the acquisition and providing an estimate of areas in which there might be synergies and their value was submitted to the board by the acquisitions team. After debating the value of the fit, the price range, and risks, the board arrived at a figure in line with Beatrice Chemicals' indicated range and registered interest on October 26, the appointed day. By the end of the month, it was learned that ICI was one of the firms left in the bidding.

Because being short-listed meant that access for on-site evaluation would be granted in about a week's time, ICI organized itself to be ready: A business director team was formed of board-level people who would be on standby. An acquisition team of five people was formed. The team immediately flew to New York and started assembling eight teams of managers, drawn from all over the company, to carry out the on-site investigation. A business evaluation team was made up of people from the units with whom the Beatrice businesses would best fit.

On November 5, access was given, and a fifty-strong ICI contingent departed in groups to evaluate twenty-one separate sites. Their job was to assess the quality of the businesses, their assets, and their people. This information and the assessment of synergy potential was pulled together in London. The expected bid date was December 10, just one month later. On December 4 Beatrice moved the expected bid date of December 10 back to December 17. On December 6, the team submitted its final evaluation and acquisition proposal to the ICI executive directors. One participant described the proposal as "not only a recommendation—there was a real debate with the Executive Directors as to what the company's response should be. It was not simply a matter of saying here's our recommendation, do you agree or not. It was a completely open sharing debate on the basic questions."

At this stage tactics become crucial and the acquisition team needs to work closely with its firm's investment bankers. For example, in the Beatrice case the ICI camp and its advisers, fearing the outcome of an unpredictable bid and sensing that the chairman of Beatrice was interested in an unconditional bid from a firm with credibility, convinced the board to make a preemptive bid.

On Saturday, December 8, the Board had its first-ever weekend meeting. After consultation with nonexecutive directors, the executive team not only agreed on the acquisition case and its price, but also decided to attempt a direct preemptive bid. At least one of the other bidders was considered dangerous, and ICI was determined not to lose out.

On Sunday, December 9, John Harvey-Jones personally communicated the offer to the chairman of Beatrice, and agreement was reached. The price ($750 million for companies with a net book value of $155 million) was high, but within ICI's range.

The requirement to gather, analyze, and integrate so much information in such a short time puts a heavy premium on a firm's ability to coordinate such an effort and to draw upon corporate resources, wherever they are, but the outcome depends on knowing what questions to ask. Once the process begins, it is easy to become completely absorbed in the evaluation of the company itself, as well as the synergy scenarios. Although the synergies are important in establishing a walk-away price, that is, a price that one will not exceed, they are of little help in determining the required bid price. In evaluating a particular business, each team must analyze the motivation, position, and likely offer of other competing bidders.

Even if a firm succeeds in putting in the winning bid, as in the Beatrice case, the role of the acquisition team is far from over.

That same day the project team flew back to New York to negotiate the final form of the agreement and see to external relations matters. In the early hours of Thursday, December 13, the documents were signed and the deal announced, four days before the formal bids were expected. The project team remained in existence until February 28, the day of the formal closing. On the financial and legal front, more than thirty-five transactions, involving thirty corporate entities in eighteen countries were completed.

Contacts had to be built between the project team and Beatrice management. Administrative matters relating to insurance, personnel benefits, and the like had to be resolved. Above all, organizational issues had to be clarified if clear messages were to be sent to Beatrice units on the first day of their new affiliation.

The ability to organize such massive efforts and to ensure depth of analysis within a short time frame has become a major source of advantage among competitors in the same business. When we interviewed managers who had been "auctioned off," we asked them how different companies had approached the opportunity to interact with them. The difference among competitors in the same industry was striking. Some send in hordes of managers from all departments; others send a small, high-powered team. Some ask very vague, apparently undirected, questions. Others from the first moment convey their understanding of the business in the questions they raise.

For example, Loral Electronics has its operating managers do the business planning. Part of their brief is to understand the industries in which they are competing. This policy had a clear payoff when Xerox Corporation announced that it would divest its Electro-Optical Systems division, and Loral won over other bidders. Chairman Bernard Schwartz explained:

> When the seller [Xerox] invited "due diligence" teams from the interested parties, I'm told that some of our competitors sent teams that spent four or five days out at the site learning about the business. We sent an executive there for one day because we already knew the industry. Xerox never thought we were serious until we made the successful offer.[13]

These differences were evident in the acquisition justifications, which we studied. The extent to which these justifications were strategic, represented shared views that were detailed, considered organizational issues, and incorporated a dynamic perspective, depended largely on the thoroughness of the process we outlined.

SUMMARY

In this section we examined the issues involved in acquisition decision making, starting from an analysis of the problems that companies encounter as they examine acquisition opportunities and prepare justifications for them. Some of these problems were specific to acquisitions; others were laid at the doorstep of more fundamental shortcomings in companies' decision-making processes.

This chapter took a pragmatic view of such problems and explored how experienced acquirers tend to remedy them. We concluded that the nature of business planning and the way a corporate function is organized and manages the acquisition decision-making process can substantially affect the quality of acquisition justifications, the ability to handle multiple types of acquisitions, and the ability to learn from them.

Instead of focusing on individual acquisitions, we have concentrated our recommendations on the broader aspects of managing an acquisitive strategy, including linking acquisition opportunities with business planning and then ensuring consistency with firm-wide objectives through the use of a corporate-level acquisitions function. With a healthy respect for the challenges in the decision-making process, we now turn to the source of value creation, the integration process.

III

Integration: The Source of Value Creation

T his part of the book focuses on acquisition integration. It analyzes what takes place during the integration process, how integration differs from one situation to another, and how the choice of integration approach should relate to both strategic and organizational requirements.

Chapter 6 first develops a general understanding of the integration process. Integration is seen as an adaptive process of interaction that takes place when firms come together in an atmosphere conducive to capability transfer. Actual strategic capability transfer and, ultimately, value creation are seen to depend on the ability to understand each other's organizational context and to create this atmosphere despite a series of problems that may arise in the process.

Chapter 7 explores three such problems in detail. Inflexibility in the face of changing circumstances, the destruction of value for employees, and a leadership vacuum that does not provide a new vision frequently limit the ability to create the atmosphere for capability transfer.

In Chapter 8 we examine how the integration process takes on a different character in different settings. Three integration approaches—absorption, preservation, and symbiosis—are proposed as metaphors for handling different situations. These three approaches provide a framework within which decisions on handling the integration process can be systematically made. Even within these approaches the process is ultimately adaptive.

Chapter 9 reexamines the integration process problems discussed in Chapter Seven in light of these three integration approaches. The section ends with an examination of the relationship between integration management and performance.

6

Understanding the Integration Process

INTRODUCTION

THE INTEGRATION PROCESS IS the key to making acquisitions work. Not until the two firms come together and begin to work toward the acquisition's purpose can value be created. The managers we studied acknowledged the importance of the integration process. Yet integration was the part of the acquisition process with which they were least comfortable. They found it difficult, time consuming, uncertain, and fraught with risks and setbacks.

In some situations we studied, the integration effort was guided by a clear logic. In others, where the operating managers were left to feel their way, the acquisition justification had left them with little guidance or had been completely unrealistic. Some managers had a starkly simple view of integration. For some, integration meant "making them like us"; others managed as if "nothing should change" in either firm. Other managers saw integration as a "black box" in which things just seemed to happen after the acquisition, but most of those we studied realized they were immersed in a complex process, full of subtleties and pitfalls. They were trying simultaneously to move two organizations forward toward a common purpose and trying to adapt that purpose to the changing situation.

Beyond these views, rules of thumb abounded, each grounded in the personal experiences of the managers interviewed. Many of these "rules" were contradictory. While some said, "The key is to move as fast as possible," we also heard, "Move carefully." "Put in your own people" had as a counterpoint: "Leave them alone; they are the ones who know their business."

Our purpose in this chapter is to offer insights into how integration contributes to value creation and what takes places during integration. We want to take the lid off the "black box" of integration and peer inside. This chapter develops a broad understanding of the integration process and its components. The next chapter identifies the recurring problems in this integration process that either destroy capabilities or block the possibility of their transfer.

FUNDAMENTALS OF THE INTEGRATION PROCESS

Although managers acknowledge the importance of the integration process, negotiators often bypass detailed discussion of integration because of its uncertainty, its complexity, and because of other pressures during the decision process. Moreover, the meaning of integration depends on the type of acquisition, who gets involved in the process, and the types of capabilities to be transferred.

Some acquisitions require a minimal amount of integration, as in the example of British Petroleum, which diversified into nutrition and brought Hendrix, a Dutch animal feed business. Others imply a complete combination, as in the case of Electrolux, the Swedish appliance manufacturer, which bought an Italian competitor Zanussi, and then had to streamline the operations of what had been two direct competitors. A third type requires a more complex mix of autonomy and integration, as in the case of ICI, the British chemical company, which, having acquired Beatrice Chemicals, had to find a way to preserve the entrepreneurial character of the acquired companies while leveraging ICI research into them.

Our research found a common set of elements in the integration process that remained the same regardless of acquisition type or differences in integration needs. Figure 6-1 points out the dynamics involved in the acquisition integration process.

Integration is an interactive and gradual process in which individuals from two organizations learn to work together and cooperate in the transfer of strategic capabilities. Difficulties in managing the integration process, however, are not just the offspring of difficulties in bringing about the capability transfer itself.[1] Creating an atmosphere that can

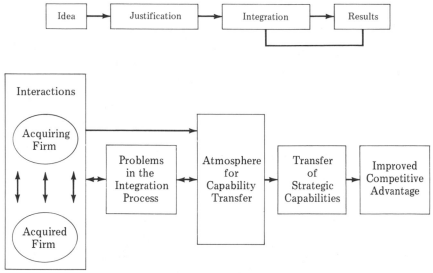

Figure 6-1 **The Acquisition Integration Process**

support it is the real challenge. Shaping such an atmosphere is especially difficult because problems in the integration process itself tend to subvert its creation. To minimize those problems and to integrate two organizations successfully, the acquiring firm must give systematic attention to the interactions between the firms that create the atmosphere needed for capability transfer and successful integration.

TRANSFER OF STRATEGIC CAPABILITIES

The heart of integration, as we discussed in Chapter 2, is the transfer and application of strategic capabilities. Capabilities may be transferred in several ways: They may be given to the new sister firm; they may be shared for common use; or they may be taught to people in the other firm. Three types of capability transfer were discussed—operational resource sharing, functional skill transfer, and general management skill transfer. Each type involves different organizational challenges. (Other potential combination benefits such as size benefits and financial resource sharing were seen to accrue with the acquisition itself.) See Fig. 6-2.

Operational Resource Sharing

The most straightforward type of capability transfer, operational resource sharing can take place through giving or sharing. Examples include combining sales forces, sharing manufacturing facilities, trade-

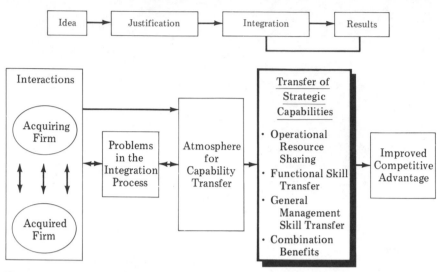

Figure 6-2 **Types of Strategic Capability Transfer**

marks, brand names, office space, or distribution channels. As we discussed in Chapter 2, value is created in such cases through economies of scope or scale. The integration challenges in sharing resources typically involve combining assets or coordinating their joint use.

The rationalization associated with resource sharing involves major organizational trauma. Even if both original resources are kept, their combination can be disruptive. Some of that disruption arises from the organizational consequences of merging two separate units. Other disruptions result from the fact that joint use of assets is not without cost. Even if two operations are able to use the same assets, their ideal use of these assets may differ. When combined, these assets may be configured and used in a way that represents a compromise for both organizations. As in the example mentioned in Chapter 2, Esselte's stationery products and Dymo's embossing tool could be sold on the same sales call. But the sales approach would be very different for the high-margined, list-priced Dymo product than for the low-margined, fragmented stationery assortment. Similarly, a bank officer may be able to sell the same client credit and insurance products, but selling insurance may be a different "art" than selling credit.

For resource sharing to create value, the benefits of sharing must outweigh these hidden costs of compromise. The importance of those costs of compromise will depend not only on how the needs of both organizations differ in terms of using the resources in question, but also on the organization's ability to manage those differences.

Transfer of Functional Skills

Even when near-term benefits may be sought in resource sharing, the primary challenge and long-term source of value creation in acquisitions is often the effective transfer of functional skills between the firms. In all cases, such a transfer of skills is neither immediate nor easy because it involves a process of both teaching and learning before the skills can be transferred.

Ironically, the more strategic the skills to be transferred, the more difficult it will be to achieve the required understanding and cooperation in this teaching and learning process. What makes a capability strategic, as we stated in Chapter 2, is that it is not easily imitated. Strategic capabilities, especially skill-based ones, are difficult to imitate because they are embedded in the skills of a group of individuals and in the procedures and cultures of firms.[2] For example, an acquisition intending to improve a firm's product development capabilities will often require an extended period of learning on the part of the firm receiving the capability. Typically, the more difficult a capability is to imitate, the longer it will take to learn and apply.

Transfer of General Management Skills

Transferring general management skills has important differences from transferring functional skills. When general management skills are transferred, the managers of one firm (typically the acquired firm) are influenced on general management issues of strategic direction, resource allocation, financial planning, and control, or human resource management. This influence can be exerted through subtle coaching, direct involvement, or imposition of systems. Transfer of general management skills implies mainly *vertical* interactions at the general management levels between the acquired unit and the acquiring organization that reports to it. In functional skill transfer, by contrast, the interactions are *horizontal* among managers at operating levels in both organizations. Because these managers do not have a direct hierarchical relationship, like the managers who pursue general management skill transfer, they are often less willing to participate in such learning.

Combination Benefits

Size-related benefits such as market power and purchasing power require little coordination to put in practice, as does the transfer of financial resources. One organization can give financial resources to the other without disrupting it in major ways.

In summary, each type of capability transfer involves different challenges. The process of capability transfer is complex because beyond simply giving or sharing resources or assets, it necessitates complex learning by both firms. To assume that the same sales organization cannot handle Esselte's stationery products, and Dymo's embossing tool, or that bank officers cannot handle both credit and insurance products, is to abdicate the responsibility to train, motivate, and reward people for complex tasks. It is because of the complexity of such learning that the context and atmosphere in which this strategic capability transfer is to take place become so important.

ATMOSPHERE

Before any capabilities can be transferred between firms, regardless of the method of capability transfer, the right atmosphere must be created. Our research suggests that this atmosphere has five key ingredients (see Figure 6-3):

- A reciprocal understanding of each firm's organization and culture.
- The willingness of people in both firms to work together after the acquisition.
- The capacity to transfer and receive the capability.
- Discretionary resources to help foster the atmosphere needed to support the transfer.

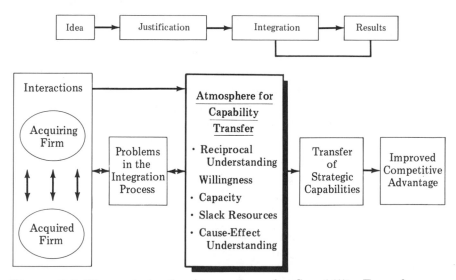

Figure 6-3 **Elements in the Atmosphere for Capability Transfer**

- A cause-effect understanding of the benefits expected from the acquisition.

Reciprocal Organizational Understanding

If a firm's strategic capabilities are embedded in the context of its organization and culture, then transferring and applying them successfully require an appreciation for the contexts from which they come and to which they will be transferred. Also required is an appreciation of any adjustments necessary to use them appropriate in the new context. Any company that is party to an acquisition should know and appreciate the other firm's values, history, organizational approach, personnel makeup, and culture. The need for reciprocal understanding depends on the type of capability to be transferred and on the acquisition's relation to the company's business domain.

Reciprocal understanding does not mean that one firm is coopted into the other's way of doing business and its culture. Instead, the organization receiving the capability needs to be able to understand how and why the capability worked in its original context. Developing such reciprocal understanding involves a two-phased learning process. First, each party learns about the other; then each learns about the capability to be transferred. The experiences of a marketing manager in a finance company acquired by a bank reflect this progression of learning:

> Immediately after the acquisition we didn't know what to think. They were bigger and had more procedures than we did. So we resisted any offers to help. After a while we learned that their procedures actually improved efficiency, and we listened more. We were then able to see how we could apply their very systematic approach to product development in our situation.

The need for reciprocal understanding depends on the type of capability transfer being pursued. The demands are highest when the capability is based on the teaching of tacit skills, which involves learning to understand the context in which these skills are embedded and learning to replicate that context or to adjust for differences.[3] For example, the ability to sell an acquired company's products through the parent's distribution system requires a great deal of detailed, channel-specific knowledge about particular customers' needs, transportation costs, prevailing norms in pricing and delivery, etc. Much of this knowledge is embedded in the acquired firm's sales force. Within the framework of capability transfer, managers in the two firms must first learn to understand each other's operations and put the capability they expect to transfer into context before they can add new products to the distribution system.

In many acquisitions despite careful planning, managers find more differences between the combined firms than they expected. Being in the same business does not guarantee either a common language or an understanding of the other organization. For example, after the merger that created the Dai-Ichi Kangyo Bank, the managers had to publish a dictionary of more than 200 words to ensure the correct interpretations of key terms. Before the merger the word for loan in one bank was a verb meaning "to loan money." In the other bank it was a noun meaning "money to be lent." These differences in the meaning of such a central concept for the business highlighted the relative market orientation and aggressiveness of the two firms, factors that could greatly influence their ability to understand and learn from each other.

Another example of the difficulty of developing a reciprocal understanding comes from the experience of a commercial bank that acquired a discount stock broker. A senior executive at the bank said:

> A big justification for the merger was to cross-sell to each other's customers. But, we made money in such different ways [fee for service versus interest income] that . . . nobody spoke the same language. For example, one of us [discount broker] serves a customer group that is price sensitive, which lends itself to a "high tech" approach [high fixed cost, high volume, low cost per unit]. The other's customers [bank's] are convenience sensitive, which leads to more people-intense, "lower" technology solutions to problems. Ultimately, we discovered what the fundamental characteristics of our customer bases were quite different and there wasn't nearly as much overlap as we had originally thought or hoped for.

Before the merger of two steel companies, one was very centralized and a highly integrated plant dominated its facilities. The other had four smaller, relatively independent plants roughly equal in size. Decisions were very centralized in the former and decentralized in the latter. A production manager said:

> Although we tried to transfer managers back and forth between [the two companies'] works, we weren't very successful because they [the managers] were either used to more authority on one hand or being told exactly what to do on the other.

Willingness to Work Together

Many firms face serious difficulties in developing the willingness of people in both organizations to work together after the acquisition. In the firms we studied, managers and employees often regarded working with people in the other organization as a zero sum game (where one group "won" at the other's expense), rather than as a chance to capitalize on a strategic opportunity. We observed a variety of motives for not working together, including fears for job security and the loss of power or control over resources. One of the integration process problems we discuss in the next chapter deals with how the destruction of value for employees limits their willingness to work together toward capability transfer.

Other factors that affected willingness to participate included differences in firm size, a desire to hold on to old ways of doing things, reward systems, and prior experience with acquisitions. Differences in firm size often made people in the larger firm less willing to help those in the smaller one. As a manager in a smaller acquired firm told us:

> . . . we could have made close to $750,000 operating profit on a project like that, but nobody at the parent would help us because those numbers were just noise level to them. To us, they were really record setting.

Some employees wanted to protect their old ways of doing things because of their uncertainty about changing or their inability to understand what the future would be. For example, a middle manager in one acquired firm said,

> We quickly backed away from synergy discussions and fought attempts to work together because we didn't want to be smothered by their bureaucracy.

This phenomenon was not related only to size differences. Similar sentiments were expressed by managers in a large, faster-growing, less bureaucratic steel company that merged with a more highly centralized firm of the same size.

Reward systems played an important role in developing a willingness to work together by the ways in which they encouraged cooperation between the firms. One manager we spoke to said:

> I wouldn't work with most of the people from the parent that called me. They got merit points on their year-end evaluation [for bonuses] just for suggesting something with us. At the end of the year I was judged on my bottom-line results, not on how many meetings I attended.

Prior experience with acquisitions or with a firm of a similar type seemed to increase the willingness to work together. The CFO of one acquired firm said:

I may have had an advantage around hereafter the merger. I had been through a couple of others when I worked for a bigger firm and understood why they [managers from the parent] were acting that way.

Even experience with merger talks that had not been consummated helped condition the attitudes of people in the organization and improve their acceptance of the merger itself, as well as their understanding of what they would have to do to cooperate once it took place. One of the executives said:

Two years before our merger we had considered a merger with another firm that didn't go through. However, it started people thinking about the need for a merger and gradually more people accepted the idea. Because our eventual merger partner didn't have a dry run that failed, I think it took their people longer to accept the fact of the merger.

Capacity to Transfer and Receive the Capability

For capability transfer to occur, the parties must have the capacity to participate in the transfer; that is, the capability must exist and the appropriate people in both firms must be able to transfer or to receive it. It may seem to go without saying that a capability must actually exist before it can be transferred, but the presence of a capability cannot always be taken for granted. It must be more than a presumed technical miracle or managerial wishful thinking. If an acquisition justification is hurriedly developed on the assumption that a capability exists, severe problems may result.

For example, Exxon Corporation bought Reliance Electric for $1.2 billion in 1979 with the understanding that Reliance could inexpensively commercialize an innovation from Exxon's research laboratories, a device to change alternating current to direct current and thus save large amounts of electricity. After the acquisition, Exxon discovered that Reliance was not able to manufacture at any cost advantage. Exxon paid a $500 million premium on its purchase of Reliance for a capability that did not exist.[4]

The firm to which the capability is being transferred must have the critical mass of intellectual and organizational abilities needed to use and apply what is acquired. For example, a bank manager who tried to apply a new marketing approach from an acquired subsidiary said:

> We tried for several years to learn how to use their direct mail, response-based advertising and failed each time. We eventually understood that the reason they could do it and we couldn't was because they had a low-cost, measurement-oriented philosophy that depended on continually bringing in new customers. We were used to waiting for the customers to come to us, and none of our people were used to thinking that way.

Often overlooked as an obstacle to participation is the time overload facing managers in smaller acquired firms. Because they have fewer staff and less management depth, these managers run the danger of being smothered by staff and functional managers from the parent who arrive to help implement the acquisition. In Chapter 10 we will return to the role that the gatekeepers can play in alleviating this aspect of the problem.

Discretionary Resources

After an acquisition was made, the ability to commit additional resources at both the parent and subsidiary levels played an important role in creating the atmosphere for capability transfer. In the firms we studied, allowing some slack in the postacquisition situation did not imply sloppy management practices.[5] Instead, it provided a basis for dealing with operating and strategic contingencies at the corporate and business unit levels. In the parent corporation, slack provided both protection and maneuvering room for the subsidiary that prevented a premature fixation on short-term results when the new subsidiary did not immediately meet performance expectations.[6] As the product development manager in the food services firm said:

> We got lucky because the parent firm had a great year and it gave us time to put some of our new product ideas in place. Two years later their profits fell off and we got a lot of pressure. Had we gotten that pressure earlier, we'd never have the product line we have today.

A less fortunate example was Pillsbury's acquisition of Green Giant, a prestigious brand name in canned and frozen vegetables. Their strategy was to develop, under the Green Giant label, a line of high-quality frozen foods that could be quickly prepared in a microwave oven by busy career people. But another Pillsbury subsidiary, Burger King, suddenly needed a big cash infusion to stay alive after Wendy's began the "hamburger wars." Pillsbury's strategy for Green Giant could not bear fruit because there was no slack at the overall firm level; the corporate resources Green Giant had expected to receive had been needed elsewhere.[7]

In the acquired firm, slack also provided maneuvering room for the middle managers responsible for integration and capability transfer. Slack gave them the opportunity to deal with unanticipated events, smooth out political problems, and make some concessions to disaffected employees. The CFO of an insurance firm told us:

> I was pretty conservative when we did our first budget, and fortunately the parent didn't know enough about our business to detect the padding. It turns out that we needed it all. We spent a lot more money than we'd ever expected to keep key people happy (beyond their salaries) and to pay for everything from extra travel to temporary staff.

Cause-Effect Understanding of Benefits

Before capabilities can be transferred, the acquisition's broad initial purpose must be clarified in operational terms for the middle and operating-level managers who must work out the details for bringing the two firms together. Our research suggests that managers need to understand the nature, the source, the timing, and the predictability of the benefits they expect from an acquisition. These issues are best clarified as part of the acquisition justification. Failure to be specific and draw up a precise timetable indicating when outcomes can be predicted may create just as many problems as an overly rigid and detailed plan when the sources of the benefits are really evolutionary and difficult to specify. The experiences of one manager at a food service company we studied reflect the often difficult, iterative process involved in understanding the sources of acquisition benefits:

> Sure, the top people had some good ideas about what we could do together. When we got down to the specifics, there were just too many problems. But, the exercise of trying to figure out how to make their [top management's] ideas work, gave us lots of ideas where we were ultimately able to work together and help each other.

Acquisition decisions are usually made with particular types of capability transfer in mind (e.g., resource sharing, functional skill transfer, general management skill transfer). But benefits from capability transfer are not gained without effort. The managers involved must understand how acquired capabilities can lead to improved competitive advantage before they can apply them. Strategic capabilities represent *potential;* once transferred, they still must be applied before they can lead to a competitive advantage.

Understanding the sources of benefits is important because different types of capability transfer require different characteristics in the atmosphere. For example, in resource sharing, management groups may be pressured to show how and when facilities will be consolidated to gain the expected benefits. In contrast, when embedded functional or general management skills are transferred, more time and patience are required before learning takes place.

In some cases the benefits are evolutionary. For example, in the process of working together, managers may discover benefits that were not anticipated when the acquisition was conceived. These discoveries usually occur at the middle management and operating levels, where the work actually gets done after the two groups have come together. These opportunities are often difficult to predict beforehand, especially if the acquisition analysis and decision process are centralized among the senior management and staff and operating-level personnel are not involved. The comments of a bank's senior planning officer point to this problem:

> As soon as it [the acquisition] looked like a "go," we quickly prepared a set of synergy arguments for the board that made sense *prima facie*. It turned out that none of these ever amounted to anything. The only ones that seemed to work were those that came from the operating guys.

In summary, the atmosphere for capability transfer is important because of its influence on the exchanges and learning that take place after an acquisition. This atmosphere is created through the interaction of the people in both firms, which are under the direct control of their managers.

INTERACTIONS: THE HEART OF INTEGRATION

Ultimately, the atmosphere necessary for capability transfer results from the stream of interactions between members of the two firms. Our research points to three types of interactions—substantive, administrative, and symbolic. Substantive interactions involve the efforts to transfer capabilities. Administrative interactions focus on developing information and control systems to bring the acquired firm into the overall corporate fold. Symbolic interactions are attempts to promote or influence certain beliefs. Although attention from senior managers and outsiders is usually focused on the substantive aspects of the merger (how value will be created), the impact of the administrative and symbolic interactions on acquisition success was equally important in the firms we studied, especially in the early period after the acquisition. While administrative and symbolic interactions can have substantive outcomes (i.e., affect the value-creating aspects of the acquisition), we will separate out their roles to highlight the differences.

Typically the initial contacts between representatives of the two organizations are formal meetings among senior executives with staff members and some operating executives who form subgroups and task teams to tackle different aspects of bringing the firms together. As time passes, the number of informal, random, and unsolicited interactions usually increases. These interactions involve managers from multiple levels in both firms who differ in status, outlook, perspective, experience, and motivation. They usually come to the acquisition with very little knowledge of the other firm and the people in it. Moreover, the knowledge they do have is often colored by rumor, accusation, or innuendo that arises during the negotiation process. Their thinking may be affected or framed by uncertainty about the acquisition's purpose and its potential impact on them, a recognition that their world will never be the same again, and that each person will be affected differently. These assumptions and opinions form the context in which the integration process begins.

We believe that a thorough understanding of these three types of interactions will enable managers to balance their attention among the three and to strengthen the atmosphere needed for capability transfer.

Substantive Interactions

Directed toward accomplishing the acquisition's original or emerging purpose, substantive interactions involve actions deemed necessary for value creation. They typically begin with senior managers from both firms developing a common agreement about areas in which the two firms should work together (e.g., technology transfer, market development, product rationalization, facility consolidation). The result is a set of plans that reflect the management groups' assumptions about the synergies that are possible and what has to happen to bring them about.

In some situations these plans have already been developed during the analysis and negotiation stage, and they are modified as more is learned about the situation.

The first substantive interactions after an acquisition usually involve well-orchestrated visits from senior line managers from both firms. A senior executive in a commercial bank said that these groups "act as scouting parties to figure out ways we can make our promises to the board and the investment community hold water."

At the same time that these planned interactions are occurring, a host of random ideas may emerge from "freelancers" in both firms. These ideas arise spontaneously when a manager, typically in the acquiring firm, contacts a presumed counterpart in the other firm with suggestions of what they could (or should) do together. As one senior vice president in a brokerage firm acquired by a bank remarked:

> A couple of days after the merger was announced we started getting calls from different people at the bank who had ideas about how to develop new products or cross-selling into each other's markets. Most of these ideas were pretty goofy, but we had to follow up.

This example also illustrates the frustration and false starts that many managers in both firms experience as they try to initiate substantive interactions; because they simply don't know whom to contact. Often afraid to ask because they will appear uniformed, they make random efforts to communicate with people in the other firm. Another manager said, "Exchanging really good ideas only happened if you tripped over the right person, and this takes time." The motives for these interactions are not always consistent. Although it is easy to cloak actions after an acquisition with the mantle of synergy, corporate reward systems also play an important role in these seemingly random contacts. A manager in the discount brokerage firm reported:

> People at the parent got brownie points on their year-end evaluations if they did something with us. But, they weren't evaluated on bottom-line profit responsibility, whereas we were. Thus, we ended up appearing pretty hard to get along with.

Administrative Interactions

The desire to "get our arms around" the acquired firm is very strong among managers in most acquiring companies. Thus they act quickly to establish reporting relationships, information flows, and operating procedures that are necessary to monitor and control the new subsidiary. Typically staff people from the parent company meet with the line managers at the new subsidiary and then staff groups from both firms meet. The imposition of parent company controls and management systems typically begins here. An operations manager in an acquired financial services firm said:

> Reporting and control issues seemed to dominate our early discussions. It was a long time before we got around to the stronger stuff.

Sometimes administrative changes are necessary before the acquisition's purpose can be achieved. For example, in acquisitions in which the facilities or distribution systems are to be combined, common accounting systems and control procedures need to be established before the consolidation can take place. Frequently, however, some firms automatically impose their administrative systems and practices on the acquired firm without considering whether these systems are right in the new setting. Such misapplication of management systems can severely limit the ability to create the atmosphere necessary for capability transfer.[8]

Symbolic Interactions

Nothing is ever the same after an acquisition; typically, the rules of the game change for everyone. People in both firms respond to these breaks with the past by engaging in a variety of activities with a high symbolic content. These actions have a dual purpose: (1) to set a general direction for the new organization, and (2) to stake out "sacred" ground that should not be violated.

As signals from top management, symbolic interactions can demonstrate and explain to both organizations the new organizational purpose and philosophy. For example, when Fuji and Yawata Steel in Japan were merged to form Nippon Steel, senior executives' quarterly meetings were rotated among the different plants for the first few years after the merger. This policy gave senior executives a chance to demonstrate the unity of the two firms and to have extensive discussions with employees at each location about the firm's future direction.

Lower-level managers and employees in both firms also use symbolic interactions to signal their basic beliefs, skills, capabilities, or positions on key issues to people in the other firm. These are intended either to gain an advantage in forthcoming negotiations between the two firms or to ward off particular types of encroachment by the other firm before they have a chance to surface. In a sense, it is less what you do than how you do it that matters. Symbolic interactions begin before the agreement is signed and continue in one form or another throughout the life of the acquisition.

SUMMARY

This chapter discussed the relation of acquisition integration to value creation. We suggested that integration can be better understood by decomposing it into a process of interactions that create an atmosphere conducive to transferring capabilities to achieve the acquisition's purpose.

Interactions between the two firms are at the heart of the integration process, because they establish the atmosphere for capability transfer and are the primary medium for exchange of ideas about how to make an acquisition work. While most interactions are originally intended to be either substantive, symbolic, or administrative, they often have elements of all three types. In addition, these interactions involve multiple actors from different levels, each with a different agenda. The senior managers of the acquired firm may have a tendency to focus on substantive and administrative interactions, as they want to get on with the strategic task and to incorporate the acquisition organizationally. For the acquired managers, the symbolic interactions, and the symbolic connotation of those that were intended as substantive or organizational, take on more weight.[9]

For managers responsible for the integration process, insight into these interactions—how they will play out by acquisition type and how they can be managed—will be critical to success. We will address these issues when we discuss the role of the interface managers in Chapter 10.

In the next chapter we turn to the process problems that can subvert the integration process by limiting the ability to create the right atmosphere. Later we will return to the ways in which managers responsible for managing the interface between the two organizations can take control of the interactions and manage the capability transfer process.

Problems in Acquisition Integration

INTRODUCTION

JUST AS THERE ARE problems related to the decision process before the agreement, there are a range of problems afterward during the integration process. Our research found three such recurring process-based problems that tended to hamper the combined firms' ability to create an atmosphere appropriate for capability transfer.[1] (See Figure 7-1.)

Determinism—the tendency to cling to the original justification in the face of a different or changing reality confronting the acquisition.

Value destruction—the impact of the acquisition on individual managers and employees themselves.

Leadership vacuum—the lack of appropriate leadership to articulate a new purpose for the combined firms.

Taken together, these problems explained to a large extent the failures in acquisition integration that we observed. In successful acquisitions the forces that brought these problems about were present, but management had been able to recognize and deal with them. In less successful acquisitions, individual managers were often painfully aware of these problems but they could not influence their company's pattern of reacting to them. We will examine each of these problems, the forces that bring them about, and their impact on the integration process.

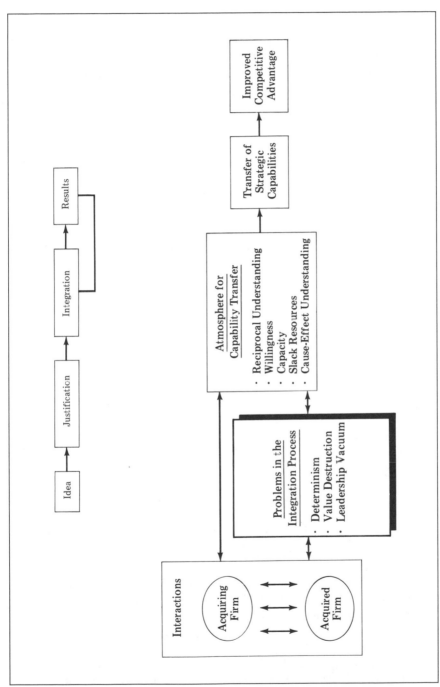

Figure 7-1 **The Acquisition Integration Process**

DETERMINISM

In Chapter 3 we discussed the acquisition decision process and how a view of the acquisition is generated and then becomes crystallized in a formal acquisition justification. Often, we argued, this is kept fairly general and simplified so it can draw support from many players in the decision-making process and provide an easily understood explanation to a variety of people. But this simplified view is often incomplete and misleading because it is based on limited information and was established under severe time pressure. Independent of the strategic assumptions, the justification is always boiled down into very specific, qualified performance expectations, as was illustrated in the Francoplast example.

Post-acquisition reality is often very different from what was expected, no matter how completely the pre-acquisition analysis has been done. These differences occur because additional information becomes available or because of unexpected events such as changes in the industry, technology, or competitors' reactions, changes in other parts of the parent firm, or resistance from competing organizational ideologies within the combined units. The problem of determinism arises when this initial justification is not altered to accommodate the changed situation in which the firm finds itself. Our research suggests that as these external events and shocks become more frequent, managers may cling to the original justification instead of trying to adapt to the changes. This inflexible outlook is rooted in a false sense of security created by the original justification and conditioned by a cycle of confusion and frustration resulting from the justification's inability to survive in the real world.

FALSE SENSE OF SECURITY

Because the acquisition idea must be "sold" to many groups, the initial justification may be developed so persuasively that it is difficult to dispute, and as a result bandwagon effect may be created because the groups involved cannot imagine how it could fail. This false sense of security clouds the managers' abilities to realize that changing circumstances can affect their prior assumptions and the acquisition's success. As a marketing manager in the discount brokerage firm said:

> All we knew about the bank [acquirer] was general and positive. We were led to believe that they had real strengths and that they could help us . . . we were very naive about their weak-

nesses. It wasn't until late in the game that we discovered they were weak just where we all thought they would be strong.

A false sense of security can also create feelings of comfort and single-mindedness about the ease with which benefits can be created. In our research, key managers often assumed that it would be easy to transfer specialized knowledge between the two firms after an acquisition. A food services company manager said of the restaurant chain:

> Until we tried it a couple of times, we thought that they'd pick up our customer-based method of product development quickly. But we didn't realize how different their customers were, which kept them from understanding what we were trying to do.

The performance expectations that developed to support the acquisition justification also reinforced this single-minded view. These expectations often grew from estimates made hurriedly during negotiations, when the tendency was to rely on judgments of savings and other assumed benefits without an in-depth examination of how the two firms could work together. High acquisition premiums sometimes forced senior managers to demand a rapid return on their investment. As a result, performance expectations for the acquisitions we studied were often so rigorous and precise that the acquisition's managers were driven to quick fixes to meet these performance hurdles.

As one of the managers in the insurance firm said,

> We had an awful time meeting our business production and profit targets. In fact, we spent more time creating profits with mirrors the first year than we did working together to develop new products.

Performance pressures were sometimes eased by offering the new subsidiary a grace period during which the performance requirements were less stringent. But promises of autonomy or grace periods are frequently forgotten as the acquisition becomes seen as a more integral part of the firm during the next planning cycle and the senior managers' attention shifts to other goals and interests of the organization that have a higher priority.

Staff planners also reinforce the pressure for performance. Corporate planning and control staffs responsible for consolidating the projections of each of the parts of the firm were less likely to be sympathetic to acquisition managers who claimed autonomy or asked for a grace period for "strategic" purposes. Everyone wanted concessions from the planners during the budgeting process, and the planners often had no incentives to treat an acquisition any differently than they did other divisions or departments. As one manager told us:

> We were acquired in the middle of a planning cycle [and didn't have to bother with planning that year]. Part of the deal was that we wouldn't be part of the planning process until the third year. But the corporate planners apparently had not heard of our agreement and barraged us with requisitions for information, data, and statistics.

UNEXPECTED EVENTS

Acquisitions are often battered by external shocks such as changes in the industry and competition. Although seasoned managers recognize these changes as normal, there is mounting evidence that managerial skills are not transferable between industries and that effective management often depends on an appreciation and understanding of the subtleties of industry and firm context.[2] This inability to appreciate other contexts is underscored by the comments of a manager from the food services company:

> Although we were both in service businesses, it turned out that we were all wet about the fundamentals of their business and what made it tick. Their asset allocation and people skills were different enough that when it came to the point where we thought we could help, we just did not understand their business well enough to offer constructive advice.

Some of the most important yet most troubling unexpected events we observed resulted from the friction and adversarial behavior that developed when the two firms were combined. In one extreme example, when a parent and its new subsidiary could not agree on the type of sign that would be displayed in front of a building they would be sharing, each brought counsel from its outside law firm to the management meeting called to resolve the issue.

CYCLE OF CONFUSION AND FRUSTRATION

These unexpected events can culminate in a cycle of confusion and frustration among managers at all levels in both organizations. Senior managers are confused and frustrated because their initial presumptions are being questioned, undermined by external factors, or proven incorrect. The middle and operating-level managers are frustrated because their bosses inflexibly hold them to the original plan without regard for the changes in assumptions dictated by changes in the firm's situation.

The problem of determinism occurs when this feeling of confusion and frustration causes managers to increase their commitment to the original acquisition justification, instead of addressing the factors causing the problems. Senior managers return to the original justification and performance targets because they are comfortable with them and committed to them. Middle managers, in turn, embrace the original justification because they were not responsible for developing it and, therefore, can hardly be blamed if it fails. Ironically, both groups that could deal with the problems stubbornly adhere to the original justification, which allows them to argue that poor performance is attributed to factors beyond their control.

Determinism undercuts the possibility of creating an atmosphere conducive to capability transfer. When managers hold fast to the original acquisition justification, they consider fewer ways in which the two firms can work together beyond those originally envisioned and tend to seek only a limited understanding of the other firm. The interactions among members of the firms are more limited, and chances are reduced that people will serendipitously discover new ways to work together. No one sees the need for discretionary resources to deal with unexpected circumstances. In fact, performance problems often lead to tighter expense controls, which reduces the availability of slack resources to deal with problems. Finally, the false sense of security created by the original justification limits the motivation of the two organizations to learn about each other because of the presumed "ease" with which they were able to pull off this particular acquisition.

Determinism and the forces that drive it were illustrated in the Francoplast acquisition, whose beginnings we described in Chapter 3.

FRANCOPLAST AFTER THE AGREEMENT

After acquiring Francoplast in December 1983, Arndt Wirtz and Stefan Wilcke moved quickly to install a management team headed by Alain Wibault, a French marketing manager who had not been involved in the original evaluation and negotiations. When Wibault arrived in April, he found a memo from Wirtz reminding him of the premises on which the company had been acquired and how it should be managed. The acquisition proposal was attached to the memo.

Wibault quickly set out to asses the situation. One worrisome piece of news was the confirmation that a claim was being filed because of faulty pipe installation. Other issues that cropped up included quality problems, a high percentage of once-only orders, and a generally poor image in the market.

A surprise visit by the corporate vice-president in charge of specialty chemicals forced Wibault to put together his views on the potential and strategy for Francoplast very quickly. With his bosses in the room, Wibault presented the list of objectives and pro forma financial statements he had inherited, mentioning his concerns to Wirtz only in private. In the meantime, his controller, digging into Francoplast's books, was discovering higher debt levels, essentially zero net worth, and increased working capital needs. During the next few weeks Wibault discovered that in some cases standard manufatoring cost exceeded competitor's list prices, that management wasn't working well together, and that the sales manager seemed ineffective.

By May, although still optimistic about the long term, Wibault was sure the company would lose money in the next year and asked for a meeting where he requested additional capital, a decision on the liability claim, removal of his sales manager, and a revision of his first year's budget. The response from Wirtz was not sympathetic. He felt it was too early to draw such a conclusion and wanted to hear *how* Wibault was going to achieve the plan. Throughout June, Wibault and his controller spent their time building a more complete picture of Francoplast's financial and market positions. They modified a projection for 1983 to now reflect a loss of $1.8 million on unchanged sales of $13 million but maintained subsequent years' objectives. Although they acknowledged some of the points put forward by Wibault, his superiors reiterated their belief that higher profibility could be achieved.

By September, urgent telexes were being sent back and forth. Wibault presented a 1984 operating plan incorporating corporate's expectations for $2.1 million profit on sales of $21.75 million, committing himself only if certain "key recommendations" that departed from the original scenario were implemented.

Wirtz, increasingly irritated at what he considered Francoplast management's complaints and excuses, called a meeting in November, relieved Wibault of his job, brought back Wilcke, and reinforced the original promises and long-term objectives, based in part on a large U.S. oil pipe order Wibault had finally secured.

After Wilcke arrived in April 1984, he soon discovered that lower oil prices and reduced government support had combined to destroy Francoplast's district heating opportunities, upon which it had expected to fall back after the large oil pipe order was finished. Despite these reversals he was confident that the R&D programs he was working on would enable the company to be competitive in the long term.

In a management meeting in the summer of 1984, the management team described the two preceding years as a phase of learning and reorganization; 1985 was portrayed as a phase for consolidation and break-even; and 1986 was expected to be a period of profitability and growth. In reality, 1983 closed on sales of $6 million and losses of $1.9 million. The results the next year, 1984, were even worse—sales of $7.5 million with losses of $7.8 million.

It took a third general manager, brought in in April 1985, to initiate a review of the situation and all options and to convince top management that it needed to sell Francoplast. In the end, cumulative losses had been over $40 million, fifteen times the original purchase price.

This extreme example highlighted many problems: Eurochem was not familiar with the business; its culture was one of opportunism and a can-do attitude; and it threw an inexperienced general manager without any corporate credibility into a situation not of his own making. The prior assessment of the acquisition was not grounded in reality; the objectives for it were unrealistic; and the market shrank when oil prices fell and government support disappeared.

Above all, this example shows how an original acquisition justification can carry over to a simplistic post-acquisition view to which top management stays committed, even when its view diverges from reality. The frustrations over this divergence often lead top management to reaffirm its adherence to the unrealistic position it has espoused. If reality does not get worked into the system, the real opportunities for capability transfer are not exploited.

VALUE DESTRUCTION

Every acquisition changes the established order and pattern of activities at both firms. These changes foster uncertainty, fear, and a tendency toward self-preservation on the part of the employees. As a result, the people who are expected to create economic value for the shareholders have value destroyed for themselves. In the firms we studied, value destruction affected the atmosphere for capability transfer in several ways. Its strongest impact was on the willingness and capacity of the employees to participate in capability transfer. As value for them was destroyed, people became unwilling to work toward the acquisition's success. They left the firm, they retreated to past behaviors, or they came to work but took no initiative. They also became unwilling to try to understand the other firm to the extent that would be necessary if they were to work together. Efforts to induce people at the subsidiary level to participate or to compensate in other ways for their lack of participation took substantial time and resources.

The value destroyed for employees may be economic or psychic. Economic value is destroyed if they lose their jobs, job security, or benefits as a result of eliminating redundancies or standardization of operating procedures after an acquisition. The destruction of psychic, noneconomic value that results from the rumors, presumptions, actions, and decisions (real or imagined) that directly affect the lives of the participants is more insidious and more subtle. We see psychic value as the nonmonetary benefits that accrue to managers and employees in an acquisition. Psychic value includes such factors as opportunities for career advancement and the status that comes from membership in a particular organization.[3]

Combining two organizations always destroys psychic value. A break with the past is caused when both are asked to accept and develop new ways of doing things and to offer allegiance to a different organization. This break causes the ideologies that represent the values of the previously separate firms to emerge.[4] In the problem-ridden acquisitions we studied, these ideologies often served as focal points for resistance to change and the rivalries that developed between the two organizations. For example, a manager from a discount brokerage firm said:

> We fought any synergy discussions because they were bureaucratic and we didn't want to be like them.

Further, a marketing vice-president from an acquired bank said:

> Everybody had his own checklist to test the parent's promises of how we'd fit in. The minute anybody from their shop tried something different, the most godawful cry went up.

Although these rivalries occurred naturally, they contributed to the destruction of psychic value because of the uncertainties, fears, and ambiguities they sparked among the employees. Individuals' moves toward self-preservation and turf protection reduced the opportunity for the firms to work together. Typical among responses was that of a senior systems manager in an acquired bank who said:

When we heard about the merger, four concerns dominated our hallway discussions:
(1) Will the president be allowed to stay?
(2) Will we still run our own show?
(3) How will this affect my career and personal ambitions?
(4) What will happen to my benefit package?
Until we got answers to these, we kept our heads down.

A more subtle loss of psychic value accompanied a reduction in prestige for managers in a new subsidiary who no longer had complete autonomy but felt superior to some of their newly found peers in the larger firm. For example, in one of the acquired firms, a senior manager had to work with a manager from the parent who had the same title but less decision authority and a lower status than he.

The [parent] sent over lower level people to work with me on different product ideas. Because they were larger and organized differently, the people they sent had the technical knowledge but weren't at a high enough level to either have the big picture or be able to commit the parent firm. Not much got done until they sent somebody at "my level."

These moves toward protection and self-preservation as a result of the destruction of both economic and psychic value occurred more frequently in the acquired firm. If the strategic capability is to be transferred from the new subsidiary to the parent, self-preservation efforts can be expected in the parent as well. These efforts resulted in reduction in commitment to the firm and to making the acquisition work, a reluctance to change, a retreat to old ways of doing things, and sometimes, even sabotage.

In situations where value was destroyed, individuals' commitment to the firm or to making the acquisition work declined because they perceived a qualitative change in the nature of their relationship with their firms.[5] The factors that had once attracted them to the firm and contributed to their productivity had been dramatically altered in comparison with the contributions they were being asked to make. Their own reduction in commitment contrasted dramatically with the increased commitment by senior managers to the performance levels in the original justification of the acquisition. As a food services company manager said,

At the same time we were trying to deal with our own careers and futures, the people at corporate seemed to be demanding more from us. They couldn't or wouldn't recognize what we were faced with on a personal level. Many of us just disengaged mentally.

No matter how much empathy managers in acquiring firms have, they usually underestimate the depth of the problem of employee value destruction. If they do recognize it, they often postpone or cancel integration steps that were planned and take only actions that will be "accepted." This slowdown in integration leads to promises and expectations that imply that real value-creation opportunities will not be pursued or that their pursuit will engender an even greater cost later on. Clearly, one key decision is when to accommodate peoples' needs and seek acceptance and when to press ahead. A more important decision is how to manage and contain the inevitable repercussions of value destruction. Both these issues will be examined later.

Acquisitions threaten, reduce, or destroy important elements of economic and psychic value such as job security, promotion, career opportunities, status, and pride of association. Problems of divided loyalties and self-preservation behavior that reduce the prospect that economic value will be created for the acquiring firm's shareholders are a natural outgrowth of this value destruction.

LEADERSHIP VACUUM

Because of the tendency for value to be destroyed, leadership becomes even more important after an acquisition, when employees in the two firms or parts of firms are brought together and are expected to embrace a new, often ill-defined concept. Our research found that unless both institutional and interpersonal leadership were provided, the possibilities for creating the atmosphere necessary for capability transfer were limited. Yet in many of the acquisitions we observed, top management attention tended to peak at the time of the deal. Once an agreement was reached, senior management typically moved on to other pressing matters, leaving implementation in the hands of lower-level operating managers.

Institutional leadership is important after an acquisition to help people from both firms develop, understand, and embrace the acquisition's purpose and to see their role in it. Senior executives need to provide institutional leadership and create a broad vision for the combined firms that will accommodate that acquisition's purpose and the respective needs of the combined firms. This new vision should yield an identity for the combined firms and foster the ability to find creative ways to transfer capabilities to fulfill the acquisition's purpose.[6]

Our research found that serious problems can arise if senior executives abrogate their responsibilities for institutional leadership after an acquisition. If the new subsidiary is not infused with values and purpose of its own, the chances are reduced that the atmosphere necessary for strategic capability transfer can be created. Without an understanding of the acquisition's purpose or ideas of how they could work together, managers and employees in the combined firms retreat to their former, more familiar behaviors. This retreat, in turn, creates organizational disruptions among the people who are expected to effect capability transfer.

In the firms we studied, institutional leadership was often missing when, after the acquisition, top management focused on performance expectations for the acquisition and delegated issues of capability transfer to operating mangers. This focus on performance resulted from three related factors. First, the analyses used to justify the acquisition provided a convenient set of targets. Although initially labeled "projections," these targets soon took on an air of precision and were offered as beacons to show what was expected of the acquisitions both to those outside and to those within the firms. Second, senior managers sometimes detached themselves from the integration process so they could make more objective judgments about the acquisition's performance.

The experience of an executive from a financial services firm reflects this senior management detachment and delegation:

> The chairman and president brought the top 10 people from both firms together and told us that we had a lot of potential if we could merge product lines and use each other's systems. They then told us that although there would be some start-up costs, they were confident that synergies would more than outweigh these and that we shouldn't have a performance dip. They then left the room and the two sides sat staring at each other, wondering why we were there and how we were going to make it work.

Another manager in a finance company acquired by a bank said:

> We were cast adrift . . . there was no support for us within the parent firm and nobody understood what we are. This was OK until the managers sent by the parent arrived with no instructions about what to do except make money.

Problems in the acquisition decision-making process discussed in Chapter 4 were a third factor that pulled top management away from institutional leadership toward a performance focus. The division of labor necessary in the analysis and negotiation and the momentum of the process precipitated and encouraged a focus on performance that did not include organizational considerations. In addition, the resolution of questions on key content aspects of bringing the two firms together was often postponed until after the agreement was signed and then delegated to middle managers who were not involved in the negotiating process. These aspects of the pre-acquisition process combined to keep senior management from developing a thorough understanding of the two firms and ways in which they might work together to create value. A finance company executive said:

> They [parent] didn't really have a strategy for us. One was developed at the time of the merger, but [it] was so far removed from the reality of what the two of us could really do together that we ended up drifting and struggled to report profits.

In the acquisitions we studied, the operating middle managers were responsible for achieving the purpose of the acquisition. But a void of institutional leadership often forced them to misallocate their time. When senior executives failed to provide a new vision and purpose, middle managers responsible for the new subsidiary had to spend a much greater proportion of their time on interpersonal leadership tasks vis-à-vis each member to insure the continued participation of key people and groups.[7] The pressures of trying to integrate two organizations that lacked a common purpose forced many middle managers to shift their focus from the substantive, value-creating aspects of the acquisition to the process issues of interpersonal leadership. As a manager in the finance company said:

> Both my boss and I agreed that I had to be responsible for the details. But there were too many people problems for me to have the time to manage the new product development ideas we had.

Such a leadership vacuum at the senior level can affect the atmosphere for capability transfer by limiting cause-effect knowledge, the willingness to participate, and organizational slack. In some instances we studied, a lack of institutional leadership led to situations in which people in the two firms simply did not interact because they did not know where to begin without knowing how the two firms could fit together; there was no chance to develop understanding of the cause-effect necessary for value creation.

This leadership void also limited the amount of discretionary resources available in two ways. More resources than expected were used up in efforts to solve individuals' problems when institutional leadership was wanting. Moreover, the lack of a common purpose led to substandard performance, which closed off the ability to attract additional resources. In summary, a leadership vacuum at the top causes a misdirection of leadership at both the top and middle management levels. This vacuum makes it difficult to create the atmosphere necessary for capability transfer because a common purpose for the combined firms is not developed. Thus, middle managers responsible for bringing the two firms together to create value must spend more of their time on interpersonal leadership dealing with organizational disruptions and less time on the real purpose of the acquisition.

SUMMARY

This chapter showed how forces present in the acquisition integration process can undermine a firm's ability to create value in practice. These forces included an overly deterministic view of the acquisition's purpose, destruction of value for the very people expected to create value for the shareholders, and a leadership vacuum. The root mechanisms that trigger these problems were present in all the acquisitions we studied. In well-managed acquisitions, however, these problems and their impact were mitigated by two factors. One was experience and the learning derived from it; the other was direction setting at the top.

Previous experience with acquisitions was an important factor in helping firms overcome process-related integration problems. Both individual experience and organizational experience were important. Managers who had been involved in prior acquisitions (at their current firm or elsewhere) had a frame of reference into which they could fit their current situation. They could recall their past mistakes and identify early warning signals that went unrecognized by others. Their effectiveness was diluted, however, unless their firm had developed a way to codify and disseminate their accumulated experience. Furthermore, at the firm level, there seemed to be less initial resistance to an acquisition (and employees seemed more willing to participate) in firms with a history of acquisitions or in which an acquisition had been considered but not taken place. We will discuss the ways in which firms develop this learning in Chapter 14.

The nature of leadership and the way top management set direction was the second key factor in overcoming these integration problems. The senior managers who provided direction regarded their acquisitions mergers as long-term arrangements and believed that employees needed both direction and protection. For example, in the mergers of the Japanese banks and of the steel companies, institutional leadership was an integral part of senior management's activities. Great care was taken to provide the broadest possible purpose for the bank merger and to discuss the benefits that the two "families would have [from] living under one roof." Top management also assured job security and stability for each employee and alternated managers from both firms in the new hierarchy to ensure power sharing. This policy was carried out at the cost of great duplication; several people in the bank estimated that there were 40 percent too many people for the work available.

In another example, when Unilever acquired Chesebrough-Pond's in February 1987 it had learned from previous acquisition experience the importance of prolonged senior management corporate attention. Consequently, a main board director moved to the United States to oversee the integration process as chairman, even though Chesebrough-Pond's operating management would remain in place.[8] In contrast, all too often, senior managers in other firms may issue press releases about the great things to come, but they pay less personal attention to developing a broad purpose coupled with long-term patience.

Part of the leadership task after an acquisition is to provide a common external focus for the members of both organizations. Making managers from both firms work together on common, external problems instead of competing with each other satisfied three key conditions for strategic capability transfer. It helped them develop cause-effect knowledge of the benefits to be expected from the acquisition; they learned to understand each other better; and they became more willing to participate. Achieving a common external focus was not automatic. Sometimes it arrived late, precipitated by problems due to internal competition. For example, when one firm sustained a substantial foreign currency trading loss at an overseas branch, the loss was traced to latent rivalries between the two firms. This event served as a catalyst for a change in attitudes as the managers realized that their old habits of antagonism and rivalry would have to cease if they were to become competitive in the marketplace.

The integration process problems of determinism, value destruction, and a vacuum in leadership limit the ability to create the atmosphere needed for capability transfer and ultimate value creation. To combat these problems of leadership void, managers need a combination of insight and organizational discipline. The exact nature of the managerial challenges involved in overcoming these problems depends, of course, on the acquisition's context and the type of integration, topics to which we turn in the next chapters.

8

Understanding Different Integration Approaches

INTRODUCTION

THE SENIOR MEMBERS OF A management team of an historically successful firm were discussing their experiences in integrating acquisitions outside their base business. When the chairman asked the management team what integration meant, the consensus answer was, "Integrating an acquisition means making them like us." Although that approach may be appropriate in a few instances, the chairman's reaction reflected the frustration felt by many senior executives involved in diversification activities: "How can we do anything different with an attitude like this?"

Integration clearly means different things to different people. Most importantly, it means different things in different situations. While there are common ingredients in the process, each acquisition presents managers with a different situation and forces a choice of integration approach. Earlier writers on acquisitions have suggested several distinctions that affect the type of integration approach. For example, it has been argued that differences in the integration task are based on the relative size of the acquired firm, the acquired firm's profitability, whether the synergies are in marketing or manufacturing, and whether the cultures are similar or not.[1] But when we compared the detailed observations from our research with such distinctions, none by itself provided a sufficient explanation of the range of integration phenomena we observed.

Our research identified two key dimensions that led to a broad logic for choosing an integration approach. This chapter examines those dimensions and presents the three integration approaches that correspond to these contexts. We do not suggest that there is one best way to integrate each acquisition. Good performance is also affected by consistency and discipline in execution of what is ultimately a managerial choice. But we do advocate carefully choosing an integration approach based on the analysis of a number of key factors and then remaining flexible to adapt the approach as events unfold. In this chapter we will emphasize a logic to guide integration choices and the analysis on which it can be based.

KEY DIMENSIONS IN ACQUISITION INTEGRATION

A firm's approach to integration can be understood by considering two central dimensions of the acquisition—its relationship to the acquiring firm and the way in which value is expected to be created. The first dimension relates to the nature of the interdependence that needs to be established between the firms to make possible the type of strategic capability transfer that is expected. The other dimension is associated with the need to preserve intact the acquired strategic capabilities after the acquisition.[2]

STRATEGIC INTERDEPENDENCE NEED

The essential task in any acquisition is to create the value that becomes possible when the two organizations are combined, value that would not exist if the firms operated separately. The analysis, negotiation, and internal selling of an acquisition candidate and ultimately the premium offered are all predicated on this central idea. Yet managers often shy away from the integration task because of uncertainties about the fundamentals of the acquired business, because of organizational or cultural differences, or because of a fear that they will be resisted.

We discussed in Chapter 2 how value is created by transferring strategic capabilities. Such capability transfer requires creating and managing interdependencies between both organizations. These interdependencies disturb the "boundary" of the acquired company, that invisible line that distinguishes them from the acquirer. This disturbance is likely to be resented, if not resisted, by managers in the acquired firm, who want to keep their identity and their way of doing things. To transfer capabilities between firms and overcome possible resistance requires that the interdependence between the two firms be carefully managed. Thus, a key determinant of the integration task is the nature of the interdependence between the two firms and how that interdependence is to be managed.[3]

The nature of the interdependence in an acquisition depends on how value will be created. In Chapter 2 we discussed three types of capability transfer (resource sharing, functional skill transfer, and general management capability transfer), as well as a number of combination benefits. Each of these four benefits implies different requirements for interdependence and, thus, for the degree to which the boundary of the acquired organization will have to be disturbed and eliminated, and, conversely, the degree to which the organizational identity of the original company should be maintained.

Some acquisitions are based primarily on *resource sharing*, which involves the combination and rationalization of operating assets. Resource sharing implies an integration process that completely dissolves the boundaries between the two subparts of the organizations that are to be rationalized. In resource sharing, value is created by combining the entities at the operating level, so that functional overlaps and duplication are eliminated. The greater efficiency of the streamlined operations is supposed to outweigh any costs associated with the rationalization. Such costs include not only those of a one-time rationalization of the firms, but also the harder-to-measure ongoing consequences of a loss of specialized focus and commitment that might derive from combining both operations.

The integration process is inherently different if the strategic capability transfer involves the *transfer of functional skills*. Skills reside in individuals, groups of people, and their procedures and practices, not in assets. They can be transferred only as people are moved across organizational boundaries or when information, knowledge, and know-how are shared. For example, the R&D capability of a chemical firm can be transferred to an acquired firm through a variety of mechanisms, including coordinated management of the R&D functions, transfer of R&D scientists in both directions, or transfer of the products or processes that are the outcome of such R&D. Although each organization retains a distinct presence in the function in question, continuing interference and involvement (or potential interference) from the acquiring company's corresponding functional managers impinge on the acquired company managers' autonomy.[4] Because that boundary disruption comes about through essentially horizontal rather than hierarchcal interactions, it is often regarded as illegitimate by the acquired managers, who want to preserve the integrity of what they still see as their firm. The transfer of *general management capability* can create value through improved strategic or operational insight, coordination, or control. These improvements can be achieved partly through direct, substantive involvement in general management decisions, or on a more permanent basis through the installation and use of systems, controls, budgets, and plans that improve both the strategic decision making and the operational efficiency of acquired management.

General management capability transfer was seen as somewhat less disruptive than the other types of strategic capability transfer. Direct involvement by hierarchical superiors was considered more legitimate than the involvement of functional counterparts from the acquirer, and after the one-time disruption of changes in systems, life inside the acquired unit could go on without further boundary disruption. Nevertheless, disruption did occur. For example, managers in the acquired firms typically regarded being subjected to the discipline of formal investment approval as a loss of freedom, even when no projects had been turned down or, to the contrary, accelerated investment had been encouraged.

Finally, any acquisition brings with it a number of *combination benefits* that are available automatically as a result of the combination and are not related to capability transfer. Some acquisitions may yield excess cash resources or borrowing capacity between the firms. In others, benefits may come from greater size, whether through the added purchasing power it provides, or through the greater market power that size brings. The merger between Metal Box of the U.K. and Carnaud of France, for example, to create CMB, one of the larger packaging firms in the world, had a clear impact on the bargaining position of the Metal Box vis-à-vis British Steel, its main source of tin-plated steel. Not only did the combined firm become the largest European customer for a product that had long been cartelized by suppliers, but it also gave Metal Box access to Carnaud's integrated capacity. Given Metal Box's prior size, the immediate cost savings on its existing volume were not dramatic, but it was able to channel its new bargaining power into obtaining much more important quality and on-time delivery benefits. At the same time CMB is continuing to make acquisitions of smaller firms, and with them opportunities for a significant raw materials cost saving.

As we discussed in Chapter 2, any individual acquisition may involve benefits from several of these sources. Yet our research suggests that in most cases, independent of the variety and number of possible synergies, it is possible, and advisable, to recognize one type of capability transfer as the *dominant* source of initial value creation.

Formally assessing the strategic interdependence needs of an acquisition has several important benefits.[5] It helps managers develop a more unbiased, objective view of the strategic task involved in creating value with the acquisition irrespective of the ease or difficulty of implemention. At the same time, by categorizing these strategic tasks in a way that reflects the required extent of interdependence, managers can go beyond identifying potential areas of synergy and examine the organizational tasks that will be needed to bring out the expected benefits. Finally, by considering only those interdependencies regarded as critical for achieving the benefits upon which the acquisition was originally justified, managers can begin to develop a clearer sense of the strategic and organizational trade-offs involved. Before making these trade-offs, however, the organizational factors that are central to the integration process must be addressed.

ORGANIZATIONAL AUTONOMY NEED

Because we regard strategic capability transfer as the precursor to value creation, it is clearly vital to preserve the strategic capability that is to be transferred. Yet one of the paradoxes in acquisitions is that the pursuit of capability transfer itself may lead to the destruction of the capability being transferred. Whereas capability transfer requires different degrees of boundary disruption or dissolution, the preservation of capabilities requires boundary protection and, hence, organizational autonomy.[6]

This paradox is especially evident in acquisitions where the acquired capabilities reside in people or groups of people. The disintegration of many of the financial firms that were acquired in London during the build-up to "Big Bang" in 1986 is an example of this problem. Key people may decide to leave simply because, as we discussed earlier, they feel that value has been destroyed for them. At the heart of this problem is the issue of boundary management. Demands for organizational autonomy and "no change" are present in every acquisition. They come from the deep-seated identification of managers, employees, and other organizational stakeholders with their original organization.

All too often, acquiring managers respond to these demands for autonomy by promising whatever it takes to make acquired managers "accept" the takeover. They then often shroud their promises in the illusion that all expected benefits of an acquisition will be realized without any disruptive changes. For example, a dispute over the integration of Blue Arrow, the British temporary services company, with its American acquisition of Manpower, Inc. in the United States led to the resignation of Manpower's CEO. The chairman of Blue Arrow said that it was time to look for "back office synergies and cost savings." At the same time, he hastily added that he would not change Manpower's culture or the way its services were marketed.[7] Statements such as this are often made for public consumption or to soothe the apprehensions of acquired managers and employees. But, as experienced acquirers well know, this sort of schizophrenic attitude often paves the way for the reverse: organizational upheaval with synergies left unrealized.

We indicated earlier that most of the organizational behavior and corporate culture research on acquisitions has focused on the issue of the impact on people and their acceptance of the acquisition.[8] The assumption often seems to be that in an acquisition no one should be disturbed or have "bad" things happen to them. We, too, believe that people are important in an acquisition and we believe they should be treated fairly and with dignity. But if managers lose sight of the fact that the strategic task of an acquisition is to create value, they may either grant autonomy too quickly or fall into the perilous "no change-all synergies expected" syndrome described above. Managers and employees in acquired firms are too smart to be fooled by this syndrome.

Dealing with the perceived need for autonomy after an acquisition is one of the most important challenges a manager will face. The manager should not deviate from the strategic task—transferring capabilities to create value—unless the argument for autonomy corresponds to a real need for boundary protection. Such a real need exists when the strategic capabilities whose transfer is key to the acquisition are embedded in a distinct organization and culture and that distinction is central to the preservation of those capabilities. That is, the other firm may have been acquired precisely because it is different.

Managers in acquiring firms can consider the need for organizational autonomy in more practical terms by examining three questions: Is autonomy essential to preserve the strategic capability we bought? If so, how much autonomy should be allowed? In which areas specifically is autonomy important?

Regarding the first question, our research suggests that autonomy should be provided the acquired unit if the survival of the strategic capabilities on which the acquisition is based depends on preservation of the organizational culture from which they came. The important question, thus, is *not* how different the two cultures are, but whether *main-*

taining that difference in the long term will serve a useful purpose.[9] For example, when BASF, the German chemical giant, bought American Enka's petrochemical operations from Akzo in 1985, its main purpose was to improve the raw materials supply position of its fiber business through acquisition of the Enka plant. The economics of that facility depended very little on the organizational culture of American Akzo.

On the other hand, when BASF bought the Celanese advanced composites materials businesses in that same year, the situation was very different. The very success of that acquisition depended on BASF's ability to keep intact both the entrepreneurial culture of the former Celanese organization and its links with important aerospace and defense clients—substantial challenges for a large foreign acquirer. In such cases, allowing sufficient autonomy to preserve the acquired capabilities constitutes more than a tactic to gain acceptance and placate employees. It is vital to the success of the acquisition.

If there is a genuine need to maintain autonomy, managers must next consider whether the capabilities are widely spread or fairly isolated in the acquired organization.[10] At one end of the spectrum the strategic capability may be embedded in a particular subunit of the organization. For example, a particular firm's value for the acquirer may derive from a specific R&D capability that, although highly dependent on a subculture within the R&D department, is fairly unrelated to the rest of the organization, from which it can be "extracted." In contrast, an acquired firm's value may depend on more generalized capabilities that extend well beyond a particular department to involve the entire organization. In the acquisition of the Beatrice companies by ICI, for example, the value of companies like LNP and Fiberite was based on the fact that they were close to the (leading edge) U.S. market, solution oriented, and entrepreneurial, properties that were spread throughout the organization. Another illustration is seen in the comment of the managing director of BP Nutrition, who, in the purchase of Hendrix, a Dutch animal feed company, realized that Hendrix had a very different dynamic and was most concerned about "keeping their flywheel going," because BP would not be able to start it again.

These considerations allowed us to distinguish among the acquisitions we studied in terms of their need for autonomy.[11] In some situations, company-wide autonomy was needed because the acquirer had virtually no experience in the business and the particular skills sought were inseparable from the culture in which they were rooted. In others, the protection of important, functionally embedded capabilities was needed, whereas other parts of the organization were less sensitive to change.

Finally, in some situations the organizational differences were not at the root of the targeted benefits and hence change would not prejudice the realization of the benefits.

Managers may not always have the information to judge how different the cultures and subcultures of both organizations are before they experience those differences. Yet, we suggest, an early focus on which strategic capabilities need to be preserved, to what extent they depend on maintaining a cultural difference, and to what extent they can be contained in a subpart of the organization focus will be of critical importance in choosing an integration approach. This focus can help managers distinguish between the strategic needs of the situation and the desire of the acquired firm's management to retain its independence. It can also help to clarify the trade-offs at stake in granting or refusing autonomy to an acquired firm and help managers define decision rules for action in each setting.

TYPES OF INTEGRATION APPROACHES

While understanding the distinctive needs for strategic interdependence and organizational autonomy can offer insights, considering them in a combined fashion helps suggest specific approaches to integration. Figure 8-1 positions integration approaches in light of the relationships between these two key factors. Some acquisitions have a high need for strategic interdependence, and a low need for organizational autonomy.

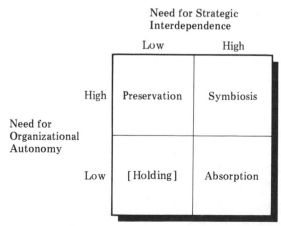

Figure 8-1 **Types of Acquisition Integration Approaches**

These acquisitions call for what we label an *absorption* approach to integration. Other acquisitions, to the contrary, present a low need for strategic interdependence but a high need for organizational autonomy. We will call the integration approach associated with these acquisitions *preservation*. Other acquisitions are characterized by high needs for interdependence and high needs for organizational autonomy. We will use the term *symbiosis* to describe the integration approach called for in such acquisitions.

These three acquisition integration approaches represent, in our experience, useful metaphors to guide the integration task.[12] In practice, of course, the degree of strategic interdependence and of organizational autonomy present in an acquisition integration depends on the choices managers make about how they perceive those respective needs.

The usefulness of choosing an overall metaphor for an acquisition integration does not change the fact that acquisitions bring with them many positions and capabilities, the integration of which, seen in more detailed perspective, might be best served by a different approach. A detailed analysis of the autonomy needs and interdependence needs of the main components of the acquisition helps a company determine how, within the dominant metaphor, they can try to differentiate the approach to each capability.[13] The choice between the compromise of a fairly blanket approach and a tailor-made differentiation depends on the capability of the organization to implement the integration approach it chooses. We will return return in Chapter 9 to the very real problems of perception and ability to implement. First we will describe each of these approaches more fully.

Of course, an acquisition's role in the acquiring firm's corporate strategy has a bearing on the integration approach that may be required. In Chapter 2 we discussed acquisitions that involved domain strengthening, domain extension, and domain exploration. The ideas developed in the chapter represent decisions about the integration approach that will best serve the strategy in the given integration setting. The correspondence between the integration approaches of absorption, preservation, and symbiosis and whether an acquisition is domain strengthening, domain extending, or domain exploring are discussed later in this chapter.

None of the acquisitions in our sample fell into the fourth quadrant in Figure 8-1, which could be labeled as "holding" acquisitions: These would be acquisitions where the firm has no intention of integrating and creating value through anything except financial transfers, risk-sharing, or general management capability, even though the two firms are presumably in such similar businesses that there is no need for organizational autonomy. The only integration in such acquisitions would, in a sense, be a mere holding activity. Given our research focus on strategic acquirers, it is not surprising that we did not encounter such acquisitions. Nevertheless, it is conceivable that such acquisitions exist. The situation of Triangle Industries, which had acquired both National Can and American Can before selling them off to the French company, Pechiney, is an example. Another is the acquisition and simultaneous holding by the financial firm McAndrews and Forbes of Revlon, Max Factor, and Barnes-Hinds, three firms in similar businesses, which were kept completely at arm's-length from each other. Such acquisitions would be made in a value-capturing perspective, as in the example of Triangle, or value creation would be based solely on the introduction of better general management.[14]

Each of the three integration approaches (absorption, preservation, and symbiosis) and the settings to which they correspond is very different. In Chapter 9 we couple them with the key integration process that we raised in Chapter 7 to point out how differences in integration approach lead to differences in the ways these problems are dealt with. Understanding these differences is a precondition to managing them successfully. How each can be successfully managed will be discussed and illustrated in Chapters 11, 12, and 13.

ABSORPTION ACQUISITIONS

Absorption acquisitions are those in which the strategic task requires a high degree of interdependence to create the value expected but has a low need for organizational autonomy to achieve that interdependence. Integration is this case implies a full consolidation, over time, of the operations, organization, and culture of both organizations.

To eliminate all differences between both original companies may take a very long time indeed, especially if one is not just folding a small unit into a large one, but combining two sizable companies in the same businesses. The distinction that matters is one of intent at the outset: in absorption acquisitions the objective is ultimately to dissolve the boundary between both units. In this light, the key integration issue becomes a question of timing rather than how much integration should take place. In absorption acquisitions the acquiring company needs the courage of its convictions to ensure that its vision for the acquisition is carried out. Wavering because of extreme sensitivity to cultural issues is likely to limit the firm's ability to get the value expected, because the management task is to bring about the interdependence of the firms.

A recognition that the decisions can be tough but necessary is illustrated by the challenge facing ICI's Agrochemicals division after the acquisition of Stauffer. The two companies had a large degree of overlap in their sales territory in the United States. Each was set up to sell and market different products to essentially the same farmers. One company had a very direct sales approach, using its own sales force, whereas the other used independent wholesalers to provide sales and service to farmers. Whether and how to integrate the sales function and according to which model were clearly crucial and complex questions, worthy of detailed analysis. Yet a decision about whether to integrate or not had to be made very quickly. In this seasonal business, product turmoil during the crucial ordering period could mean the loss of an entire year.

PRESERVATION ACQUISITIONS

In preservation acquisitions there is a high need for autonomy and a low need for interdependence among the combining firms. In such situations the primary task of management is to keep the source of the acquired benefits intact, because deterioration in the acquired (and sometimes acquiring) company's ways of managing, practices, or even motivation would endanger success. Even though needs for interdependence are low in preservation acquisitions, this sort of autonomy and the protection it implies are often difficult to provide. In these situations the acquired operations are managed at arm's length beyond those specific areas in which interdependence is to be pursued. The latter typically consist of financial/risk sharing and general management capability transfer to the extent that such capability is not industry-dependent.

In preservation acquisitions it is important to understand how sufficient value can be created to offset the acquisition premiums paid. The typical conception is that the main benefit is to be derived from the ability to bring funding to the acquired company. However, in the successful preservation cases we studied, money was not the main factor. In fact, all were successful enough to finance their own development completely. In these cases, as we shall discuss in Chapter 12, value was created through a series of interactions that brought about positive changes in the ambition, risk-taking, and professionalism of the acquired company's management group. The metaphor that best captures the way value is created in preservation acquisitions is that of *nurturing*.

Nurturing the acquired firm represents only part of the value-creation potential that may be realized through a preservation approach. Another important source of value creation, which we will discuss later, is the *learning* that for the acquiring company might derive, both in terms of making further acquisitions in the newly explored area and in terms of learning for its base businesses. This learning is typically central to the purpose in the case of platform acquisitions. Exxon's ill-fated acquisitions in electronics companies; BP's entry into the nutrition business; the acquisition of Burndy, the American connector manufacturer, by Framatome, the French nuclear company; and the acquisitive development of Lafarge-Coppée New Materials' division into decorative paints are all examples of situations requiring preservation.

Symbiotic Acquisitions

The third type of acquisition integration approach presents the most complex managerial challenges. Symbiotic acquisitions involve high needs for both strategic interdependence (because substantial capability transfer must take place) and organizational autonomy (because the acquired capabilities need to be preserved in an organizational context that is different from the acquirer's).

In symbiotic acquisitions the two organizations first coexist and then gradually become increasingly interdependent. This coexistence and mutual dependency are slowly achieved despite the tension arising from the conflicting needs for strategic capability transfer and the maintenance of each organization's autonomy and culture. Symbiotic acquisitions need simultaneous boundary preservation and boundary permeability.[15] These needs can be kept in balance by protecting the boundary between both firms that shields the broad identity and character of the acquired firm at the same time that it is becoming increasingly permeable to a whole series of interactions aimed at functional as well as general management skill transfer.

The needs to preserve autonomy in symbiotic acquisitions can be gradually lifted only to the extent that the acquired company itself changes its own organizational practices to adapt to the new situation. To succeed in truly amalgamating the organizations symbiotically, each firm must take on the original qualities of the other.

IMPACT OF OTHER DIFFERENCES

The dual needs for strategic interdependence and organizational auton-omy captured were by far the most important factors that we observed determining the integration approach. Two other factors, the quality and size of the acquired firm, were also found important. Their impact can be better understood in light of their relationship to the needs for interdependence and autonomy.

QUALITY OF THE ACQUIRED COMPANY

When asked to single out the factor that relates most to acquisition success, operating managers will frequently point out to the condition the target is in prior to acquisition. Earlier research confirms that man-agers' experience with less profitable target firms is not as good as it is with profitable ones.[16] This fact suggests a number of points. First, in terms of the trade-off between price and quality, there are not many real bargains in acquisitions. Second, managers may overestimate their ability to turn an acquired firm around. It is not clear, however, whether these judgments reflect better economic returns on the purchase price for high-quality situations, or that it is easier for managers to integrate a well-run company than a poorly run one.

There are, of course, exceptions to this optimism with respect to turnaround capability. For example, Electrolux, in its core business of household appliances, has turned around a score of competitors in dire straits, including Electro Helios in Sweden, Arthur Martin in France, Zanussi in Italy, and White Consolidated in the United States. But, even for an experienced turnaround specialist like Electrolux, this ability is very domain-specific. Indeed, on a few occasions that the company ventured outside the major home appliance business, it did not fare as well. Two acquisitions outside their core domain, Facit, the office equip-ment maker, and Granges, a Swedish power generation and mining company, sent Electrolux's profits into a three-year slump.

Our research suggests that the quality of the acquired company does make an important difference, especially with respect to the quality of its general management team. There are many definitions for quality of management. We define quality in relative terms as the ability of the acquired company's management to bring about the strategic purpose of the acquisition. The real difficulty with a lack of quality in the acquired firm is that it makes it difficult to preserve the autonomy that the integration may strategically require.

In absorption acquisitions the fact that one of the two companies has weak management needs to be addressed quickly but it does not pose any particular problems as long as the other company has capable management available, or can merge the operations swiftly. But in situations that require autonomy, such as preservation or symbiotic acquisitions, any serious weaknesses in management quality pose a special challenge. The increased involvement by the acquiring firm that poor-quality situations beg for often sets off a cycle of permanent capability destruction as the acquirer engages in an irreversible process of "colonization."[17] Acquisitive firms can avoid this pitfall, as we shall discuss in Chapter 10, by focusing on improving the acquired company's quality on a stand-alone basis early in the integration process, before they turn to the actual integration of the two organizations.

ACQUISITION SIZE

The issue of acquisition size involves both the absolute and relative sizes of the firms involved. There is a fairly fixed cost in making any acquisition, irrespective of its size, especially in organizational terms. Prior research has found that the reported success of smaller acquisitions is indeed less than that of larger ones.[18] Some of the same studies also report that acquiring managers were more satisfied with targets that had a higher market share,[19] which suggests there is not only an organizational, but also a market performance dimension to size. Other observers suggest that, beyond a threshold, it may be the acquired units' relative size vis-à-vis both the acquiring company and the absorbing unit within that company that presents the greatest challenge to integration.[20] There are several reasons for this. One is the greater tendency to fall automatically into the "make them like us" syndrome because the de facto power balance is clearly in favor of the larger firm when it is integrating a much smaller organization.[21]

Our research suggests that, at a more fundamental level, the significant differences among firms have more to do with the stage of the acquired business's development in both a market and an organizational sense than they do with pure size. Acquisitions that represent only a platform that will need substantial further investment to become viable, will impose more requirements on the maturity and quality of the acquirer's decision making than will an investment in a business position that essentially can look after itself.

Differences in the organizational maturity of the two companies also can cause integration problems. At the time of integration, each firm will have reached a different stage of development or complexity.[22] Successfully integrating firms at different stages of maturity is problematic. For example, integrating an owner-managed family business smoothly into a multinational firm with a matrix structure (the task Eurochem faced with Francoplast) is a much more difficult task than bringing the same company into the fold of a more entrepreneurial diversified group with a much simpler organizational approach.

But companies can turn this sort of problem to their advantage. For example, Lafarge New Materials, the new business arm of French cement-maker Lafarge-Coppée, has defined its business concept successfully as "federating" a large number of geographically diverse family businesses in decorative paints. The management group is using Lafarge's relatively entrepreneurial and decentralized culture to offer small decorative paint companies an alternative to selling out to the large chemical companies like Akzo, BASF, Du Pont, Hoechst, ICI, or PPG, which are making scores of acquisitions in their quest for leadership in the business.

In summary, size and maturity differences do matter and useful lessons can be drawn for each setting. But, we suggest, the role these factors play in shaping the nature of the integration process is not as great as the pressures that arise from the need for strategic interdependence and the need for organizational autonomy, which as described earlier, lead to three very distinct integration approaches.

INTEGRATION APPROACHES AND ACQUISITION PURPOSE

We have noted that there is a relationship between the different acquisition purposes outlined at the beginning of this book (domain strengthening, domain extension, and domain exploration) and the integration approach that may be required. That correspondence is not always a direct one, primarily because the integration approaches developed in this chapter, although each corresponds with a certain setting, represent managerial *decisions* on how best to integrate.

Domain-strengthening acquisitions usually imply an absorption approach to integration, because the benefits expected from the acquisition often revolve around achieving greater economies of scale resulting from the combined operations. Examples are legion. They include those already mentioned, such as the Stauffer acquisition by ICI and others like Wells Fargo and Crocker.

Within domain-strengthening acquisitions, however, the benefits of continued differentiation and competition between two entities of the same group sometimes outweigh possible integration benefits. Even when two companies overlap geographically, the preferred integration approach may call for a market share-based logic predicated on separate sales forces rather than a cost-based logic of full integration. For example, the French food group BSN acquired control of both the number one and the number three brewers in France, Kronenbourg and Société Européenne de Brasseries (SEB), respectively. A full absorption approach might have brought very important resource-sharing benefits, given the overlap in sales forces, distribution logistics, and costly brewing capacity. Instead, in a beer market that was then fast growing, BSN chose a strategy intended to maximize market share in the French market and to keep out companies like Heineken or Stella Artois, who were trying to enter the market. By doing so they decided to forgo not only the benefits of scale economies but also the multiple opportunities for functional skill transfer in areas such as marketing or brewing.

The logic used was that the coordination and transfers that a full absorption approach would require could only blunt the autonomous competitive drive of both organizations. For several years the integration process between these acquisitions was primarily a preservation process, with the benefits deriving from combined market power and strategic coordination through the corporate general management role. In the mid-eighties, after the competitive situation reached a new equilibrium, with Heineken entering the market and others staying out and the market maturing, BSN began giving more priority to cost position, and hence, to integrating the two companies.

Similarly, acquisitions motivated by *domain extension* can involve a wide range of integration approaches. Some acquisitions may present a symbiotic challenge, e.g., the acquisition of an advanced composites firm by a chemical company, the acquisition the biotechnology firms by pharmaceutical companies, or the merger of two software firms.

Other domain-extending acquisitions may require an absorption approach. This is often the case when a firm acquires an additional product line to offer through its distribution system. Many acquisitions of brands in the food sector fall in this category, for example, the acquisitions by Seagram of such brands as Martell cognac. Another example is an acquisition to gain a sales organization in a new territory for one's products, for example, the acquisition of Miles Laboratories by Bayer, AG, a firm with excellent products but no strong American distribution presence.

Finally, *domain-exploring* acquisitions are always likely to require the ability to manage a preservation process. Acquisitions outside a firm's core businesses are expected to lead into an area in which performance depends on a completely different way of doing business, one that needs to be protected from the acquiring firm's ways.

SUMMARY

This chapter examined differences in integration context and suggested the usefulness of distinguishing among three approaches to integration that correspond to different requirements for strategic interdependence and for organizational autonomy: absorption, preservation, and symbiosis. This framework keeps the focus on the fundamental tasks necessary to create value: on the one hand preserving and on the other hand transferring and applying the strategic capabilities that have been identified as the purpose of the acquisition. As such, they are partly a matter of choice and partly determined by the situation.

In the next chapter we will explain in more detail just how the integration process challenges discussed in Chapter 7 differ among these three approaches. We will also clarify the complex relation among the choice of an integration approach, its implementation, and performance.

9

Integration Approaches and Integration Process Problems

INTRODUCTION

HAVING DISTINGUISHED AMONG absorbing, symbiotic, and preserving integration approaches in Chapter 8, we can begin to focus on the more managerial implications of our process view. While there are commonalities in each integration—interactions that lead both to the creation of an atmosphere and the transfer of strategic capabilities—the precise nature and issues involved in these elements differ substantially depending on the integration approach taken.

In this chapter we first return to a number of key managerial challenges that were implicit in the process view of capability transfer during acquisition integration discussed in Chapters 6 and 7. Next we will examine how they differ according to our integration approaches. Finally, we examine the relationship among acquisition approaches, their implementation, and their performance.

KEY INTEGRATION CHALLENGES

From the process view developed in Chapters 6 and 7 three interactive issues stand out that capture the most central managerial concerns for integration:

155

- Balancing expectations between determinism and adaptation.
- Providing enough of the right kind of institutional leadership.
- Ensuring the presence, quality, and support of interface management between the two firms.

Balancing Expectations. One of the most difficult tasks for corporate management is managing the varying sets of expectations present after an acquisition. Post-acquisition reality is always different from the original acquisition justification, no matter how well the homework and analyses were done. Often, we argued, companies suffer from excessive determinism, an inability to come to grips with reality. Of course, not all companies exhibit problems of determinism. In fact, we observed the opposite behavior in some situations where managers' excessive caution or open-endedness sapped the firm's ability to focus the integration process. Developing the right balance between determinism and adaptation, which, in turn, is connected to the timing of decision making, is one key challenge in managing the integration process.

Institutional Leadership. A second challenge is ensuring the presence and quality of institutional leadership. The key role of such leadership is to reformulate and credibly communicate the new purpose of the combined firms and its implications to all affected parties. Such leadership is the only broad force available to counteract the effects of uncertainty, insecurity, and value destruction, which affect all managers and employees (especially those in the acquired firm).[1] Yet, as we noted, institutional leadership is often absent when it is needed most. Its content and style depend greatly on the type of acquisition integration approach required and whether one firm, both firms, or neither firm faces a major reformulation of its purpose.

Interface Management. The third managerial challenge derives from the central role played by interactions between the two firms in the value-creation process. We suggested that creating value in an acquisition requires creating the atmosphere within which capability transfer can take place. In addition to creating the atmosphere, the individuals responsible for integration must filter out interferences that are often well-meaning, but usually counterproductive. The quality of interface management therefore becomes a key to unlocking acquisition value. The presence of "gatekeepers" who assume this role, the quality of the job they do, and the support top management provides for their task are vital, and often missing, ingredients. The individuals who manage the interface are squarely in the middle, and they must deal with most of the integration issues we discussed. How they play out their constellation of roles again depends on the integration approach adopted by the firm.

HOW INTEGRATION ISSUES DIFFER BY INTEGRATION APPROACH

Although these issues are central concerns in *all* acquisitions, they take on a very different character and require a different orientation of management in each of our integration approaches (see Figure 9-1).[2] In the sections that follow we will examine how they range across the spectrum of acquisitions. In Chapters 11 to 13 we shall see how these issues relate to each other as we study each acquisition approach in depth.

INTEGRATION AND EXPECTATION MANAGEMENT

Managers may become so strongly wedded to their pre-acquisition views that they insist on implementing them at any price without considering major changes in environmental conditions or the imperfections of prior evaluation. At the same time, there is a great cost if a management group hesitates to move forward with integration because it lacks complete confidence in its original acquisition justification. Beyond the opportunity cost of not making the decision is the continuation of the value destruction caused by further uncertainty. Any attempt to soothe people's fears by promising that no changes will be made only makes the impact of later changes more dramatic.

Our conceptualization of different integration types enables managers

	Absorption	Symbiosis	Preservation
Expectation Management	Predetermined	Adaptation	Learning
Institutional Leadership	Transfer of Affiliation	Redefinition of Purpose	Reconfirmation of Purpose
Interface Management	Transitional Management	Membrane Regulation	Boundary Protection

Figure 9-1 **Acquisition Integration Approaches and Integration Process Issues**

to develop a clearer perspective on the relationship of pre-acquisition goals to post-acquisition management, on the timing and announcement of post-acquisition decisions, and on implementation paradoxes.

Absorptions: The Acceptance Paradox. In absorption acquisitions the risk of excessive determinism, which we described in Chapter 6 as a common problem, is relatively less important. Indeed, the acquiring firm's ability to develop an adequate pre-acquisition view in a business they presumably know, together with limited needs to preserve the acquired organization's original culture, should allow it to adopt a fairly predetermined, programmatic approach to implementation. Experienced absorptive acquirers have a clear plan of action ready, and they pursue it at a fairly fast and consistent pace. A good example, which we will examine in more detail in Chapter 11, is Electrolux. A veteran of more than 300 acquisitions, it has routinely moved quickly at the start of the integration process, having identified key action areas beforehand. Typically, joint task forces are created, objectives specified, milestones identified, and a first phase of integration completed within three to six months of the acquisition so as to create momentum.

A useful rule of thumb in such situations is "move as fast as possible." There are two reasons for this. The benefits of waiting for extra information are limited and the costs of inaction are high, because postponing forseeable rationalizations will prolong uncertainty.

It should be no surprise that performance problems in absorption acquisitions tend to arise when decisions about combining the firms are tentative, hesitant, or not clear-cut. In one of the acquisitions we studied, the paints division of a British firm bought an overseas paints company active in the decorative and automotive refinish businesses. The integration of what was to be an absorption was permeated by a very cautious management style. At the outset, almost three months went by in "intellectual hesitation" before any action was taken on the important rationalization decisions that were waiting within the acquired business. This caution retarded the integration process. The decision to replace the acquired company manager, although decided in principle, also took time to implement.

Overall, the caution in decision making was exacerbated by a cultural gap that engendered miscommunication. For example, what to "trained" British ears was a perfectly clear order was interpreted by the acquired company managers as a mere suggestion.[3] By not acting forcefully and by bending over backward to accommodate the people and culture in the acquired firm, the acquiring firm may have made its task of absorbing the unit more difficult and disruptive than it would have been had they initially acted more decisively. At the same time, it is important to note that precisely the same cultural characteristics were helpful in other types of acquisitions.

It is this indecisiveness which in absorptions all too often leads to the paradoxical outcome that integration proceeds the least in those areas of the business where strategic logic dictates it is most needed. The paints acquisition described above provides a clear example of this paradox. It consisted of two business segments: decorative paints, a highly local business that needed to be run fairly autonomously, and automotive refinish, whose sales and marketing functions were to remain local, while at level of paints technology and color assortment it was to be a much more international business. From the outset the managers in the refinish segment, who could see the handwriting on the wall, were the most protective of their own turf, whereas their counterparts in the decorative business felt they had more to gain and less to lose from interacting with the acquirer. At the time of our investigation, strategic capability transfer had proceeded much further in the local decorative business, whereas in the international business, the zeal of the international product managers at headquarters had to be kept in check by their senior executives, who were concerned about the acquisition's acceptance by managers in the acquired refinish business. Thus, when one is not determined enough, the pace and degree of absorption end up being dictated by the degree of acceptance, which is often inversely related to the actual need for interdependence.

Preservations and the Independence Parodox. In preservation acquisitions, the relation between pre-acquisition views and implementation takes on an evolutionary nature, which can best be described as learning. Preservation acquisitions are essentially experiments and opportunities for learning, particularly when a firm is making an initial platform acquisition into a new domain. Strategic capability transfer to the acquired company is brought about by the development of a general management context that fosters the acquired company's prospects for development and professionalism.

In contrast, benefits accrue to the acquirer primarily from an increased knowledge about the industry in question and from learning the nature of the general management task in that industry. In that sense such acquisitions help the acquiring firm's management team form opinions about whether the company would do well if it expanded its commitment to that business area. From a timing perspective such acquisitions demand an early decision not to make initial changes, followed by a willingness to hold to that principle until the learning benefits lead to a reformulation to the commitment to this domain.

In the firms we studied, the ability to benefit from such learning in preservation acquisitions depended on the acquiring firm's ability and willingness to leave decision-making autonomy with managers in the acquired firm. But autonomy did not mean complete independence. Moreover, the success of an autonomous business did not imply that learning had taken place. For example, when British Petroleum acquired Tensia, a Belgian detergents manufacturer, the rationale for the acquisition was largely BP's experience with a highly successful previous platform acquisition, McBride's, in the U.K. But after its purchase, BP had left McBride's almost completely alone, under the continued management of the McBride family. Soon after the acquisition of Tensia, however, it became apparent to BP management that precisely because McBride's had retained this autonomy, BP had learned very little about the detergents business from this first platform.

In contrast, BP's acquisition of a platform from which to observe the nutrition business, a small Dutch company called Trouw, was much more problematic. Several operational problems had to be overcome, so a BP manager was put in as managing director. Although it was not intended at the time of the acquisition, BP's involvement in a platform acquisition gave it a much broader basis from which to assess and understand subsequent acquisitions in the field of nutrition.

These examples raise an interesting paradox that occurs when firms make platform acquisitions in new areas. The acquired firm's performance may be a function of the autonomy granted. But granting too much autonomy to the acquired platform limits the acquiring company's learning about the nature of the business, industry, or technologies in use. From a broader perspective, first steps that are very successful may cause the management team to misconstrue this success and encourage major resource commitments in an area where the firm has little in-depth knowledge. There may be more of a danger in this than in platform experiences that fall far short of prior performance expectations and thereby lead the company to decide not to invest in a position subsequently. That, after all, is one of the reasons why firms make platform investments.

Symbiosis and the Action Parodox. Symbiotic acquisitions, on the other hand, imply an adaptive attitude on behalf of both organizations. In these situations careful attention must be paid to issues of both interdependence and autonomy. The main strategic capability transfer in such acquisitions revolves around the transfer of functional skills such as R&D, marketing know-how, and product design. It is more difficult to predict what skills will be useful, how they will be transferred, and what benefits will be derived from symbiotic acquisitions than from those involving resource sharing. Hence there is a continuing need for reassessment and adaptation as results of earlier decisions are assessed. In a sense, in this type of acquisition, managers are constantly testing and modifying their hypotheses about how things actually work or should work. Although the original vision of the areas in which strategic capabilities would be transferred may remain, actual acquisition benefits are often quite different from those originally projected. They result from autonomous interactions that spring up in a carefully created symbiotic atmosphere.

As we shall discuss in more depth in Chapter 13, the open-endedness required for success with symbiotic acquisitions is not easily achieved and often runs counter to management's instincts. The patience required conflicts with internal pressures to adhere to the performance objectives sold in the pre-acquisition phase.

Yet another paradox arises when firms make symbiotic acquisitions. The more managers of the acquired firm have clarified the expected benefits and take action to bring them about, the more the walls around the acquired company may harden and chances for benefits to be discovered over time diminish. By contrast, firms that took the time to induce interactions slowly and at the initiative of the managers in the acquired firm ended up with richer patterns of interdependence that evolved more rapidly.

Acquisition Expectations and the Planning Paradox. All acquisitions have components that are partly deterministic, learning-oriented and adaptive. Achieving the proper balance among these attitudes in relation to the type of acquisition was strongly associated with the performance of the acquisitions we studied. Yet when examining how closely post-acquisition management was coupled with pre-acquisition goals, we found that the ability of management to strike the proper balance was strongly related, in a rather unexpected way, to the quality of pre-acquisition analysis. We found that the ability of management to strike the proper balance was strongly related to the quality of pre-acquisition analysis.[4]

In Chapter 3 we typified some acquisitions as planned, strategic, or opportunistic, depending on the relationship between prior strategy and the acquisition opportunity. One would expect that the greater the planning for an acquisition, the more deterministic post-acquisition management would be, because all levels of management would be very clear about what strategy to implement. Conversely, one would expect that opportunistic acquisitions would lead to very adaptable post-acquisition behavior.

In fact, our research found the opposite to be the case. The more opportunistic the acquisition, the more deterministic post-acquisition management tended to be. In the absence of a shared understanding of a clear strategy, top management's insistence on negotiated quantitative performance expectations tended to be higher. Conversely, the more strategic the acquisition, the more adaptive post-merger management was, because the agreement on an overriding priority made it easier to revise initial expectations and to agree on a new course to preserve the strategic objectives while incorporating reality. It is in this seemingly paradoxical relationship that lies one of the strongest carryovers of the pre-acquisition process onto the quality of post-acquisition management.

Top management's ability to share responsibility for an acquisition with operating management and to set appropriately flexible and broad expectations about performance, in which qualitative and long-term contributions were not driven out by short-term financial expectations, related to the second key area in integration management: the need for institutional leadership.

Integration and Institutional Leadership

We discussed earlier how institutional leadership is always a crucial factor, yet one that is often absent, in creating a successful atmosphere for integration. Here, too, our typology of integration approaches helps us to clarify the exact nature of the leadership task to be accomplished.

Absorption acquisitions require top management of the acquiring firm to create conditions under which members of the acquired organization can transfer their affiliation to the parent firm. Sometimes this happens when a "join up or leave" attitude is adopted. But such an affiliation transfer typically requires transforming the original allegiance through another vehicle, rather than abruptly replacing one set of values with another. For example, after Zanussi was acquired by Electrolux, a gradual identification by Zanussi members with the Electrolux group was fostered by developing an integrated, yet differentiated, European strategy. This strategy gave the former Zanussi organization responsibility for developing a more technically innovative product line and left the basic-value product line to be developed by Electrolux.

Evenhandedness in the exercise of leadership is indispensable in symbiotic acquisitions regardless of the relative size of the units. To create the atmosphere for capability transfer in such acquisitions, clear signals must be sent to redefine the purpose of both organizations and to encourage capability transfers in both directions.

In particular, the combination of almost equal-sized companies requires a commitment to a new purpose, a new organization, and a new set of values on both sides, rather than the orchestration of the "surrender" of one organization to the other. In other words, both sides must be asked to transfer their affiliation equally toward an entity that has yet to be defined. Activities by the senior executives following the merger of Sperry and Burroughs, which resulted in UNISYS, and the ASEA Brown Boveri merger were directed toward providing institutional leadership that could reformulate purpose on both sides.

Institutional leadership, at first blush, seems less needed for preservation acquisitions. Yet in practice we observed that one of the most frequent errors in such acquisitions, where there is no intention to change the acquired company's purpose, was the failure to confirm clearly and reconfirm the acquired firm's purpose, and thus alleviate the ever-present apprehension that things will change.

Providing the right kind of institutional leadership for a particular acquisition is difficult. In preservation acquisitions, as just stated, managers in the acquiring firm, and sometimes senior managers in the acquired firm, may forget to reconfirm a purpose that has never been questioned in their own mind. In symbiotic acquisitions, the tendency is often to exert leadership mainly in relation to the acquired company. Yet strong leadership will also be needed to change the acquiring organization. In absorption acquisitions, the lack of skill in creating a vehicle for transfer of allegiance tends to create problems. Thus, each type of integration poses its own leadership challenges.

Types of Integration and Interface Management

The distinction among the three types of integration becomes most vivid when we consider the different demands imposed by the task of managing the boundary between the firms. In absorption acquisitions, interface management essentially involves managing the transition toward the creation of a single company within which operating and functional units of both former companies are fully combined into single units. Although a formal gatekeeping structure is typically not established, a temporary responsibility structure needs to be established to control the pace, nature, and timing of interactions.

As we shall describe in Chapter 11, the repertoire of actions involved in a preservation integration differs dramatically from the interface management challenges inherent in absorptions. Interface management in preservation acquisitions implies the structuring of a gatekeeping function to protect the identity and character of the acquired firm by enforcing continued respect for its boundary.

More complex are the processes required to manage the interface in a symbiotic acquisition, which requires both a preservation of the distinct character for the acquired company and an active exchange and flow between the two organizations. This exchange and flow must be regulated in keeping with the acquisition's purpose. This regulation can be likened to a semipermeable membrane through which the passing of certain resources, capabilities, and ideas is fostered while others are contained.

INTEGRATION APPROACHES AND PERFORMANCE

Earlier in this book we proposed that although the strategic fit of an acquisition is the basis of the potential for value creation, it is managing the acquisition process well that underlies actual value creation. The relationship between integration and acquisition performance is obviously a complex one, with many factors playing a role. Nevertheless, our research, which contrasted successful acquisitions with unsuccessful ones, identified some strong patterns of factors associated with that performance.[5] We suggest that performance is associated with (1) having an initial view of the integration approach that corresponds to the integration setting, (2) being able to adjust one's initial view of the integration approach to be followed (i.e., the absence of determinism), and (3) the organization's ability to deliver on the intended approach.

To see how these elements interact, we needed to understand the contrast between the logic, or lack thereof, that drove the integration approaches in our sample of successful and unsuccessful acquisitions. To do so, we analyzed each integration situation from three different angles:

- What was the *planned* integration approach, that is, what views were shared at the time of the acquisition as to how the acquired firm should be integrated?[6]
- What was the *de facto* integration approach, by which the acquiring firm managed the integration process?[7]
- What was the *integration setting*—the actual demands of the situation as perceived by the research team?[8]

A first observation emerging from this analysis was that in all high-performing acquisitions, there was a high degree of consistency among the assessment of the integration setting by the researchers, the integration approach that was planned ex ante, and the actual integration approach at the time of research.

By contrast, in acquisitions with poor performance, these assessments were inconsistent in one of two ways. Once was a "misperception gap"—an inadequate assessment before the acquisition of the real integration needs. The extent to which this gap led to performance problems was a function of the organization's capacity to change its integration mode over time as better information became available. Contrast the case of Francoplast, which we described earlier, with that of European Hydrocarbon, EHC, another chemical firm entering advanced composites through the acquisition of a small firm.[9]

Like Eurochem, EHC made an acquisition in advanced composites with the expectation that it would provide a strong technological base in a yet to be developed industry, as well as an established R&D unit that could develop and help bring to market some research projects funded in EHC's central R&D. Like Francoplast's managers EHC's managers had to face the fact that the acquisition justification had been flawed in many ways. Acquisition of the company had been justified because of its technical reputation, its end market diversity, its high-value-added production, its prospects to sell to the automotive industry, and its involvement in carbon fibre research. Within a year after the acquisition, several facts were clear. The horizon for composites' use in the automobile industry lay much farther ahead than expected; much of the current business was not in the sought-after high value-added aerospace, but in low-skilled manufacture of products like pipes; the carbon fibre research effort needed to be written off; and the weak financial performance could be ascribed not to heavy investment in the future but rather to serious operational difficulties and managerial weaknesses.

Unlike Eurochem, however, EHC did not suffer from determinism, and was able very quickly to adjust its integration approach to the reality of the situation. Within a year, an experienced operating manager recruited from within the industry had put the company back on the road to profitability, its role had been scaled down from being the vehicle for expansion in this area, to that of providing the learning about industry requirements before investing in the critical U.S. market for advanced composites. On the basis of a more realistic insider's picture of the various segments and the capabilities required and the credibility from a turned-around operation, EHC later backed its advanced composites managers in a major U.S. acquisition.

Other firms were plagued by a more fundamental problem, which we call a "mismanagement gap"—the inability to bring about what they perceived to be the correct integration approach. Developing the ability to determine a viable integration approach during the acquisition decision-making process is indeed not enough. Firms need to be able to manage according to the approach in question. A dramatic example was that of Francoplast, discussed in Chapter 3. It was recognized that to achieve enough organizational autonomy, this acquisition would have to be a freestanding venture outside the matrix organization. But this autonomy was not granted because of the deep-seated reflexes and practices of managers in the parent firm's matrix organization. A less dramatic example was the paradoxical integration of the decorative and automotive refinish paints segments, which we discussed earlier in this chapter. The integration approach that was called for in the acquisition justification ended up being reversed because of management's emphasis on caution and acceptance.

The role of integration in acquisition performance thus is multifaceted, because the perception of the required integration approach, the ability to adjust to changed perceptions, and the ability to deliver on the intended approach are all important. How to manage each approach in practice, and hence what capabilities are needed for doing so, will be discussed in the following chapters.

SUMMARY

Although no two acquisitions are alike in practice, we believe the types of integration approaches we have outlined represent a useful framework for managers considering approaches to integration. They maintain a focus on the essential tasks necessary to create value: preserving, transferring, and applying the strategic capabilities that have been identified as the basis of the acquisition. As such, they are both a matter of choice and determined by the strategic need of the situation.

Our discussion also highlights the different ways acquisition integration can go wrong: by incorrectly perceiving the requirements of the situation, by not adjusting to the firm's needs after integration has started, and by not being able to deliver on the intended approach. Rather than focus on what can go wrong, we will examine in the next four chapters what characterizes successful acquisitions in each integration approach.

IV

Managing Integration for Value Creation

We have argued throughout the book that the integration process is the real source of value creation in acquisitions. A detailed examination in the preceding chapters of the integration process itself, as well as of different integration approaches, has made clear the complexity of the management task involved. With that understanding, we can now turn to the managerial lessons that can be drawn from our research.

The post-acquisition management task is extremely complex for several reasons. First, as we discussed in Chapter 6, integration must be both detail oriented and subtle. Integration involves interactions between the firms that directly affect capability transfer, and interactions that indirectly affect and are directed at, the general integration atmosphere and context.

Second, as we noted in Chapter 7, the managers' integration task is complicated by the underlying tension between forces that require the dissolution, or at least the permeability, of the organization's boundaries and forces that call for protection of the separate identities of those same organizations. An imbalance in either direction may completely impede value creation, either because capabilities are destroyed or because integration does not take place. This complexity is deepened because the balance between these forces has to vary selectively, not only among subunits, but also over time.

Acquisition integration is pregnant not only with intricacy, but also with incomplete information and unexpected problems and opportunities. It must, therefore, be viewed as a highly dynamic process of adjustment. While some firm decisions have to be made, flexibility will always be required. Integration requires decision making by skilled executives in the midst of a constantly changing situation where new information is becoming available. Consequently, it requires that top management empower these executives with the necessary authority to manage those interactions.

We will argue in this part that, no matter what type of acquisition one is dealing with, acquisition integration should be seen as a two-phase process. The first phase sets the stage for the actual integration, largely by addressing the interaction issues that determine the atmosphere and shape the context in the period immediately following an acquisition. Only in a second phase should managers pursue the realization of synergies across both organizations. In practice, the distinction between both phases is not precise and the duration of the first phase may vary greatly. But it is, in all situations, a critical ingredient in value creation.

Although the importance of the stage-setting phase is undeniable, as we will describe in Chapter 10, it is only in the subsequent operational integration of both firms that strategic capabilities are transferred. As we pointed out earlier, the choice of integration approach depends on balancing each acquisition's needs for interdependence and for autonomy. Sometimes an absorption approach is called for; at other times a preservation approach; and in other cases a symbiotic approach. Clear patterns for each of these approaches emerged in our study of the contrast between successful and unsuccessful integration. Firms that were successful at integration were able to handle a number of tasks directly related to the integration approach they took. Chapters 11 through 13 will describe and explain each of these coordinated approaches to integration, illustrating them with detailed examples of situations where they were successfully handled.

10

Integration

The Initial Steps

THE NEED FOR A STAGE-SETTING PHASE

EVERY ACQUISITION, after the agreement, involves a transition period before the actual integration of the two companies begins. We call this period, which may vary from a few days to many months, the stage-setting phase. Although it may involve briefly postponing the pursuit of actual integration synergies, it is not a time in which to procrastinate or lose momentum. On the contrary, it is a time filled with many simultaneous activities, all intended to underpin the integration dynamic and facilitate later capability transfer. It is also a period when many actions are taken within the acquired firm (and it is hoped, a few within the acquiring firm). Figure 10-1 shows where the stage-setting phase fits into the overall acquisition integration process, as discussed in Chapter 6.

The time required for stage setting will depend on a number of factors. One is the type of integration approach followed. For example, in absorption acquisitions the transition will be as short as possible, whereas in symbiotic acquisitions a thorough investment in this phase may be essential to ensure the quality of the later value-creation process. The acquired company's health is another consideration. If the acquired company needs a turnaround, substantial efforts to improve the company by itself may be needed before any operational integration is attempted.

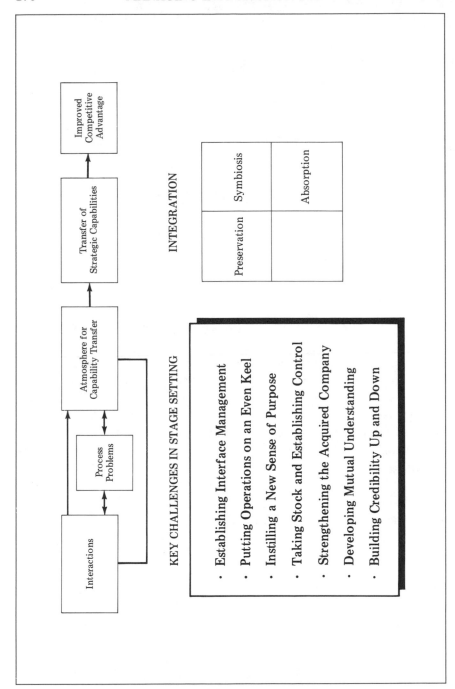

Figure 10-1 Setting the Stage for Acquisition Integration

It is easy to take a detached view and agree intellectually that a transitional, stage-setting period is needed, but in practice it may be hard to stick to this principle. The need for a period of reflection or a detour may seem superfluous to managers who, after making an acquisition, feel pressured to deliver the quantifiable benefits expected from the acquisition.

The importance of resisting these pressures for quick integration and of making sure the stage is set correctly first is illustrated by the debate within ICI after the company succeeded with its $750 million preemptive bid for Beatrice Chemicals in January 1985. The Beatrice acquisition is particularly relevant because it involved different businesses, which ultimately would require different integration approaches. Yet all shared the need for a stage-setting phase.

ICI/BEATRICE:
SETTING THE STAGE FOR VALUE CREATION[1]

In Chapter 5 we introduced the Beatrice Chemicals case in our discussion of the role of ICI's acquisition team. The acquired company was really a miniconglomerate of ten businesses, which, from the perspective of ICI, fell into three groupings—resin products, reinforced plastic compounds, and advanced composite materials.

One of the Beatrice businesses, Polyvinyl, manufactured resins used in the formulation of paints, inks, and coatings. As such, it was a natural extension of ICI's own activities in the Resin Products group of its Mond division. The acquisition investigation had brought to light substantial benefits to be realized through providing Polyvinyl with raw materials integration and Mond's strong R&D capability. At the same time, it was expected that Polyvinyl's application strength in the United States would mean better marketing of the products developed by ICI. Mond's managers were anxious to absorb Polyvinyl into their businesses.

Two other businesses, LNP and Fiberite, were suppliers of reinforced plastic compounds and advanced composite materials, respectively. They were regarded as the jewels in the acquisition because they might provide ICI's recently set-up advanced materials business with capabilities that ICI's own technology-driven efforts lacked. These capabilities included access to U.S. aerospace and defense industry for Fiberite and a more general market-oriented and entrepreneurial problem-solving attitude in both firms. Many of the synergy expectations that had underpinned the $750 million price tag for Beatrice Chemicals were based on expected synergies with these two businesses.

The remaining seven businesses occupied chemical specialty niches that did not relate so directly to any of ICI's activities. Stahl/Paule, for example, was the world leader in leather finish chemicals, a business unconnected to ICI. Although these businesses were not the reason for the acquisition, they appeared to be well-run, well-positioned, mainly U.S. businesses that might be an addition to ICI's own growing specialty chemicals business. It was clear though that the benefits ICI could bring to them would be limited to improving their general way of managing. All these businesses had a similar entrepreneurial and market-driven management style. They were highly successful, though suffering somewhat from underinvestment, having been operated over the years as cash cows by Beatrice.

During the preacquisition phase, everyone in ICI agreed that the Beatrice businesses presented very different needs for alignment with ICI businesses. The debate over what to do with them was strong. At one extreme, some senior managers felt that breaking the company into its ten component parts and slotting them into the various ICI units was the only way to go. As an ICI manager said:

> If you don't, you don't get any synergy. You have to go for integration, not everywhere, not all the time, but you must stop worrying about the problem you create and get on with it.

At the other extreme were members of the acquisition team that had coordinated the investigation work. They insisted that the companies could be effectively protected from ICI interference only if they were kept together for several years. As far as the acquisition team went, the vital need was to preserve not only the identity of the Beatrice companies, but also the administrative philosophy that stood behind them.

In the end an agreement was reached that the Beatrice companies would be kept together for one year during a transition phase. On the day of the acquisition, a clear set of objectives was distributed both within ICI and the acquired companies. Most of these objectives addressed the need to protect the acquired businesses:

- To achieve 1985 profit cash forecasts.
- To motivate and retain key people.
- To preserve inherent growth and profitability characteristics.
- To maintain the lean market-responsive style of companies.
- To ensure that the companies continue as self-sustaining entities while they are provided with essential ICI or external resources on a strict cost-of-use basis.

- To ensure that minimum ICI standards are met for finance and accounting, legal, health and safety environment, and that ICI will not be subject to surprises.
- To establish robust links with relevant parts of ICI to achieve maximum synergy.
- To achieve maximum benefit from interchange of experience and knowledge between companies and ICI.

To manage that transition year, a special gatekeeping structure was set up to isolate these acquired businesses from ICI's regular corporate environment and to set the stage for subsequent integration. As we shall discuss later, the priorities and actions of the managers involved in this gatekeeping effort illustrate the tasks that need to be performed to manage the stage-setting phase successfully.

CHALLENGES IN THE STAGE-SETTING PHASE

The successful acquirers we studied tackled this stage-setting phase by pursuing seven key tasks:

- Establishing interface management.
- Putting operations on an even keel.
- Instilling a new sense of purpose.
- Taking stock and establishing control.
- Strengthening the acquired organization.
- Developing mutual understanding.
- Building credibility up and down.

Though conceptually different, these tasks are by no means sequential. If anything, as we shall discuss, they represent simultaneous activities on many fronts. One theme runs through all of them: communicate and then communicate again.

In this section we will first distinguish the nature of interface management by type of integration. Next we will examine the gatekeeping roles in more detail, and finally we will describe how these roles are distributed among the group of managers that forms the gatekeeping structure.

Establishing Interface Management

The very first step in any acquisition integration is to assure the ability to direct and control the interactions between the organizations—in other words, to establish interface management. To do so, top management of the acquirer must decide how to manage the boundary between the firms and select the individuals for these boundary management roles. Once appointed, the executive or the team that will manage the interface must determine the extent to which filters need to be put in place to shield the acquired firm and decide how these filters will evolve.

As we discussed in Chapter 7, the requirements and nature of interface management depend entirely on the integration approach that is required. In *absorption* acquisitions the transition toward a single organization needs to be managed in such a way that the pace, nature, and timing of the interactions can be controlled. Transition management involves members of both organizations from the beginning and immediately addresses issues involving the combination of the firms. Thus it can be seen as part of the integration process as much as it is part of the stage-setting phase. Transition management requires a *temporary* structure that will elaborate and implement the absorption process up to a point where ongoing operating management can take over and the two organizations operate as one. Coordinated by a single executive who is responsible for working out the integration plan, such a temporary structure may vary in both size and composition, depending on the complexity of the integration and the resources available on both sides. The transition manager may set up a small team, a task force, or a series of task forces with representation from both organizations, which are coordinated by a central steering committee. Key decisions include how to structure the task force organization, how to staff it, and how to support the process.

Preservation acquisitions are driven by the need to continue to protect the distinct identity and character of the acquired firm; the acquired capabilities are typically central to success. A *durable* gatekeeping structure is required to ensure that the acquired firm is managed according to its own needs, rather than on the basis of routines of the acquiring organization, not just in the early stages, but indefinitely.

Interface management in *symbiotic* acquisitions aims to achieve semipermeable membrane-like properties between the organizations to allow for capability preservation and, at the same time, extensive capability transfer. This requires an *evolving* gatekeeping structure that can slowly transform itself from one used in preservation acquisitions in the stage-setting phase to the ongoing management of the joint organization as the two units amalgamate.

In the stage-setting phase then, what are the typical roles and composition of such a gatekeeping structure?

Gatekeeping Roles

Gatekeeping involves three interrelated roles: filtering unwanted interactions, channeling acceptable ones, and fostering desirable ones.

If the separate identity and culture of the acquired organization are to be preserved, then one role of gatekeeping is clearly to filter and restrict the type and number of contacts or compliance demands that are imposed on the acquired company to those that do not unintentionally threaten its identity. The legitimate excuses for managers from all areas in the acquiring company and its functions, territories, or businesses to become involved in an acquisition know no bounds. What seems to the parent company managers to be prudent, minimal involvement often appears as a blizzard of costly, unrealistic demands to the smaller acquired company. As one acquired general manager commented:

> There are really only five of us in our management team. If we were to attend all the meetings where we are requested or invited to attend, there would be no time left for running the business.

While the extent and quality of filtering is important, restricting the channels through which acceptable demands are formulated is even more essential. The impact of any imposition or request by the acquirer derives as much from the process by which the demand reaches the acquired organization as from the actual impact of that demand. That is why it is so essential to channel all demands through a gatekeeping structure and why, as we shall discuss, it is important that there be a clear host structure into which the acquisition reports.

In addition to a clear gatekeeping structure, distinctness from the mother company may be assured through a separate location and management practices. For example, in ICI/Beatrice, the senior executive, Ben Lochtenberg, faced a major decision whether to maintain Beatrice's Wilmington, Massachusetts headquarters, despite strong expectations that he move into ICI America's offices in Wilmington, Delaware to eliminate the costs of duplication. At the same time, he fought hard to keep the Beatrice companies out of the ICI overhead structure and to preserve their freedom from ICI's territorial organization around the globe.

The need to respect agreed-upon channels to filter out any interactions that run counter to what is required for the strategic purpose is only part of the program of gatekeeping. Gatekeeping has another side as well—to foster the interactions and acceptance of the demands that will contribute both to the proper atmosphere and to the capability transfer required. What those actions and interactions in the stage-setting phase are will be discussed in the next sections.

At this stage we will restrict ourselves to emphasizing that allergic reactions always occur, no matter how disciplined the management of the early interface, because any new demand may reawaken the fears of individuals and the perceived threat to the organization with which they identify. Even with the strong gatekeeping role of Lochtenberg and the buffer of Wilmington "North," strains were close to the surface, as the Beatrice companies interpreted any action as a breach of the "no change" policy, which they liked to redefine more broadly than ICI intended. Because each of the Beatrice companies was rather small, they felt burdened even by the filtered claims on their time. Bob Schultz, general manager of LNP, commented on this:

> There is an expectation that we can work miracles, but we have very limited people resources. There are more claims on our time that were just not there before (including interviews with professors). We have to put our foot down as I see it. I cannot tell my people to keep ICI out, but I can tell them that at the end of the day they have a plan to meet and it is up to them to say no.

Beyond pointing out to acquired managers that ultimately it is their responsibility to stand up and resist excessive demands, succeeding in this delicate period will require an inordinate amount of communication in all directions from all people involved in the gatekeeping effort. This must begin with clear backing from the top.

Gatekeeping Structure

How are these challenging roles best fulfilled? A typical gatekeeping structure consists of three sets of individuals, working as a team, that divide these roles, yet cooperate closely: the head of the host structure, the head of the acquired unit, and a small number of support/resource people.

The head of the host structure is the executive to whom the acquired unit reports. This executive's primary function is to keep the acquiring corporation at bay, focus the acquired units on a renewed purpose, build credibility in both directions, and orchestrate the efforts of the other members of the gatekeeping team to create the right atmosphere. As discussed earlier, the parent firm typically has a host of people who appear from all corners of the firm in an ostensible, usually genuine, effort to "help" the acquired firm. The head of the host structure must stem this flow and inspire the actual interface group to accomplish the purpose of the acquisition.

Ben Lochtenberg, the executive officer of ICI's U.S.-based speciality chemicals business and an Australian citizen with many years experience in ICI, embodies some of the personal characteristics that may be helpful in this position. Being neither British nor American, he was more conscious than most managers of the differences between the national and corporate cultures he would have to deal with. As someone whose career had been in specialty chemicals, he could understand the context of both ICI, which was large and complex, and these small Beatrice companies.

The second part of the gatekeeping role structure is the head of the acquired unit. In addition to this person's regular role in running the business, he or she must make a very active effort to shield the people in the acquired firm so they can remain focused on the operating task. Perhaps no factors are as important after the acquisition as the character and caliber of the person running the acquired firm and that person's ability to relate both to the demands and expectations of the acquirer and the needs of the acquired organization. This is truly the manager squeezed in the middle, who needs all the support—and sometimes comfort—that others can provide.

The roles this person will play, the amount of support needed, and the difficulties that will be encountered depend on several factors:

- Is this the previous manager who has been reconfirmed?
- Has he or she been sent in from within the acquirer?
- Is the new manager coming in as an outsider to both organizations?

Choosing the manager for the acquired unit is both crucial and difficult. A situation in which top management can stay is, of course, always preferable. Yet always to keep the manager, as some companies are doing, all too often invites problems. Whether previous owner/managers can remain motivated and adapt to working within a corporate framework is just one of the difficult questions. An equally serious question is whether the existing top manager can bridge both perspectives, particularly when the acquirer has a more complex organizational and strategic context than the manager was familiar with. In the Beatrice acquisition, all general managers were confirmed in their jobs, with no successions planned from inside ICI. Although each worked out satisfactorily, some did better than others, and that factor alone explained much of the difference in how well integration progressed. In all cases, general managers of acquired companies need help and guidance to understand how the parent's system operates, as we will discuss later.

The common solution when a new general manager is required is to bring in an executive from the parent for the general manager position. Yet two caveats are necessary. First, this person must bring general management expertise to the job. As was illustrated in the example of Francoplast, acquisitions are no place for a functional manager to learn how to be a general manager. How the transferred manager will be able to create acceptance will depend not only on that manager's personal skills, but also on the role he or she played in the pre-acquisition period. Second, even an experienced general manager can fail if asked to solve a problem in a business with a patently different strategic logic from those with which he or she is familiar. We witnessed many problems caused by putting internal people in charge of domain extension and exploration efforts, and our research supports the view that general management skills are not as general as many firms would hope.[2]

Especially in domain exploration acquisitions, it may often be preferable to do something companies do not easily consider—bringing in an experienced manager from another firm in the industry. In the short run this person's industry expertise and credibility may make a more effective contribution than management from either the parent or subsidiary can. This advantage must be traded off against the long-run Achilles heel of such external managers—their lack of an effective network in either the parent or the subsidiary company.

No matter where the new head of the acquired unit comes from, he or she will have to be assisted by a few resource people who are brought by the acquiring firm into the acquired company or into the host structure. These people may have a formal job or responsibility in the acquired firm, such as controller or planning manager, or they may just be placed at the disposal of the new subsidiary with less formal responsibility. In all cases, however, their primary role is to help solve the acquired company's perceived problems, to make themselves useful in fostering reciprocal understanding, and to be a focal point for questions and communication.

An example of an effective resource person comes from the Beatrice acquisition. Rex Palmer, a member of the original pre-acquisition team, became the gatekeeper in an operational sense and used his considerable knowledge of ICI to try to help Beatrice managers see how they could use ICI's worldwide resources. An experienced manager who had been the controller for many companies within Beatrice stayed on to work with Lochtenberg and Palmer. In addition, two other managers were brought into the host structure later. One had an excellent overview of ICI R&D, and the other was very familiar with ICI's international network. An experienced human resource consultant completed the group. Nobody was assigned to any company in particular, although each started working closely with a few, depending on the issues.

These gatekeepers have complementary roles and must operate as a team. As we shall discuss later, the selection and empowerment of this team are crucial. Our research suggests that the style, insight, and actions of these few individuals will largely determine the atmosphere of the acquisition and ultimately its outcome.

PUTTING OPERATIONS ON AN EVEN KEEL

The immediate post-acquisition period is one of vulnerability stemming from factors both inside and outside the organization. Managers and employees for whom uncertainty has been created mentally disengage and must be reenlisted. Equally important, competitors who sense a moment of potential weakness will redouble their efforts and focus on the market franchise of the acquired organization. Suppliers begin to question the firm. Customers wonder if their levels of service will change. A new sense of purpose (to which we turn in a moment) contributes to addressing these questions. But, beyond these more lofty aims, it is essential to pay immediate, explicit attention to get the company operating on an even keel as soon as possible by concentrating managers' and employees' attention on the details of the daily business and gearing up to fight the devils "outside" instead of each other.

The first thing required is to focus attention on outside competition by providing immediate performance targets. These need not be based on extensive analysis, but should be simple and, depending on the managers' sense of the situation, challenging or in line with prior results. In one of the situations we studied, where the acquired company had "lost its way" and performance was slowly deteriorating, the acquirer walked in with fairly arbitrary expectations for improvement across the board. Not only were the cost improvements and sales targets met, but the rapid action orientation pulled the organization out of its languor.

In ICI, performance was dealt with by focusing the Beatrice companies on reaching their own original budget objectives, an item that also would maintain the credibility vis-à-vis ICI. Yet, while Lochtenberg clearly announced his expectation that budgets should be met as originally planned, it was also agreed that, after that date, the acquisition premises would be reassessed. This policy allowed him to steer a middle course between achieving credibility and avoiding the trap of falling into a deterministic pattern.

Quick attention to getting the boat sailing again also has to extend to the firm's business partners. When Electrolux took over cash-strapped Zanussi, it used its financial resources to extend credit to the trade and to create the feeling that "Zanussi was back." Similarly, in the UNISYS merger, a critical role for Michael Blumenthal was personally to reassure key Sperry and Burroughs accounts.

The second and concurrent action is to alleviate concerns by carefully communicating and confirming what will not change, especially in regard to the managers and employees of the acquired firm. Especially in areas such as executive compensation, bonuses, pension schemes, and employment decisions, it is important to differentiate the areas in which there will be "no change" from those where adjustments will be made. The cost of making changes despite earlier assurances to the contrary increases over time.

INSTILLING A NEW SENSE OF PURPOSE

We discussed earlier how institutional leadership capable of instilling a new sense of purpose was needed to activate managers and employees in both firms after the merger. Indeed, while quickly providing clear, short-term objectives is a critical ingredient in putting the acquisition on an even keel, it does not suffice if one cannot create a much deeper driving force: a new vision for both companies in the light of the acquisition that translates into a clear mission.

Mission statements must be credible if they are to motivate the organization and to reenlist the participation of managers and employees. They must make sense to the managers of the acquired company, who understand the strengths and weaknesses of their own organization and are beginning to understand the acquirer.

Sometimes acquiring executives may not have many of the answers about precisely where the organization will have to go and what changes this implies. Most problems arise when managers either provide no guidance at all, or to the contrary, make unfounded statements intended to assure people in the acquired firm. In such cases it is better to acknowledge that a process is beginning that will develop a new mission to which both organization's members will be able to contribute. It is important, however, to combine this process in the meantime with a clear effort at understanding and listening and a willingness to make general-purpose resource commitments, which are logical irrespective of the future path. Both these efforts can substitute for the temporary lack of a clearly defined new mission.

TAKING STOCK AND ESTABLISHING CONTROL

We discussed how one of the big dangers in acquisition integration is determinism: holding on to a fiction, rather than acknowledging reality and working with it. One of the first areas of attention for the interface management team is establishment of an information basis to verify, complement, amend, and detail the pre-acquisition view. This effort has to entail a conscious checking of both the internal and external premises upon which the acquisition was based. We are not suggesting the imposition of control system, but cultivation of a systematic attitude of listening and drawing out the facts and opinions of a broad spectrum of employees and also of distributors, customers, and other stakeholders. Managers need to seek out potential problems rather than repress them. Clearly this is not always easy, especially when the managers themselves and their bosses were recently involved in selling the acquisition idea.

Lochtenberg took up his job, traveling extensively, getting to know the people and the businesses. He had two main messages: "We want to learn about the business and have you learn about us, so that we can start to build bridges towards synergy" and "Keep doing what you are doing, meet objectives, and make the budget."

Introducing the parent's basic systems for corporate control is also a must. It is a prerequisite for establishing de facto control and often for meeting legal reporting requirements. Much depends upon how selectively those systems are introduced and used.[3] Decisions about which management systems to introduce and when to do so requires great care, as systems are very task-specific, especially if they are for corporate information purposes and not for operational use by the unit in question. In situations we studied, successful host structures often went out of their way to buffer the subsidiaries and to absorb corporate demands for information at their own level.

STRENGTHENING THE ACQUIRED ORGANIZATION

After the interface management team has developed a detailed sense of the weaknesses and shortcomings of the acquired company, the next priority is to remedy them as quickly as possible. Most acquisitions have several intrinsic weaknesses, some of which are known and some of which are uncovered as time passes. Our research found that such weaknesses need to be remedied in the stage-setting phase, before starting to integrate the two organizations operationally. In real turn-around situations, remedying weaknesses may take an extended period of time. In such situations the stage-setting phase may become as important an ingredient of value creation as the subsequent integration effort. Before dealing with operational problems, the right people must be in place. The first place to start to remedy weaknesses is in staffing or staffing depth.

In the Beatrice case the companies did not need much operational improvement because they were typically well run by their general managers. The main strengthening came from a willingness to commit resources, in sharp contrast to the cash-cow role executives felt their businesses had been playing under Beatrice. This again helped them overcome their apprehensions and they felt that "there is much more interest in the company, and a lot more opportunities."

Another ICI acquisition, that of the French paint manufacturer Valentine, illustrates well the need for strengthening before integrating and also how the acquirer's expertise and legitimacy for change can provide the momentum for an accelerated restructuring and strengthening of the acquired company.

In 1984, the ICI Paints division had acquired Vernis Valentine S.A., a leading French decorative paint manufacturer with a small presence in the automotive refinish business. In contrast to its strong brand image and market presence, the company's manufacturing capacity was in need of drastic restructuring. The company had begun to build a new plant, but it had not faced the tough decision of whether to rationalize its existing site in Paris, which suffered from excess manpower and underinvestment. The previous owner, a French financial holding company, was reluctant to make the investments and, even more, to risk the social conflicts thought to be inevitable when a company is to be restructured in France. Although a fairly detailed restructuring plan had been drawn up before the acquisition, it was left on the shelf.

After the acquisition, ICI decided to press on with the rationalization of the company, largely using the existing plan. ICI proceeded to close most of the production operation in Paris, reduced manpower levels, and divested the automotive segment. The rationalization plan, contrary to initial expectations, did not lead to labor strife, largely because of a continuing process of information, dialogue, and efforts to tackle any problems that emerged over the next few months. The plan was presented through a massive effort of communications both outside and within the established French process of communication to employees, works councils, and labor unions in a way that (1) covered a detailed strategic, organizational, and economic analysis diagnosing the problem and its causes, (2) outlined a plan for recovery including investment commitments and employment and (3) offered a social plan to deal with the employment consequences. The social plan was presented as an effort to do the utmost to help staff weather what was described as a "difficult and damaging, but inevitable period."

Beyond the sheer number of job losses involved, it is how a firm communicates and handles the repercussions of any restructuring that determines the extent of resistance to integration. The combined efforts of a line management that communicated clearly, a truly professional personnel and labor relations staff, support from outplacement firms, and a willingness to be humane and generous succeeded again and again in the firms we studied, despite environments where unions had not yet lost their power.

DEVELOPING MUTUAL UNDERSTANDING

As we discussed in Chapter 6, the development of a reciprocal understanding is a key element in creating the atmosphere in which capability transfer can take place. Yet the natural tendency of executives in the acquiring firm is to focus the early acquisition process on tackling and deciding substantive issues. After all, they have typically paid large premiums for the new firm and need to provide results to justify their decision.

Acquiring managers often underestimate how differences in perception on substantive issues are rooted in poorly understood differences in the wider context of both organizations. They also tend to underestimate, regardless of the agreements reached, how implementation may be confounded by those differences.

An important element of setting the stage for acquisition integration is spending time educating managers about each other's organizational and cultural contexts. There are often pressures to limit efforts at building this understanding. Many managers will consider the time and slack resources required for these activities superfluous in the light of all that is on their agendas after an acquisition takes place. But our research suggests that it it the subtle but important actions taken to improve this reciprocal understanding that tend to influence both the comfort level and the effectiveness of managers with the other organizations.

The classic efforts of most companies to bring the managers of both organizations together, "so that they get to know each other," fall far short of what is required. Two other efforts need to take place under the broad umbrella of communicating a new purpose. The first is a program to raise the consciousness about the importance of these differences in broader context and to build an awareness of what the main differences are. The main effect of this is not just a reduction in ill-timed interactions. It is also to reduce the negative impact of such events. The side that feels "wronged" may no longer interpret what happened as an intentional act and be better able to raise the issue dispassionately. A second effort is to take a very broad and open-ended perspective of where future capability transfer may come from by multiplying the opportunities for people to interact by providing them with challenges and problems.

In Beatrice, with the situation under control and with an atmosphere in which people had reenlisted, Lochtenberg tried to interest Beatrice managers in discovering what ICI could do for them. The members of the gatekeeping team had been carefully selected and introduced as resource people in those areas where it was felt that ICI would be of assistance to the companies: through its R&D, its geographic network, and its general resources. Lochtenberg used the 1986 budget process as a transition toward increased contact with the future host units. He brought in the Mond division's Resins and Intermediates managers to help shape and discuss next year's budget for Polyvinyl and asked LNP and Fiberite to work out their plans with Hal Logan, the manager of ICI's Advanced Composites subsidiaries.

The support received from ICI in different areas and the respect and competence they had sensed in the budget and plan discussions with their ICI counterpart slowly nudged the Beatrice managers along a new path. At the same time, they were reluctant to be pushed faster or further, clinging proudly to their past identity, for which the corporate name and logo was a clear symbol.

> People are scared they will replace the LNP logo with the ICI logo. If they are going to do that, they should cut out the baloney and do it straight. But to our people things would not be the same if the logo went.

Their feeling was strong: "We are a company, not a business."

At the end of the year, Polyvinyl was formally required to report to Mond's Resins and Intermediates group; LNP and Fiberite became part of the Advanced Composites business. Lochtenberg, as new principal executive officer (PEO) of the Specialties businesses, retained the other companies. As we shall discuss later, each new host structure brought its subsidiaries along a different path in the integration phase.

BUILDING CREDIBILITY UP AND DOWN

Another key challenge in the early integration phase is the need for the gatekeeping team to build credibility with both the acquired organization and their own superiors. Establishing credibility is a major challenge in acquisitions. Indeed, within the context of existing parts of the company, a division's or a manager's credibility is typically well established and changes slowly. In contrast, acquisitions and their managers typically begin with a credibility slate that shows no credit on either side. In fact, from the perspective of the managers of the acquired company, the acquirer's emissaries may start with a serious debit position.

Our research identified a number of common factors associated with building credibility. Vis-à-vis corporate managers, gatekeepers build credibility with perceived truthfulness of communication, demonstration of personal competence and fairness, and the ability to deliver resource commitments. In contrast, gatekeepers build credibility in the acquired firm from early results and the perception of a healthy post-acquisition atmosphere.

To gain the cooperation of acquired managers, it is very important, as we stated before, that early statements about the acquisition's purpose and activities have credibility. They must ring true and be borne out by actions. Interface managers must generate a level of respect for their personal expertise and perceived fairness. Managers in the acquired organization must also begin to regard the acquiring organization as one they can depend on. Thus, it is very important to provide what acquired managers perceive as real help and to deliver on early commitments. The personal qualities required of such managers will be examined in more detail in Chapter 13 after we discuss the challenges interface managers face in the later integration phase.

The gatekeeping team needs to preserve its credibility with corporate management as well. The acid tests tend to be actual results and the sense that the integration atmosphere is healthy, with turnover of key people serving as the thermometer. Later we will discuss in more detail how the pressure for rapid performance may subvert the quality of post-acquisition management. But to counter a regression to such simple parameters as operating results and turnover, the gatekeeping team will have to strive constantly to demonstrate a sense of control, a sense of direction, and a sense of progress.

ALL THINGS FIRST

Although one can conceptually distinguish these seven tasks, in practice the job of setting the stage is complex because each dimension is important and is interactive; solutions in one might create problems in another. Clearly, the first task is to set up the interface management structure. After that, all the other tasks befall the team at once. It is very difficult for an acquisition team to recover from an initial failure to filter out unnecessary interactions. Any later efforts at strengthening the gatekeeping will have to swim against the tide of already-established norms of involvement and "help." Although beefing up the quality of the acquired company may take time, the effort benefits greatly from a quick start. Early moves to build and strengthen become crucial in getting people to reenlist. Moving quickly to cut or weed out what is not essential minimizes uncertainty and resistance. From day one people will be looking for clues as to what the new game will be. Unless efforts to develop reciprocal understanding are made early and often, mutual suspicion will fill the void.

The importance of hitting the ground running after an acquisition puts a substantial premium on thorough and detailed preparation during the period between the signing of the agreement and the closing date, when the attention finally shifts to how to integrate.

SETTING THE STAGE IN DIFFERENT ACQUISITIONS

So far we have stressed the commonalities in the stage-setting phase independent of the integration approach. The Beatrice example was used because in one acquisition, ICI ultimately needed three different integration approaches to realize the expected strategic capability transfer. At the same time, however, it is clear that each stage-setting task and its relative importance are quite different, depending on whether the stage is being set for an absorption, a preservation, or a symbiotic acquisition and depending on whether the acquired firm is in good shape or not.

All other things being equal, symbiotic acquisitions present a much greater challenge in this phase than preservation acquisitions, which are in turn more challenging to begin than absorption acquisitions. The role of the early phase is an absorption acquisition is clearly important, but it is less a determinant of the success of the fairly massive integration task that follows. In contrast, for preservation acquisitions the essence of the preservation task needs to be established in this early stage.

The difficulties of stage setting in symbiotic acquisitions stem from the fact that while early preservation is crucial, it must take on another quality to prevent the capability protection from being achieved at the cost of a hardening of the companies' respective boundaries. Even more subtlety and sophistication are required in the methods and the means for doing so than in preservation acquisitions because isolating mechanisms cannot be applied so easily. At the same time, the gatekeepers in symbiotic acquisitions face legitimate pressures for interference, which they have to resist even as they acknowledge them.

The duration and importance of this stage-setting phase also vary with the condition of the acquired company. In turnaround situations, the need to strengthen the acquired firm before undertaking any integration with operating units of the acquiring firm is critical.

SUMMARY

The immediate post-acquisition period is pregnant with expectations, questions, and reservations, among the personnel and the managers of both the acquired and acquiring organizations. The first interactions, communications, and decisions made by the acquirer bring with them a certain legitimacy, that of the "new owner." They occur at a time when personnel and managers in the acquired firm may be unsettled, not yet having decided how they will react.

We described seven challenges that acquiring company managers must meet quickly and simultaneously if they are to benefit from the early "grace" period, during which changes may be seen as more legitimate than later efforts to address problems. If successful, the stage-setting period leads to a realistic and sensible integration road map or plan and an atmosphere in which individuals have begun to reenlist in a new sense of purpose.

Even if stage setting is successful, the interactions that will be called for in the later integration phase will be met by apprehension and will require careful guidance. We turn next to the integration phase as we describe how successful acquirers create value in each type of acquisition. We will start with absorption acquisitions and then move to acquisitions in which the integration process is less dense (preservation), and on to those in which it is more subtle (symbiosis).

11

Creating Value in
Absorption Acquisitions

ABSORPTION IS THE INTEGRATION APPROACH that most naturally comes to mind for managers and most of the public when they think of what happens after an acquisition—two firms truly consolidating. Probably the most prevalent form of integration, absorption is the appropriate choice when the benefits from the acquisition come from high interdependence between the firms and there is less concern about maintaining the autonomy of the acquired (usually) firm. Our research found that successful absorptions are characterized by four basic tasks: drawing up a blueprint for consolidation, managing the combination, moving to best practice, and harnessing the complementarity between the two firms (see Figure 11-1).

A first set of tasks involves *drawing up a blueprint for consolidation.* Of all acquisitions, absorptions come closest to the idea that one should first plan and then implement. We explained in Chapter 10 that we would treat integration planning for absorptions conceptually as a part of the actual integration phase because of the need to involve managers from both sides and because of the early focus on actual capability transfer. Drawing up a first integration blueprint should start long before the acquisition is completed. Ideally, managers from both sides are involved, if not always before the acquisition, then as soon as possible after an agreement is reached.

The second set of tasks involves what is normally seen as the essence of the integration process: *managing the rationalization* of both

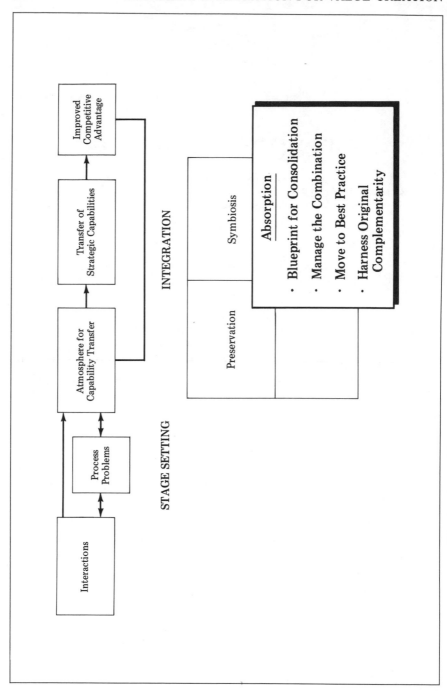

Figure 11-1 Key Integration Tasks in Absorption Acquisitions

organizations. This is the difficult, but necessary, task of realizing the resource-sharing benefits that underpinned the merger justification and that are spelled out in the integration plan.

Successful acquirers, however, do not merely try to eliminate duplication. A third set of tasks involves getting the combined firm to *move to best practice* in all areas of complementarity, whether they be systems, manufacturing practices, or human resource management. Such skill transfer can be pursued simultaneously with the elimination of duplication, but is usually emphasized after the basic resource sharing-benefits are being realized.

A final task in getting the most out of absorption acquisitions is *harnessing the complementarity between the two firms* for long-term competitive advantage. Whereas the previous tasks are based on the view that the organizations should be made more similar, this task involves the ability to capitalize on their differences.

Before examining each of these tasks in detail, we will illustrate the basic approach to dealing with an absorption through an example of a company that has more experience of this process than most—Electrolux. Its acquisition of Zanussi represents a significant acquisition in terms of size; a situation with strong complementarity and significant overlap in activities and markets; and an acquired company with some outstanding qualities, but also many problems. This example, which covers not only the actual integration but also the decision-making and early stage-setting phases, provides another illustration of the acquisition decision-making issues we discussed in Chapters 4 and 5.

ELECTROLUX'S ACQUISITION OF ZANUSSI[1]

Electrolux of Sweden has come a long way since Hans Werthén became its CEO in 1967. A small Scandinavian firm with a narrow product line and partly outdated technology, the company grew to become the world's largest household appliance manufacturer (larger than GE, Matsushita, Whirlpool, or Bosch-Siemens). This growth was spurred primarily by more than 300 acquisitions, including those of Zanussi in Italy and White in the United States. Most of these acquisitions were in the company's core business; often they were competitors in serious trouble.

Electrolux's Acquisition Approach

Electrolux seldom targeted specific acquisitions. At the same time, however, the corporate planning process was very thorough in its emphasis on competitive analysis. This analysis included looking at each competitor as a possible acquisition candidate and examining the specifics of an eventual integration with Electrolux. This approach led to a philosophy of acquisitions expressed in the words of Anders Sharp, who had succeeded Hans Werthén as CEO: "You never choose an acquisition; sooner or later opportunities just come." The financial aspects of each acquisition were considered very important by Electrolux, and the company typically tried to ensure that it would keep the full amount of synergies on its side of the bargaining table.

Once an agreement was reached, Electrolux moved quickly to identify key action areas and create task forces to tackle them on a timely basis. Such joint task forces, the company believed, helped to solidify confidence and commitment and created avenues for reciprocal information flows. Objectives were clearly specified, milestones identified, and integration generally proceeded fast to maintain momentum. Top management of the acquired company was often replaced, but middle management was kept intact.

After they were integrated into an existing Electrolux division, companies became part of Electrolux's highly decentralized organization, in which the small headquarters maintained a very direct control over strategic decisions and return on asset performance. The acquisition of Zanussi provides a good example of how the company went about this integration process and what being absorbed into Electrolux meant.

Zanussi

Zanussi was the second largest private company in Italy, with more than 30,000 employees. Most of its growth had come in the 1950s and 1960s when Lino Zanussi acquired a series of Italian producers of appliances and components. It became one of the vertically integrated and full-line manufacturers in the industry and established a strong export presence in sales and service. At some point, Lino Zanussi considered a takeover bid for Electrolux, then a struggling Swedish company less than half Zanussi's size.

After Lino Zanussi's death in a plane crash, his successors embarked on an unsuccessful and costly program of unrelated diversification, which left the core business languishing for want of capital. Despite efforts to cut back, by 1984 the company was losing money very rapidly, collapsing under its debt burden, and in urgent need of a capital infusion.

The Acquisition Process

Although Electrolux's management was surprised that Zanussi would come up for sale, when Zanussi's banker approached Hans Werthén at the end of 1983, Electrolux, as a result of their ongoing competitive analysis, knew very well where the main complementarities between the companies were. The fit seemed very good because Zanussi was strong where Electrolux was weak: It was Europe's largest producer of "wet" products, such as dishwashers and washing machines; it was the market leader in Italy and Spain, with a strong presence in France and Germany, two markets in which Electrolux had not done well; and it had significant capacity in key components.

Negotiations took more than a year, and agreement was reached in December 1984. By August 1984, however, Electrolux had already drawn up a specific action plan for the turnaround and eventual integration. The plan emphasized a reduction in Zanussi's overhead and marketing costs by integrating sales operations and shifting at least 600,000 units to Italy to enhance capacity utilization. As stated by one manager: "When we make an acquisition . . . we have a definite plan worked out when we go in, and there is virtually no need for extended discussions."

Immediate Post-acquisition Actions

Hours after signing, Electrolux announced a complete change in Zanussi's top management and appointed as chairman and CEO two Italians with experience in working with Swedish companies: Giovanni Rossignolo and Carlo Verri. Together, they had turned around the Italian subsidiary of SKF, another Swedish multinational. Actions were initiated immediately to introduce Electrolux's financial reporting system, which was to become fully operative within six months.

In the usual Electrolux style, a number of task forces were formed to come up with short-term and long-term recommendations in different functional areas. Immediate actions were geared to improve capacity utilization, cheaper purchasing, and revitalizing sales through improved credit terms.

In February, management turned its attention to the medium term, presenting a complete restructuring program, as promised to the unions, who accepted a work force reduction of 4,848 employees over the next three years. (This is a good example of attention to symbols in communication; 4848 is Italy's emergency telephone number.)

Restoring Competitiveness

Electrolux realized that sustainable profits could not be realized through work force reductions or improved capacity utilization alone. After careful analysis, three areas were chosen for the strategic transformation of Zanussi: improving production technology, spurring innovative product development, and enhancing product quality. While Electrolux was impressed by the quality of Zanussi's technical people, it was surprised by the complete absence of robotics or computers in product development units and plants. A major investment program was begun to restructure Zanussi's two major plants. Heavy emphasis was put on achieving flexibility and quality improvements rather than on saving labor costs.

In a separate effort the new Zanussi management team moved to revive Zanussi's innovative spirit. The organization responded quickly, and a torrent of product ideas and improvements poured forth. The first major product was the "jet system," a new washing machine design that cut detergent and water consumption by a third.

Quality enhancement was the third leg of the revitalization of Zanussi. The technical staff organization at Electrolux provided the guidance and assistance needed to set up the parameters for a comprehensive quality improvement effort. A Total Quality Control (TQC) project started in May 1986 extended from suppliers to the field service organization.

Changing Attitudes

Throughout these turnaround efforts, one of the biggest challenges lay in the area of revitalizing the Zanussi organization. During the troubled years, conflicts had become a way of life at Zanussi. Information flow had been constrained because it was considered a major source of power. Most issues were passed up to the top, and operating managers felt bypassed by the bosses, who were making deals with the unions. The acquisition had, in addition, created a strong barrier of defensiveness in employees who ascribed the companies' problems to the practices of previous owners, rather than to any strategic or organizational shortcomings. Rossignolo and Verri were initially seen by Zanussi managers as "closer to Stockholm than to Pordenone."

In an attempt to overcome these barriers, Verri and the entire management group participated in a number of team-building sessions facilitated by an external consultant. A direct outcome of these sessions was a statement of mission, values, and guiding principles that was to serve as a charter for change. The statement identified the four main values of the company: (1) to be close to the clients and satisfy them through innovation and service; (2) to accept challenges and develop a leader mentality; (3) to pursue total quality, not only in production but in all areas of activity; and (4) to become an international competitor by developing an international outlook.

The statement also confirmed the new management's commitment to creating a context that would ensure consistent, goal-directed behavior under all circumstances. As described by a manager:

> We adopted the Swedish work ethic—everybody keeps his word
> and all information is correct. We committed ourselves to be
> honest with the local authorities, the unions and our customers.
> It took some time for the message to get across, but everybody
> has got it now.

To develop a flow of information with the senior management group and to co-opt everybody into the new management approach, a set of management development workshops was organized, first for the top 60, and then for the next tier of 150 middle managers. Structurally, Zanussi's operating companies were given full operating responsibility as the central staffs of former sector managers were cut back.

Integrating the Companies

Electrolux had drawn up a broad integration plan before agreement was reached. Throughout the early period after the acquisition, eight task forces involving managers from both companies worked to find specific opportunities for integrating the activities of the two organizations. Their recommendations formed the basis of the actions that were taken to (1) integrate the production and sales operations of the two companies, (2) rationalize component production, and (3) develop specialization in product and brand development within the total Electrolux group. These task forces represented more than an integration plan for Zanussi. At the level of individuals, these meetings also built a bridge between the top management team of Electrolux and senior managers of Zanussi. And in many areas they also led to a new way of thinking for Electrolux as a whole.

Sales and Production

Until the merger with Zanussi, Electrolux had integrated production and sales country by country. After the Zanussi acquisition, it decided to reorganize the company into international product divisions and national marketing companies. Each product division carried full responsibility for the development and production of its specific product range, such as dishwashers, refrigerators, or ranges. The product divisions themselves were set up as a network of plants with each plant specializing in a single product. For example, within the washing machine division, the Italian Porcia plant specialized in front-loaders, whereas the French Revin plant made top-loaders. Other plants in each division were to be specialized in niche products. One plant in each division was also given primary responsibility for technology development. Porcia, for example, was chosen to develop washing technology.

Within its local market, each marketing company was responsible for marketing and selling products from all divisions. It was planned that in each market where the companies overlapped, the stronger subsidiary would absorb the weaker one. The sales forces themselves were kept separate, but such aspects as stocking, transportation, order taking, invoicing, and service were integrated. By 1988, Zanussi was operating four sales subsidiaries directly, instead of the nine subsidiaries it had had before the acquisition.

A number of systems were changed to facilitate the integration process, including launching the Electrolux forecasting and supply systems in 1987 to act as the interface between commercial and production units. Evaluation systems were changed to assess both factories and sales companies on RONA (return on net assets).

Electrolux Components Group

Following Electrolux's acquisition of White Consolidated in the United States in March 1986, the company turned to worldwide coordination issues. It set up a task force to examine opportunities for global synergies between the three companies. Though the task force concluded that opportunities were relatively limited, there was at the component level much greater scope for standardization and rationalization, given the similarities in needs. As a result of this analysis, the Electrolux Component group was formed in early 1987 with responsibility for all strategic component production worldwide. It was decided that half of the sales should go outside the group, and at least 20 percent of internal needs should continue to be sourced elsewhere. Because more than 50 percent of the group's component production came from Zanussi, Verri was appointed head of this group, in addition to remaining as Zanussi's managing director.

New Product and Brand Development

In Europe a new organization was created to coordinate product development, marketing strategies, and brand positioning of all household appliance brands. The group was lead by a Zanussi executive reporting directly to Leif Johansson, head of Electrolux's household appliance division.

The group established four broad design families: Alpha, Beta, Gamma, and Delta. Alpha was to be the "prestige" range and its development was to be the responsibility of Electrolux. Beta, assigned a "warm and friendly" appeal, was to be developed and marketed under the Husqvarna umbrella. Gamma, which was to be "young and aggressive," was the responsibility of Electro Helios. Finally, Delta, with an image as "innovative," was under the overall charge of Zanussi.

By 1988, Electrolux could clearly be satisfied with its acquisition. After going from a massive loss of $120 million to a profit of $60 million, Zanussi was well integrated into Electrolux's ongoing operations, upon which it had had a major impact. Electrolux had become much more balanced in product range and market presence, and it had built a vertical strength in components.

Vis-à-vis the senior management of Zanussi, Electrolux had made efforts to portray the acquisition not as a takeover, but rather as a partnership. As a senior Zanussi manager commented: "We have had a lot of exchanges, and learned a lot from them, but we have not had a single Swedish manager imposed on us."

At the next level down in management, the links were still weak and apprehensions remained. A senior manager at Zanussi said:

> We don't know them, but our concern is that the next level of Electrolux managers considers us as a conquest. In the next phase of integration we must develop bridges at the middle, and I frankly do not know how easy or difficult that might be.

Most companies would have shied away from an acquisition like Zanussi, deeming the financial risks too substantial, the labor climate too difficult, and the lack of organizational fit too great a gamble to realize the strategic benefits that were clearly present. Financial risks and organizational challenges always accompany the strategic fit of an acquisition, though not always to such a great extent. The challenge is to develop the organizational capability to manage those risks and to handle the absorption process. Few acquirers have built up more experience at absorbing companies than Electrolux, which has developed a proven corporate routine for doing so. In the Zanussi acquisition it excelled at each of the four tasks we outlined as key in absorptions: preparing the blueprint for consolidation, managing the nationalization process, moving to best practice, and harnessing the complementarity.

PREPARING THE BLUEPRINT FOR CONSOLIDATION

The first task in an absorption is to work out the integration plan. However, if the acquiring firm knows the business, even a one-sided integration plan can be developed in quite some detail, to be ready when the acquiring firm takes charge. Leif Johansson of Electrolux remarks on this:

> When we acquire, we go in with a clear plan. We try to be well prepared before the acquisition. We have a list of actions ready for twice as much impact as we need. And we have a strong sense of what we want to achieve in three months, in six months and in nine months. The fact that you have a plan does not mean that you cannot change it. But to go into an acquisition without a plan usually becomes a disaster.

There are five aspects to an integration plan:

- Choosing a single leader to manage the integration process.
- Choosing the management team that will lead.
- Setting up a transition structure including specific task forces in the key integration areas.
- Managing to an integration calendar.
- Communicating throughout the process.

One leader. The first step is to choose top management. To manage the integration process, a single manager has to be clearly in the lead. Electrolux's choice of a team of two that had worked together does not invalidate the main point: neither a collegial "business board" approach nor the multiple advocacy present in a matrix organization is an effective structure for integrating an absorption acquisition.

Tough Choices. A second task is to choose senior managers from both sides and involve each of them in clarifying the choices of individuals for the next level. Absorption acquisitions, by definition, always involve difficult people choices. For many jobs there will be two viable individuals, while functions may be candidates for downsizing because of changing practices. Our research found that these appointment decisions, more than anything else, shape the direction of the future organization, as well as managers' and employees' perceptions of what the new organization is about.

Although a cascade system may be used whereby every rank that is appointed gets involved in decisions one level down, this is an area where top management attention is crucial. Percy Barnevik, CEO of ABB (ASEA Brown Boveri) commented on this process:

> Everybody must be perfectly conscious of his role and responsibility. In our case we had to appoint 500 managers. We did it in three months, during the summer of 1987. I and my colleagues at ASEA knew the Swedish managers but not those of Brown Boveri and vice-versa. I spent sixty days in hotels in Baden, in Mannheim, and elsewhere interviewing hundreds of people. Then came the time to decide and nominate those who would be responsible. Leaving a position unfilled for too long only creates turbulence.[2]

Keeping to a selection system based on competence often requires that managers disappoint members of their own organization. When there was no clear basis for choosing one executive over another, experienced acquirers we studied tended to choose the acquired company's executive over their own. This policy not only sent positive signals to the acquired company but also saved human resources for use elsewhere in the parent firm. In a relative sense, the acquiring firm's own managers can be more easily placed in another position within the parent firm; an acquired manager who is equally capable but without the reputation or the network to find a position easily in the parent would probably be lost as a resource.

Task Forces for Critical Functions. Setting up a transition structure is the third step. It should be reemphasized that the current organizations remain responsible for managing the current business and for ensuring budget performance. Beyond that, the task is to create a temporary structure, defining its tasks, and supporting its functioning.

Sometimes it is already clear who the new management team will be when the transition structure is set up, and sometimes it is not. Typically the decisions are linked because for many of the slotted individuals the transition work is a testing ground and a chance to earn credibility with the managers from the other side.

Typically, the temporary structure consists of a number of task forces that report to a steering committee (which may itself have set up some management committees). The steering committee, composed of senior managers, not only oversees the long-term integration planning effort carried out by the task forces, but also makes the short-term coordination decisions that will affect future business and should not be left to the current operating organizations. For example, in R&D both organizations may be facing short-term decisions on the grouping of some long-term projects.

The role of the task forces is to identify and evaluate potential synergies and to recommend ways to achieve them. In some situations we studied, these task forces developed a much more productive process than others. The key differences were in the ways that these task forces were established and managed. Sophisticated acquirers used task forces selectively, rather than automatically setting one up for every function. They also invested attention and resources to monitor the task force process.

A fruitful way to approach the structuring of integration task forces is to ask two key questions about every function or area of operations. The first is "How critical is the integration of this function to the success of the acquisition?" The second is "How compatible or difficult to combine are the two firms' operations in that function?" Indeed, not all functions are equally crucial to integrate in an acquisition. For example, in the merger of two banks, the integration of the management information systems (MIS) may be critical to the success of the acquisition. In the merger of two manufacturing firms, it may be much less important. At the same time, two firms may have an identical approach to the management of some functions but very different approaches to other aspects. Figure 11-2 points out the four broad situations that are possible, given these two considerations.[3]

There are typically one or two critical functions in which the firms have used very different approaches. These should be the true target of the task force process. Any urge to postpone solution of the difficulties they present must be resisted. For example, when ICI's Agrochemicals division bought Stauffer in 1988, it had to integrate the firm's herbicide businesses. Two of the most urgent decisions were whether to merge the two sales forces and what approach to take. The sales organizations overlapped almost completely; both companies sold products to the same farmers, albeit for different crops. Yet the sales approaches and philosophies were very different. One company used direct selling, and the other used dealers.

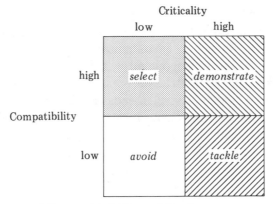

Figure 11-2 Use of Task
Forces in Integration

Whenever critical functions are handled very differently in the firms, the risk is great that the issue will be resolved on purely political and power grounds or be left to the operating managers of each unit, who will continue to use their different approaches. Only an in-depth, factual analysis can provide the basis for development and acceptance of a sensible choice.

A second focus of task forces should be on critical functions that are compatible. This focus can early demonstrate the merger benefits and can greatly contribute to a positive merger dynamic. Whether secondary but compatible areas should be tackled depends on the resources available. Managers must be selective and make trade-offs between the benefits of involving more people in the process and protecting the ability of top management to monitor progress and deliver key benefits.

It is important to avoid creating task forces in functions whose combination is relatively unimportant to the success of the merger (which is not the same as saying that the function is unimportant). For example, in one of the mergers we studied, the two firms' approaches to management information systems were radically different. The hardware was incompatible, and one firm used centralized data processing and the other used distributed data processing. At the same time, the MIS function was not essential to the functioning of both entities, two basic manufacturing operations. The management group set up a task force to plan MIS integration. The turmoil and organizational confusion generated by this task force seriously impeded the integration process.

Acquisition task forces have a great deal of impact on future policy and on the role and jobs of the people involved, as well as others in both firms. As a consequence, these task forces become the focal point of enormous political tensions. To minimize this politicization, the task force process needs to be supported with facts and analysis and to be overseen by a manager who has a sound view of how value will be created but has no hidden political agenda or organizational axe to grind. It is ironic that when facing such critical decisions about combining the capabilities after the acquisition, firms tend to pinch pennies. The same companies who spent millions on investment banker, legal, and consulting fees before the acquisition often are loath to spend the resources needed to examine such crucial trade-offs on the basis of factual evidence and analysis.

Apart from providing legwork and a neutral analytical focus to the process, external support can help to sustain it. Very often managers of both organizations join actively in the early analysis phase but are reluctant to press for conclusions. They fear that these decisions may force the "other side" to give up something, which would lead to stirring up controversial areas they want to leave untouched. To break this de facto coalition of managers on both sides who try to protect old habits and practices, somebody has to keep pushing the issues.

Managing to an Integration Calendar. Announce and adhere to a workable integration calendar that provides credible milestones and helps maintain the pressure for progress.

This comment from Leif Johansson illustrates both the need to involve managers deeply and to keep up the pressure on the process:

> We usually say that we have a window of around a year to make the major changes that are needed. We set up task forces involving management at different levels, and give them two weeks to work and then report to us and to the acquired company (at that stage we are still two parties). Then, we keep doing this at a very quick pace: study, report back, get new direction, go back, study, etc. That gives us a continuing process.

Communication. The preparation of an integration plan involves an inordinate amount of communication. Its logic and timing must be sold to employees and outside stakeholders of both organizations. This typically occurs in an environment of suspicion, confusion, and rampant rumors, most of which have little basis in fact. Thus an essential task of the general manager is to communicate honestly, clearly, and frequently. Praising and promoting progress achieved, while reminding participants of what still needed to be accomplished and its urgency, were important practices we observed.

MANAGING THE RATIONALIZATION PROCESS

Rationalizing the operations of the two firms is traditionally regarded as the crux of the integration process. Depending on the blueprint that emerges from the planning phase, a number of functions must be merged over a certain time span.

In the planning stage the clear costs and benefits of rationalizing a function have to be carefully weighed. The expected benefits can often be quantified because they involve assumptions about identifiable cost savings or sales growth. Much of the cost, however, may comprise the less tangible costs of compromise whenever the rationalization of assets or integration of functions diminishes entrepreneurial drive, managerial attention, or employee enthusiasm.

Sometimes the logic of resource sharing may run counter to the logic of skill transfer. In the acquisition of Dymo Industries by Esselte, a key issue was integration of the sales force of Esselte's Business Systems division with that of the Dymo division. Many of the benefits of eliminating the overlap in sales forces could have been lost because of the very different marketing and sales approaches used for the low-margined Esselte office products and the high-margined Dymo embosser. Sales of the Esselte products involved order taking and bargaining, whereas selling the Dymo tool involved mainly marketing and merchandising.[4] Companies that approach integration planning superficially may not realize the dangers they may encounter. What is needed is not just the combination of the two firms' resources, in the Esselte example, the merging of the two sales forces. In addition, for example, a whole program of devising incentive schemes, control systems, and sales force education is needed to guarantee the proper attention to each product range.

Once a decision to integrate functions has been made, the experience of successful acquirers suggests, a fairly determined and fast-paced execution is preferable. In the Esselte-Dymo integration, sales forces were merged within three months. Fred Chiswell, the manager in charge of that integration, said, "My only regret is that I did not do it faster."

Acquiring managers with less experience sometimes let the perceived difficulty or resistance expected determine the speed of integration. This reflects the acceptance paradox which we discussed in Chapter 9 and which was illustrated with the example of a paints acquisition. In this acquisition we saw fast integration in the decorative segment, where acquired managers saw no threat but slow integration in the automotive after-market segment because threatened managers were putting up barriers that were not overridden by an acquirer who was trying to avoid resistance from people in the acquired firm. Two years after the acquisition, considerable progress had been made through exchanges of people in the local business, but none of the resource-sharing benefits in the global segment had been realized.

Johansson captures well what is key about actual integration and how to get acceptance.

> The key is first to concentrate on real issues. We generally don't hold big discussions about principles or what organizational structure will be needed in the future. Rather we concentrate on what creates the real improvement in results, and those are generally tough decisions, like whether to make investments, or to get one service organization out of two, etc.
>
> The way we get acceptance is to talk about it, argue, explain in a clear voice, never be political and be extremely clear. Secondly, to see to it that the acquired company managers actually grow, that they get more, that they are also winners in this change.

MOVING TO BEST PRACTICE

The immediate focus of most absorption acquisitions is an effort to reduce costs by sharing resources in certain functions. The cost benefits that result from this elimination of duplication can be substantial. Absorptions, however, also offer a good deal of potential for functional skill transfer.

Sometimes the pre-acquisition justification is based on the expectation of such skill transfer. But even when it is not, a systematic search for islands of "best practice" and their subsequent adoption by the combined operations can pay off handsomely. Part of the payoff will be in dollars, yen, pounds, or deutsche mark. The rest of this payoff comes from the new ideas that are generated when each side has the opportunity to show its best to the other.

For many international acquisitions among firms in the same industry, in such diverse areas as retailing, cement, and insurance, this move to best practice may be the main source of value creation. Increasingly, long-term competitiveness on a global scale is driven as much by the ability to transfer learning as by economies of scale or scope.[5] In cement industry acquisitions, for example, the scope for resource sharing is rather limited, because each plant serves its own local market. Yet the scope for transferring best practice is vast. Kiln productivity is largely dependent on the unit's ability to apply experience and make small improvements. A systematic program to determine best practice on the basis of technical parameters and then to share and transfer that practice is a major source of value creation.

Such long-term efforts to transfer skills and move to best practice imply, as we shall discuss in Chapter 15, a network approach to the organization. Johansson of Electrolux calls this the "microstructure" in contract to the earlier rationalization process which involves "the macrostructure":

> The second wave is then to create an international network to go after other benefits such as savings on development of the incorporation of more innovative features, what we call the microstructure. That we do by organizing international network structures coached by a very small central group.

Harnessing the Complementarity

The earlier phases in absorption acquisitions correspond to efforts to manage the key strategic capability transfers in terms of resource sharing and skill transfer but pay little attention to organizational or cultural differences. They imply that the organizations should be treated as if they were uniform or made as similar as possible. Creating the maximum leverage from an absorption acquisition, however, requires not only the ability to bring about uniformity but also the simultaneous ability to turn complementarity into a permanent advantage.

The line between uniformity and complementarity can be easily blurred and result in the destruction of capabilities. Some firms, however, are able to seek out complementarity on a few key dimensions while they ensure uniformity on all the others. Very often an absorption that homogenizes two corporate cultures may be very productive in one area, for example, manufacturing, but destroy value in other areas. For example, if the combined firm adopts a uniform marketing and sales approach, it may appeal to a smaller total customer base than the firms did individually before the acquisition. Companies need to be able to drive very hard on some dimensions yet accept and use the fact that there will be continuing differences.

Electrolux is a good illustration of the ability to harness complementarity. After acquiring a number of competitors, each with full product lines, the firm faced a difficult problem. The Component manufacturing and sales forces could be largely integrated. But moving away from developing and manufacturing a fairly full line of appliances in each company would fundamentally change the character of each organization. Yet the group was well aware that carrying many different product lines would entail internal duplication and competition.

The group decided to establish four broad product-design families. This allocation of responsibilities and brand positioning recognized the differentiation of the group's products in what marketing managers would call the brand space—thereby increasing the combined market share potential. More important, it also corresponded to a conscious exploitation of existing differences. Market research clearly showed, for example, that the average Zanussi customer was younger and was an earlier adopter than the Electrolux customer. At the same time, the approach helped to revive and stimulate Zanussi's innovative culture and drive, which had languished somewhat during the difficulties that preceded the takeover. That the company did this consciously is reflected in the following comment from Johansson:

> What we tried to do was to build on the know-how and the strengths that existed in the Zanussi group, as it related to brands, as it related to innovative capacity, etc. I think what we have done is to build on the old strengths of Zanussi and get more emphasis on that, rather than change too much. The skills necessary were there, but what was lacking was both financial resources and a strategy as it relates to the European market.

Developing the management skills to harness complementarity is a critical ingredient in a long-term approach in absorption acquisitions. It provides the opportunity to make the necessary transition from managing acquired companies to managing an integrated network of complementary operations, to which we will return in Chapter 15.

ABSORPTIONS AND THEN ABSORPTIONS

In our discussion we have stressed the commonality among absorption approaches. Although all absorption acquisitions represent the dissolution of the acquired firm's original identity, not all absorptions are the same. Absorptions are characterized more precisely by the extent of resource redundancies, the relative size of both firms, and the quality of the acquired firm.

Some absorptions take place between organizations with a high degree of geographic and product overlap, while others involve firms with more complementary market positions. Clearly, the more overlap between the companies involved in an absorption, the more extensive the rationalization process will be. Nevertheless, combining organizations that are geographically very complementary may represent a true absorption when the two entities evolve into a single organization. One such example is the 1989 merger between the packaging arm of the British firm, Metal Box, and the French Carnaud group, who together became the largest packaging group in Europe and the third largest in the world. While the geographic base of both companies scarcely overlapped, the resulting CMB Packaging is operating under completely unified management.

The relative size of the organizations also affects the nature of an absorption. In a typical acquisition, the smaller acquired company is absorbed into the much larger acquirer and the absorption process represents a fairly one-way transfer of affiliation. In a competitive context that forces increasingly bold strategic moves upon competitors, mergers between equal-sized partners, let alone reverse takeovers, are increasingly common. In such cases, relative power considerations and the need to preserve capabilities, especially in voluntary mergers, tend to make the integration decisions more complex.

The third factor that affects the nature of the absorption process is the quality of the acquired company. As we discussed in Chapter 9, if the acquired company has fundamental managerial or operational weaknesses, a much longer period will be required in the stage-setting phase to shore up and consolidate the quality of the firm's management. For example, in the early stages of the Zanussi acquisition, the whole focus was on putting Zanussi back on its feet again, strengthening management, providing business, investing in manufacturing and changing attitudes. Such a turnaround process often accounts for a major part of the value created through the acquisition.

SUMMARY

The ability to manage an absorption process effectively becomes increasingly important as industry restructuring pressures drive acquisitions that call for such integration. Of course, skill and determination at managing the actual rationalization process are important. But equally important are what come before, and after, the rationalization process. We discussed the importance of a dispassionate and well-supported integration task force process, as well as the need to go beyond rationalization to focus on moving to best practice and learning from evolution. The most important mark of a truly successful absorption may well be that there are no winners and no losers, and that, to the contrary, the outstanding qualities of both sides are harnessed in an effort to reach a common objective.

12

Creating Value in Preservation Acquisitions

PRESERVATION LIES at the other end of the integration spectrum from absorption. A preservation approach is appropriate when capabilities are acquired that require protection from the embrace of one's own organization, and there is a low need for interdependence between the two firms. At first blush the integration task in preservation acquisitions might seem easy—establish the proper gatekeeping structure during the stage-setting phase (as we discussed in Chapter 10)—as little or no integration is called for. In practice however preservation acquisitions remain difficult to manage throughout. Not only is providing adequate protection a continuing effort, but the value-creation process itself is one of subtle nurturing and careful learning.

Our research has identified four tasks in preservation acquisitions that need to be managed well by the gatekeeping team and by the host structure (see Figure 12-1).

The first is *continued boundary protection*. In preservation acquisitions, the gatekeeping challenge is a continuing one.[1] The need to preserve a distinct culture in which the acquired capabilities are embedded will in essence remain unchanged. An important aspect of continued boundary protection is making managers and employees in both firms more tolerant of continuing differences within the firm.

The second task is to *nurture the acquired company* because the value that is directly created in this type of acquisition stems from accelerated business development. This nurturing is a subtle process in which the

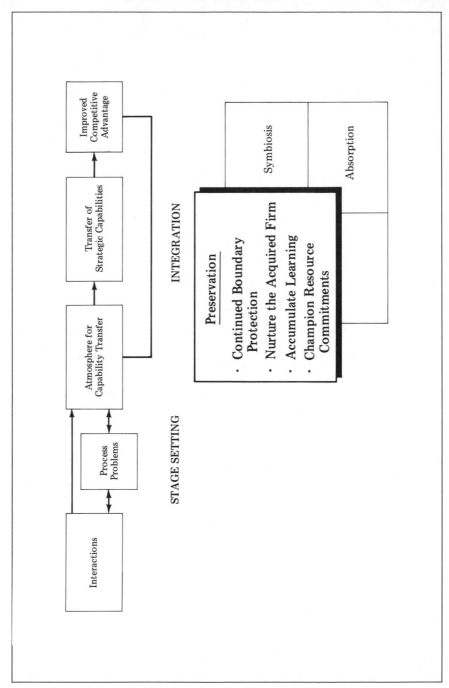

Figure 12-1 Key Integration Tasks in Preservation Acquisitions

acquirer must use resources and, above all, general management skills to help the acquired company develop better and faster than it otherwise would have.

The next two tasks flow from the need to fulfill the corporate strategy objective that usually underlies the preservation acquisition: the exploration of a new domain.[2] One task is to *accumulate learning* of two types. First, the management group learns about the industry as a prospective new business domain. In the long term the value of a first acquisition in a new area derives as much from helping the acquirer decide whether and how to make further commitments as it does from the development of the acquired company itself. A second type of learning comes from the exposure of the acquiring firm to a different business that may be relevant to the company's existing core business.

Domain exploration often begins with small, platform-type acquisitions, rather than the immediate acquisition of a full-blown position. In such cases, preservation brings a fourth challenge for the managers of the host structure. They need to *champion increased resource commitments* to that new domain, to cluster the resulting acquisitions, and combine them with internal development projects into a broad-based business position that has the critical mass required for the industry in question.

These tasks, as well as the challenges to execute them in the context of a domain exploration effort, are well illustrated by the way British Petroleum handled its acquisition of Hendrix, a £267 million Dutch feed company, as it built up the BP Nutrition division. The case also illustrates the important contribution of the pre-acquisition process to establishing the mutual trust that effective preservation will require.

BP NUTRITION: MANAGING A PRESERVATION ACQUISITION[3]

Because the oil business has always been cyclical and oil prices have tended to swing wildly, oil company executives have intermittently considered diversification, only to refocus on their core business, because its prospects have improved, and because so many of these diversification efforts prove unsuccessful.[4] In the early sixties, when oil was cheap, BP researchers discovered a way to make protein from oil. Technical difficulties and the 1972 oil crisis led them to abandon the idea, but not before a couple of very small acquisitions were made in conjunction with the effort, including that of a Dutch feed company called Trouw. In the late seventies, when the oil business once again looked cash-rich but mature, the area of nutrition again aroused interest at senior levels in the company. Nutrition was not only societally attractive, but it seemed to offer the stability and magnitude that would make it worthwhile, given the dollar magnitude of the oil business. Moreover, it seemed to be dealing with what, in contrast to oil, was a renewable resource.

Although Trouw became moderately successful after Tom Walker, a BP manager, was installed, by 1978 it had become clear to BP that the fledgling nutrition business was too insignificant in group terms. At the same time that the overall organization was being restructured into business streams, BP senior management felt there was a need to reexamine the commitment to the nutrition area and requested Eddy Brouwer, the respected country manager of BP Holland, to become head of the newly formed BP Nutrition. Brouwer thus became the only expatriate in BP to head a business stream, albeit the smallest one.

Originally quite skeptical about the chances of successful diversification within BP, Brouwer initially retained his position as country manager and launched a number of studies into the opportunities in nutrition. Slowly he became convinced of the potential in this area, and after the 1978 five-year plan review, he was given the green light to look for an acquisition. After extensive screening, Hendrix, a Dutch family business with sales of £267 million and pretax profits of £14 million, became the leading target. It was a proud, successful company, with an internally grown, loyal management team rooted in the agricultural environment of the company's feed business.

Brouwer was not without concerns about the acquisition. He was not certain that Hendrix would want to sell to BP, let alone that the oil giant would be able to cope with such a different business. He knew that Hendrix was seriously considering at least two other companies. During March 1979, Brouwer had preliminary talks with Bert Hendrix and Henk Lodders, his number two man. It was clear to Brouwer that for Hendrix the issues at stake were their identity and their independence. He would never be able to buy the company unless he could convince Bert Hendrix and Henk Lodders that BP would respect both. He also knew that if Hendrix was acquired, he would have to transform its rudimentary planning and control system into formal and lengthy five-year plans with frequent reviews and strategy meetings. As he considered how BP operated, he wondered how he would be able to "keep Hendrix's flywheel going," and at the same time to satisfy BP's "insatiable hunger for detailed forward planning and control."

During the preliminary talks, Hendrix had informed Brouwer that he had retained two respected advisers to assist him, one of whom was the head of McKinsey & Co.'s Amsterdam office, who was McKinsey's leading acquisition specialist. Having come up with the counterproposal to use these "wise men" as neutral advisers to both parties, Brouwer started negotiations.

The Policy Statement

The negotiations lasted four months, most of which were spent on hammering out a policy statement outlining how Hendrix would be run after the acquisition. Price was not even mentioned until the end, and only a couple of meetings were required before agreement on price was reached. The policy statement, which captured the preservation spirit of the agreement between the parties, began with a statement of intent by both sides and then covered the following areas:

1. BP's reasons for wanting to acquire Hendrix.
2. Hendrix's reasons for wanting to sell.
3. Control procedures within the BP group.
4. Specific policies governing the relationship of the two companies in the future.
5. The duration of the policy statement (five years).
6. The disposal of shares.

Reflecting later on the significance of the policy statement, Brouwer said:

> The Policy Statement went into the drawer and never came out again. It's importance was that through protracted negotiations over every clause, each side came to understand the primary concerns of the other and most importantly that trust and commitment were built up. Hendrix accepted the need for BP to satisfy its control requirements. By focusing on the future management of Hendrix, both sides became committed to a common vision: that of seeing Hendrix at the center of BP Nutrition's expansion on the Continent.

The size of BP Nutrition was tripled overnight by the acquisition, making it one of the twenty largest feed companies in Europe. There was still a long way to go, however, to meet BP's target for sales of £1.5 billion by 1990 and achieve significance in group terms.

Because fast growth could come only from further acquisitions, Brouwer knew he would have to establish a way to run the diverse companies making up BP Nutrition so they performed better than they could on their own. At the same time, he knew there would be continued questions about the value of this business in the BP portfolio. His perspective was that he just had to prove he could outperform other companies in that industry but also to make sure that nutrition would not get so interwoven with the rest of BP that it could not be disposed of.

Organizing BP Nutrition

Brouwer's first task was to determine the structure and role of the BP Nutrition host structure. In essence, he wanted to keep the staff lean and operate along the lines of a nutrition company, not an oil company. Besides supervising and assisting the development of the acquired businesses and keeping the mother company's numerous central staff at bay, BP Nutrition would have to develop a broader nutrition strategy.

Brouwer's other task was to integrate Hendrix into this structure. He made as few changes as possible. There were no changes in letterheads, company literature, or building inscriptions. In keeping with the logic of the policy statement, Henk Lodders (who succeeded Bert Hendrix) was made to report directly to Brouwer, and Trouw (the original platform) became a new division of Hendrix. The only hesitance came from Hendrix managers, who were reluctant to incorporate a company that they thought suffered from weak management and poor results.

Only one manager joined Hendrix from BP. When Hendrix needed a planning manager, it invited Chris Pritchard, an experienced BP Nutrition staff member, to take up this role in a three-year assignment. Speaking of his role at Hendrix over the next few months, Pritchard said: "We made quite a few changes, but we very much hope that they do not feel those changes have come from us."

Inevitably, there was something of a culture clash between the oil company and the small family company. The BP head office staffs and the national affiliates expected to fulfill their traditional roles, whereas Hendrix managers expected Brouwer to be the sole contact point. Brouwer found himself constantly having to act as gatekeeper vis-à-vis BP operations, who found his strict instructions against unauthorized involvement hard to take.

On the whole, however, the company was relatively unencumbered by BP, and it started developing faster than anticipated, generated returns above its industry, and, as we shall discuss later, embarked on its own acquisitive development.

CONTINUED BOUNDARY PROTECTION

In preservations, gatekeeping is not confined to the stage-setting phase. Permanent vigilance about protecting the boundary of the acquired firm is required if the parent company is not to break its pact of noninterference. Ian Steel, then CEO of BP Ventures, calls this "the need to keep fighting the corporate immune system." Gatekeepers in Brouwer's position may have to use their influence again and again to keep the acquired subsidiary free of the influence of the territorial organization or to fight off forced incorporation in general overhead structures. At the same time, corporate staff needs may have to be met or dealt with. As a member of the host structure team in another successful preservation acquisition told us, holding up the corporate planning and control forms: "I make sure these don't go down [to the newly acquired firm], by filling them in myself." After a while, corporate management or other affiliates may not be the only source of interference: even the host business staff itself may be tempted to become involved in an operational role rather than the strategic one.

NURTURING TO ACCELERATE BUSINESS DEVELOPMENT

The second task in preservation acquisitions is to create value by nurturing the acquisition to accelerate its development. Common wisdom suggests that this nurturing can be accomplished both by leaving the acquisition alone and by being generous with funding. Neither was true in the Hendrix acquisition or other successful preservation acquisitions we examined, which generated the resources to finance their own growth and development. Although these acquisitions were operationally autonomous, the strategic choices that led to their development were arrived at in a highly interactive fashion between the parent and the subsidiary being nurtured. There are two key elements in this nurturing process. One is the induction of a changed, more ambitious vision. The other is practical support for the implementation of that vision.

Instilling Ambition. The key to nurturing is not to throw resources at a company, but to lift its managers' horizons, to change their perceptions of risk, and to make them more ambitious. In Hendrix's case, this ambition amounted to implementing the intention of the policy statement: to transform Hendrix from a Benelux company into the biggest continental European feed company. Companies that have operated for years on a particular scale and have been constrained by their own resources wear self-imposed strategic blinders, the effect of which may be reinforced by negative experiences of earlier growth. Ambitious as Hendrix managers were in their familiar markets, they had considerable self-doubt about expanding in other markets, describing their first such experience with a move into Germany a few years earlier as "quite traumatic."

Being part of a large concern may change the perceptions of risk. If the changed perception can lead to a more ambitious expansion (rather than to resource requests for all pet projects hereto deemed postponable), then the nurturing process has begun in earnest. In other words, what is important is not the use of the parent firm's financial resources, but the fact that they are there. Removing these self-imposed blinders may require continued questioning from the parent firm. As Lodders, the general manager of Hendrix, stated: "Without the constant encouragement and prodding from BP Nutrition, we would have lacked the confidence to go into other markets."

Practical Support. Inducing a more ambitious vision must be accompanied by the practical support that ensures that the vision is strategically sound and that the capabilities for implementation are acquired. Central to this support is the informal transfer of managerial expertise, especially in the areas of strategy development and human resource management. It is not the imposition of formal systems that creates the value in nurturing, but person-to-person dialogue and patient education. No formal BP planning or human resource management systems were imposed on Hendrix, because the BP Nutrition staff took care of any demands coming from the group. The BPN staff engaged in a continual, informal process of clarifying strategic objectives and encouraging accelerated investment in the depth and professionalism of management. The most extensive role in this was played by Chris Pritchard, who not only helped them make their own thinking more strategic, but also served as a key resource to help them understand what a large organization like BP was all about, for example, with respect to preparing and selling investment projects.

Between 1980 and 1985, Hendrix completed its own acquisitions, one in France (a highly successful company called UFAC/NORIA) and one in Spain (the biggest Spanish feed company, Nanta). Like the original

Hendrix acquisition, these were preceded by protracted negotiations with owners who were not necessarily interested in selling and by initial contacts mostly "to see if we spoke the same language." The division's attitude toward their acquired companies was similar to BPN's original attitude to Hendrix. Brouwer commented:

> Hendrix's external board members, still in place, always urge us to break the shell of acquired companies and integrate them into the existing business structure. But we saw that breaking that shell is too risky in terms of dampening the motivation of their managers and undermining the reasons for their success.

Throughout this period, the BP Nutrition staff still provided support with the financial evaluation and with selling the acquisitions to corporate management. The former manager of Trouw, a BP appointee then in the corporate planning department, was a valuable link in this.

Staying Vigilant. As long as acquired companies do not become too successful or do not dramatically alter their scope, the vigorous early gatekeeping can be effective. Every significant new expansion, however, is likely to energize the claims of the acquiring company's units. Hendrix's success in geographic expansion set off another round of boundary conflicts to be managed. Encounters with the BP associates in the countries it was entering revolved around concerns such as the demand for change of ownership to the local affiliate. The desire to benefit from tax pooling in the country was certainly legitimate. But it was difficult to divorce ownership for tax purposes from other types of involvement that emerged from many quarters. As Brouwer commented:

> Once you own the shares, even if it is for tax reasons only, all sorts of excuses can be found: to visit, to query figures, to ask for more information, and so on.

Although a pragmatic attitude has to prevail in the preservation of the new business, each agreement should be the occasion to reiterate the basic principle: This is a different business that should be managed according to its own needs.

ACCUMULATING BUSINESS LEARNING

The third task in preservation acquisitions is to accumulate learning both about the business and from the business. Preservation acquisitions are often part of a domain exploration effort and hence are typically made to seek out new business areas. The industry and business knowledge that can be derived from a platform acquisition managed in a preservation mode can be a key part of the learning leading to a firm's decision whether to move further in an area.

Learning about the Business. Gatekeepers perform the key role in accumulating, translating, and disseminating this learning. Resource people in the acquisition or the host structure offer the best opportunity to learn from within. As they convey knowledge about the mother company and about business method to the acquired company, they, in turn, learn to view the business from an insider's perspective.

On the basis of such first-hand experience, the host structure can develop a much better perspective on the industry, as well as a more specific development strategy, and sell it to corporate management. Of course, learning must actually take place, and the managers must not be myopic. We will return to what it takes to foster and transfer learning in Chapter 14. Clearly, unless there is a restrained but rich involvement by a limited number of people, no real learning will take place. Moreover, unless the position of the acquired company in the overall industry context is clearly perceived, the wrong lessons may be learned.

Learning from the Business. Domain exploration also helps managers learn from the business. This learning accrues to the long-term benefit of the company's current business domain, as in the example of CIBA-Geigy's early entry into the household products business through the acquisition of a number of small companies, which were later merged into the stand-alone Airwick organization. The development of a viable household products business itself may not have been the major benefit of this domain exploration. The long-term benefits included helping the overall organization become more comfortable with marketing- and advertising-based competition, and preparing it for the changes involved in the over-the-counter trend in pharmaceuticals. The success of this effort would not be measured by the success of the household products business itself (which was, in fact, divested and sold to Reckitt and Colman in 1985). The key question is the degree to which the business, during its days as part of the CIBA-GEIGY organization, contributed to a cultural and organizational change process, starting with the exposure it provided top management to this very different business.

Learning from an acquired business is more complex than learning about a business. The knowledge to be achieved is not between the business and its immediate and reasonably like-minded host organization. Rather it is between the new business and a suspicious, if not downright hostile, base business. The main dilemma is to balance the isolation required for protection of the new business culture with the proximity and acceptance by the base business required for transfer of learning.[5]

We observed how in practice the resolution of this dilemma hinges mainly on two factors. First is the ability of top management to balance over time the demands by the host structure champion for "special status" with the demands by the base business for "equal treatment" of the new business. This balance is a function of the acquired company's ability to provide financial support for such "equal treatment." Second is the ability of the host structure champion to create the confidence and excitement around that new business to attract young, fast-track managers to it, as well as the willingness over time to lose them again to the base business.

ORGANIZATIONAL CHAMPIONING

Closely related to the gatekeeping role of accumulating and disseminating learning is a fourth role—organizational championing. Because most initial domain exploration acquisitions tend to be of the platform type, their viability within a large company is rarely stable. Internally they are too small to represent a durable commitment by the parent. Externally they are not big enough to provide for their own long-term stability. Most of the momentum for greater commitment has to come from the host structure, which plays a role akin to that of organizational champions in internal ventures.[6] Host structure managers gain support for increased commitment to the acquisition by slowly building confidence that their area presents a sensible diversification effort.

In our research into domain exploration efforts, we found that a number of factors influenced the ability of the championing host structure to persuade the corporate parent to make the sizable resource commitments needed to transform the new business into a full member of the portfolio.[7] In addition to the projection of strong leadership and the presence of a solid corporate sponsor, the ingredients typically included:

- The ability to demonstrate early control over operating performance.
- The ability to frame the development strategy of the platform in planning language that corporate managers can relate to.

- The ability to retain good relationships with corporate staff units such as strategic planning and R&D, important friends to have at court.

In the BP Nutrition example, business development took place in three ways. First, there was continued internal development within Hendrix. Second, Hendrix itself began to grow via acquisitions, acquiring French and Spanish feed companies. Third, BP Nutrition made major acquisitions that deepened its presence in animal feed (they acquired Purina Mills, the largest U.S. animal feed supplier) and broadened the nutrition product base (they entered into such segments as processed foods and plant breeding). By 1989, BP Nutrition had exceeded its pre-Hendrix target and had a turnover in excess of £1.8 billion and a trading profit of more than £41 million. Moreover, it survived the refocusing of the BP group portfolio in the late 1980s and emerged as one of the four core businesses with a growth mission in the 1990 corporate reorganization.

Acquisitions Drive Out Internal Development. In other cases that we observed, however, this championing process, which was intended to accelerate new business development, detoured into a vicious cycle in which internal development efforts were driven out. Indeed, to gain the credibility to commit the company to larger acquisitions, most managers felt obliged to emphasize short-term operating results in the smaller acquisitions they had just made, often at the expense of the investments in people and strategic expenses that were needed for internal growth. Thus, the successful business development pattern tended to become one of growing by larger and larger acquisitions, each immediately managed for operating results. The need to commit the company to a larger acquisition before the operating results of a platform reflected its weak structural position became a real pressure on many of the host structure managers who were shepherding acquisitive business development.

Planning Drives Out Adjustment. Apart from the phenomenon of "acquisitions driving out internal development," another danger lurks in this championing process. Domain exploration efforts by large companies are not always made in already well-established areas where these companies are late entrants. Instead, they enter areas of business that are still embryonic or rapidly evolving, such as biotechnology, advanced materials, or other new fields. In such areas, the pressure on the organizational champions to cast the strategy making in corporate planning language, including a review process based on monitoring deviations from plan, may not be compatible with the rapid adjustments and learning required in the context of these new industries.[8] This gap between corporate requirements and business needs is often aggravated by the insistence of corporate on seeing such businesses in a high-technology light. To make substantive progress, a more down-to-earth, market-driven approach may be appropriate. Host structure managers often struggle to minimize the gap between the corporate fiction that they are dealing with R&D-based, high-technology businesses, which allows them to draw upon corporate resources, and the business reality, which is often that of fragmented marketing- and service-based competition.

CONCLUSION

We examined the key requirements for managing the integration process in preservation acquisitions. In these acquisitions, value is created in two ways. One is through nurturing the acquisition for accelerated business development. Equally important, however, is the learning derived from such acquisitions. This encompasses learning about the business—critical to the success of subsequent major commitments in this new domain—and learning from exposure to a different business.

Even if the exploitation, strengthening, and broadening of a company's current domain have primacy over the exploration of new domains, the diversity of exposure resulting from preservation acquisitions may be an important ingredient in a healthy renewal process in large organizations. In that sense, both the earlier broad-based diversification trend and the more recent refocusing trend seem to be unnecessary swings of a pendulum. Ultimately the continued existence within a large organization of a number of domain exploration efforts relates to the diversity of values embodied in this core management team.[9] Moreover, the repertoire involved in successful preservation, described in this chapter, also becomes an important ingredient for successful domain extension because it is key in the early stages of many other acquisitions, such as the symbiotic ones to which we turn next.

Creating Value in Symbiotic Acquisitions

SYMBIOTIC ACQUISITIONS PRESENT the most substantial challenges to managers, who find themselves torn between the twin needs of preserving the acquired company's culture and encouraging interdependence to fulfill the acquisition's purpose. As a member of the ICI-Beatrice gatekeeping team commented: "We knew from day one that they had to retain their entrepreneurial, market-oriented culture and be run at arm's length. Yet at the same time, we had to find ways to get the synergy."

In our research, the companies that succeeded in this unnatural act were those whose interface managers were able to shepherd a carefully evolving pattern of interactions (see Figure 13-1).

The pattern *began with preservation* of the acquired company (as we discussed above), while the acquiring company made changes in its own organization so it could be better juxtaposed to the acquisition. Next, the acquiring company gradually encouraged interactions between the two organizations, preferably at the initiative of the acquired company's managers, a process we will call *reaching out rather than reaching in.*

After that, strategic control over the acquired firm was gradually affirmed, while operating responsibilities of the managers of the acquired firm were increased, a process we call *swapping operating responsibility for strategic control.* This process set the stage for a gradual *amalgamation* of the organizations, which is the essence of symbiotic acquisitions.

A good illustration of effective management of a symbiotic acquisition

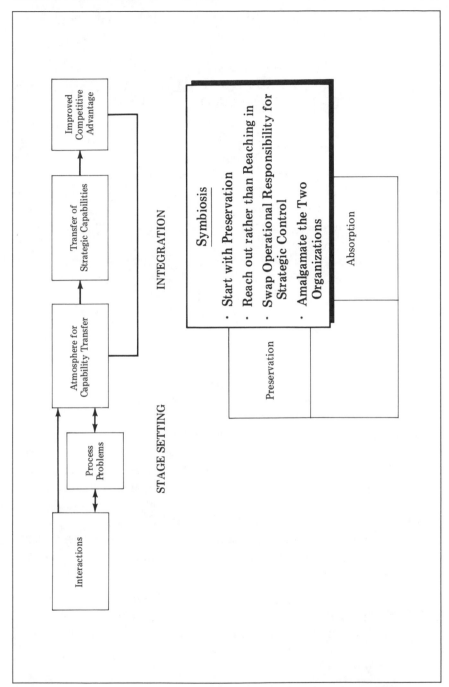

Figure 13-1 **Key Integration Tasks by Integration Approach**

is ICI's movement of two Beatrice businesses (LNP and Fiberite) into its Advanced Composites business:

AMALGAMATING BEATRICE CHEMICAL COMPANIES AND ICI ADVANCED MATERIALS[1]

Starting with Preservation

For subsidiaries like LNP and Fiberite, the first year of the Beatrice acquisition (described in Chapter 10) represented a situation of de facto preservation. They were kept completely at arm's length from ICI and run by Ben Lochtenberg through the buffer of their own former small headquarters organization, Wilmington North.

Original objectives had been reemphasized. Any operational contact with ICI was clearly initiated by LNP or Fiberite people, even though ICI managers like Rex Palmer and his colleagues, with whom they discussed strategic and operating issues, continued to suggest people in ICI who might be useful to talk to.

Juxtaposing the Organizations

At the end of the first year, formal reporting responsibilities changed. The former Beatrice Polyvinyl operations began to report to ICI Resins and Coatings; LNP and Fiberite reported to ICI Advanced Materials; and the remaining six into ICI Speciality Chemicals. The composite materials businesses (LNP and Fiberite) were headed by Dick Bucher and juxtaposed to ICI's own operations in the advanced materials field under Hal Logan, with whom they shared a common boss in the person of Hugh Miller, PEO Advanced Materials and Electronics.

With the original gatekeeping gone, initiative for cooperation increasingly came from the ICI side. Commented a wary Robert Schulz, the general manager of LNP:

> ICI should recognize that the accidental bullet kills just as surely as the intended one—they say they want to leave us alone, but at the same time they want to collaborate on this and then on that. They do try not to smother us however, and we try to live this day by day.

At the same time, Schulz clearly was optimistic about the outcome of such collaborations:

ICI has the answers, but not the questions; LNP has the questions. Merging has given us access to world-class technology. In the UK we now interface not only within Advanced Materials but also with the New Sciences group. We have spent the whole year working out what we can use from them. One result is a fiber that combines the properties of stiffness and toughness, which used to be mutually exclusive. We are comparing formulae with the advanced materials group (Logan's operation) and have found that some of their grades are better and some of ours are better.

LNP people felt a strong commitment from ICI in several ways. "There is a lot more interest in the company and a lot more opportunities," commented one manager. Operationally they were being asked to take over the marketing of Victrex, an ICI product that had not been doing well in the United States. Also, all capital investment projects were approved very promptly. Commented Bucher: "ICI resources have allowed us to continue growing; we would have plateaued otherwise."

No pressures were exerted to have LNP buy from ICI, even when the mother company had the equivalent new materials. At the same time, LNP of its own volition began to experiment with using the ICI sales forces in some countries where their distributors were not working out well.

Throughout, ICI's expectations of performance results seemed balanced, with some managers complaining: "ICI has the right strategic vision, only it expects it a bit too fast for reality," whereas others noted: "For the next year, budget expectations have been slowed, something which was unheard of under Beatrice. It is understood that emphasis will be on the progress towards long-term objectives."

As time went by, Logan had more frequent direct discussions with Schulz and Bucher spent more of his time on Fiberite. While LNP slowly developed a practice of working with its ICI counterpart, its sense of identity remained unchanged: "LNP is a very special company and will continue to be so under ICI, if it is handled right."

Another manager commented: "We would like to continue the growth of the past year with the same choice over use of the ICI infrastructure and very little if any integration or loss of identity. Were we to become part of Advanced Materials, it would severely affect people in the organization."

The Amalgamation Stage

In February 1987, LNP was formally shifted from Composite Materials (Bucher) to Engineering Plastics (Logan), and all engineering plastics activities were consolidated under one individual. While this could be construed as putting LNP under the control of ICI, LNP people like Schulz spoke of it differently:

> ICI was not doing well in plastics in the U.S. before the acquisition. The business was badly managed and the technical calibre not very high. As a result, LNP has been given stewardship for what ICI already had in the U.S. We are trying to upgrade their quality with the least upheaval possible.
>
> My task has been to make LNP, Victrex, and other ICI products combine into a cohesive engineering plastics organization and to give ICI enhanced visibility without losing the previously separate images. The view in the U.S. is that ICI looks to LNP to help the other pieces over here. We have the influence, not them.

In September 1987, a geographic organization was set up with three general managers (Europe, Far East, and the United States). Appointed U.S. general manager, Bob Schulz assumed responsibility for selling all product lines in the United States. Hal Logan stated:

> We are trying to bring LNP into ICI Advanced Materials. The U.S. organization for Engineering Plastics *is* LNP. So we are trying to change the name affiliation to ICI Engineering Plastics, but retain the market responsiveness.

Bob Schulz commented on this change:

> With the shift in businesses (and some others which were lifted from other parts of ICI), there was a doubling in the size of this part of Advanced Materials, which everybody realized led to a need for restructuring.
>
> So we met in Long Island in June to decide how we would structure and how we would call ourselves. By involving me, they cleverly involved LNP. Engineering Plastics was born at this meeting—with three regional general managers, with all products under their aegis for their territory, and four business managers with responsibility for the worldwide strategy drive. After much debate it was decided that these business managers would be made

subordinate to the territorial managers so that the local market flavor would never be overridden.

Schulz's comments illustrate ICI's success in helping people adjust to new realities:[2]

> At the time of the Long Island meeting, it was assumed that if I took the U.S. position, I'd relinquish my LNP presidency (the title should be International Business Manager—it's just a legacy). I had an emotional reaction—it was like cutting the cord; I didn't want to lose my baby. It was probably an immature reaction, but after all, I had grown LNP from $3 million to $100 million. Anyway, I created an impromptu logic to keep it, and they let me. But in August, at the time of preparation for announcement, I started thinking maybe I should not be wearing both hats. Maybe both are full-time jobs. My boss said, "no, we agreed; let's try it." But last week I told him it was time we started looking seriously at a timetable for me to relinquish LNP, as I'm not doing justice to either position.

By that time (January 1988), Schulz clearly saw himself in the middle, contributing to protecting what was productive in LNP and helping ICI to be more successful in this kind of business:

> I have been trying to keep ICI out of LNP in this sense (in the sense of not taking on big-company habits). You have to be wary; it's like slicing a baloney; each slice is so thin it does not matter, but in the end you are left with nothing. Someone like me is needed to bridge the gap, run ICI and LNP. I can ease things, build confidence, create less fear.
>
> I hope we can manage a middle ground. There is a preservation need: we have a dedication, almost an obsession, to giving the customer what he wants. The market interface skills of LNP are vital. ICI's plastics culture would have been a disaster. For example, their salesmen have no expense budget; they do not make their own sales forecast. Where is the pride of ownership in that?
>
> On the other hand, if the ICI pieces start to take over this culture and get successful, maybe they need less independence. If there has been any surprise, it is that LNP has so soon been driving the ICI plastics business.

In the meantime, the amalgamation was proceeding, step by step. ICI committed resources for a modern headquarters for the engineering plastics business in the United States about twenty miles from LNP's Malvern, Massachusetts site. Talking about the new building, an LNP manager commented:

> It will really be an LNP building up there; we will have 110 LNP people for a couple of dozen Victrex and Fluor people only. LNP Malvern will be closed down. It is bursting at the seams anyway; we have people in rented trailers and rented offices on the other side of town.

The move was expected to usher in further changes:

> We are still on the LNP incentive plan. In 1988 we will have to bring LNP/ICI plans closer. We will be in the same building, and it would be difficult to have different systems.

Despite this increasing amalgamation of the two organizations, it would be misleading to say that by 1988, LNP had been absorbed into ICI. Indeed, the company had retained all its original qualities, which ICI had been (relatively) lacking: customer orientation and entrepreneurial drive. It was, in fact, largely ICI's Advanced Materials organization that had become more differentiated from ICI's core business mentality. Less discussed, but equally important, this facet of the integration allowed the two acquisitions to come together without destroying LNP's original capability.

STAGES IN SYMBIOTIC INTEGRATION

The slow evolution of LNP's integration into ICI illustrates the challenges present in symbiotic acquisitions. The pattern begins with preservation steps and then moves through an intensive process of amalgamating the two organizations. As can be read between the lines in the example, the texture of the relationship between the acquired and acquiring company; the atmosphere created; the respect for differences and for the acquisition's purpose alike; the continuous evolution toward the future vision; and the continuous concern to bring people along define more than any specific actions what a symbiotic integration is all about. Four stages can be recognized in this evolving process: (1) starting with preservation, (2) reaching out rather than reaching in, (3) trading operating responsibility for strategic control, and (4) amalgamating the organizations (see Figure 13-1).

STARTING WITH PRESERVATION

The initial steps in a symbiotic acquisition are the same as in a preservation. The same issues that we discussed in Chapter 10 and Chapter 12 dealing with preservation acquisitions apply. At first, all contacts need to be channeled through a formal gatekeeping structure that emphasizes the capabilities for which the company was acquired in the first place and keeps managers focused on achieving their original operating objectives. In the Beatrice example, that was literally the case, as the LNP and Fiberite companies were initially kept together with those Specialty Chemicals companies that would remain in a preservation mode.

There are some differences in this stage from a pure preservation situation, however. Expectations for symbiotic acquisitions tend to be higher. More attention needs to be paid to managers' reactions in the acquirer in symbiotic acquisitions and to the organizational reporting of the new unit.

Premiums Paid and Patience Needed. It is difficult to begin a symbiotic integration with a clear preservation orientation because the premiums paid for the kind of acquisitions that require a symbiotic integration tend to be substantial. For example, in ICI's acquisition of the Beatrice companies, a price of $750 million was necessary to top competing offers from competitors like Akzo, BASF, AMOCO, and others. Most of the synergy such a figure implied had been imputed to LNP and Fiberite, the two businesses that provided the potential to reinforce the newly created Advanced Composites business. This created pressure within ICI to pursue those synergies. It also created initial fear among managers in the acquired firm that they would be stretched to make up for the price that had been paid for their company.

ICI was able to allay those fears, first by holding them to their own budgets and later by focusing on long-term progress. Increasing resource commitments in the absence of financial results put high demands on the corporate system. Some of the same qualities we discussed in Chapter 5 as key to acquisition decision making carry over in the integration phase. In this phase the quality of the strategic vision and the degree to which it is shared in the acquirer become important. There has to be a clear understanding between the corporate level and the interface managers about the strategic objective, the kind of time horizon that will be needed, and the organizational path that should be followed.

Turning the Tables on One's Own Troops. We noted earlier that in symbiotic acquisitions the legitimate claims for involvement by the acquirer's operating units are much stronger. They have been asked to help support the justification by identifying the synergies that could be expected with their own area of business. We described in Chapter 9 how the ICI Advanced Composites people (just like their colleagues from the Mond division) argued against the acquisition team and wanted to split up the Beatrice companies immediately. The acquiring managers will have to agree not only to a delay, but also to go one step farther—to prepare their own organization for the fact that if it is on the receiving end of a new capability, it may have to change its own way to become a good "receptor."

Side by Side. In addition to preserving the acquired company from uncontrolled interactions, the gatekeeping structure is typically set up so that the acquired unit and the operating units with which it interfaces become adjacent, reporting to a single executive. In the Beatrice example this change came in two steps. First, ICI and the Beatrice Advanced Composites businesses were put under the same senior executive; subsequently they were put side by side under one operating manager (Logan). The role of that single senior executive is to develop and push the strategic vision and also to start reformulating the purpose on both sides, especially on the side of the host organization. The heads of both operations, in this case, Bucher and Logan, should offer assistance. The senior executive will have to be a statesman, providing the required overall vision and pressuring both organizations for awareness and change.

REACHING OUT RATHER THAN REACHING IN

After an initial emphasis on setting the stage properly on both sides and controlling any urge for headquarters staff or operating unit involvement, it is time to pursue the real purpose of the acquisition: achieving a rich capability transfer between both sides. The boundary between the two firms must be transformed into a semipermeable membrane. The key to this in the situations we studied was in the style and the direction of initial and subsequent contacts. The initial substantive interactions between the firms were originated by the managers in the acquired firm as much as possible. As already discussed, to facilitate this, the acquiring firm put a few experienced people at the disposal of the acquired units to point to resources in its organization that could help solve some of their problems. In this way, the acquired company could perceive benefits accruing to it from early interactions. As one acquiring manager commented: "The idea is that we open our hands and let them walk in the candy store and refrain from pushing anything in particular on them." If the complementarity of resources and problems is really there, the time lost in exercising such restraint will be small.

TRADING OPERATING RESPONSIBILITY FOR STRATEGIC CONTROL

Voluntary interactions, even if nudged along, will go only so far. Over time, as some of the early contacts and interactions began to bring results, symbiotic acquisitions required a gradual stepping-up of the influence over the acquired company. This involved the managers steering a middle road, between the expectations of the mother company and the reluctance of the acquired organization. The earlier comment of Schulz, who acknowledged the benefits of the collaboration and his concern for the preservation of LNP, illustrates the ambiguity of this process, an ambiguity that reaches deep in the organization. One of the LNP managers, after discussing a number of positive developments, returned to his fear: "They must realize we are a company, not a business. If they ever were to change our name, it would not be the same place anymore."

The ability to exert increasing influence over the acquired company, and to avoid getting hung up on "symbolic" issues such as names and logos, was typically a function of the degree to which managers in the acquired firm felt that the capability transfer was operating in both directions.

Handing over significant responsibility for part of the acquirer's own business to the acquired organization, as ICI did by making LNP responsible for marketing its Victrex and other product lines in the United States, is often the most effective way to start pulling the strategy and priorities together. More operating responsibility is entrusted to the managers in the acquired firm, while the acquiring firm begins to take firmer control of strategy. At the operating levels both organizations remain distinct. The managers in the acquired firm still identify largely with their own company, yet a few people and resources have moved to the other side.

Amalgamating the Organizations

Ultimately, the whole process must lead to a true amalgamation in which the two organizations combine to become a new, unique entity. This combination must be accomplished without losing the character that underlies the capabilities of the acquired company, and superfluous differences must be reconciled. The Beatrice example illustrates a number of mechanisms that can accelerate such a gradual evolution. Senior managers in the acquired unit can be assigned double roles: One is to act as the traditional guardian for their units, and the other is to take an overall perspective that involves them in the broader strategic outlook.

Another mechanism is physically or geographically to regroup the individuals, if not the organizations, for example, by investing in new buildings, such as a headquarters or R&D labs.[3] Our research suggests that the increased understanding bred by geographic proximity lessens demands for maintaining other differences, such as retaining separate benefit structures.

Whether an acquired company succeeds in transforming itself without losing its intrinsic characteristics depends on the caliber and ability of business managers, who can make the transition from a smaller- to a large-company setting. Not everyone combines the entrepreneurial ability to grow a $3 million operation into a $100 million one and the managerial ability to adjust to operating within a complex multinational with a matrix organization structure. Such managers must continue to care deeply for their own organization, yet become realistic and careful never to obstruct the purpose of the acquiring company.

Successful transformation also depends greatly on the long-term perspective of the acquiring company, which must be willing to add the required resources and adopt the time horizon that will be most productive. Above all, the quality of the integration process in symbiotic acquisitions, as in absorptions or preservations, depends on the quality of interface management.

MANAGING THE INTERFACE

Irrespective of whether an acquisition is an absorption, preservation, or symbiotic, integration is a highly complex process. The difficulties in bringing two organizations together are legion. The people in one company, by virtue of the acquisition, are often set to claim their ownership rights, whereas the people in the other company are frequently alienated and defensive. The ensuing problems affect capability transfer both directly and indirectly through their impact on the atmosphere. The balance between pushing for capability transfer and protecting the acquired organization's identity is a delicate trade-off among the demands of the situation, the intended evolution, and the dynamic at a given time.

Because of the complex and dynamic nature of this process, the essence of value creation is really assured by the group of managers who manage the interface and perform the gatekeeping role.

We suggested in Chapter 10 that it is better to think not of one individual, but of a number of people who jointly fulfill a constellation of roles. Three types of individuals are an integral part of the gatekeeping unit: the head of the host structure, the head of the acquired unit, and a small number of resource people. Managers who head the host structure like Leif Johansson at Electrolux, Eddy Brouwer in BP, and Ben Lochtenberg and Hugh Miller in ICI, successfully steered the integration process, relying upon their own skills and the support of their top management in dealing with corporate colleagues. Others like Stefan Wilcke in Eurochem, had neither the foresight nor, more importantly, the support to mobilize the necessary forces in the situation.

The success of these individuals at managing the acquisition process upwards, downwards, and laterally hinges a great deal on their credibility within both organizations and (except in absorption acquisitions) their ability to be mavericks who can set their own rules (and have them tolerated). Interestingly, many of the successful gatekeepers we studied were bicultural. For example, Brouwer was the only Dutchman managing a BP subsidiary, and Lochtenberg was an Australian working for a British company in the United States. Others were bicultural in the sense that they had not, like most of their colleagues, spent their entire career in the firm. They were sensitive to the reality of life in the smaller organization, even while working for the huge one and to differences among national cultures. They could perceive, for example, that what to an American ear seems a small suggestion may be interpreted by a British manager as an order from his boss.

A second key player in the gatekeeping team was the head of the acquired unit. Sometimes the existing manager was kept on, as were Schulz at LNP, Lodders at Hendrix, and Chiswell in Dymo. In other situations, a manager was brought in from the parent firm, such as Wibault in Francoplast and Walker in Trouw, or from the outside, such as Verri in Zanussi. The decision whether to confirm the existing manager or to recruit the new one is crucial. It depends on the relative importance of preserving continuity of management in the acquirer, providing industry, know-how to the acquired and acquirer alike, and being trusted and experienced in one's own organization. In all cases the managerial burden imposed by the acquisition requires an individual of a character and caliber well above that required to run a similar business independently or within one's own company.

The third set of players in the gatekeeping team comprised the resource people, experienced managers from the acquirers' organization, who are recruited into the acquired company or generally made available to it. These are the people who, like Palmer in Beatrice, or Pritchard in Hendrix, and many others we interviewed are assigned to positions that are often subordinate to the rank they would have in their own organizations.

In many ways their real role is not the one reflected in the lowly formal position they occupy. Seeking to allay the mistrust of the acquired company, they must build credibility by being helpful and by sharing their expertise. It takes a certain modesty and much interpersonal skill to play this vital role, as they must constantly walk a fine line between the positions of the two companies. As one of them commented:

> It is a great challenge to balance affiliation. I try to tell myself and others that my affiliation is neither with the acquired unit nor with the division of our company that it interfaces with. My affiliation is with our Board and its goals.

> The delicate balance is between what is perceived by the managers in the acquired firm, and what is perceived by our managers. At first, in this job, you seek credibility with the acquiree. Later on, it is with corporate that you must assure credibility. It is then that the declared support and authority that you have been told you are given become important.

Another manager described his gatekeeping task in very similar terms, at the same time reflecting its intrinsic orientation:

> Our first job was to establish credibility, both with the managers in the acquired firm and with corporate. Our next task was to get their people to see what our company had to offer. Our third task was to get our organization to learn from them.

The qualities required of the members of the gatekeeping team and their crucial impact place a great premium on the way in which acquisition staffing decisions are made. The de facto criterion seemed to be (as in Eurochem) the normal internal job market of who is up for a new assignment. Other companies in which such staffing decisions are a matter for executive committee consideration are likely to make better choices.

Beyond the choices, these situations also make heavy demands on the leadership of top management. Having appointed these managers, they must be willing to back them up and provide them with the resources needed to bring in long-term results.

SUMMARY

We discussed how the integration process in different types of acquisitions takes on a very different character, each requiring from the acquiring organization a different repertoire of skills in interaction management. We also described how the process can be managed. Although for each type of acquisition there are some clear steps, the real quality of the integration process lies in the subtleties required to respond to the different needs for interdependence and autonomy.

Regardless of the type of acquisition, the overriding image deriving from the successful integration efforts we observed is one of corporate-level managers, interface managers, and acquired company managers engaging in a continuous process of adaptation and learning. They have substantial responsibilities, and while immersed in a constant stream of action, they must keep their eyes fixed on the strategic mission of the acquisition and the firm itself. In the next chapter we will step back and examine this acquisition activity in its broader context.

Linking Acquisitions
Back to Strategy

In this last section we summarize the main thrust of our research and put it into broader perspective. Chapter 14 summarizes our conclusions about how to manage the acquisition process and returns to the role acquisitions are to play in the overall corporate strategy. It also picks up a theme that has been running throughout the book—how acquisitions contribute to learning.

Each research opens doors to new issues and each solution brings new problems. As we were examining some of the active acquirers, "strategic assemblers" as we call them, we saw them invariably confront a whole new set of challenges beyond those of integration we discussed in this book. Chapter 15 discusses some of the problems and opportunities active acquirers face as they move beyond making acquisitions to managing an integrated network of operations.

14

Managing Acquisition Strategies

INTRODUCTION

THE EXPERIENCED FIRMS that we studied for our research did not develop their capability to handle acquisitions well overnight. Their acquisition management capability was based on hard-won learning and often, dismal early acquisition track records that left quite a few skeletons hiding in the closet. Many of these companies had gone through a period of major diversification at the corporate level, followed by another period of pruning, if not dramatic refocusing. The fact that many of their early acquisitions had subsequently been divested did not imply that fewer new acquisitions were made. To the contrary, the same firms were often most active in both acquisitions and divestments, both of which the continuing work of repositioning and renewal implies.[1]

The combination of these ongoing shifts in acquisition activity among geographic regions, industries, and companies and the internal turnover in management teams provide both a vast source of, and a dramatic need for, the transfer of learning in how to manage acquisitions. Many industries (e.g., automotive tires, chemicals, and electrical products) have largely undergone or are well into the major industry restructuring associated with a dramatic technological change or with globalization. In some countries with a relatively unconstrained market for corporate control, such as the United States and the United Kingdom, acquisition activity has reached a high plateau as a fully developed mergers and acquisitions industry of investment bankers, acquisition lawyers, and capital providers seeks to sustain the acquisition momentum in the face of less obvious targets, more competition, and more skepticism.

In contrast, other companies are only beginning to make their first acquisitions; other industries are still in the very early phase of restructuring; and the managers in those firms are beginning acquisition programs with just as much enthusiasm (and associated naiveté) as their fellow executives in sister companies a few years earlier. At the same time, deregulation, the expansion of the maturing mergers and acquisitions industry into new geographic and product markets, as well as more structural factors, are increasing acquisition activity in heretofore quieter countries.[2]

A Call for Caution and an Encouragement

We began this book expressing the hope that we might provide managers with words of both caution and encouragement. Caution, we said, is required, because making successful acquisitions is much more complex and entails many more problems than managers assume before they begin. Our emphasis was both on analyzing the problems and on showing how they can be overcome.

Encouragement is warranted because the strategic benefits from acquisitions may be high for firms whose management teams can learn from their own experiences and from the experiences of others. We saw how British Petroleum built a multibillion dollar nutrition business that outperformed its industry, in the face of many oil company diversification efforts, including some of BP's, that had failed. We saw how ICI's acquisition of Beatrice Chemicals became a key factor in the making of the "new" ICI. The acquisition of Zanussi dramatically changed the product and geographic position of Electrolux and became the stepping-stone to the restructuring of the overall company. We explored how the combined impact of acquiring the Inmont paint business, the advanced materials businesses of Celanese, and Akzo's American fiber business gave BASF a critical mass in the United States as a chemical company. The impact of many acquisitions should be measured not only in the direct financial returns, or in the market position gained, but also in terms of the effect on the overall capabilities of the combined organizations, their competitive positions, and the new strategic options open to them.

An Integrated Process Perspective

This book has suggested a new perspective on acquisitions that incorporates the relationship among strategy, a firm's capabilities, competitive advantage, and organizational issues. We believe that the use of this richer, expanded perspective can offer insights into key managerial problems that may not be apparent when acquisitions are viewed from more limited perspectives. Moreover, we believe that this perspective has the potential to encourage more robust, integrative academic research.

We discussed how focusing exclusively on the financial and deal-making aspects of an acquisition opportunity frequently limits acquisition benefits to capturing value from other stakeholders. But value capturing is not the mission of most companies. Although the immediate financial benefits may be appreciable, the philosophy behind such acquisitions does not address a firm's fundamental corporate renewal needs, nor does it lead to ongoing value creation.

We also warned against adopting a narrow, overly rational view. This perspective takes too literally the well-meaning prescription to first develop a clear strategy; define acquisition objectives; formally search and screen candidates; engage in strategic and financial evaluation; and finally, after negotiating the deal, turn to implementation. Such a segmented, sequential view is incomplete in situations where opportunities, emerging strategy, championing, and evaluation mix in the decision-making process, and where adaptation and learning are key to implementation and the value creation process.

A final caution was offered against overemphasizing organizational or cultural problems in acquisitions. Such a focus can often make acquirers shy away from making an acquisition, even when it is dictated by the strategic logic of the circumstances. Strategic fit and organizational fit often point in different directions. In these instances the challenge is to manage the organizational dimension in a way that acknowledges the strategic logic of interdependence, the autonomy needs of the acquired firm, and the need to treat each person involved with dignity, respect and fairness.

Tasks for Corporate Management

Corporate executives face two intertwined tasks as they manage an acquisitive strategy. The first is to develop a coherent view of their renewal strategy and to define the role that acquisitions will play in it.

The second task is to ensure that their company has an organic process in place that allows it to manage acquisitions effectively.

This book has mainly focused on the latter issue of how to manage an acquisitive strategy, not on how to develop one. We have made the important assumption that the company's top management knew what course to set. In fact, we believe that too many companies do not spend enough time thinking about the nature, type, and quality of the firm's *corporate* strategy. To guide acquisitive development, top management needs to have a good sense of several interactive factors—their corporate strategy, how acquisitions fit into this strategy, and the corporate capability to manage its implementation.

In this chapter we will examine the first challenge that we took for granted: defining a corporate-level acquisition strategy. Next, we will revisit some of the corporate capabilities required to manage the acquisition process effectively. Finally, we will discuss how acquisitions can contribute to organizational learning.

ACQUISITIONS' ROLE IN CORPORATE STRATEGY

A STRATEGY FOR CORPORATE RENEWAL

The fundamental responsibility of senior executives is to sustain and renew their firm's capabilities and its ability to compete. Developing a shared view among the top management group of the role that acquisitions should play in the company's strategic evolution and renewal is part of the broader challenge of developing a corporate-level strategy. Over the past decade or so, corporate-level executives have become accustomed to expecting from their business managers well-articulated business plans that clarify how they expect to achieve a competitive advantage. Typically such plans are supported by the use of business strategy tools and frameworks such as strategic segmentation; industry and competitive analysis; value chain analysis; experience curves; and the like. The end result of this process of two-way communication is a set of well-developed and agreed-upon business strategies and thinking for how to compete at the business unit level.[3]

There is much less clarity among senior managers over what could be called the corporate strategy.[4] This vagueness may be accounted for in several ways. First, corporate managers are typically not reviewed, evaluated, and expected to meet identifiable performance targets in the same sense as business-level managers. As a result, their statements about corporate strategy often inform the financial analyst community and brighten annual reports to shareholders more than they provide direction for the firm. This lack of articulation may also result from the paucity of clear conceptual frameworks to frame senior executives' thinking about corporate strategy as opposed to business strategy.[5]

The use of tools to allocate resources among businesses such as portfolio techniques are by themselves too simplistic to capture the richness of required corporate strategic thinking. Because corporate executives are subject to constantly shifting external pressures as well as numerous internal decisions and demands, they may prefer to keep their options open. Because they have to rely on their operating managers to deliver results, they may choose to rely on them also to advocate choices. Whatever the contributing factors, the perception at the business levels in many of the companies we studied was that there was a paucity of clear guidance coming from the top.[6]

Although a detailed discussion of corporate strategy issues falls outside the scope of this book, two dimensions critical to understanding the role and contribution of acquisitions to a corporate strategy have been developed. One was the need to develop a clear understanding of the firm's corporate domain—the product-markets within which the firm can effectively deploy its core capabilities. A second dimension was the need to examine acquisitions in terms of their contribution to the corporate renewal strategy by which both capabilities and product-markets are renewed.

NEED FOR A CAPABILITIES-BASED PERSPECTIVE

A major theme of this book is an argument that managers should shift the emphasis in their thinking about their firm's strategies from a sole focus on product-market positions to one that explicitly includes the capabilities that underlie their competitive positions. Such a shift in perception is also related to a conscious choice of the means by which the corporate level intends to add value to its units. Conceptually there are three ways (discussed below) that a diversified company can add value to its businesses: through operating discipline, through portfolio strategy, or with a horizontal strategy.[7] The first two hinge on arguments of relative efficiency vis-à-vis the discipline imposed by outside markets.[8] Only the latter, through the deployment of capabilities across units, provides an absolute benefit.[9]

The limits of operating discipline as a source of corporate value creation are apparent. Many firms can benefit from cost reductions brought about by increased efficiencies. But the operating discipline brought by a large corporate structure does not easily outweigh its costs (both in terms of overhead and the loss of motivation).[10] As the history of conglomerates shows, recently acquired and less professionally managed businesses may provide opportunities for disciplining benefits that outweigh the costs. As these businesses become more efficient and internalize this general management discipline, the balance between continued monitoring costs and added value may shift. Thus conglomerate acquirers must continue to add to the "stable" of businesses onto which they can impose discipline or by failing to add value, they may find themselves ripe for "deglomeration."

The same healthy skepticism exists with respect to the ability to add value at the corporate level through business portfolio management. By this we understand a corporate level's ability to improve the strategies of its individual business units and to develop an internal resource allocation flow across the business units in the portfolio that supports these strategies.[11] That approach assumes that the diversified company can allocate cash to high-yield uses more efficiently than the external capital market. Portfolio planning may still be a useful way to stimulate a dialogue about the nature of business strategies during the business-corporate planning process.[12] But the benefits it offers in allocating resources among businesses may be less applicable with freely available external funding and an active market for corporate control that has become a more efficient "discipliner" and allocator of resources.[13]

The only corporate value-added that provides a sustainable advantage originates in the sharing of hard-to-imitate capabilities and competences across units. This sharing requires the ability to develop a learning organization where the transfer of capabilities can take place.

While the theoretical arguments for a capabilities-based approach to strategy are becoming well-developed, as we discussed in Chapter 2, the real challenge remains in the implementation of such an approach. Such implementation requires both a clear perspective on what those core capabilities may be and how to deploy them organizationally. Even in the firms we studied, where acquisition evaluation clearly reflected a capabilities-based orientation, no formal assessments were made of the cluster of core capabilities that the company was implicitly nurturing.

Although it is not easy, the task of clarifying core competencies is very important. The conceptual and organizational difficulty of this task is analogous to the difficulty of defining the business which most corporate managers faced earlier.[14] Just as an analytical definition of a business is at the heart of effective current resource deployment, an analytical definition of core capabilities is central to the ability to set long-term resource allocation priorities. A clearly articulated decision about the set of core capabilities on which the company will build its uniqueness provides important guidance for decisions about investing in renewal, the direction of that activity, and the vehicles to use in such renewal.

A capabilities-based perspective requires most companies to reexamine their organizational approach to enrich the current focus on profit centers and business units with a process that recognizes that core capabilities are corporate resources that have value that transcends the organizational unit of the firm in which they reside.[15] There is a need to encourage the transfer of existing capabilities across product-market opportunities in different units and also to foster capability recognition, generation, redeployment, and renewal. In practice, core capabilities are embodied in the teamwork of skilled individuals; this implies a far-reaching change in the organizational roles and responsibilities of key middle-level managers and specialists and the ways in which they are managed. A management team's ability to evaluate possible acquisitions and to understand what would be involved in transferring capabilities to and from them must begin with a recognition of its firm's own core capabilities and how they are embedded in its organization.

Clarifying the Renewal Strategy

Renewal strategies and the role of acquisitions in them can now be seen in a broader, more fruitful context of the firm's existing capabilities. In this light three areas for decision stand out:

- The balance between renewal and ongoing operations.
- The relative importance of acquisitions in renewal.
- The type of acquisitions that the firm should pursue.

An assessment of the overall situation of each of the company's business units allows the senior executives to judge the degree to which a shift is needed in the *balance between ongoing operations and renewal*, not only in terms of businesses, but also in terms of technological, functional, or general managerial capabilities. That is, given an overall assessment of the threats and opportunities in the company's core domains, what resource commitments should it encourage to strengthen its competitive posture or enter new business areas?

We use the word "encourage" purposefully rather than "allocated." We believe that senior management should set the ground rules and provide support to those in the organization who understand and champion new commitments. We do not advocate prescribing activities from a lofty corporate vantage point without the benefit of a business-level understanding of the market, technical, or political realities inherent in an opportunity.

Unfortunately, the pressures driving the balance between ongoing operations and renewal activities are often the wrong ones. Too often the rate of renewal activity depends on whether diversification is either in or out of fashion, apparent needs for current performance, considerations of risk spreading among businesses (which does not add value by itself for the stockholders), or the personal whims of a key manager. We suggest that the balance between continuity and renewal should be driven by more strategic considerations such as the munificence of the current business domains; the rate at which the firm generates capabilities and their applicability to other areas; and the rate at which the firm's capabilities and its competitiveness are eroded in the marketplace.

A second decision area relates to the *relative importance of acquisitions,* as opposed to internal development or alliances, in accumulating, expanding, or redeploying capabilities. There are no easy ways to define this role. Individual firms' choices will depend on the preferences and personal style of management, the heritage and organizational experience of the company, the firm's experience with acquisitions, its ability to develop organizational capacity to manage the capability transfer process, and on national differences.[16] In practical terms the decision to pursue acquisitions often rests on the fact that they promise (in theory) faster results than internal development and allow more control than alliances.

Although there are no clear a priori prescriptions for deciding on the role of acquisitions in renewal, one message that flows from our research is that the various renewal modes (e.g., acquisitions, joint ventures, license agreements, technology-sharing arrangements) are not only conceptually similar but also highly complementary. They are similar in that in each type of renewal, capabilities are transferred to improve competitive advantage. They are complementary in the sense that most internal development relies on some acquisition of capabilities. By the same token even the acquisition of a complete business position needs to be made in a developmental perspective if it is to create the most value—the acquisition price is the first installment on a future investment program. Joint ventures and partial equity stakes as well require concurrent internal investment if one is to appropriate and leverage the value created in the joint venture.

Not only does each renewal mode imply a complementary dose of the other, but sometimes one leads to the other. In many cases collaboration is the first productive step toward understanding the business, market, or industry before a complete acquisition, or the way to overcome a firm's reticence and open the way for a discussion of a potential merger. In other cases it is the instability of collaboration over time that drives one of the partners to buy out the other.

The third set of questions addresses *the type of acquisitions* that the company wants to engage in. At one end of the spectrum acquisitive renewal is accomplished through a single (or a few) bold corporate-level acquisitions that reposition the firm. We have suggested throughout this book that there are important limitations to the view that such corporate acquisitions are miraculous, deus ex machina, solutions to a company's long-term renewal problems. At the other end of the spectrum are small divisional acquisitions that can be a powerful strategic development tool at the business level, but also consume vast amounts of management time.

When focusing on business-level acquisitions, managers must decide whether they will approach domain extension and prospection through building on platform acquisitions or make major commitments by purchasing existing business positions. We suggested that all too often the scale of the initial commitment is governed by internal political considerations in the firm rather than by needs to acquire learning or improve market position.

Platform acquisitions have a unique ability to foster learning and offer the firm a place where capabilities can coalesce in the development of new business domains, but they are frequently mismanaged because of the disparity between the sizes and stages of development of the two organizations. Above all, however, the problems stem from imposing onto platforms performance expectations that are more appropriate for fully developed businesses.

The decisions top management makes about the role of acquisitions must come from juxtaposing competitive pressures and opportunities on the one hand and the organizational repertoire that shapes the options on the other. In a world where a substantial aspect of corporate-level and business-level competitiveness revolves around the ability to manage the acquisition process, building broad-based corporate capabilities in managing that process is an important responsibility of senior management.

MANAGING THE ACQUISITION PROCESS
FOR VALUE CREATION

The corporate capabilities to manage an acquisitive strategy develop slowly and deliberately over time. They include three interactive elements: orientation, context, and skills.

Orientation

Perhaps the most fundamental ingredient in managing an acquisitive strategy is a capability-based perspective on corporate success. This perspective is necessary to ensure that all aspects of the acquisition process are devoted to identification, acquisition, preservation, transfer, and application of capabilities. Management must identify the capabilities that are required to build competitive advantage and judge prospective acquisitions against this yardstick. It must carefully learn where and how core capabilities are embedded in acquired firms and safeguard these acquired firms when necessary to encourage capability transfer between the two organizations. Such a capabilities-based perspective is necessarily also a process perspective: Management's key role is to manage interactions over time, to balance implementation with adaptation and proaction with change. It also must recognize that key aspects of the decision-making and integration processes can affect the outcome of the acquisition and capability transfer.

Another aspect of this orientation is the willingness to exert leadership to develop a new vision for the combined firms. Building a vision about the role of acquisitions in the corporate renewal process is one thing. Building up the corporate capabilities to implement this acquisition-based strategy is, as we have argued in this book, an equally critical but much more complex task. Finally, there is a need to encourage learning from acquisition experiences. Firms must be willing to see initial problems and mistakes as investments in learning; be determined to use and lever that learning; and to recognize that the immediate results of an acquisition may not be as important as its contribution to the company's overall capabilities and options.

The role of senior executives does not stop here, because their task is to envision the next challenges the firm must face. Strategic managers do not acquire or integrate companies for the sake of acquiring them, but to implement a renewal strategy for their business operations. At some point the focus has to shift from the requirements of making acquisitions to a more broad-based management of what has become an integral network of operations. This shift will be a big transition to make, especially for companies that are rapidly assembling an industry position through a series of acquisitions. We will discuss in the next chapter the foresight required from top managers of such companies, who must guide this shift in mind-set and organizational practices.

Context

Mastery of the acquisitions process starts with the creation of the appropriate decision-making context. We stressed how the acquiring firm's strategic agenda needs to drive the decision-making process, rather than outside advisers who are often, as one manager put it, the corporate equivalent of a one-night stand. The same holds true for the organizational set-up that the company adopts for acquisition decision-making.

We suggested that in most firms, the regular resource allocation process is not equal to the special demands that decisions like acquisitions (and divestments or joint ventures) impose on it. Consequently, we argued, companies that wish to have a more active acquisition process and to develop the capability for a broad range of acquisitions are well advised to build a separate organizational capability for acquisitions.

The main ingredients of such a capability, we suggested, were the formal incorporation of acquisition planning in the business planning process and the creation of a corporate acquisition function. This function, we suggested, should stay in close contact with the top and with a broad network of business development managers. While the exact nature and composition of the acquisitions function depend on the size of the company and the intensity and nature of its acquisition strategy, we described a number of roles that in all cases need to be institutionalized in the firm. These roles include stimulating proactive acquisition thinking, clearing acquisition leads, fostering internal learning, and bringing professionalism to the process. The contribution of the acquisition function derives from the ability of its managers to establish a working process in which they service both operating business management and the CEO more than it does from any formal authority assigned to it.

The specific context of each acquisition was seen to call for an acquisition team set-up in the decision-making phase and a crucial interface management set-up in the integration phase, with, it is hoped, some continuity between the two. A major consideration regarding acquisition teams was that they should be led by operating managers.

Interface management was seen to depend on the roles of at least three groups of individuals: the head of the host structure, the head of the acquired firm, and resource people made available to the acquired firm. Formalizing these roles to some extent was a prerequisite to exerting them effectively and consistently.

Skills and Attitudes

For a management team to capitalize on a capabilities-based renewal orientation and to make such a context effective requires the ability to tap a broad set of skills at different levels in the firm. We described the practice of interface management as especially demanding because of the needs for a broad range of personal qualities on behalf of interface managers, an attitude of empowerment on behalf of top management, and a process perspective of both. An attitude among managers of the acquiring firm that conceives of acquisition integration as a two-way process of moving to best practice is not easy to develop. In fact, owning the acquired company makes the emergence of a true partnership attitude harder to accomplish. Top managers must take charge of the acquisition process themselves and ensure that it is driven by the company's strategic agenda and organizational capabilities, not by opportunism or the deal-making interests of outsiders. They must also spur their own organization to transform itself.

ACQUISITIONS AND LEARNING

Learning has been a pervasive theme throughout our discussion of acquisitions: learning *which* acquisitions to make (or not make), learning *how* to make them, learning *about* the acquired business, and *incorporating learning* in the acquiring firm's own organization.

The importance we place on learning in acquisitions reflects the fact that from an organizational perspective, acquisitions are in some sense experiments, whose outcomes inform practice even when they are unsuccessful. Most of the examples we used were of successful acquisitions, but we also got a good look at the skeletons from earlier acquisition failures that are datapoints in the statistical studies of our financial economist colleagues. A comparison between the early acquisition record of these companies and their later acquisitions encourages us to be optimistic about companies' capacity to learn how to handle acquisitions better. At the same time, some companies seemed to learn from their acquisition experiences faster than others.

LEARNING WHICH ACQUISITIONS TO MAKE AND HOW TO MAKE THEM

Lessons about which acquisitions to make (or not to make) and learning how to make them are inextricably linked. As the companies we studied "experienced" the success and failure of acquisitions, their reactions varied on the basis of their ability to interpret that experience analytically, as well as their subsequent reaction to this learning.

A candid, analytical evaluation of acquisition experiences is often difficult in firms. Few decisions rival acquisitions in their propensity to label a manager's career. As a result, the retroactive interpretation of acquisition events serves the political ends of protecting some managers' careers or attaching a stigma to others. In many cases the reputation of an acquisition that we picked up in occasional conversation was far from what close attention to the original documents and interviews with the direct actors would yield. Nevertheless, the reputation of an acquisition matters, because it becomes the basis for justifying or influencing future acquisition decisions.

Some organizations have the discipline to conduct postmortems with integrity. Yet even in those cases, we observed, learning was hindered either by a tendency to overgeneralize—what worked well or not well should be applied to all acquisitions—or to the contrary, from a lack of generalization, for example, acquisition lessons were framed in very industry-specific terms. Framing acquisition experiences at the right level in terms of distinctions to be drawn and then drawing those distinctions are central to learning from these experiences. While each company should develop its own insights, acquisition categorizations in terms of why companies buy and what they buy as we developed in Chapter 2 and the integration typology that we developed in Chapter 7 may prove more helpful than the distinctions of size, country, or industry that we found in many corporate documents.

Companies differed not only in their ability to interpret similar acquisition failures meaningfully, but also drew very different conclusions from their failures. In some firms such introspection led to a commitment to augment the organization's capability and do better next time. In other companies each bad experience seemed to reduce the willingness to undertake such an acquisition again. After the Francoplast debacle, for example, Unichem top managers concluded the firm would no longer make small platform acquisitions. If Unichem were to enter a new area, they concluded they would rather wait and acquire a larger firm. While it would reduce the chances of similar acquisition failures in the future, this attitude also implies that a firm forgoes important strategic options. Our description in Chapter 5 of how an effective acquisition decision-making process can be shaped, and the discussion in Chapters 10 to 13 of the integration challenges in different types of acquisitions, was premised on the fact that firms would want to build up as broad-based an acquisition capability as possible to service their future strategic requirements.

LEARNING THE BUSINESS

Acquisitions can be an excellent way to learn a business. Two important drawbacks of complete internal development, besides the time it takes, are the fact that a market test comes relatively late in the development process and that the market is approached with the same competences and skills that were already characteristic of the company. In contrast, an acquisition gives a firm access to a set of capabilities embedded in an organization grown in the milieu in which the acquiring firm is interested. In Chapter 12 we described at length how platform acquisitions managed in a preservation mode may, in conjunction with internal development, provide the basis for exploring new domains.

The role of acquisitions in business learning is not constrained to new domains. One of the messages in our discussions of both symbiotic (Chapter 13) and absorption integration (Chapter 11) approaches was that the acid test for true success is how much learning can be derived from the acquired organizations, even when they are in the same domain or adjacent to it. Mediocre acquirers acknowledged all the outstanding features of an acquisition candidate to support the acquisition justification but ignored them during integration. Successful acquirers were able to foster a two-way learning process.

INCORPORATING LEARNING

The most lasting payoffs from acquisitions that we have described were in the learning benefits that can accrue to one's organization. Granted it is important to pursue quickly the immediate benefits flowing from the combination and the resource-sharing opportunities that may immediately improve a cost position. Yet the real benefit of the successful acquisitions we observed derived from the transformation of the acquirer's own organizational capabilities and competitive strategy. This transformation depended on the extent to which managers were open to the acquired capabilities and were able to leverage them in their own organizations.

Such a transformation involved two separate processes. One was the reconfiguring of the acquiring company's strategy and organization prompted by the acquisition. The Beatrice acquisition, for example, led to the restructuring of ICI's overall advanced materials business, which evolved out of the gradual symbiosis of its own engineering plastics activities with LNP and Fiberite; the organizational set-up under Ben Lochtenberg of its worldwide specialty chemicals business, in which a number of ICI activities were now run in a similar mode as the Beatrice companies. At a broader level it led to the institutionalization of the acquisition team and gatekeeping approach in the company and became a symbolic example for the "new" ICI that John Harvey-Jones and his successor, Dennis Henderson, were attempting to create. In Electrolux, the Zanussi acquisition was not only the trigger for a whole new strategy with respect to vertical integration, manufacturing, and marketing, but over time became a major factor in the evolution of its overall organizational approach. Not surprisingly the companies that derived the most learning from incorporating acquisitions in their organization were those in which, through a history of prior restructurings and acquisitions, organizational change had become an accustomed part of the organization's culture.

A second, much slower, process in which learning from the acquisition affects each organization, stemmed from the long-term impact on the organization of new patterns of coordination among different operating units. We will return to this learning in the epilogue, which takes us beyond integration issues.

CONCLUSION

Acquisitions can contribute to corporate growth and renewal in a variety of ways. Perhaps the most subtle yet lasting impact of an acquisitive strategy is on the evolution, over time, of the firm's overall management approach. By bringing in new ideas as well as exposing parts of the firm to new capabilities, markets, and regions, the senior management can test and introduce innovations in management approach that can themselves be an important source of competitive advantage.

Broader managerial concerns such as the quality of decision making in general are brought into sharper focus through the lens of acquisitions.

The advent of globalization has increased the need for managers to become aware of the differences in how decision making takes place in other economies.[17] When they look closely, they will discover important differences in time horizon, capability view, analytical perspective, and risk sharing among international competitors. We suggest that these differences have a far-reaching impact on resource allocation decisions and ultimately the competitive position of the firms. To move an organization toward a more long-term, capabilities-based perspective, a more analytical view, and more risk sharing will require strong leadership. Bringing about the changes in these fundamental factors may be as crucial as it is difficult.

Acquisitions are a revealing litmus test that highlight the quality of leadership and decision making in a company. We hope that the perspective offered here will be a catalyst for managers, prompting them to consider their firms' corporate renewal needs and to learn how acquisitions can be managed to contribute to that renewal.

15

Epilogue

Beyond Acquisitive Development

INTRODUCTION

THE CHALLENGES OF integration management discussed in this book are not an endpoint, because acquisitions are only a means to accelerate ongoing corporate renewal. In this final chapter we will step beyond acquisitions and provide an epilogue to our main arguments: *Once a firm has assembled a series of acquisitions, how can they be harnessed into an integrated network of operations?* We will argue that shifting from managing acquisitions to managing ongoing operations implies a real transition, a transition that is especially problematic for "strategic assemblers," firms that have amassed an important industry position through acquisitions during a period of industry restructuring.[1]

If acquisitive firms can handle this transition successfully, however, they may have a relatively stronger position vis-à-vis their more internally grown competitors. After all, acquisitions bring with them a broad variety of capabilities, the potential for local adaptation, sources of new ideas, and a rich set of subcultures that other firms cannot replicate through internal growth.

INDUSTRY RESTRUCTURING AND STRATEGIC ASSEMBLERS

In some industries the pace of restructuring is slow and acquisitions are few. Companies that make a limited number of acquisitions in such industries may find the process of moving beyond integration almost

255

imperceptible, as the acquired company's identification recedes, employees become socialized, and new recruits enter who are ignorant of old distinctions.

Often, however, industry restructuring is fast paced, as industry after industry goes through a window of strategic change. In some industries this restructuring involves a shift in regional scope, as competition shifts from local to national, or from national to global. In other industries the restructuring involves a blurring of industry boundaries, as previously distinct business segments become engulfed in broad-based competition.

In the face of such pressures for rapid industry restructuring, an increasing number of companies have embraced rapid acquisitive development to leapfrog their competitors in this process or catch up with early leaders. These "strategic assemblers," as we will call them, attempt to put a significant industry position together through multiple acquisitions. On a global scale, examples include the Swedish Electrolux in white goods, the Finnish Valmet in paper machinery, the British Saatchi and Saatchi in advertising, the French Rhône Poulenc in agricultural chemicals, the American General Electric in medical equipment, the French Thomson in consumer electronics, and many others. Within a single geographical market, companies like BancOne and NCNB in United States regional banking or Thompson International in technical magazine publishing are similarly pursuing a strategy of assembling an industry position through rapid acquisitions. For other companies, such as the American Computer Associates, strategic assembly is a way to build up broad-ranging capabilities.

At some point, we will argue, such companies face a difficult transition. The logic of strategic assembly, the top management orientation it implies, and the organizational capabilities it develops are very different from the logic of ongoing management. These companies need to be able to move beyond the assembly mode and to compete in a more integrated fashion.

It is the challenge of this transition, which for most strategic assemblers still lies beyond the horizon, to which we turn in this chapter. We will discuss and illustrate this challenge in the context of global competition. But its elements apply almost equally to many other situations of rapid acquisitive restructuring. Before turning to the transition problems strategic assemblers face and examining elements of a response, we will discuss some of the special issues these firms already face in the assembly phase and the organizational capabilities developed in this phase.

CHALLENGES IN THE ASSEMBLY PHASE

Behind every strategic assembly there is a logic rooted in a view of industry structure and its evolution. Often, as we shall illustrate in the Saatchi and Saatchi example, that logic takes shape only as successful acquisitions are made, which reinforce top management's belief of what is possible.

In some companies the underlying economic logic driving the assembly concept is clearly articulated, while in others it is reduced almost to the urge to be "number one." Independent of its articulation, the key strategic question is whether the concept corresponds with future industry economics. In Saatchi's case the merits of its initial "Global Agency" concept may have been partially borne out, but the economic logic of its later "Global Service Firm," including financial services seems more tenuous.

Beyond the strategic merit of the assembly logic, the timing of its implementation is also critical. Attempts to restructure an industry that is not ripe for it may spell disaster, whereas waiting too long to respond may squander valuable first-mover advantages. Such advantages include the choice of acquisition candidates, inattention by competitors, and interest in the financial community. Otis's rapid acquisitive development and standardization strategy during the late sixties and early seventies in what was the fragmented local elevator business in Europe illustrates the importance of moving first. Spearheaded by Otis's general manager France, the company made a series of acquisitions across Europe, providing it with the volume and customer base to make its standardization strategy pay off. Before Westinghouse, Schlindler, Kone, and other competitors reacted, the company had taken a commanding lead which still forms the basis for its competitive edge in Europe. Yet a similar concept by a competitor had failed only a few years earlier, when the industry apparently was not ripe for standardization.

SPECIAL INTEGRATION CHALLENGES OF STRATEGIC ASSEMBLERS

Assembling and integrating a series of firms adds complexity to the integration issues we discussed in Chapters 10 through 13. One factor is the *relative size of the combined acquired units* vis-à-vis the size of the original acquirer. Saatchi and Saatchi's original agency and Electrolux's original white goods business represented only a minor part of the assets of these groups in the end. Such size disparities place a heavy premium on the ability of the original business to remain a driving force as a result of its clear competence, or in the case of Saatchi, its continued creativity. Acquiring many companies rapidly also leads to a shortage of management talent in the acquirer's ranks, especially when operating problems emerge in some of them.

Other complicating factors for strategic assemblers include the *multiplicity of cultures* across the newly acquired subsidiaries. The parent firm often ends up acquiring more cultures than the number of acquisitions would indicate, because newly acquired units themselves are frequently the result of recent prior combinations, as in Electrolux's acquisition of White in the United States, or Whirlpool's two-step acquisition of Philips' white goods businesses in Europe. This multiplicity makes it easier to argue for the genesis of an entirely new, overarching culture, but it also adds complexity to any integration work, particularly if these units vary widely in size or strategic and operational importance.

Finally, the continuing acquisition activity may have a very destabilizing effect on previously acquired units. After every new agreement, strategic missions that were just recently established may have to be reviewed, and recently settled organizational arrangements may have to be reexamined. Frequently, as we discussed in the previous chapters on integration, smaller activities acquired earlier end up being folded into more recently acquired, but larger, organizations.

ORGANIZATIONAL APPROACHES OF STRATEGIC ASSEMBLERS

Very often, strategic assemblers consciously or unconsciously reduce the complexity brought by these integration challenges by adopting a relatively simple organizational approach by which a small headquarters organization monitors a large number of acquired subsidiaries on a fairly autonomous basis.[2] What could be the full absorption of a number of acquisitions within a sector is, in fact, more a collection of several preservation acquisitions among which coordination is limited.

If coordination among units remains rather limited, the small corporate center nevertheless can exert a strong substantive influence, because all positions are within the industry that is familiar to the corporate center. As a result, the organization does not suffer from the strategic distance that is prevalent among other firms that are managed with small corporate centers, but that are composed of more diversified businesses.[3] One illustration of this is the Electrolux case, which we described in Chapter 11. At the time of the Zanussi acquisition, when the company was already running 25 product lines in 5 business areas, its corporate headquarters in the old factory south of Stockholm did not exceed 100 people, clerical staff included.

Inevitably, strategic assemblers are decentralized. As Anders Scharp, Electrolux CEO, commented: "I believe we have at least two hierarchical levels less than most companies of our size, and all operational matters are decentralized to the subsidiaries."

Both group-wide strategic decision making and coordination in strategic assemblers tends to rest with a small, high-powered, and tightly knit general management team that plays a high-profile role in the acquisition process. They are joined by a cadre of capable unit general managers to whom the tasks of integrating the acquisition and improving its internal operations are delegated.

In the description of the Electrolux case in Chapter 10 we alluded to the fact that whereas senior Zanussi managers were fully involved in the integration process, acquired company middle management, which had developed fewer links with Electrolux, was more apprehensive. As we will further illustrate in the Saatchi and Valmet examples, integration in strategic assemblers frequently rests on corporate and senior acquired managers and on the incorporation of the acquisition into the acquirer's systems. The vast majority of middle managers in acquired firms initially tend to be unaffected by what happens in other units of the group, and the original cultures of the acquired companies tend to be preserved, as communication is vertical only and coordination limited. As we shall discuss further, such an organizational approach, which works for acquisitive assemblers in the assembly phase, is a mixed blessing beyond the early integration.

A STALLING DYNAMIC

We witnessed how a powerful dynamic builds in companies that are using acquisitions successfully to reposition themselves in their industry. The years of rapid-fire acquisitions are exhilarating; with every new acquisition the organization seems to adjust its horizon as to what can be achieved. The objective of becoming "number one" takes on more weight and begins to seem more achievable. Every acquisition adds to the size and reported earnings and in turn makes it easier to attract the funding and other resources required for the next acquisition.

Individual acquisitions made by strategic assemblers are accompanied by all the integration challenges we discussed earlier and may from time to time present real operational difficulties. But these annoyances are likely to be submerged on a company-wide basis for several reasons. First, the acquisition dynamic builds an excitement and momentum when the focus is on the goal of achieving a number one position. This creates a tendency to downplay bothersome aspects of reality. Secondly, as long as larger and larger firms are acquired, the growing sales and profit figures tend to counterbalance the impact of any internal operating problems.

At some point, however, the dynamic stalls. Often it is because no other candidates are visible or because candidates are not accessible either for ownership or antitrust reasons. In other cases, prices for firms in the industry have been pushed beyond what is reasonable. Finally, in many cases firms may have reached the point where resistance to further concentration begins to come from the customers themselves.

The logic of assembly must now make way for new logic geared to ongoing management. Fundamental changes are needed, not only in the method of growth, but also in the degree and nature of coordination and ultimately in the management's entire orientation. Unfortunately, management groups are often too caught up in their acquisition logic to envision early enough the need for the nature of this change.

Two illustrations of this dynamic and its inevitable stalling are Saatchi and Saatchi, the British advertising group, and Valmet, the Finnish paper machinery manufacturer. The acquisitive growth of Saatchi and Saatchi was more flamboyant, more concentrated in time, and had a more dramatic aftershock. Valmet is a more typical example of successful acquisitive development followed by a slow and difficult transition to more integrated management.

The Rise and Stumbling of Saatchi and Saatchi[4]

Maurice and Charles Saatchi's success in growing their firm from a modest 9-person agency in 1970 to a 10,000-employee global advertising group by 1986 was the result of creative talent in the base business, an aggressive acquisitive strategy, and a sharp financial orientation.

The brothers' conviction that size was important was manifest from the beginning, and the agency grew not only through its creative talent, but also through some smaller early acquisitions. The 1975 reverse takeover of Garland-Compton, then the only listed advertising agency in the U.K. fueled their ambition and provided the means for it. Their stock's price/earnings ratio became about 20, compared with the 4 to 5 p/e multiples typical for the large (mainly American) multinational agencies. This allowed them to finance the acquisitions by stock swaps. At the same time, the use of earn-out contracts delayed the dilution impact of their acquisitions, and underpinned post-acquisition profitability. The use of this technique had drawbacks, however, as it clearly became less possible to implement changes in these acquired companies that might affect their bottom lines.

With the means for rapid growth available, the Saatchi brothers set their sights on becoming the largest agency group in the world extolling their vision of a global agency. With the acquisitions of Backer and Spielvogel and of Ted Bates, that objective was achieved. In the meantime, the brothers' ambition had broadened into providing one-stop shopping for management services, which led to diversification into marketing services and the acquisition in 1984 of Hay Consultants, the executive compensation specialists.

The 1984 Ted Bates acquisition, however, while helping the Saatchis realize their original ambition, marked the firm's zenith and then began the unraveling process. The stock market's reaction to the acquisition price for Ted Bates was negative. More importantly, clients representing $450 million of billings deserted the agency, fearing conflict of interest. Some key corporate managers left, including the man behind Saatchi's strong financial planning and control systems.

Rather than reorient their management approach and focus on streamlining the core advertising business, the Saatchi brothers continued their acquisitions, broadening their ambition even further. Beyond consulting services, they saw financial services as an area where they could "successfully globalize." They made an unsuccessful bid for Midland Bank, the U.K.'s third largest clearing bank, which deepened the apprehensions of the financial community. Saatchi's stock price tumbled as deferred earn-out payments on earlier acquisitions were coming due, and relaxed controls were undermining operating results. By 1989 the company had scaled down its ambitions and brought in an external head, trying to get its internal act together without close involvement of the Saatchi brothers. A positive counterpoint in the situation was that, underneath it all, the core advertising agencies had retained their creative skills and ability to attract accounts, so they could set out to rebuild their strategy, organization, and credibility.

FROM ACQUISITION GROWTH TO INTERNAL DEVELOPMENT AT VALMET
PAPER MACHINERY[5]

Another, less flamboyant illustration of this dynamic and its stalling is
the case of Valmet Paper Machinery, the main subsidiary of the Finnish
state-owned Valmet group. After a dramatic turnaround in the early
eighties, Valmet embarked on an acquisitive conquest of an industry-
wide global leadership position, only to find that acquiring and integrating were only the beginning of the road.

In 1981 the Valmet group as a whole was losing money. The projections were especially dire for its Paper Machinery division, which had
succeeded in getting only one new paper machine order in 1982, compared with 6 in 1980, and a (highly cyclical) world market of around 60
to 100 per year.

In response to this crisis, the board named a new CEO, Matti Kan-
kaanpaa. In 1983 he turned the organization around, divisionalized operations, shortened chains of command, improved operating efficiency,
and installed strategic planning. Valmet then embarked on an acquisitive
development path of paper machinery-making firms in Canada, Finland,
Germany, Italy, Sweden, and the United States.

In less than four years, Valmet had assembled a broad-based position
in the paper machinery industry, covering most aspects of machines for
all paper-making segments. Rivaled only by the American Beloit and the
German Voith, the company had market shares of between 25 percent
and 50 percent in various segments, and had the number one position in
paper machinery worldwide. Its sales grew from FIM 1.6 billion in 1984
to FIM 4.4 billion in 1988.

The integration of the various subsidiaries had, on balance, proceeded
relatively well. But Valmet found it difficult to translate its leadership
position quickly into better financial results. By 1988 it was suffering a
small loss despite a booming business cycle and record sales. It also
became evident that, for several reasons, leveraging the economic benefits from their position would not come quickly. In boom times, the
firm relied heavily on expensive subcontractors. Moreover, they were
investing heavily in the acquired businesses. The limited number of
machines sold, coupled with the specificity of paper machines by segment and the complexity of each machine, precluded dramatic scale
benefits, even on a worldwide basis.

The company still undertook to eliminate manufacturing duplication in
component parts such as reels and rolls. But these were low-volume,
small-value components, and achieving such rationalization depended on

costly investments in design standardization and computerized design and manufacturing technology. Nevertheless, the company pushed ahead, knowing that the benefits of integration would come over time.

A better-coordinated strategy necessitated a more streamlined organization. After internal task force work, the company in 1989 adopted a more streamlined product-based organization in which each major product line would integrate its manufacturing and development, and sales and service would be territorial. The biggest challenge was to achieve coordination across these profit centers, whose previous operation as independent subsidiaries had been based on tough profit controls and the management of their own subcontractor relationships. Without increased pressure from senior management, integration would not accelerate, as the benefits to subsidiary managers of collaborating were not yet demonstrable.

Top managers in the company were slowly changing from a focus on direct involvement in major sales and engineering decisions and reliance on a cadre of Finnish collaborators to an emphasis on the organizational engineering of a more integrated culture incorporating the acquired middle managers.

FROM ASSEMBLY TO INTEGRATED MANAGEMENT

The Saatchi and Valmet examples illustrate the strategic and organizational problems and opportunities with which many active acquirers find themselves confronted after the assembly phase spree and initial integration of these firms. Major shifts in emphasis are called for in strategy as well as organizational orientation. The need for a shift in strategy stems partly from the fact that dramatic expansion through acquisitions has ended. The firm has reached a stage where further major acquisitions are ruled out, for reasons we discussed earlier, or because the organizational challenges have caught up with them. At the same time, internal performance pressures tend to rise when ongoing operating performance can no longer be masked by dramatic acquisition results.

As the acquisition engine grinds to a halt and the pressures for operating performance increase, a second, more profound set of demands arise from the competitive realities of the newly acquired position. In comparison with competitors who develop steadily through internal growth, the strategic assembler is likely to have inherited a number of partly overlapping and competing product ranges and brand names. Some degree of incompatibility may exist, and there may be conflicts in dealing with competing customers, as illustrated by Saatchi and Saatchi's loss of $450 million worth of Ted Bates' billings. In other cases it is difficult to maintain the development of incompatible technologies. Above all, there is a need to streamline the collection of designs, product lines, and brands to achieve the order and logic inherent in the strategy. For example, in Europe alone, Electrolux ended up with a collection of more than twenty brands, some national, some international, most with different positioning in different countries.

While streamlining may be an economic imperative, the process itself is fraught with organizational difficulties and competitive risks. The elimination of duplication is hard to achieve without an attendant loss in market position, particularly as local competitors may be exceptionally active during the transition process. Whether such streamlining involves the elimination of brand duplication or choices among competing technologies, it involves discarding what are, after all, dearly paid-for and valuable assets.

For a firm to capitalize on the competitive potential of its newly assembled position requires a much more integrated strategy. For strategic assemblers who seek to achieve competitiveness in a global business, it becomes imperative to be able simultaneously to exploit system-wide economies to exploit learning and facilitate renewal without losing their original ability to adapt to local requirements.[6]

The increased need for coordination inherent in the pursuit of such a complex strategy presents a substantial administrative challenge, even to long-standing multinationals that have grown through internal development.[7] But for the strategic assembler, whose coordination capability has been outpaced by rapid external growth, this administrative challenge is particularly acute. The mind-set and simple organizational approach that once facilitated the rapid acquisition and incorporation of many firms now runs counter to capabilities needed to develop such a complex multinational management approach. Moreover, the reorientation problem may be magnified because the need for it was masked for a long time by the very dynamic of acquisitive development. Driving at full speed, managers of acquisitive assemblers often fail to see either the sharp turn or the uphill road that lies beyond it.

Embracing Tomorrow's Market Requirements

Notwithstanding the organizational challenge, the partially overlapping but broad product lines and multicountry positions that strategic assemblers inherit in their acquisitive quest give them an important strategic opportunity. They have a chance to capitalize on the increasingly complex nature of their markets in a way that internally developed competitors with a narrower range of capabilities would have a hard time matching. This opportunity is based on the fact that many markets, as we shall discuss, are becoming increasingly segmented within countries, yet more homogeneous across countries.[8]

Although the forces for globalization are numerous and powerful, the vision of one homogeneous world marketplace may be a mirage. As described by Theodore Levitt, this scenario is one in which "companies must learn to operate as if the world were one large market, ignoring regional and national differences."[9] In practice, countervailing economic and political forces that require local responsiveness resist such blanket homogeneity and, in fact, are on the rise.[10] In competitive (as opposed to politicized) marketplaces, this emerging complexity is, in our view, characterized by two simultaneous phenomena.

Increased Segmentation Within Markets

Many national markets are becoming increasingly segmented. Earlier, markets were rather simply segmented, often with a single basic segment accounting for the bulk of the market. Such a marketplace provided the well-entrenched local competitor with the scale economies to compete for the bulk of his local market. In many markets, however, segmentation is becoming more finely grained, with each individual segment becoming smaller.[11] This phenomenon is driven by the increasing sophistication of customers, who expect their needs to be met more precisely, by greater competitive pressures on suppliers, who attempt to gain share by being more finely attuned to customer needs, and by technological evolution that makes product variety more feasible. In this evolution, local competitors have difficulty achieving scale in a single segment, and they tend not to be able to afford the investment that a differentiated approach to each segment would require.

Increased Homogeneity Across Markets

The other trend is that toward increased homogeneity of segment needs across international borders.[12] This occurs for several reasons. Sometimes the customers themselves are global, requesting the same product specifications in different countries, as in the case of automotive supply companies. In others it is because the attitudes and needs underlying a segment are becoming similar internationally. A classic example is the buying behavior of the international yuppie. But the same phenomenon extends to other segments, as illustrated by the successful appeal of "the international colors of Benetton" to young customers throughout the world.

The Opportunity for Strategic Assemblers

The combination of these two phenomena—increased segmentation within countries and increased homogeneity across countries—drives the restructuring of many industries. Moreover, it provides strategic assemblers with their biggest challenge and opportunity: to present the broadest, best adapted offering in each national market and exploit the fact that these segments, when summed across country boundaries, provide the potential for economic efficiency. In Electrolux, which is pioneering this philosophy, Leif Johansson, head of the white goods business, points to the "Quatro" refrigerator as a case in point. This product, which provides the user with several compartments with different temperature ranges, appeals to too small a segment in each country to make its design and production economical. However, on a Europe-wide basis, sufficient volume can be obtained to make it a worthwhile product investment.

Strategic assemblers must reject both the easy route of allowing acquired firms to continue their autonomous strategies and the simplistic route of forcing these acquisitions into a uniform global strategy. Combining efficiency, local adaptation, and learning benefits across a range of newly acquired businesses is foremost an organizational challenge. First, we summarize the general nature of that challenge, which has been extensively examined by multinational management scholars.[13] Then we reexamine this challenge from the vantage point of the acquisitive assemblers whom we studied.

THE ORGANIZATIONAL CHALLENGE

The organizational requirements to shape an appropriate decision environment to handle such a complex strategy are substantial. Diversified multinationals are accustomed to coping with these trade-offs, and scholars have described these requirements.[14] Yet for strategic assemblers, which have so far developed limited coordination capability, the task is huge.

MORE COMPLEX COORDINATION REQUIREMENTS

Consider, for example, the implications of Electrolux's decision to streamline its operations along the lines of four brand families, as discussed earlier. The potential benefits are huge. We mentioned how it allows them to tap into the original entrepreneurial strengths of companies like Zanussi, which, in this case, was entrusted with the "innovative" product range. This decision also allows Electrolux to cover multiple segments in each market, not only at the customer level but also in terms of distribution channels. At the same time, however, the grouping and streamlining of local brands offers standardization potential across countries, with potential benefits from efficiency in sourcing, manufacturing, and engineering.

Implementing this simple yet powerful idea entails tremendous coordination requirements. Beyond the traditional need for coordination among different brands within each country, the four brand groupings must be coordinated across countries in at least two ways. One is to ensure consistency of positioning within the brand families across countries, avoiding, for example, the fact that the Zanussi brand, while perceived as innovative and high quality in the U.K., may be seen as less so in Sweden.

A second thrust of coordination is to organize the differentiation among these brand families to capture as much of the total market as possible. To truly implement such a differentiated brand strategy, however, it is not enough to differentiate brand positioning in the market. That positioning has to be translated into differentiated product development for each range. Firms cannot merely attach a different brand label to the same products and then sell them through different channels at different prices. For each brand family, international marketing and product design capability must be integrated.

The resulting marketing/product development units must interface with manufacturing, which, as explained earlier, has been organized in separate divisions by product to achieve scale economies. Every brand family thus consists of products made in different divisions whose product and process engineering skills have to be involved at the product development stage. Thus, while Zanussi may be entrusted with the "innovative" product line, each product in that line belongs to another division, each of which is organized as a network of specialized plants, with one designated as the center of engineering excellence for its division.

Electrolux is not unique in the complexity its strategy demands. Its products at least lend themselves to a fair amount of standardization and modularization. Provided manufacturing capacity is sufficiently flexible and product design sufficiently standardized, component and product manufacturing can be largely uncoupled from market responsiveness in the pursuit of efficiencies. Companies like Valmet, on the other hand, face the same coordination needs among the overlapping yet different product ranges and market positions of their acquisitions. Yet the immediate benefits of coordination are much smaller, as component series are small, and each machine is uniquely designed for the customer.

Horizontal versus Vertical Coordination

Two approaches are possible to achieve such challenging coordination in a company. The traditional approach has been to coordinate from the center. Alternatively, responsibility for coordination can be pushed down to the operating units themselves. Recently several authors have argued that the latter approach, leading to a view of the multinational as a differentiated network of subsidiaries and operations, is inherently superior, because it is less likely to stifle local initiative and responsiveness by not removing responsibility from those who are in contact with the marketplace.[15] Yet such a networked approach may yield the same benefits in terms of coordination, not only in terms of economic rationalization, but also with respect to the transfer of learning. At the same time, different authors point out, the effective functioning of such a networked approach is predicated on the internalization of objectives and ways of operating that only a shared corporate culture can bring.[16]

CAN STRATEGIC ASSEMBLERS COPE?

What do these organizational challenges mean for strategic assemblers? On the one hand, it is not obvious that strategic assemblers will recognize the need for a reorientation before a performance crisis forces them into it. Even when they do recognize the need, the gap between the organizational approach they have typically adopted in the assembly phase and the coordination capability we just discussed is huge. On the other hand, their organizational approach predisposes them to use a decentralized network to build the required coordination capacity, which may ultimately make them more nimble competitors.

It is not obvious that a reorientation process will be generated proactively without the pressure of an externally induced performance crisis or a change in management. The firm's prior acquisition dynamic, a habit of conceiving their organization as a collection of subsidiaries to be individually managed, the organizational approach we described at the outset, and the personal orientation of managers who are successful deal-makers all conspire to limit the firm's ability to change. Ultimately, the latter factor, the profiles of the managers at the helm and other managers at the center, may be the most important barrier to a reorientation.[17]

THE NEW AGENDA

The reorientation implies a major change in the role and agenda of top management. From the exciting work of making major strategic and structural decisions, they have to move to more gradual and patient issues that will underpin such long-term competitiveness as quality, product renewal, and marketing plans. At the same time their personal involvement in details of the issues has to diminish as they need to focus on providing the vision and leaving operating managers to work out the action plans. They need to become the process engineers that build group-wide cohesion, create the necessary coordination mechanisms, and draw subsidiary middle management into this coordination process. This cannot be accomplished by a few short-lived measures such as an annual group-wide conference. A careful sequence of integrating mechanisms needs to be planned, layering different dimensions of coordination into the organization. Beyond accelerating the development of coordinating mechanisms across units, it may be necessary to enrich the perspectives on performance and on individual contribution to move beyond unit performance. Responsibility for coordination across units will have to be defined and clarified vis-à-vis the rest of the organization. Broad investments will need to be made in group-wide education and other integrating devices.

Building such management capabilities and their effects is necessarily gradual. The effectiveness of the lateral coordination these mechanisms seek to achieve depends on achieving a group-wide orientation and cohesion. At the same time, involvement in these mechanisms is what brings managers that orientation. Top management thus has to carefully pick up the coordination needs, one dimension at a time, and provide the full support of surrounding mechanisms to make them work.

The original predisposition of strategic assemblers may mask the need for such coordination. But, because of the way they have learned to deal with acquisitions, strategic assemblers are more likely than internally developed firms to seek coordination in a decentralized network form, rather than through build-up at the center. Their small headquarters mentality makes them more resistant to the build-up of central staff activities, and the buildup of a horizontal network approach is seen as the only way to forge a corporate culture because there is no clearly dominant one into which the others can be absorbed. Furthermore, in comparison with internally grown firms whose organizations have become complex and diffuse, strategic assemblers are less likely to lose sight of the need to maintain clarity of authority and clearly allocated responsibilities.[18]

SUMMARY

The strategic and organizational tasks that lie beyond acquisitions require a substantial change in orientation from what was needed for successful acquiring. These tasks are a reminder to other acquisitive firms that acquisitions are a means to an end. Acquisitions may be a way to accumulate capabilities quickly and to put a business position together. But to achieve lasting competitiveness, top managers must become adept at managing an integrated network of ongoing operations.

If the top managers of strategic assemblers, like those in Electrolux, have the foresight and ability to turn their full attention to the gradual integration of their operations, their firm will be stronger competitively. One reason, we argued, is that they may have incorporated a broader range of capabilities than they could develop internally, and this fact may become increasingly important as customer requirements become more varied and specific. A second reason is that their original, small headquarters orientation makes it less likely that they will seek to achieve coordination through heavy staff buildup in the center. They are more likely to embark on a horizontal networking approach, which is also the way to build a more integrated culture. Finally, because of their earlier reflexes, they are more likely to preserve clarity of responsibility and focus on individuals, without which coordination mechanisms tend to stall the dynamism of the organization's growth.

To master these tasks, top management, even amid the euphoria of a successful acquisitive growth record, must exhibit the leadership to visualize the new strategy and to identify the gap between current organizational capabilities and those that will be needed. This requires top management to sell deep into the organization a crisis which is not there and, it is hoped, will never occur.

Whether to make acquisitions, to integrate them, or to move beyond them, the need for visionary and effective leadership remains an indispensable factor in organizational success.

A

Research Method

OUR RESEARCH HAS SPANNED five years and has encompassed three separate field research projects involving 20 acquirers from 6 countries, and acquisitions in 10 countries, ranging in size from $3 million to well over $1 billion. In total we interviewed more than 300 managers in 10 countries on 3 continents. This appendix will describe the research process and methodologies used in each of the projects and help the reader to understand how our insights were developed.

David Jemison conducted two distinct studies on acquisitions. A first study in 1983–1984 was done in collaboration with Sim Sitkin when both were at Stanford University. It used cross-sectional interviews to explore broad questions of why acquisitions do or do not work. From this research came initial insights about the impact of the acquisition decision-making and integration processes on acquisition outcomes. This study encouraged further exploration of aspects of the acquisition process and formed the basis for the ideas in Chapter 4 of this book. The second research project by Jemison in 1984–1985 used an in-depth field study to examine what actually happened during the integration process in firms where strategic acquisitions were made to improve the competitive position of one or both firms. This study explored how transferring capabilities from acquisitions can lead to value creation (Chapter 2). This study also led to a grounded theory of the integration process and of the problems that emerge in this process, discussed in Chapters 6 and 7.

Separately, at INSEAD, Philippe Haspeslagh was conducting a research project on the management of acquisitive development. The fieldwork for this project was carried out in three phases in the period from 1985 to 1989. The first phase, with research collaboration mainly from Alison Farquhar and Sarah Williams, was carried out from 1985 to 1987. It involved an in-depth examination of decision-making and integration processes in a structured sample of eleven acquisitions in three large multinationals in the chemical sector. A second phase in 1987–1988, also carried out with the research assistance of Farquhar, tested the emerging findings in three further acquisitions in a fourth site.

Beyond an independent corroboration of Jemison's observations, these phases led to an examination of the role of acquisitions in corporate and business strategy (Chapter 2), an examination of how acquisitions affect the resource allocation process (reflected in Chapters 3 and 4), how experienced acquirers organize for acquisition decision making (Chapter 5), and a contingent approach to acquisition integration, presented in Chapters 8 and 9. In a third phase in 1988–1989, Haspeslagh concentrated further data gathering on acquisitive assemblers, firms who through a series of acquisitions are rapidly building a leading position in a restructuring industry. This data gathering led to the observations on management beyond integration presented in Chapter 15.

We note, of course, that the joint process of sharing our observations and findings and writing them up allowed us to refine many of the ideas from our respective research streams.

RESEARCH ON THE ACQUISITION DECISION-MAKING PROCESS

A basic question stimulated Jemison's initial research: "With so many sensible prescriptions available for making acquisitions work and so many managers who want to succeed, why do so many acquisitions seem to have disappointing results?" Suggesting that a would-be acquirer could succeed simply by avoiding the mistakes committed in acquisitions that had failed seemed specious. Although there were no data yet to back the presumption, it was suspected that the most important reasons for success would be quite different from those that led to failure.

To answer the original question, a research project was designed, in collaboration with Sim Sitkin, to understand the broad issues associated with acquisition success and failure. Because of the complexity of the issues, an exploratory field study was structured around the following open-ended questions:

- What factors have contributed to the success of the acquisitions or mergers with which you have been involved?
- What has led to the failure of these acquisitions?
- What departments or people in the two companies have been important to success or failure? Why?
- At what point did the managers involved recognize that an acquisition was a success or failure?

Interviews were conducted in 1983 and 1984 with twenty-seven senior and operating managers involved with acquisitions and investment bankers and consultants who provide advisory services to such managers. The bulk of the interviews were conducted by Jemison in the managers' offices in New York, San Francisco, Paris, and London. Most of the interviews lasted between one and two hours.

At each meeting, respondents were asked for detailed descriptions of situations where acquisitions with which they had been involved had been particularly successful or unsuccessful. Respondents emphasized that the methods of successful, acquisition-oriented companies exemplified the classic prescriptions for acquisitions by diligently ensuring a good strategic and organizational fit between the two businesses. In contrast, acquisitions that had failed achieved neither strategic nor organizational fit.

While these answers supported prevailing theories, an important pattern began to emerge as Jemison and Sitkin studied the interview data in greater depth. Although the research had not been directed toward the process of making an acquisition, the results indicated that the aspects of the acquisition process could influence the eventual outcome of the deal. While managers interviewed dwelled on the unique circumstances of each situation, it became clear that although the particular problems of strategic or organizational fit differed, the same problems in the acquisition process kept emerging. Jemison and Sitkin identified several of these as fundamental to the acquisition process. The findings of this first study were published in a series of articles outlining the process perspective on acquisitions including (Jemison and Sitkin, 1986a, 1986b).

RESEARCH ON ACQUISITION INTEGRATION AND STRATEGIC CAPABILITY TRANSFER

During the research that led to the initial insights about the acquisition decision-making process, the importance of integration came up repeatedly. Anxious to learn more about the actual integration process, Jemison set out to design a study to explore what took place during acquisition integration. Again, because there were no theories of acquisition integration, a qualitative field method was chosen to study the phenomenon. Although this type of method places important demands on the researcher (Kimberly, 1979; Miles, 1979), the nature of the phenomenon and the state of theory development indicated the appropriateness of such an approach.

As Glaser and Strauss (1967) suggest, theories grounded in empirical evidence are superior to those developed by one's imagination. In addition, with respect to complex phenomena such as acquisition integration, where no theory existed before, or where the process is not well documented, a grounded theory of acquisition integration is likely to be both useful (Mintzberg, 1979) and interesting (Davis, 1971). Because the period of acquisition integration takes many years (Kitching, 1967; Mace and Montgomery, 1962), a longitudinal study was not possible. Instead, a longitudinal processual design was used where real-time data collection was coupled with retrospective data collection of both an interview and archival nature (Pettigrew, 1979).

Sample Selection

The purpose of this research was to study the integration process in acquisitions between related firms where the acquisition was made to improve the competitive position of one or both of the firms. The sample had to be selected carefully to ensure that firms chosen met theoretical and methodological criteria. The theoretical criteria were that the firms had to represent strategic capability transfer in related business acquisitions. Accordingly, situations were chosen where the avowed purpose of the acquisition in public documents was the transfer of capabilities between firms. This criteria led to the exclusion, for example, of oil company acquisitions made to increase reserves or expand the number of retail outlets.

The sample firms selected for study in this research had made acquisitions to transfer strategic capabilities in hopes of gaining a competitive advantage. Often the actual capabilities to be transferred in acquisitions are tacit, i.e., they are embedded in individuals and organizations who have difficulty articulating them. As Polyani suggests "it is a well known fact *that the aim of a skillful performance is achieved by the observance of a set of rules which are not known to the person following them*" (Polyani, 1962, p. 49, emphasis in original). Capabilities studied in this research included, for example, the transfer of specialized operational knowledge about customer groups, manufacturing processes, product development processes, or R&D practices; management systems including inventory, planning, and control systems; and general management knowledge about managing growth into a broader realm where the strategic logics of the related businesses intersect. In addition, there had to be managers remaining in the firm who were involved in the integration process, who could provide the perspectives of both the acquired and acquiring firms, and who were willing to discuss their experiences.

The basic methodological criterion governing the selection of comparison groups for discovering theory is their relevance for the category and the properties they possess in which the researcher is interested (Glaser and Strauss, 1967, p. 49). With this in mind, the sample firms were chosen to minimize the variance on the phenomenon being studied (strategic capability transfer during acquisition integration) and to maximize variation on situations where that phenomenon could be found.

The acquisition integration process was studied in seven acquisitions or mergers among twelve firms.[1] Initial contact was made with senior line or staff executives in eight firms that were thought to meet the criteria above. A preliminary interview was conducted with the senior executive to verify the criteria, explain the purpose of the research, and secure firm participation and cooperation. All eight firms met the two criteria. Cooperation was received from seven firms. In one firm, the acquisition had been made only six months earlier, and the CEO felt that data gathering at that time would be disruptive.

The sample included seven acquisitions or mergers representing four industries—commercial banking, food services, steelmaking, and financial services. The acquisitions represented strategic renewal activities among the acquiring companies in banking (2), insurance (1), restaurants (1), retail credit (1), securities brokerage (1), and steelmaking (1). Each acquisition or merger was intended to transfer capabilities to improve competitive advantage. None of the acquisitions was a hostile takeover. Of the seven combinations studied, five were in the United

States and two were Japanese (commercial banking and steelmaking). The need to provide anonymity to the firms and to their managers precludes a detailed description of these sample firms here.

Data Gathering and Model Development

Qualitative, theory-building research is very much a product of the interaction of the researcher with the data. Accordingly, it is important to expand here on the processes of data gathering and model development to allow replication of this study and provide support for the rigor and logic on which the model is based. Data analysis followed the constant comparison method of Glaser and Strauss (1967), which involves simultaneously collecting, coding, and analyzing the data. This method requires the researcher to begin with as few theoretical preconceptions as possible and allow broad abstractions and theory development to emerge from the systematic and comparative analysis of the data. The researcher is constantly comparing additional data with insights developed from previous data. This involves careful interim development of concepts and the relationships among them as they emerge from the data.

As the interviews progressed, preliminary hypotheses about concepts present and the theoretical relationships among them were developed, reformulated, and either retained or discarded, depending upon the data. While the method is intentionally nonlinear and interactive (Eisenhardt, 1989), this approach is distinguished from abstracting from a collection of case studies, since each interview in grounded theorizing builds upon the others (Miles and Huberman, 1984; Yin, 1984). The interviews progressed until theoretical saturation was reached, that is, the point at which the incremental learning from additional data is minimal because researchers are observing phenomena seen before (Glaser and Strauss, 1967).

During the first interview in each firm, a senior executive was asked to recommend an initial group of middle and operating-level managers or corporate staff who were directly involved with the integration process and who would be the primary focus of data collection. Additional managers were also interviewed when their colleagues recommended that they be contacted or if they were mentioned in interviews as being key individuals in the process. A total of seventy-five interviews were conducted with sixty-three managers over an eleven-month period in 1984 and 1985. Exhibit A-1 indicates the number of interviews by firm, interviews by level in the firm, and the number of years since the acquisition at the time of the interviews.

These interviews lasted from one and one-half to three hours. A total of 327 typed, single-spaced pages of notes were transcribed from the interviews. None of the interviews was taped. Two of the interviews with the Japanese steelmaker were conducted with the assistance of a translator. All others were conducted privately, in English, with only the researcher and the informant present.

The interviews were guided by a set of unstructured questions designed to elicit observations and comments about particular events, incidents, and behaviors that occurred as the integration took place. In particular, informants were asked about (1) what the two firms and people in them did to work together (or not work together) after the acquisition, (2) who the key participants were from both firms, and (3) what the outcomes (both benefits and problems) of working together were and the reasons for those outcomes. Archival materials furnished by the firm and publicly available documents about the acquisition were studied to prepare for the interviews.

As the interviews progressed, each informant was asked to relate his or her comments to colleagues' comments on particular aspects of or incidents in the integration process. Thus data were provided on the expected and realized content of the decisions made, as well as on the process by which various integration initiatives were undertaken. Follow-up interviews were used where time had run short or to get managers' reactions to events and phenomena described by their colleagues. This iterative process of following up comments about particular phenomena or continuing interviews with certain people was an important part of the confirmatory process in the development of the grounded theory presented here.

Three types of archival data were used to prepare for the interviews and to compare with the interview data in the theory development process. The first were publicly available documents in newspapers and magazines that referred to the acquisition or to the firms' strategic situation. The second included company-prepared background documents that were used by the firms either as a part of their pre-acquisition analysis to justify the acquisition or as post-acquisition analyses that explored how to bring parts of the firms together. These included internal memos and presentations as well as officially sanctioned press releases. Other archival data centered on the incidents discussed with the managers and were typically interoffice memos or memos to the file.

In some instances the existence of certain internal documents was

Exhibit A-1 **Interview Frequency Across Sample Firms**

Firm Type	Number of Managers Interviewed	Number of Interviews	Number of Managers Interviewed at These Levels			Number of Years Since Merger or Acquisition at Time of Interview
			Top Management	Staff	Operating Management	
Commercial Bank						
Acquired Discount Stockbroker	20	29	3	5	12	2
Acquired Finance Company	3	4	—	1	2	8
Acquired Commercial Bank	2	3	—	1	1	1
Food Products Company						
Acquired Restaurant Chain	3	4	1	1	1	4
Commercial Bank						
Merger	16	16	1	3	12	13
Steelmakers						
Merger	11	11	1	2	8	15
Financial Services Firm						
Acquired Insurance Company	8	8	—	3	5	2
Total	63	75	6	16	41	

revealed during the interviews and they were subsequently requested. While these documents were usually provided quickly, in some situations several requests were necessary before they were made available. In other instances, internal documents were provided during the interviews without being requested.[2]

The process of model development was iterative and involved several stages. Interview notes and impressions were transcribed the same day, while they were still fresh in the researcher's mind. These transcriptions were then typed for further study. Handwritten notebooks with hypotheses and observations that led to the elements of the theory were kept and updated as patterns emerged during the interviews and after further study of the data. As the data collection progressed, the preliminary model was refined and modified on the basis of the transcribed and archival data. While the model developed in an iterative fashion, the first set of insights that emerged from the data were those regarding the interactions among members of the two firms. Beyond the actions that were directed toward the acquisition's purpose, other behaviors were observed, studied, and compared. These formed the basis for the three different types of interactions described in the model—substantive, administrative, and symbolic.

As the interactions were studied and understood more clearly, a sense emerged of how the parts of the firms worked (or didn't work) together to transfer strategic capabilities. This led to another set of insights about conditions that facilitated an atmosphere in which strategic capability transfer could occur. These facilitating conditions are salient in two respects. First, they provide a conceptual link between the interactions and the transfer of capabilities. Second, they emerged directly from the data and thus could be observed and validated as a necessary antecedent to capability transfer in each of the acquisitions studied.

During the interviews, examples emerged of instances where the facilitating conditions were present, as well as those where they were absent. This provided a third set of important insights that involved the process constraints to strategic capability transfer, organizational phenomena that prevented the facilitating conditions from emerging and, thus, acquisition integration from taking place. Specific aspects of these process constraints were directly traced to ways in which they limited strategic capability transfer by inhibiting the presence of the facilitating conditions. While interactions and facilitating conditions are important, this research suggests that these process constraints are the heart of the model, because they offer important insights into why integration does or does not take place.

RESEARCH ON ACQUISITIVE DEVELOPMENT

Philippe Haspeslagh's research interest in acquisitive development dates back to 1981 when, together with Dominique Heau, he developed INSEAD's senior executive course, Strategic Issues in Mergers and Acquisitions, as well as an MBA elective in the broader issues of management of diversification. Broad-ranging interaction and interviews with experienced corporate managers provided an appreciation for the organizational dimension within which acquisition evaluation took place. Fieldwork for pedagogical material, including the Esselte-Dymo case series, provided detailed exposure to several integration processes. From this exploratory data gathering emerged a conviction, which he would later discover that he shared with Jemison (and a few other researchers like Sitkin and Shanley), that in large organizations acquisition success and failure had more to do with the processes of decision making and integration than with the variables captured in the then prevailing performance-oriented studies.

In addition, his attention was drawn to the impact of the corporate domain and the corporate organizational approach on the acquisition process, whereas the prevailing literature focused on business-level relatedness. He had formed the hypothesis that the acquisition process for a given acquisition would differ not only by how it related to the company's corporate-level strategy, but also by the extent to which the corporate level was dominated by a single domain.[3] Preliminary data gathering also drew his attention to the distinction between business-level relatedness, which other researchers tried to capture, and the interdependence actually managed between both firms, which could coincide or not with relatedness because it was a managerial choice.

Formal Research Design

During 1985 a research project was designed to address three broad question areas:

1. What factors determine success and failure of individual acquisitions?
2. How are acquisitions initiated, evaluated and committed to? How does this acquisition decision process differ from the internal development process? How does the design of the process affect generation of leads, speed of decision making, and quality of strategic and organizational fit?

3. How do companies learn about their domain and discover its limits? How can domain issues be usefully conceptualized?

For similar reasons, as described under the second research project above, intensive field research was chosen because it corresponded to the purpose of the research, the nature of the topic, and the state of knowledge about the topic.

The research purpose was indeed to examine acquisition performance in the very broad context of acquisition decision making, which itself was embedded in the broader context of a company's domain and organizational approach. This broad definition of purpose was conscious and derived from the impression that the inconclusive research on the relation between strategic variables and acquisition performance derived precisely from the neglect of these wider variables.[4] We did not understand, for example, how an unrelated acquisition made by a conglomerate and by a dominant firm could be classified alike, hence the choice of a holistic clinical approach to the topic.

The nature of the topic also reinforced the need for clinical observation. The nature of acquisition decision making required a research process that tapped multiple levels in the firm and was longitudinal so that it could capture process dynamics. The nature of acquisition integration likewise required data gathering on both sides and an even more longitudinal perspective. It was expected that it would be important to capture informal aspects of the process.

The nature of knowledge about the acquisition process was, in Fritz Roethlisberger's (1977) words, "still low on the knowledge tree." This does not mean that no hypotheses could be formed and tested in more structured ways than through the field research methods we employed. The point is that there is a rather inverse correlation between the relevance of questions that could be asked and the state of knowledge about them. The questions we wanted to ask were still very much in the exploratory field.

The foregoing elements not only pointed toward intensive field study, but also made quality of access an important criterion in site selection. The intensity of investigation also implied we would have a limited number of companies if we were to have a structured sample in each.

SELECTION OF THE RESEARCH SITES

The following criteria were used to select companies for investigation:

1. They should be *experienced* acquirers in order to allow for a sufficiently rich choice for a matching sample of acquisitions. Only experienced acquirers could be expected to provide insight in effective ways of coping with the acquisition process.
2. They should be broadly present in *similar domains* in order to control for variances that might derive from differences in strategic logic other than the ones we would try to maximize: the companies' organizational approach and the acquisitions' relatedness to corporate strategy.
3. Within the same domain set we wanted to maximize the *variety of corporate organizational approaches* companies exhibited to manage an equally wide-ranging set of businesses. Ideally, we wanted to be able to compare truly "diversified industrials" with "dominant business" firms.
4. We equally wanted a *variety in their acquisition decision-making approach,* including companies who treated acquisition decision making through their regular resource allocation process and others who treated acquisition decision making quite separately.

The broadly defined chemical and petrochemical industries were chosen because of their large number of sizable companies, their multinational character, their rich and broad-based history, and not unimportantly, the openness of some of their companies to collaborate with an INSEAD research project. ICI, BP, and "Unichem," three companies in the $10 billion-plus category that matched the other criteria, agreed to participate in this first phase of the project. The nature of their businesses, their organizational approach, and the handling of acquisitions are summarized below.

Imperial Chemical Industries (ICI), a British chemical company, was, as of 1986, truly diversified in that it had several core businesses, albeit of a related-linked[5] nature, such as: agrochemicals, fibers, explosives, petrochemicals and plastics, polyurethanes, general chemicals, pharmaceuticals, specialty chemicals, and paints.

In terms of organizational approach, ICI was run in 1986 as a true "diversified industrial" (Berg, 1971) or M-form (Williamson, 1975) organization. Its corporate level was clearly distinct from its operating divisions. Each division represented one of its core businesses and was headed by a business board. Although strategic direction was ultimately set by the corporate level, each of the divisions operated under a great deal of autonomy.[6] The company's past experiences with acquisitions had recently led to a separate acquisition decision-making process with a small but influential corporate-level acquisition function.

British Petroleum (BP), a British petrochemical company, was equally diversified in businesses such as oil exploration, oil refining and marketing, chemicals, minerals, coal, nutrition, detergents, and ventures.

Its formal organization had a similar M-form structure with each of these activities represented by "business streams." In many respects, however, the company's corporate level had a stronger substantive role toward the businesses, and the way it exerted that role was considerably influenced by the management approach developed in the company's original oil business.

BP did not have, as of 1986, a distinct corporate functional unit for acquisitions. Acquisitions as a "special investment" did face additional hurdles and lower approval limits than did internal investment decisions. A tradition of acquisition postmortems existed as part of the broader brief of a corporate post-project appraisal unit.

"Unichem," an American chemical firm similarly diversified across a broad range of chemical areas, including agricultural products, petrochemicals, plastics, pharmaceuticals, and some consumer products, was the third firm studied.[7]

Whereas some of its nonchemical businesses were managed on a stand-alone basis, Unichem's chemical businesses were, within its multibillion dollar European division, managed through an integrated functional/geographic matrix, dominated by strong functional management in R&D, manufacturing, and sales.

Unichem did not treat acquisitions significantly differently from other investments, except for additional due process areas.

Cooperation was gained from these companies to select a sample of both successful and unsuccessful acquisitions and to provide broad-based and prolonged access. The companies also contributed in part to the expenses of the study in return for limited feedback on their observed acquisition practices. Because of the competitive overlap among these companies, the research process in each remained confidential to the other until such time and to such extent that the material to illustrate the learning was formally released.

SELECTION OF THE ACQUISITION SAMPLE

Within these companies with a rich history of acquisitions (particularly BP and ICI), a sample of acquisitions was identified that corresponded to the following criteria:

1. They should be *divisional* rather than corporate acquisitions, not necessarily in terms of where the idea originated, but in terms of how they would ultimately be incorporated. Our purpose was to examine the organizational process of decision making, as well as the integration process with existing operating units. Our preliminary investigation had led to the judgment that corporate acquisitions are characterized by a very different process.

2. They should have taken place *more than two years but less than five years* from the start of the research. This window was seen as the best trade-off between allowing time for the integration process to occur and not too far in the past to allow for the presence and recall of key actors. Whereas one of the acquisitions selected was only a year old, the data-gathering phase itself would take two full years, and a special point was made of revisiting the site much later.

3. Across companies we would seek to pair a sample of acquisitions that, with respect to corporate strategy, represented *domain strengthening, domain extension,* and *domain exploration,* as defined in Chapter 2.

4. Within each of these categories in each company we would attempt to select two acquisitions, one clearly *successful* and one clearly *unsuccessful.* This approach was chosen to maximize the variance in the sample and to sidestep the conceptual and practical difficulties of defining acquisition success precisely. To make the practical selection, a judgment was based on three combined criteria. An acquisition was considered clearly successful if (1) its performance exceeded the expected performance in the original form acquisition justification, (2) its returns outperformed the average of its industry, and (3) it was considered successful by well-informed managers without direct responsibility for the acquisition, such as strategic planning and corporate control staff.

5. Among the diversifying acquisitions (domain extension and domain prospection) we would try to include in our sample sequences both *platform* acquisitions and *position* acquisitions (see Chapter 2 for a definition). Our preliminary data gathering had led us to observe that new domain building in practice proceeded through sequences of acquisitions, complemented with internal development.

On the basis of the resulting grid, which implied ideally six acquisitions per company (see Exhibit A-2), discussions were held with corporate staff managers informed about the companies' acquisition history.

	DOMAIN STRENGTHENING	DOMAIN EXTENSION	DOMAIN EXPLORATION
SUCCESSFUL	(1)	(3) Platform/Position	(5) Platform/Position
UNSUCCESSFUL	(2)	(4) Platform/Position	(6) Platform/Position

Exhibit A-2 **Acquisition Sample Selection Grid**

A number of acquisitions were jointly selected, incorporating the pragmatic considerations of location and organizational sensitivities. On all of them, access to original acquisition justification documentation at the corporate center was obtained. In the case of BP's acquisitions, this access was more extensive, because the companies internal postproject appraisal unit had conducted its own internal audits and kindly made the source material accessible. With the prospective sample identified and explored, access was sequentially negotiated and cooperation secured from operating management of each acquisition selected within these firms.

DATA-GATHERING PROCESS

Between June 1986 and January 1988, data were gathered in all three companies for eleven acquisitions, including four that were domain exploring, three that were domain extending and four that were domain-strengthening. The research team consisted of Haspeslagh and a research associate (either Alison Farquhar or Sarah Williams), who conducted scheduled sets of interviews. Often the research associate remained at the site to make sure that promised archival data or documents not to be removed from the site were fully accessed and to conduct follow-up interviews suggested during the meeting or prompted by the data. Interview notes were typed out on the basis of the comparison of handwritten notes of both researchers. The research associates also assisted in drafting research cases on which subsequent analysis, as well as pedagogical material development, was based.

To obtain insight into the formal and informal corporate acquisition decision-making processes, several avenues were explored. Data were gathered on the investment approval procedures, and interviews were conducted in each company with the corporate (European, in the case of Unichem) staff managers responsible for strategic planning, finance, internal control, and the secretaries to the capital expenditure committee. In ICI, we also interviewed members of the corporate acquisition team, and in BP, members of the post-project appraisal unit.

Data gathering on each acquisition began with prolonged meetings with the designated "gatekeeper" for each acquisition to obtain further access to original acquisition justification data, as well as a number of later memos and reports, mainly reorganization data and subsequent performance data. At the same time, a chronology of main events was prepared and a group of people to be interviewed was selected. The initial interviews for each acquisition involved between ten and twenty people per acquisition and included: the head of the host structure and his key staff, the heads (including prior heads or selling owners) of the acquired companies and some of their key staff, managers from the acquirer appointed in the acquired company in interface management roles, plus, in most cases, managers and personnel managers of the geographic side of the matrix where the acquisition was located.

A second round of interviews was made in each acquisition more than a year after the first interviews. The second round involved all heads of the host structures, the gatekeepers, the general managers of the units, and some other staff. These interviews clarified conflicting or missing data and updated the researchers on developments and performance.

During this second round, the researchers departed from their detached data-gathering mode; this phase included a feedback component for each firm. A brief summary of observations was presented in the ICI and BP businesses, whereas in Unichem feedback took the form of a Francoplast case discussion with all the original actors involved.

Strategic Interdependence/Organizational Autonomy Framework

In June 1987, with complete case dossiers on the first seven acquisitions, a period was set aside by the research team for analysis and comparison of a broad range of variables that had emerged or had been used by other researchers, including size, platform versus position, quality of management, financial performance, relatedness, managed interdependence, and cultural difference. From these informal discussions, in which Haspeslagh's insights greatly benefited from Farquhar's and Williams's questioning and comments, the conflicting needs of *strategic interdependence* and *organizational autonomy need* tentatively emerged as the most significant variables in understanding available acquisition integration approaches.

The issue of interdependence had been central to our thinking from the outset of the project, but it achieved its impact only when combined with the insight that continued cultural difference might be both functional and dysfunctional. The three integration approaches that these combined variables defined, which we labeled absorption, preservation, and symbiosis, seemed to best capture the integration processes we had observed. More importantly, as we distinguished between our successful and unsuccessful acquisitions, they seemed to provide most clues on the link between integration and performance.

During the summer of 1987, the data from each of the first seven acquisitions were re-analyzed in light of these emerging variables, and an accompanying review of the organizational theory literature was made. Following our earlier work, the strategic interdependence variable was operationalized as varying in density depending on whether the main strategic capability transfer involved: resource sharing, operational skill transfer, general management skill transfer, or automatic benefits.[8]

The organizational autonomy need variable was operationalized through two concepts. One, which was termed the *functionality* of this distinct cultural embeddedness, responded to the question whether the strategic capability would be in peril if the difference in culture was not maintained. If so, a further distinction was made with the notion of *specificity,* which examined whether the strategic capability was embedded in a well-defined component of the acquired organization or was tied to diffuse properties. Using this relatively crude operationalization, we investigated three aspects for each of the acquisitions: the planned integration mode, the de facto integration mode, and the objective integration mode.

The *planned* integration mode was determined by excerpting organizational integration intentions and arguments from the documents related to the acquisition justification, with particular emphasis on planned interdependencies and considerations of autonomy.

The *de facto* integration mode was determined by examining the actual interdependences that had been managed, and the degree to which the acquired unit, or parts thereof, had been left autonomous. Both retroactive analysis over time and a snapshot at the time of the research were made.

The analysis of the *objective* integration mode represented a necessarily subjective attempt by the researchers, with the benefit of hindsight, to determine the objective needs for integration and autonomy that were called for, given the companies' stated strategic objectives for the acquisition. Depending on the acquisition, two or three of the researchers who had been intensively involved scored each acquisition separately. These individual views were then reconciled to come to a consensus judgment. This resulting judgment remained subjective and imprecise, especially in light of the fact that the choice of integration approach is, to an extent, discretionary. The procedure was maintained, however, because it provided interesting insight into the relation between integration and performance (see Chapter 8). And precisely because our sample consisted of extremes, it allowed us to feel comfortable with our judgments when they differed from those practiced by the firms involved.

The resulting conceptualization formed on the basis of the first seven acquisition dossiers was first written up and presented in October 1987 (Haspeslagh and Farquhar, 1987) and a later version upon completion of all eleven dossiers in October 1988.

VALIDATION IN A FOURTH SITE

Because of decreasing returns to further acquisition data gathering in our sites, length of stay in the sample companies, our interest in validating of the emerging integration framework, and the desire to obtain a wider range of observations on corporate acquisition decision making, we decided not to examine further acquisitions that would have completed the grid in the three companies. Instead, we chose to seek access to a fourth company known to be different on several key dimensions.

Readers less familiar with clinical research may raise the issue of comparability of sites. In clinical field research, adding a site is not an issue of statistical sampling. It derives from finding out whether the properties of a model that was constructed and the behavior of its elements hold in situations that are known to be different from the one in which the model was developed. Validation comes in a Popperian sense from putting the model at risk in the environment of experience. The value of comparative field research relies on the fact that, in addition to giving the model another test, it helps to sharpen it by allowing further contingencies that fit closer with the observed variants of the system under scrutiny (Christenson, 1972). The following characteristics were sought:

- Same industry environment.
- A reputation for effective acquisition decision making without resorting to a separate acquisition function.
- Access to three additional acquisitions whose settings might provide a test of the emerging integration framework.

Research access was obtained to study the BASF corporation, a $10 billion-plus diversified chemical firm with related linked diversification in such areas as raw materials and energy, dyestuffs, fibers, plastics, paints, agricultural chemicals, etc.

The company's organizational approach consisted of a very integrated management style in which three sides of the matrix—business, area, and function—reported to a member of the *Vorstand* (management committee), whose responsibility included oversight of some businesses, some areas, and some functions. The company's acquisition decision process did not have a corporate acquisition function. Although it did have a separate committee for special projects such as acquisitions, the corporate finance function had a different involvement in acquisitions than in other investments. The same manager in corporate planning followed up on all the acquisition dossiers.

Within BASF the three acquisitions that were selected included the acquisition of Inmont Paints by BASF Paints, the acquisition of American Enka by BASF Fiber, and the acquisition of Celanese Advanced Materials Business by BASF Advanced Materials. Data gathering, which took place between October 1987 and January 1988, emphasized the corporate decision-making process for acquisitions. In addition to selective document access, all members of the *Vorstand* in the companies' matrix who were business wise or geographically responsible for the acquisition in question were interviewed, as well as those who oversaw finance and R&D. Interviews included all three division managers, several of their staff, and several of the BASF North America area's staff. Whereas the acquisition integration framework was largely corroborated in the subsequent data analysis, our thinking on acquisition decision-making approaches was vastly enriched by the contrast brought by a non-American, non-British company. Differences in acquisition decision making could be traced to the much more deeply rooted differences in resource allocation processes in our research sites, which we described in Chapter 4. From this reanalysis of our data also stem our observations on the dimensions of quality of the observed acquisition justifications, which we discussed in Chapter 3.

EXTENSION OF THE RESEARCH

The last phase of Haspeslagh's data gathering, which took place as this book was being written, sought focus on two related issues that had emerged from the prior research as important areas, but for which no rich material was yet available. One was the special issues implicit in the making of numerous and rapid acquisitions, which we came to call the problems of "strategic assembly." The second was the transition from acquisition integration to ongoing management of operations. While extending the data gathering outside the chemical industry, we were able to obtain access to two experienced acquirers coping with exactly those issues.

One was Valmet, a Finnish paper machinery manufacturer, and the other (investigated in collaboration with INSEAD colleague Associate Professor Sumantra Ghoshal) was Electrolux, a Swedish appliance manufacturer. In each a series of interviews was conducted at the corporate level and within one domain-strengthening acquisition: Valmet acquired KMW, a Swedish paper machinery maker; and Electrolux acquired Zanussi, an Italian white goods firm. The research teams (which included H. Mattila in the Valmet-KMW acquisition and L. Andersen, N. De Sanctis, B. Finzi, and J. Franzan in the Electrolux-Zanussi acquisition) conducted about twenty interviews in each organization, including senior operating management, senior acquired company management, and corporate staff members in charge of planning, human resource management, finance and acquisitions. Investigations at these two sites refined our insights into absorption acquisitions and led to the ideas described in Chapter 15.

CONCLUSION

Throughout these research projects, informal discussions with other researchers, other managers with the members of the various research teams, and between the authors sharpened questions and concepts at each stage. A number of executive audiences have responded to the ideas in ways that provide face validity to them. Nevertheless, this remains small-sample, theory-building research, inviting replication and extension. Both Jemison (with Sitkin) and Haspeslagh are in the process of replication within the financial services sector, with the American savings and loans restructuring and the European banking restructuring as fertile ground.

Other issues for further research include the differences in management approaches among firms using acquisitions, joint ventures, license agreements, and other forms of strategic alliances as forms of renewal.[9] Our examination of acquisition decision making in American, British, French, German, Italian, and Japanese companies brought strong cross-cultural differences in corporate investment decision-making processes that merit systematic pursuit. The investigation of the organizational coordination challenges of strategic assemblers as they compete against more integrated firms merits much fuller study, possibly in contrast to the local adaptation challenges faced by their more integrated counter-parts.

Every research stream builds on previous work and is likely to open more doors than it closes. We look forward to joining in continuing studies of these phenomena, which are intellectually interesting and have important implications for practice.

B

Prior Research on Mergers and Acquisitions

A BRIEF SUMMARY AND OVERVIEW

As THE FREQUENCY, number, and size of acquisitions have increased, acquisitions have inevitably drawn the attention of many groups of scholars, each of whom studies the subject from a unique perspective. This appendix provides an overview of the research on mergers and acquisitions. Provided as a broad background document, it assumes that the reader has little prior knowledge of the topic. The scope of research on acquisitions is much too broad for an in-depth coverage in this limited space. Accordingly, our intention here is to provide a representative sample of the research contributions of different areas so that interested readers can pursue these questions in more depth at their convenience.

Three broadly defined schools of thought exist that offer insights into merger and acquisition activity. For the sake of reporting convenience, we refer to them as the *capital markets* school, the *strategy* school, and the *organizational behavior* school. Recently also a number of scholars have combined strategic and organizational considerations, adopting what we will call a *process* school on acquisitions. Although all of these schools pursue questions related to mergers and acquisitions, each line of research is anchored in a different central question, and each approaches its question from a particular perspective, with different sets of assumptions, and with a different set of methodologies.

The central question asked by financial economists on whose research the capital markets view is based, is, "Do mergers and acquisitions create value and if so for whom?" Their broad conclusion after studying stock prices of acquiring and target firms during periods surrounding the merger announcement is that, in general, the shareholders of the acquired firm benefit but those from the acquiring firm do not. Overall they conclude that acquisitions create value, and hence, that an active market for corporate control should be encouraged.

Strategy researchers look at two issues of interest to individual firms. Some empirical researchers examine what types of acquisitions are more likely to be successful for an acquiring firm. This group often focuses on the extent to which an acquisition is related to the firm's existing businesses. Other strategy researchers are interested in providing firms with logical advice on how to search for and evaluate acquisitions so as to have a proper "strategic fit."

Organizational behavior scholars in turn are concerned with the broad question of what effect acquisitions have on individuals and organizations. Their studies generally focus on determining the impact of acquisitions on the individuals in each firm and on the problems relating to a lack of "organizational fit" or "cultural fit."

Finally, some researchers are combining strategic and organizational considerations to address how the acquisition *process* affects the attainment of strategic objectives.

THE CAPITAL MARKETS SCHOOL

The financial economists' perspective on acquisitions focuses on the net wealth gains that are achieved when a firm's assets are purchased by a different group of investors. Ownership is changed because the new investors believe that they can put the assets to better use than can existing management. By following changes in stock price after adjusting for overall market fluctuations, these scholars attempt to determine whether wealth has been created as a result of a merger or acquisition.

Financial economists base their work on several fundamental concepts: the efficient markets hypothesis, agency theory, free cash flow, the market for corporate control, and the capital asset pricing model. Efficient market theory suggests that the market value of a firm's stock price reflects an unbiased estimate of all publicly available information about the firm's future cash flows and their related risks. Thus, it is argued, any acquisition that causes an immediate increase in market value (after normal market fluctuations are adjusted for) is good, and one that causes an immediate decrease in market value is bad. Using this perspective, financial economists have concluded, after extensive research, that acquisitions on the average do not create value for shareholders of the acquiring firm. The same studies reveal, however, that, on the average, a significant premium accrues to the acquired firm's shareholders.[1]

Agency theory views managers as the agents of stockholders and avers that agency problems arise when managers' and stockholders' interests are not congruent (Holmström, 1979; Fama, 1980). It has long been recognized that managers' interests may diverge from those of the firm's owners (Berle and Means, 1932). For example, a manager's pay, power, and prestige typically are closely related to the size of the company. Consequently, the manager, acting in her own self-interest, may choose to invest company funds in projects that increase the size of the company, even though doing so will not always be profitable (Mueller, 1969). To limit this self-interested behavior, firms must incur costs to monitor the agent's behavior. See Eisenhardt (1989a) for an excellent review of agency theory and its application to strategic and organizational research.

If a firm has cash remaining after all projects on which the returns equal or exceed the cost of capital have been funded, it is said to have free cash flow (Jensen, 1987). Since any investment beyond this should be expected to destroy shareholder value, free cash flow, financial economists argue, should be paid out to shareholders so that they can reinvest it in other more productive uses. To the extent that agency costs are high, and companies have a free cash flow, the threat of a takeover may be an effective disciplining mechanism to force managers to return the free cash flow to the shareholders.

Manne (1965), who first introduced the concept of the market for corporate control, proposed that "the control of corporations may constitute a valuable asset; . . . that an active market for corporate control exists, and that a great many mergers are probably the result of the successful workings of this special market" (p. 112). Corporate control can be defined as the right to determine the management of corporate resources, including the right to hire, fire, and set top-level management compensation rates (Fama and Jensen, 1983a, 1983b). The market for corporate control exists because one group of investors is willing to pay more than another group for the right to manage the firm. The market for corporate control, then, is "the arena in which alternative management teams compete for the rights to manage corporate resources" (Jensen and Ruback, 1983, p. 6).

The capital asset pricing model provides a framework for assessing the rate of return that the market expects an asset to earn, given its riskiness.[2] Riskiness is seen to consist of an unsystematic component that is company-specific and can be diversified away by investors and a systematic component that cannot be diversified away. To measure the latter component, the model compares the volatility of the companies' earnings with the volatility of the stock market. This measure of systematic risk is referred to as the beta coefficient. The model essentially postulates that the opportunity cost of equity is equal to the risk-free rate of return plus the firm's systematic risk (beta) multiplied by the market price of risk (the market risk premium, which is the difference between the average market return for equity, and the risk-free rate.)

The methodology financial economists use to study the performance impact of acquisitions measures the changes in stock prices that occur over a short period surrounding the acquisition announcement to determine net stock price gains or losses through so-called event studies (Brown and Warner, 1980, provides an overview of event study methodology). When the market values of the acquiring and target firms change after the acquisition announcement, and the net change (beyond that attributed to movement of the market in general) is positive, financial economists conclude that wealth has been created.

The rationale for focusing on the period of time around the announcement of the acquisition comes from the efficient market hypothesis. Once an acquisition is announced or becomes known, the present value of the expected benefits of a bidder's acquisition program is considered to be immediately incorporated into the share price of the acquiring and target firms (Malatesta, 1983; Schipper and Thompson, 1983). Financial economists do not consider it necessary to wait for the acquisition to be consummated to determine the result or for integration to take place.

The financial economists are consistent in their key findings, which are that, on average, shareholders of target companies earn significant gains and shareholders of acquiring companies neither gain nor lose. Surveys by Jensen and Ruback (1983) and Jarrell, Brickley, and Netter (1988) bring together a variety of different studies and find that in the United States, on average, target company shareholders gain between 20 and 30 percent. Shareholders of bidding companies, on the other hand, gain between 0 and 4 percent. Similar findings result from studies in other countries, including Australia (Dodd, 1976), Belgium (Gagnon, Brehain, Broquet, and Guerra, 1982), Canada (Eckbo, 1986), France (Eckbo and Langohr, 1985; Husson, 1986), and the United Kingdom (Franks, Broyles, and Hecht, 1977). For an overview, see Husson (1987, pp. 53–81). From these findings financial economists conclude that acquisitions and mergers benefit society by creating wealth.

Sources of Gains in Takeovers

The source of gains in takeovers in general has been another area of study by financial economists. If the gains are merely the result of some other party's losses (what we called in Chapter 2 value capture or transfer, for example, from previous shareholders, the government through tax benefits, or bondholders), the financial economist cannot state that resources have been re-allocated so as to improve efficiency and create wealth. But if the researchers cannot find a plausible theory to explain target gains in takeovers in terms of losses to another party, they can conclude that it is reasonable to believe that wealth is not merely redistributed in takeovers but is created.

Some suggest that stockholders' gains come from bondholders' losses—an event that some theorists state will occur when the acquiring firm pays cash for a riskier target. An extensive study by Dennis and McConnell (1986) does not support this view. Another view is that gains result from tax-related manipulations of the target company's assets. The evidence on tax motivations of mergers is mixed. Auerbach and Reishus (1987) found tax benefits to be significant enough to influence the merger decision in potentially 20 percent of mergers in a study of 318 mergers between 1968 and 1983. Gilson, Scholes, and Wolfson (1988) explored the circumstances under which acquisitions might be tax motivated. They concluded that a host of definitional problems regarding tax favoritism, information costs, and transaction costs make it difficult to argue that tax benefits are indeed motives for acquisitions or that acquisitions are the best way in which firms can capture certain tax advantages. Another study of leveraged buyouts from 1980–1984 (Lehn and Poulsen, 1988) found a direct relationship between potential tax benefits and premiums paid. Jarrell, Brickley, and Netter (1988), after a review of a variety of studies, concluded that much of the takeover activity in the last twenty years has not been tax motivated.

Shleifer and Summers (1988) argue that gains from takeovers arise as new management breaks the implicit contracts that exist between the firm and stakeholder groups. These gains come from transferring wealth from stakeholders (such as employees or suppliers) by changing employment conditions, wages, or prices for purchased goods. Shleifer and Vishny (1988c) reviewed studies that link acquisitions to poor target company management performance. Their review shows that companies have not been successful in instituting controls to prevent managers from performing activities that do not maximize shareholder wealth. Moreover, the study of hostile takeovers by Mørck, Shleifer, and Vishny (1988) suggests that such takeovers occur in rapidly declining or changing industries in companies where managers fail to shrink operations rapidly enough or to make other adjustments. These findings support the propositions that agency costs exist which new investor groups believe they can reduce.

The finding that acquiring firms do not gain as a result of a takeover begs the question as to why merger activities continue. Lubatkin (1983) offers several possible explanations for this apparent riddle. He proposes that perhaps mergers do not actually provide real benefits, but that mergers continue to take place either because managers make mistakes when estimating the value of proposed mergers, or because managers seek to maximize their own wealth at the expense of stockholders' wealth. Alternatively, Lubatkin proposes that perhaps mergers do provide real benefits, but that administrative problems accompanying the merger may wipe out its benefits. Consistent with Jensen's discussion of the difficulty of measuring returns to bidders is Lubatkin's explanation that perhaps the methodologies employed have not been adequate to reveal the benefits. A final reason Lubatkin offers for the continued frequency of acquisition activity in spite of the evidence of the absence of returns to bidders may be that only certain types of merger strategies benefit the stockholders of the acquiring firm.

Along these lines, Roll (1986) accepts the efficient market hypothesis but finds empirical studies that assess the combined value of the target and bidding firms after a takeover to be inconclusive. In response he has proposed the "Hubris Hypothesis," which states, "If there actually are no aggregate gains in takeovers, the phenomenon depends on the overbearing presumption of bidders that their valuations are correct" (p. 199). In other words, management persists in overvaluing target companies.

These findings illustrate how financial economists combine the concepts of efficient markets, agency theory, the market for corporate control and free cash flow with the technique of event studies to develop explanations of merger and acquisition activity.

Alternative Viewpoints

Some finance scholars do not accept the basic assumptions of the financial economists including the view that the market for corporate control is the primary mechanism to discipline managers, that event studies are a valid means of measuring wealth creation, and that the stock market is efficient in accurately valuing companies.

Researchers who apply techniques other than event studies to available data draw different conclusions about the benefits of mergers and acquisitions. For example, Ravenscraft and Scherer (1987) argue that longer time-based findings show that on average, tender offer targets were underperformers by about 8 percent relative to their home industry norms, and that profit performance neither improved nor deteriorated significantly following takeover.

These scholars, who do not accept the premise that the stock market is always efficient, offer different explanations of acquisitions from those offered by financial economists. Scherer (1988) theorizes that if the stock market does not always properly value stock, then at any given time some companies will be overvalued, empowering them to acquire new companies, and some companies will be undervalued, making them attractive targets. Overvalued firms will examine selected potential target firms to determine whether they are undervalued. As potential targets are scrutinized prior to an acquisition, their stock prices rise. Companies that are found to be undervalued are acquired, and their new stock price merely reflects a market correction. Companies that are not acquired after being scrutinized are not undervalued, not acquired, and their stock prices return to pre-acquisition levels.

Using the Capital Markets Perspective for Strategic Purposes

There are two major problems with applying a capital markets perspective when considering acquisitions from a strategic perspective. The first is that important assumptions in the model do not reflect the realities of the managerial world. The second is the conception of the firm that this perspective implies.

The capital markets view makes several important assumptions about both internal firm operations and external market efficiency. Regarding market efficiency, it assumes that shareholders can understand the way in which a firm's strategy will evolve and thus value the firm according to their risk preferences for that strategy. This assumption contradicts a good deal of what we know about strategy, how it is developed, and how it evolves. Recent research suggests that strategy is not a predictable, deterministic process but an evolving set of decisions about how a firm will relate to its environment.[3] Even if they were completely predictable, many of the managerial decisions about how the firm will relate to its environment are proprietary. To reveal them to the investment community would weaken the firm's competitive position.

In addition to assuming that a firm's strategy is predictable, the capital markets perspective assumes that the probable cash streams associated with an acquisition can be predicted. Although analysts may make their best estimates, these estimates may not be informed enough or robust enough to reflect adequately the cash streams expected from an acquisition. As a consequence, the less able we are to understand or predict the actions needed to change the firm's cash stream, the less able we are to predict whether an acquisition will create value.

Finally, the capital markets view assumes more internal firm efficiency than is present in the managerial world. In particular, the assumption that managers and employees consistently act on behalf of the shareholders contradicts a powerful stream of research that points to many motives for managerial behavior other than maximizing shareholder wealth. Donaldson and Lorsch (1983) argue that managers are committed to corporate survival and maximization of corporate wealth—financial assets, human assets, and competitive position. Other research points to the moral hazard problem in managerial decision making, managers' inability to maximize outcomes, and the prevalence of satisficing behavior.[4]

The surge of management buyouts in the United States and Great Britain during the late 1980s may reflect, in part, the inherent assumptions of the capital markets model. A firm's managers who are familiar with its potential see the opportunity to buy the assets of their firms at bargain prices. Their firms are undervalued because investors either don't understand the business portfolio well enough to value it properly or because they lack the perspective or patience to hold the shares long enough for the managers' strategy to bear fruit. Thus the managers, with better information about the strategy and its implications, are willing to stake their personal capital on a belief in the firm's true value.

Despite these and other problematic assumptions, the American and British business environments largely accept the capital markets perspective and the impact on current shareholder value as the overriding benchmark by which to judge the quality of acquisition decisions. This view may have become predominant in the United States because most acquisitions research has been financially oriented with an emphasis on measuring the outcome. Changes in the share price provide a convenient but hazardous and single-minded measuring stick. Beyond the United States (and among a minority in the United States), the acceptance of these elegant but restrictive assumptions is by no means universal. A dispassionate comparison of managerial practices in other business environments, e.g., Japan, Germany, and Switzerland, suggests that corporate boards are much more reluctant to use this yardstick, which is tied to short-term performance. The measurement and rewards systems for managers in this group tend to focus on long-term firm performance and the accomplishment of strategic objectives over time.

THE STRATEGIC SCHOOL

In contrast to the financial economists' perspective, which is primarily interested in the efficiency impact of acquisitions on the economy, the strategic school is interested in their impact on individual firms. Among strategy researchers studying acquisitions, two subgroups can be distinguished. One group of researchers shares the financial economists' interest in performance, sometimes using their methodology of event studies, to uncover variables that might discriminate between different types of acquisitions and consequent performance levels. We will call this group the *acquisition performance* group. Another group of writers has been interested in developing strategic analysis concepts to improve acquisition performance. In this broad category, which we will call the *acquisition planning* group, one finds a number of academics, consultants, and reflective practitioners who draw on their acquisition experience to prescribe a better way of analyzing acquisitions.

THE ELUSIVE STRATEGY PERFORMANCE LINKAGE

Claiming that the average performance findings of financial economists are of little relevance to the strategist in individual firms, strategic performance researchers have set out to examine the performance impact of a whole series of characteristics of the acquirer, the target, or the relation among them. The variables deemed to be associated positively with performance include relative size, market share, pre-acquisition profitability, and pre-acquisition growth and pre-acquisition experience (e.g., Kitching, 1967, 1974; Fowler and Schmidt, 1989).

The issue of relatedness has received the greatest attention. The antecedents of the research on relatedness in acquisitions are found in the studies on corporate diversification (Gort, 1962; Rumelt, 1974, 1982; Jacquemin and Berry, 1979; Bettis, 1981; Montgomery and Christensen, 1981; Bettis and Hall, 1982). Ramanujam and Varadarajan (1989) provide a comprehensive review of diversification and performance; also see Kim (1989). These studies found a clear association, though not necessarily a causal relationship, between relatedness among activities of the firm as a whole and its performance.

Rumelt's original findings (1974) pointed to the relative superiority (in terms of capital productivity) of related-constrained firms over related-linked firms, which outperformed unrelated diversified firms. Rumelt (1982), in a subsequent re-analysis of his earlier findings, pointed to the industry effect (related diversifiers tend to be in high-barrier industries that are more profitable). Christensen and Montgomery (1981) further found that market structure variables moderated the relationship between diversification and performance. Bettis and Hall (1982), who also explored this industry effect using Rumelt's sample, pointed to an overrepresentation of pharmaceutical companies in the related constrained category, an industry noted for high profitability. Most subsequent studies have supported both the robustness of Rumelt's classification scheme (Montgomery, 1982) and its basic finding (Bettis, 1981; Palepu, 1985).

In contrast, however, support for relatedness as a determinant of *acquisition* performance is inconclusive at best. Early acquisition studies using managerial judgment as performance variables reported that related acquisitions outperformed unrelated ones (Kitching, 1974). These studies have not been supported by research focusing on operating or stock market performance data. In an event study of 439 acquiring firms and 430 targets, Elgers and Clark (1980) found that conglomerate mergers offered superior wealth effects for both acquiring and selling stockholders than did nonconglomerate mergers. Similar findings are reported by Chatterjee (1986), who concluded that targets in unrelated mergers perform better than those in related mergers.

Yet Singh and Montgomery (1987), in an event study of 203 target firms covering the period 1970–1978, report higher abnormal returns for related targets. Shelton (1988), in a study of 218 acquisitions in the 1962–1983 period, comes to similar conclusions, showing significant returns for both horizontal acquisitions and related-supplementary ones (same products to new customers), whole unrelated acquisitions show a negative, though not significant, correlation. Lubatkin (1987), on the other hand, in a sample of 340 target firms between 1948 and 1975, concluded that related mergers do *not* create more value than unrelated ones.

A number of explanations have been offered for these mixed findings on relatedness (Haspeslagh and Farquhar, 1987; Kim, 1989; Seth, 1990). Some are methodological, including sampling biases and problems of measurement. Several of the studies, for example, focus on acquirer gains, as opposed to the sum of gains to both bidder and targets, which confounds the value creation of the acquisition with its appropriation by the acquirer. In addition, some important variables may not be controlled for. For example, as Kim and his colleagues have pointed out, the large companies in the sample of the diversification researchers have very different profiles in terms of international diversification, and none of these studies controls for the degree of internationalization (Kim, 1989; Kim, Hwang, and Burgers, 1989). Yet a strong association has been observed between international diversification and performance (Wolf, 1975, 1977; Rugman, 1979).

Another issue concerns the relatedness categories themselves. Categories originally conceived to examine notions of corporate-level relatedness, such as Rumelt's classification, are in this research used to categorize acquisition relatedness at the business level. Unless corporate and business-level diversification are considered simultaneously, acquisition categories fail to capture vital distinctions. For example, unrelated acquisitions by a diversified industrial company (the type of acquisition we described as domain exploring in this book) are very different from similarly unrelated acquisitions in a conglomerate (which is in the business of unrelated diversification).

The most pervasive issue for us, however, is the implicit equation in the strategic performance literature on acquisitions between relatedness and managed interdependence. We have argued elsewhere (Haspeslagh, 1986b; Haspeslagh and Jemison, 1987) that relatedness gives an ex ante indication of potential sources of value creation, but it does not determine the nature, scope, and probability of actual value creation. Taking synergies from relatedness for granted is symptomatic of a more fundamental weakness of the strategy school: its disproportionate emphasis on the strategic task, leaving aside practical impediments to value creation such as interpersonal, interorganizational, and intercultural friction. Even where the exploitation of relatedness through the management of interdependence is intended, acquisitions are characterized by widely varying degrees of success in realizing that potential (Haspeslagh and Farquhar, 1987).

STRATEGIC PLANNING OF ACQUISITIONS

Some strategic management scholars and practitioners have addressed the difficulty of acquisition implementation through a concern for better pre-acquisition analysis and planning (Searby, 1969; Howell, 1970; Salter and Weinhold, 1979; Bradley and Korn 1981; Berman and Wade, 1981) or post-acquisition planning (Howell, 1970).

Central to these prescriptions is the logical decomposition of the acquisition process to a number of steps which include: the definition of acquisition objectives, acquisition search and screening, including the selection of criteria, and the design of a screening/search method, strategic evaluation, financial valuation, and negotiation. The most significant contribution in this stream is Salter and Weinhold's (1979) rich exposition of acquisition analysis. They extensively discuss and illustrate each step and were the first to relate the strategic assessment back to stockholder value creation in light of modern financial theory. In particular, they drew attention to the risk dimension (variation in cash flow), as well as to the return dimension (level of cash flow) in such value creation.

The prescriptions of the strategic planning group are logical and useful to the practicing acquisition analyst, but find their limits in the fact that acquisitions are not ultimately amenable to a planning/implementation approach. The extent of this limit is brought home by one of the performance studies (Souder and Chakrabarti, 1984), which showed how even though acquisitions in the sample were associated with value creation, the dimension along which benefits were reported did not correspond with the original acquisition motivations nor with the expected specific benefits.

THE ORGANIZATIONAL BEHAVIOR SCHOOL

Although the strategy research, on balance, has not considered the problems of implementation, there has been an extensive and eclectic stream of research that has focused on the people aspects of implementation, often to the neglect of strategic requirements. Whereas the financial economists are interested in the impact of the acquisition on the economy and strategic researchers study its impact on a given firm, organizational behavior researchers focus on acquisitions' impact on individuals. Because there is no prevailing paradigm in this literature, we have arbitrarily grouped these contributions into three groups. A *human resource management* tradition has focused on the human problems created by acquisitions and ways to prevent or minimize them. A *crisis* literature focuses on acquisitions as an example of organizational crisis. Finally, *culture* researchers have focused on the cultural compatibility between the two organizations. In addition, individual work has been directed to many other perspectives, such as the effects of communication on acquisitions (Bastien, 1987; Schweiger and DeNisi, 1987; Napier, Simmons, and Stratton, 1989) or the use of symbolism in acquisition language (Hirsch, 1987; Schneider and Dunbar, 1987).

HUMAN RESOURCE IMPACT OF ACQUISITIONS

Numerous articles have been written focusing on the human resource impact of acquisitions and on how this impact can be managed. The tradition ranges from reflective practitioners (Leighton and Tod, 1969; Pritchett, 1987), to academics (Bastien, 1987; Buono and Bowditch, 1989; Hayes, 1979; Ivancevich, Schweiger, and Power, 1987; Levinson, 1970; Marks, 1982; Marks and Mirvis, 1985; Shirley, 1977; Sinetar, 1981; Walter, 1985). For a comprehensive review, see Schweiger and Walsh (1980). The human resources writers cover both the issues associated with the pre-acquisition period, and the impact of post-merger events. Typically only the negative impact is examined, because issues of career opportunity and financial or nonfinancial advancement are never touched upon in these studies. Rather these articles discuss employees' typical feelings of conflict, tension, alienation, career uncertainty, behavioral problems, stress, loss of productivity, concerns about financial security, geographic relocation, and co-worker trust (Sutton, 1983; Sales and Mirvis, 1985; Marks and Mirvis, 1985, Buono, Bowditch and Lewis, 1988).

Some studies have not focused on the impact on those who stay, but on the relation between acquisitions and turnover (e.g., Walsh, 1988). Schweiger and Walsh (1990) note in their review that this complex relationship is moderated by a host of contextual variables. It is interesting to note how different the interpretation of turnover is between the financial economist school and the organizational behavior school. Financial economists view turnover as a potential source of financial gain to acquiring company shareholders, because it implies that inefficient previous management is replaced by value-maximizing new management. In contrast, organizational behavior writers tend to see turnover as the ultimate symptom of a decaying work environment resulting from a poorly managed integration effort (Pritchett, 1985).

The issue of whether the new owners and managers are accepted by managers and employees of the acquired company has also been studied (Shirley, 1977; Graves, 1981). The underlying assumption of these studies is that the identification of the major human problems in an acquisition will facilitate a fairer and less conflictive resolution of the implementation issues.

CRISIS LITERATURE

Another line of organizational research focuses on the collective experiences of individuals in an acquired company. Rooted in the crisis literature, this research views negative consequences of acquisitions, at least to some extent, as rites of passage, a necessary organizational crisis requiring individual members to progress through several stages including shock, defensive retreat, acknowledgment, and finally adaptation (Jick, 1979; Marks, 1982; Devine, 1984). This perspective is translated into the prescriptions of some consultants for the organization of appropriate "mourning" opportunities (Pritchett, 1985).

CULTURAL COMPATIBILITY

Many researchers have seen acquisition integration primarily as a culturally driven phenomenon. Drawing on a literature that examines interorganizational and intraorganizational culture differences (Martin and Siehl, 1983), these researchers argue that when a decision upon a merger is being made, great weight should be given to cultural compatibility between the organizations (Sales and Mirvis, 1985). From the cultural conflict perspective, one reason acquisitions are a conflictive process is that they are likely to involve a one-way imposition of cultural elements by a more powerful group despite the resistance of a less powerful one (Sales and Mirvis, 1985). The degree to which changes are made solely in one organization or distributed across both organizations then becomes an important variable (Bastien and Van de Ven, 1986; Napier, et al. 1989).

In addition to company culture, company history is taken as an influencing factor to the extent that each employee group's history shapes its actions and its understanding of its surroundings. Groups that share a history of conflict and then are called upon to cooperate may already have erected a significant barrier to such cooperation (Blake and Mouton, 1984).

Concerns within the acquired company center around the question of the extent to which it will retain its own identity (Sales and Mirvis, 1985). One proposed response to such cultural concerns is to foster an understanding of the elements of the two firm's cultures and mutual understanding and respect across both organizations (Sales and Mirvis, 1985). Another is the establishment of a high level of communication about the transformation that is to take place (Buono, Bowditch, and Lewis, 1988).

Although they provide an antidote to the financial or strategic perspective on acquisitions, these studies tend to fall into the opposite corner, that is, they let organizational issues outweigh an acquisition's strategic potential and consider integration issues primarily from the standpoint of whether individuals accept the new situation.

THE PROCESS PERSPECTIVE

Recently a fourth research stream, the process perspective has begun to address factors affecting acquisition outcomes. Historically, acquisition outcomes had been seen as a result of achieving both strategic fit and organizational fit between the two firms. But mounting evidence that acquisitions do not yield the desired results calls these perspectives into question. In response, the process perspective has arisen that recognizes that the acquisition process itself is a potentially important determinant of acquisition outcomes (Jemison and Sitkin, 1986a). This perspective retains the important role of issues of strategic fit and organizational fit, but it adds the consideration of how aspects of the acquisition decision making and integration processes can affect the final outcome.

It is in this tradition that the research reported in this book is situated. Jemison's (1986) work was the first to link acquisition outcomes (improvements in competitive advantage) with the integration processes through which those outcomes are achieved (interactions between members in both organizations leading to strategic capability transfer) and to detail some of the problems and facilitating factors arising in the process (Jemison, 1988a). Haspeslagh's work reported here was the first to develop a contingency framework for acquisitions integration that matches the strategic needs with organizational task requirements (Haspeslagh and Farquhar, 1987). Appendix A describes the research methods used in these studies.

The antecedents of a view that balances strategic and organizational considerations are found in Mace and Montgomery's classic work

(1962). On the basis of 275 interviews, the authors develop a perspective that is sensitive to the impact of an acquisition on personnel, which is seen as "sharp and real. . . . Existing work anxieties are compounded by the possibility of possible changes and the entire organization may be diverted from its everyday tasks" (p. 227). Yet the authors do not shy away from the strategic task: "The headquarters executive to whom the acquisition reports must accept the responsibility, and take an active and time-consuming interest in seeing that the newly added company becomes part of the total operating structure" (p 243). They clearly focus on the importance of the process as they conclude (p. 230):

> The value to be derived from an acquisition depends largely upon the skill with which the administrative problems of integration are handled. Many potentially valuable acquired corporate assets have been lost by neglect and by poor handling during the integration process.
>
> Each organization acquired is composed of a unique combination of human and physical assets, and it is the job of the acquiring company management to motivate and administer the unique group to achieve the objectives which made the arrangement appear to be a good deal in the first place.

Another eminently practical narrative is provided by one of the rare corporate-sponsored merger accounts that is detailed and painstakingly balanced. In detailing the merger decision-making process of the CIBA and GEIGY merger, supported by facsimiles of the original documents, Erni (1979) details the overriding importance of the interaction process between members of both firms and the role of top management leadership in keeping the merger on track.

Recently a number of academic researchers have addressed process-related issues or espoused a process view. Haspeslagh and Farquhar (1987, p. 6) note:

> A useful framework for conceptualizing acquisition issues cannot be divorced from either a strategic task or an organizational perspective. . . . [Analyses of the] sources of synergy can only yield an evaluation of the potential sources of benefit, since it takes no account of the constraints inherent in the process of benefit realization.

Lindgren (1982) examined both the pre-acquisition decision process and the strategic aspects of post-acquisition management in a sample of acquired subsidiaries of Swedish multinationals. His observations point to the importance of both external and internal consistency and of synergistic effects. External consistency is defined as the extent to which the coordination and control systems meet the need of the strategic and environmental context. Internal consistency corresponds to the extent to which the system fits in the internal systems configuration. Synergistic effects are believed to depend on the extent to which the integration of operating systems achieves potential coordination benefits.

Jemison and Sitkin (1986a), in one of the studies incorporated in this book, addressed a series of process impediments to achieving the expected strategic and organizational fit. They examined the pressures that lead to the segmented nature of pre-acquisition analysis, the escalation of momentum, and the presence of ambiguous expectations. A fourth factor to which they refer, misapplication of management systems, addresses post-acquisition issues.

Duhaime and Schwenk (1985) point to a number of biases in the process, including drawing the wrong analogies, the illusion of control, and the escalation of commitment.

Bastien and Van de Ven (1986) proposed an acquisition process typology based on comparative size (as a proxy for relative power) and institutional affinity between the two organizations involved. Their case studies of eight acquisitions highlight the need for a process-based contingency theory if implications for managers are to be drawn.

Shanley (1987) has tested the performance impact of four different organizational approaches to acquisition integration. He found an autonomous approach to be associated with the best performance and centralized intervention with the worst. Though survey-based research is intrinsically limited in its ability to inform the understanding of a dynamic process, and though the lack of linkage to a strategic purpose results in pooling of data on very different acquisitions, his work provides a very detailed understanding of the administrative post-merger issues.

SUMMARY

In this appendix we contrasted the observations of researchers from financial economics, strategic management, organizational behavior, as well as acquisition process researchers. Each addressed different questions with a different methodology and different objectives. While scholars from each of those schools continue to examine their partial, albeit important, questions, managers themselves cannot afford the luxury of separating out the questions in their daily decision making about acquisitions. Yet an understanding of the findings of those diverse schools and the limits of those findings can be an important aid to managerial decision making.

C

Assessing an Acquisition's Attractiveness

INTRODUCTION

THIS APPENDIX IS DESIGNED to serve as a template to highlight important questions that should be addressed before an acquisition is made. Its focus is on the *strategic evaluation* of the acquisition opportunity and on the aspects of the acquisition *integration approach* that need to be clarified to make such strategic evaluation realistic. Answers to these questions should result in a valid set of assumptions for subsequent financial valuation. For financial evaluation, other sources are available which explain in detail various approaches that can be followed.[1]

USING THIS APPENDIX

We wish to emphasize that because of the complex nature of acquisitions, using this set of questions will provide a *way of thinking* and a sense of how an acquisition opportunity may fit rather than a set of precise answers. The process of a management team working together to discuss and answer these questions should offer important insights into an acquisition opportunity. The end result of the evaluation process will be a meaningful justification for an acquisition which can form the basis of an acquisition dossier. The process is also a valuable vehicle for communication between operating divisions and corporate headquarters.

The components of an acquisition justification (Chapter 3) include answers to these questions:

How *strategic* is this acquisition opportunity in terms of its potential impact on the firm's strategies and competitive positions?

How *shared* within our organization is the view of how this acquisition will be managed to create value?

How *specific* are our insights into the sources of expected benefits and costs of this acquisition?

How far have we thought through the *organizational approach* that will be required to create the value?

How clear among decision makers is the *timing* and the *path* that integration will have to follow?

Because each company is organized differently and faces different acquisition challenges, our questions should be modified to suit those needs.[2] We have cross-referenced this appendix to different chapters in our book and provided a variety of references.

Depending on the situation, or on the stage in the acquisition evaluation process, complete answers to all the questions may not be available. It is important to pinpoint important unanswered questions, so that additional data gathering or the negotiation process itself can be used for clarification.

We have organized our template for acquisition assessment into nine parts as indicted below. In all the questions, the form "we" is used to suggest that an acquisition analysis and the resulting acquisition justification are perceived as an internal process and document.

OUTLINE OF AN ACQUISITION ASSESSMENT

1. Executive Summary.
2. The Acquisition Logic in General.
3. Assessing Industry Attractiveness.
4. Assessing Country Attractiveness.
5. Assessing the Company by Itself.
6. Acquisition Logic: The Company with Us.
7. Managing the Integration Process.
8. Scenarios for Financial Valuation.
9. Financial Valuation of the Target Firm.

SECTION 1: EXECUTIVE SUMMARY

The executive summary provides a concise logic for the acquisition. Because it is the first item in writing, the executive summary sets the tone for what the reader will expect. It should be written in prose and emphasize the strategic impact of the particular acquisition candidate. The prose is important because it will help limit the tendency toward mechanical thinking. The questions we provide throughout this appendix are intended to be woven into a logic by the team preparing the dossier. Sources of items for the Executive Summary are indicated by the section of Appendix C where they are discussed in detail.

1.1 Summarize the acquisition logic from Section 2.

What is the relation between this acquisition and the corporate or business strategy? Discuss in broad terms (domain penetration versus extension or prospection; platform versus position) as well as more specifically.

Does the acquisition imply a need to revise the strategy of the business? What elements, other than the acquisition opportunity itself, have brought about this need?

What other alternatives, including acquisitions, partnership possibilities, and internal development, were considered?

1.2 Provide a short description of the opportunity:

Name

Activities

What would we be buying? (a business, a part of a business, a diversified firm where we would keep only part of it, key skills, fixed assets . . .)

Size (assets, sales, people, . . .)

Performance: How healthy both competitively and operationally is the firm?

1.3 What is the origin of this acquisition opportunity?

1.4 Which operating manager is proposing this acquisition? Who are the members of the evaluation team?

1.5 Summarize your assessment of the industry (Section 3). Include in your assessment:

Main strategic segments.

A picture of the industry structure.

A prognosis of its evolution (identify your main assumptions).

1.6 Summarize any country-specific considerations (Section 4).

1.7 Summarize your assessment of the company by itself (Section 5):

What are the main strengths and weaknesses of the company in the light of your assessment of the industry evolution?

What is your assessment of the quality of its current management?

What risks does this acquisition expose us to? What has been done to investigate or reduce those risks?

1.8 Summarize how we propose to create value in this acquisition (Section 6):

Through improvements in the company by itself. Which ones?

Through strategic capability transfers between the company and our business(es). Which ones?

Describe briefly how you see this process over time and in organizational terms.

What costs will be involved? What risks? What subsequent investment needs?

1.9 Describe the overall integration approach (Section 6).

1.10 Summarize your assessment of the:

Stand-alone value.

Quantifiable synergy value (operating and nonoperating).

Unquantifiable benefits and risk component.

1.11 Summarize key environmental, legal, fiscal issues, or any other broader aspects that need investigation.

1.12 Conclusions and recommendations:

What are the next steps in the acquisition process?

What key ambiguities need to be resolved?

What approach to the company or the bidding process is recommended?

SECTION 2: THE ACQUISITION LOGIC IN GENERAL

2.1 What is the broad strategic logic behind this acquisition? How does this logic correspond with the approved strategy for this business area? (see Chapters 2 and 6.)

If the acquisition's purpose is *domain strengthening,* please clarify:

> The foreseen industry evolution.
>
> What you see as requirements for a viable competitive position. What are key lags or leads in our current competitive position and capabilities?
>
> What would be the broad impact of acquiring this firm on these lags and leads in competitive position and capabilities?
>
> The main sources of the acquisition's impact (combination benefits, resource-sharing opportunities; functional skill transfer; general management improvements).
>
> The magnitude of further investments or acquisitions required to reach a viable position.

If the acquisition is a *domain extension,* please clarify:

> What is the nature of the complementarity in business positions and capabilities?
>
> What strategic capabilities can we bring to the acquired company? From which unit in our organization? To which unit in the acquired company?
>
> What strategic capabilities can the acquired company bring to us? To which units in our organization?
>
> What opportunities for learning from best practice are foreseeable in both directions?
>
> What further strategic options does the acquisition open or fore-close?

If its main purpose is *domain exploration,* please clarify:

> What motivates this unrelated diversification?
>
> What is the potential for nurturing this as a stand-alone business? Why would we be the appropriate host?
>
> Are we likely to be able to provide the funding over time that successful growth may absorb?
>
> What learning do we hope to derive about this business? What is

the potential to leverage this learning in later commitments to this business area?

What learning do we hope to derive for our current business? Why not develop that capability within the current business?

On a very long-term basis, what are the potential synergies between this business area and our current business?

2.2 Choice of renewal mode:

Why should we consider achieving the strategic objective through an acquisition, rather than internally or through a partnership?

What would be the best internal development scenario?

What would be the best partnership scenario?

2.3 Why this company?

How did the opportunity come about?

Why is the company possibly for sale? What are the sellers' motives?

Why this particular company?

Which better alternatives have we dismissed as impossible or impractical?

2.4 What are the strategic implications of *not* acquiring this company?

SECTION 3: ASSESSING INDUSTRY ATTRACTIVENESS

Acquisition evaluation often focuses unduly on the acquisition opportunity itself, rather than on the broader industry in which the acquired firm is a participant. The purpose of this section is to develop a broader understanding with which to evaluate the positioning of the company itself.[3]

Assessing industry attractiveness is particularly important not only in diversifying acquisitions, but also in any international acquisition, because international horizontal acquisitions often imply important differences in strategic requirements.

3.1 What are the *strategic segments* in the target's industry?

(Strategic segments are segments that serve different user needs and have a segment-specific cost structure, and as a result, represent separate competitive arenas.)

In which is the target firm present or absent?

3.2 Provide *by segment* a *current picture* of the industry:

What is the return potential of this industry? By what is it limited?

What are the customers' needs? How do they buy? How loyal are they?

What is the structure of distribution? What are their needs? How powerful/dependent are they?

Describe the buildup of the cost structure in this business, from raw materials through customer service.

What is the range of competitive weapons used to compete?

Who are the competitors? Group them in types of competitors that use similar strategies. For each competitor in the strategic group of the target and for relevant key competitors in other strategic groups, describe briefly:

– Their performance in this segment.
– Their objectives/commitment to this segment.
– The strategic approach they have to it.
– The resources they have available.
– Their relative cost position.

Any substitute products? Any substitute segments?

What are the core technologies underlying this product market? What are the key technology issues?

What position and capabilities seem required to be a viable competitor?

What artificial barriers or regulations, if any, underpin or limit industry development and profitability?

What management capabilities are crucial to succeed in this industry?

3.3 What is, *by segment,* your *prognosis* about the evolution of the target industry?

How will the segmentation evolve?

What expected growth do you see for each segment? Why?

How do you see the evolution of returns in this business? Why?

What could destroy the industry as it is? What could destroy its profitability? Consider major threats of any kind (regulatory, environmental, substitution, foreign competition, etc.).

How will the competitive forces in the industry change:

- Relations with suppliers?
- Relations with customers?
- Relations with distribution?
- Substitution trends?

Among the factors that influence the industry, which ones are:

- *Controllable* (e.g., barriers to entry/exit, distribution channels, . . .)?
- *Influenceable* (e.g., customer preferences, power of the suppliers, competition characteristics . . .)?
- *Uncontrollable* (e.g., economic fluctuations, demographic trends . . .)?

To sum up, the industry is:

- Very attractive.
- Attractive.
- Moderately attractive
- Not very attractive.

Outline from three to five main reasons that support this opinion and that could be used for a public announcement of our decision to enter this industry.

SECTION 4: ASSESSING COUNTRY ATTRACTIVENESS

This section deals with a *geographical diversification:* how a company can compete in another country. For firms making their first move beyond the borders of their home country, these questions deserve a good deal of attention. Experienced international managers may want to check their experiences against these broad categories.

4.1 What are the main relevant differences between this country and the country(ies) in which we are currently operating? On what dimensions can we understand them?

In the immediate industry environment:
– Growth.
– Customer needs.
– Price levels.
– Nature of competition.
– Cost structure elements: e.g., raw materials, labor, transportation, energy.
– Technology used and technical sophistication.
– General management approach.
– Other key factors.

In the broader environment:
– What is the availability of skilled labor?
– Labor relations policies and issues.
– Environmental policies and issues.
– Regulation (employment law, taxation, dividend repatriation, local content, export subsidies, financing, etc.).
– Business practices.
– Political risk factors.
– Other key factors.

4.2 What impact could these differences have on the performance of the combined companies?

4.3 What restrictions to our strategic freedom would we be operating under in terms of:

Funding?
Repatriation of dividends?
Local content?
Taxation?
Other?

4.4 How do we evaluate the overall political and economic risks of the country?[4] How is the business tied to those risks?

4.5 Can we find experiences by other foreign entrants in the same industry?

Who was involved in these acquisitions?
Why have they (not) been successful?
What does it seem to take to succeed there?
What else can we learn from these experiences?

4.6 Have other firms from our country made acquisitions in this country (in other industries)? What can be learned from them?

4.7 To sum up, having such an activity in the country would be:

Very attractive
Attractive
Moderately attractive
Not very attractive.

Outline three to five main reasons that support this opinion of country attractiveness and that could be used for a public announcement of our decision about the acquisition.

SECTION 5: ASSESSING THE COMPANY BY ITSELF

5.1 Provide a brief description of the acquisition candidate:

Short history of the development and performance of the firm

Main activities and locations

Size of the company (sales)

Nature and description of the assets (both human and balance sheet)

Its management and organization

Main strengths and weaknesses?

Relevant relationships with governmental or regulatory groups.

Has the business previously been sold or has it been for sale? If so, what happened?

5.2 Product/service strategy by segment:

What are the main products and services and their histories (volume, sales, unit price)?

What is the profitability by product line?

What is the level of quality and the reputation for quality compared with those of competitors' products?

What are the objectives of R&D?

Are there some potential new products?

Are there some major projects to be started?

Assess the strengths of patents and trademarks.

5.3 Position in the market:

What is the firm's market share by strategic segment?

What is the relative position by segment?

What changes can be expected?

What image and reputation does the target firm have among the customer and professional groups? Why?

If it is a distributor, how is it rated by its suppliers?

5.4 Customers:

What are their needs?

How are those needs changing?

Who are the main groups of customers?

Assess the quality of the brand franchise.

How is the company perceived by its major clients?

What would be the influence of our acquisition on these customers?

5.5 Suppliers:

Who are the key suppliers?

How dependent is the company on these suppliers?

To what extent does the company receive best client price levels?

5.6 Distribution Channels

Through what channels do they distribute?

What is the structure of these channels?

What are the main characteristics?

How are the channels evolving?

How much does it cost to use the various channels?

What are the main logistics operations? How are they handled?

5.7 Cost evolution[5]

What is the evolution over the past 5 to 10 years of:
- Sales (price and volume)?
- Manufacturing costs?
- Contribution margins?
- Selling costs?
- Administrative expenses?
- Capital structure (debt/equity)?
- Depreciation and interest?
- Profit before taxes?
- Net profit?
- Cash flows?

5.8 Compare the competitive position of the firm in relation to the competitors identified in Section 3 on each of its key functions:

In sum, what is the competitive position of the firm in relation to its most profitable and successful competitors?

What is the potential for improvement?

What is required to realize that potential (for instance: specialization, industrial rationalization, productivity and organization, investments, technology, etc.)?

	Strong	*Relatively* Strong	Adequate	Weak	*Leading* Competitor
General management					
Purchasing					
Product R&D					
Process technology					
Production					
Logistics					
Distribution/sales					
Marketing					
Service					
Innovativeness					
Image					
Finance					

5.9 Ratio analysis: Ratio analysis enables a firm to compare its performance with that of other firms in the same industry. It can also provide an insight into some of the firm's difficulties. What stands out from an analysis of the following financial ratios (for the firm and for the industry)?[6]

Efficiency ratios:
- Sales to total assets (sales/total assets)
- Inventory turnover (cost of sales/average inventory)
- Average collection period (accounts receivable × 360/net sales)
- Average payment period (accounts payable × 360/cost of sales)

Profitability ratios:
- Net profit margin (net income/net sales),
- Return on total assets (net income/total assets)

Leverage ratios:
- Debt ratio (long-term debt/total assets),
- Times interest earned (net income/interest)

Liquidity ratios:
- Current ratio (current assets/current liabilities).
- Quick ratio (cash + short-term investments + accounts receivable)/current liabilities).

Market value ratios:
- Price/earnings ratio (market price per share/earnings per share).

- Market-to-book value ratio (market value per share/book value per share).
- Dividend yield (dividends per share/market price per share).

5.10 If it is a public firm, what is the market's perception:

How is the company perceived by its shareholders?

How has the stock been traded for the past one or two years (price and volume)?

What is the firm's credit rating? Has it changed recently?

5.11 Organization and management:

Formal organizational chart.

Beyond the formal chart, what does the real "informal" organization look like?

Who are the members of the board of directors (names, positions, powers)?

What are the profiles and competencies of the key managers?

What are the motives of the key managers?

How are their compensation packages structured?

5.12 Culture:

Characterize the management style.

What kind of group spirit is there?

How are decisions made?

How are the main business functions and their role defined by the firm (e.g., marketing, production, finance, control)?

Historically, are there some dominant functions?

What is the philosophy of management on matters such as growth, industrial relations, organizational planning, industrial engineering, merchandising, educational selling, advertising, accounting and budgeting, R&D, product design, dividends, financing expansion, etc.?

On what dimensions is the firm's culture compatible with, the same as, or different from our culture? How great are these differences?

5.13 Human resources:

What are the strengths and weaknesses of the management team?

What are the skills/capabilities of the workforce?

How disciplined and motivated are the employees?

How strong is their identification with the current owner or management team?

How are the jobs classified (for instance, skilled/semiskilled, salaried/hourly, full-time/part-time)?

What is the number of employees by job classification?

What is the wage level? How does it compare with the industry?

Age and seniority in the company.

What education do the employees have?

What is the employee turnover? Does it vary by level? How does it compare with the industry average?

Is it appropriate to adjust the workforce to the volume of activity (overtime, seasonal schedules, temporary work force, . . .)? How much does it cost?

Do any employees hold special employment contracts? What are the employees' pension rights and benefits?

How compatible are they with those of our firm?

What other fringe benefits are present?

– Vacation.

– Health.

– Profit-sharing.

– Stock-purchase plans.

What is the overall cost of fringe benefits?

What are the strengths and weaknesses of the management team?

Are the employees organized? Which unions are representing them? What is the history of labor relations at the firm? If there are some contracts currently in force, what are the key terms?

5.14 Relation to other stakeholders:

What is the importance of the company's various operations in different local communities?

What is the history of the company's relation with these communities?

Who are the opinion leaders in this respect?

5.15 Ownership structure:

What is the structure of the firm? (proprietorship, partnership, private or public corporation, trust . . .)

Who exercises control of the company and how?

Who are the shareholders?

Are there any voting agreements?

How widely is the firm's stock held?

Are there some warrants, rights, or options?

Who wants to sell and what do they want to sell?

Why do they want to sell?

5.16 Legal considerations:[7]

How and where is the firm registered?

Are there any current active lawsuits?

Does the firm have any particular liabilities (e.g., damages, compensation, product liabilities)?

Are there any mortgage provisions or liens that could affect the sale of some properties?

Are there other contracts or informal agreements that should be taken into consideration for the sale?

Has it been completely clarified what is and what is not part of the sale in a legal sense?

5.17 Environmental issues:

Are there environmental problems resulting from the firm's operations or from the use of its products or services?

Are the premises, equipment, and working conditions safe?

Does the company have proper insurance coverage?

5.18 Overall, in light of Sections 3 and 4, how do you assess the competitive position of the target on its own? What are the major areas where improvement is possible? What resources would be needed?

SECTION 6: ACQUISITION LOGIC: THE COMPANY WITH US

This section details the argument for making the acquisition. The quality and clarity of the acquisition justification will be critical not only for the decision but also for valuation and the negotiation process.

6.1 Restate in more detail the acquisition logic discussed in Section 2:

What are the main areas in which the firms might create value together?

Given our own business positions and capabilities, are there *different strategic logics* that could be followed in this acquisition?

For each of those logics provide a brief scenario of integration, investment, benefits, and timing.

Which of these scenarios or combinations thereof is the *chosen logic* to guide the evaluation and integration? Explain your choice.

6.2 How specifically are we going to *create* value in this approach?

What is the relative emphasis on:
- Resource sharing.
- Functional skill transfer.
- General management improvements.
- Combination benefits?

Describe the trade-offs that need to be made for these to occur.

Provide your arguments for making the trade-off you advocate.

How do you see the sequencing of benefits over time?

6.3 List the expected benefits that will be detailed in the synergy scenario, the time horizon within which they are achievable, and, most importantly, the organizational interdependence requirements without which these benefits will not be achieved. (See Table.)

6.4 What costs and negative synergies might be associated with the acquisition?

Restructuring costs.
Customer conflict.
Supplier impact.
Image impact.
Etc.

6.5 What are the main commercial and noncommercial risks? How can they be contained?

6.6 What are the risks and costs of not making the acquisition?

6.7 If a competitor were making the acquisition; for which competitor would the fit be best? How does that compare with our expected benefits?

Table C.1 **Expected Synergy Benefits**

	Description	Financial Estimation of Expected Benefits	Organizational Conditions for Implementation	Time Horizon
Resource sharing				
Sales				
Production				
Service				
Logistics				
Overhead				
Other				
Functional skill transfer				
R & D				
Production				
Marketing				
Other				
General management capability transfer				
Operating efficiencies				
Better strategic focus				
Other managerial improvements				
Combination benefits				
Market power				
Purchasing benefits				
Financial benefits				
Fiscal benefits				
Other				

6.8 What options is the acquisition likely to open up? Which does it foreclose?

SECTION 7: MANAGING THE INTEGRATION PROCESS

The purpose of this section is to think through the integration approach that will be required to preserve and transfer the strategic capabilities that underlie not only the synergy expectations but also the value of rest of the company to us. (See Chapters 8–13.)

DECIDING ON THE INTEGRATION MODE

7.1 Complementarity of acquired positions and core capabilities

List the product-market positions and the core capabilities that would be available to us if we acquired the firm.

Do the same for our business(es) with which the acquisition is to be integrated.

Explain the degree of overlap, complementarity, and benefits expected.

7.2 Strategic interdependence required (see Chapter 8):

Given the extent of this complementarity and overlap, and given the synergy expectations, what is the need for strategic interdependence among the two firms for each capability, each position, and for each individual function?

7.3 Organizational autonomy required (see Chapter 8):

Is there a need to preserve distinct cultures after the acquisition? Specify which of these capabilities and business positions could be destroyed.

Can these capabilities and positions be preserved in distinct subunits or do they depend on broader organizational qualities?

7.4 In light of this need for interdependence and organizational autonomy, *what is the best metaphor for the overall integration?*

Absorption (low autonomy, high interdependence). (See Chapter 11.)

Preservation (high autonomy, low interdependence). (See Chapter 12.)

Symbiosis (high autonomy, high interdependence). (See Chapter 13.)

7.5 Within this overall choice of integration approach, how could the integration approach best be *differentiated* for each of the different business positions and capabilities:

Which ones, ideally, need strong preservation?
Which ones, ideally, require full absorption?
Which ones, ideally, need to evolve symbiotically?
To what extent is such differentiation manageable? How?

MANAGING GATEKEEPING (SEE CHAPTER 10)

7.6 Preparing the interface management:

In case of an absorption approach:

Who will be in charge of the transition process?
Who will be on the steering committee that makes the policy decisions with respect to the acquisition integration?
What temporary integration structure is envisioned?
What timetable is seen for the integration process?
What attitude will be taken vis-à-vis the acquired company and vis-à-vis our own units?

In the case of a preservation approach:

Who will be the gatekeeper?
IIow will this be communicated to our organization?
Which managers will be seconded to the host structure or the acquired firm? Why were they chosen?
What needs to be done to protect the acquired firm's dynamic?

In the case of a symbiotic approach:

Who will be the gatekeeper?
How will the need for initial preservation be communicated to our own organization?
How long will the initial preservation period last?
Who has been identified to assist the acquired firm? Why were they chosen?

Deciding on the New Organization

7.7 How will the acquired company initially report into our existing organization?

7.8 Will the acquired firm be reorganized? If so what will the new organization look like? How fast should such a reorganization be decided? How fast should it be implemented?

7.9 What organizational changes does this acquisition call for *in our own* company? What will the new organization look like? How fast should this be implemented?

7.10 The managers:

How clear is it whether the acquired firm's management will be able and willing to stay?

What are the management team's key strengths and weaknesses?

If management talent is needed, do we need to staff them from outside, from within the acquired firm, or with our own people?

Does the acquisition give us a surplus of managerial talent? Is this surplus qualified for other opportunities in the firm?

When do we plan to exchange managers between our company and the acquired company? In both directions?

7.11 Other employees:

What are the functions that represent critical skills?

What will be done to maintain those skills?

What is the possible redundancy impact?

How will the impact of this redundancy be managed?

Creating the Appropriate Atmosphere and Context
(see Chapters 6 and 10)

7.12 What actions can be envisaged vis-à-vis employees, distributors, and customers to put operations on an even keel?

7.13 What immediate actions will we take to strengthen the acquired company?

7.14 What will we communicate as the new purpose to both sides? How?

7.15 What systems and processes will or will not be implemented in the acquired company?

7.16 What actions will be undertaken to foster mutual understanding?

Preparation of the Subsequent Integration Phase

7.17 Outline the status of our current planning for the actual integration phase. Who will need to become involved beyond the initial gate-keeping team?

SECTION 8: SCENARIOS FOR FINANCIAL VALUATION

The purpose of this section is to narrate briefly the scenarios that are developed for the financial valuation of the acquisition. These scenarios are important because they focus attention on the assumptions underlying the numbers and because a realistic approach to best and worst cases requires a coherent scenario, instead of merely adjusting all the financial variables lower or higher.

If the acquisition is a *platform,* it may be preferable to base the acquisition decision on a complete strategy scenario for decision purposes, rather than a stand-alone value plus synergy value.

If the acquisition involves a business *position,* the development of a stand-alone value plus synergy value may be the most practical.

8.1 Develop a base case scenario for stand-alone value and synergies.

8.2 Develop a pessimistic scenario for stand-alone value and synergies.

8.3 Develop an optimistic scenario for stand-alone value and synergies.

8.4 Develop the appropriate competitive scenarios. This would typically include:

The scenario of an LBO bid for the company.
A synergy scenario with relevant competitors.

SECTION 9: FINANCIAL VALUATION OF THE TARGET FIRM[7]

Financial valuation is an imprecise and subjective exercise, and it should be recognized as such. Several methods can be used to value a business. Each technique can lead to very different prices depending on the assumptions. Among the most used methods are *accounting*-based methods such as book value, written-down replacement costs, or book value plus goodwill; *market*-based methods such as price/earnings ratios, adjusted price/earnings ratios, price to sales ratios, dividend yield; and *economic* methods such as return on assets, net present value of earnings, and net present value of free cash flows.

Financial valuation can serve several purposes. For the purpose of negotiation, one obviously wants to use any method that advances one's own interests and is understood by and acceptable to the seller. To establish one's own walk-away price, however, we strongly advocate the use of net present value of free cash flows, not only because it is theoretically the correct method, but because it is the only one that forces managers to state their assumptions about the future.

For detailed treatment of the discounted cash flow method, we refer readers to Rappaport (1986) and Copeland, Koller, and Murrin (1990). We limit ourselves here to some basic remarks.

ACCOUNTING-BASED METHODS

Accounting-based methods are not very helpful in establishing the value of a firm. The only practical implication of the still much-regarded book value, for example, is that it determines the tax implications of the acquisition, because any value above book will be considered goodwill. The practice of valuing a company as consisting of book value and goodwill results in a completely arbitrary assessment of what that goodwill is.

One accounting-based method that might be useful in the case of asset-oriented acquisitions, such as the acquisition of capacity, is the *written-down replacement cost*. By valuing all the firm's assets and liabilities at their replacement value and writing down the assets according to age, one obtains a reasonable estimate with which to compare the cost of internally investing in capacity with the cost of acquiring, especially after incorporating the benefit of time gained.

Market-Based Methods

Market-based methods are much used, especially in the form of *price/ earnings multiples,* or, for nonpublic companies, *comparable price/ earnings multiples.* Though these may be helpful for establishing at what price (after inclusion of a premium) a firm could be bought, they are not very relevant to determining one firm's value to another firm. Apart from serious comparability problems, which necessitate numerous re- statements in the earnings factor, and the instability of the p/e multiple over time, their most fundamental weakness is the simple-mindedness of expressing all future value of the firm in relation to its last year of earnings. No matter how elaborate a comparative study of p/e-based prices is made, the information content for valuation is very limited.

Under the assumption that a company will not be carried on as a going concern, its *liquidation value* can be estimated. This is the cash value of the assets minus the cash value of the liabilities if the firm were to be liquidated.

Economic Methods

One method by which to develop a realistic perspective on the op- erating improvements required to justify a price would be to start from a market-based estimate of the necessary acquisition price and then to work back into the *return on capital* improvements that will be required to justify this price.

In general, however, the *net present value of the discounted free cash flows* is the most practical, most informative, and theoretically and op- erationally the most correct method. The application of this method involves judgments in five areas: what is to be sold and what to be kept and hence modeled; which time frame to project; the elaboration of free cash flows; the determination of a discount rate; and the determination of a terminal value.

A first step is to decide which activities are to be kept and sold, how to model the activities and into what detail of segments to separate the model.

Next a time horizon must be chosen. This should be done in terms of the nature of the business (longer if the business is cyclical or capital intensive). In practice, the decision is a trade-off between the lack of comfort in detailed projections beyond a certain horizon and the lack of comfort in a valuation in which the end-value method weighs heavily.

The free cash flows are best determined through detailed nominal value projections that start from the market (market growth, market share, sales, etc.). That way realism in assumptions is encouraged; all too often the estimates of growth and share turn out to be far less accurate than the cost estimates. A second key area for attention are the lines below the earnings statement: the estimates for working capital needs and reinvestment. The free cash flow must truly be free.

The discount rate is another important decision, especially when considering diversification into another business area. The rate should indeed be the cost of capital estimate of the acquired business, an important distinction in the case of diversification. The estimate is the result of weighing the cost of equity and the after-tax cost of debt in a proportion equal to the target debt/equity ratio. The cost of equity itself is determined by adding to the risk-free rate a risk premium that corresponds to the nature of the business. See again Rappaport (1986) and Copeland et al. (1990) for more detail.

The terminal value is the estimated net present value of the free cash flows beyond the planning horizon. Again caution is required because estimates of terminal value can vary widely, and especially in the case of growing businesses, they have a strong impact on the total value. Assumptions can range from conservative projections that beyond the horizon, all investment will take place at the cost of capital, and no additional value will be created, or that the last year's free cash flow will remain constant, to more optimistic ones that see continued growth in cash flow. In any case one should be careful about projecting growth into infinity by assuming that a (currently) growing business will be sold at the end of the planning horizon at today's high p/e's.

BEYOND NET PRESENT VALUE

The net present value of free cash flows would correctly value a company if it were true that we could express all benefits and all costs in terms of cash flows. Though the discipline of financial valuation is a healthy one, not all benefits of an investment are embedded in the scenarios. In particular the *option value* which the acquisition has in terms of future investments in this or other businesses is not represented in the scenarios. Beyond the result of the net present value calculation, it may be useful to think through the existence of such nonquantifiable benefits.

Notes

Chapter 1
Mastering the Acquisition Process:
The Key to Value Creation

1. Throughout this book we will use the terms merger and acquisition almost interchangeably. Although the word merger tends to be used for the combination of equal-sized firms and acquisition tends to be used for the takeover of one firm by the other, such distinctions are largely in the eye of the beholder. Our focus will be on the process of combining both organizations irrespective of size or legal distinctions.

2. Stigler (1950), described the first wave of acquisitions, around the turn of the century, as "mergers for monopoly," leading to the emergence of dominant firms through amalgamation of several competitors in industries such as steel (U.S. Steel), the electrical products industry (General Electric), and the oil industry (Standard Oil).

   In the thirties, a second wave was characterized as "mergers for oligopoly." In many of these industries remaining competitors regrouped to form a strong number two firm, such as Bethlehem Steel and Continental Can. Several authors have described the third or "conglomerate" wave in the sixties (Scherer, 1970; Picini, 1970; Lynch, 1970), in which a large number of conglomerates like Textron and Gulf & Western grew rapidly through acquisition of scores of unrelated businesses, often in exchange for stock. In Europe the period of the sixties corresponded to an increased acquisition level, as U.S. multinationals developed their European base. For a review of historic acquisition trends and performance, see Haspeslagh and Berg (1979) and Golbe and White (1988).

   There have been waves of diversification as well as waves of refocusing. The economic argument for diversification is that firms should deploy their capabilities into other fields where they can be leveraged into producing competitive advantage. Clearly diversification entails costs, the most important one, in our perspective, the loss of effectiveness of the companies' general management function. See Prahalad and Bettis (1986), Penrose (1959), and Williamson (1975) for a discussion of this point. An argument can be made that many companies have overdiversified, because they have overestimated the applicability of their general management approach (Kotter, 1982; Chandler, 1990b) and because improvements in external capital markets have shifted the extent to which internal resource allocation is superior to external resource allocation. Bhide (1989) and Markides (1990) discuss the issue of refocusing.

3. Securities Data Co. Mergers and Corporate Transaction Data Base, February 1990.

4. Bhagat, Shleifer, and Vishny (1989). The research of Bhagat, et al. (1989) raises an important point about the ultimate disposition of the assets involved in hostile takeovers. They found that in most cases, raiders and management buyout specialists are just brokers who allocate assets to the eventual strategic buyers (p. 3). In addition, they found that in these hostile takeovers, 72 percent of the assets were eventually owned by corporations with other similar assets. Thus, the ultimate owners of most of the assets that change hands in financial acquisitions seem to have strategic motives.

5. Source: Amdata/Acquisitions Monthly database.

6. For descriptions of the differences in national acquisition contexts, see Haspeslagh, Neven, and Armstrong (1988), Franks and Mayer (1990), and Edwards and Fisher (1990).

7. Source: Yamaichi Securities Co. Mergers and Acquisitions Strategy Group, presented at the Conference on Japanese Securities Markets, New York University, March 1990. *Nikkei Business* (1988, no. 6, p. 9) reported that acquisitions among Japanese firms had grown from 122 in 1982 to 219 in 1988. Japanese companies took to acquisitions even more quickly overseas, where acquisitions rose from only 28 in 1982 to 228 in 1988, as they started to move beyond internal development and asset purchases to broaden their international presence.

8. By 1988, before the enthusiasm for "junk bond" financing cooled off, $109.2 billion or 30.5 percent, of that activity was finance oriented (i.e., involving corporate restructuring and buyouts), rather than strategic, up from $10.4 billion in 1984. At the same time, more strategic acquisitions were being made in the same or related businesses, than unrelated ones. Source: Morgan Stanley.

9. The conventional view is supported by academic research from a variety of disciplines (e.g., financial economics, strategic management, and organizational behavior). Yet, while individually offering important insights, each of these schools leaves key questions unexplored. None seems to examine acquisitions from the perspective of the general manager's complex job and the challenges we introduced earlier.

The most visible research stream on acquisitions is financial research, using changes in firms' stock prices as indicators of whether acquisitions create value. The main conclusion seems to be that, on average, acquisitions have not created value for the acquiring firm's shareholders, whereas shareholders of the acquired firms do benefit. Unfortunately, this research is silent on the reasons for this disparity and offers no insights on which acquisitions do better than average nor *a fortiori* on why they would do so.

Research from strategic management has addressed questions of "strategic fit" and has tried to explain which types of acquisitions perform better than average. Yet there is no conclusive support so far for a primary hypothesis—that related acquisitions outperform unrelated acquisitions. Although seasoned practitioners would tend to support this assumption, they know that a lot depends on the quality of implementation. Developing a sense for what is related and what is not is a tricky thing. It misses the point that the same acquisition can be considered in different ways, depending on how the combined firms are actually managed. We suggest that by focusing on *a priori* measures of relatedness, most strategic fit research has addressed potential, rather than actual, value creation.

Organization constraints, cultural differences, and implementation problems are well recognized by managers and some scholars as important elements in acquisition success. The organizational behavior and culture research on acquisitions focuses almost exclusively on the interpersonal issues of having the acquisition accepted by key employees and other constituencies. In an overriding pursuit of the question of acceptance, this research often loses sight of the fact that the acquisition's strategic task must have primacy. Avoiding situations that may involve strong cultural differences is naive in a world where strategic objectives can often be fulfilled only by combining people and capabilities from firms with many different national, industry, and corporate heritages. In sum, though each of these research streams offers a number of interesting partial insights, they do not seem to address the manager's overall problems with acquisitions. Appendix A presents a more detailed summary and discussion of the findings of these various research streams.

Chapter 2
A Capabilities-Based View of Value Creation

1. Appendix B summarizes research on merger and acquisition activity from three perspectives—financial economics, strategic management, and organizational behavior.
2. See Rappaport (1986) and Salter and Weinhold (1979, Chapter 6) for a discussion of how firms are valued.
3. A summary of the capital asset pricing model based on the efficient market hypothesis is presented in Mullins (1982). To study the seminal papers in CAPM, along with a detailed treatment of the model, see Markowitz (1952), Sharpe (1964), and Lintner (1965), and the paper by Fama (1968). See Jensen (1972) for a compendium of important earlier papers.

4. The financial economics research on this issue is summarized well in Jensen and Ruback (1983). Their results suggest that shareholders of acquiring firms do not benefit or benefit only marginally, whereas shareholders of acquired firms enjoy substantial abnormal returns to their holdings. Jarrell, Brickley, and Netter (1988), who explore similar questions about the value-creating aspects of acquisitions made in the United States from 1980 to 1987, come to the same conclusions. Similar findings result from studies in other markets, including Australia (Dodd, 1976), Belgium (Gagnon, et al., 1982), Canada (Eckbo, 1986), France (Eckbo and Langohr, 1985; Husson, 1986), and the United Kingdom (Franks, et al., 1977). For an overview, see Husson (1987, pp. 53–81).

The conclusions of these studies may be somewhat attenuated because they neglect the size effect. On the average, acquired firms are significantly smaller than acquirers; hence their impact on the acquirer's stock price should be expected to be small. Asquith, Bruner, and Mullins (1983) found that "abnormal" returns to bidders depended on the relative size of the target firms. In general, the smaller the target, the lower the returns to the bidder.

Financial economists' studies use an "event study" methodology that examines the net "abnormal" returns associated with a particular security around an "event" such as an acquisition announcement. See Brown and Warner (1980) for an excellent discussion of this methodology and its strengths, weaknesses, and uses.

Magenheim and Mueller (1988, p. 190) suggest that studies of merger and acquisition results are "sensitive to both the choice of time intervals used and the choice of benchmark against which performance is measured." They suggest that ". . . an acquisition is a sufficiently complex event that it might take the market more than a single month or year to form an accurate estimate of its future effect. These considerations suggest to us the need for a longer-run view of the consequences of acquisitions."

Roll (1986) suggests that, contrary to the assumption of economists that individuals make rational decisions, merger decisions are individual decisions. He suggests that the lack of gain to bidding firms is a result of hubris.

Industrial organization economists have a different perspective on the results of acquisition activity. For example, Ravenscraft and Scherer (1987) studied 5,822 mergers and acquisitions in the 1950–1977 time period and concluded that "on average profitability declines and efficiency losses resulted from mergers of the 1960s and early 1970s" (pp. 211–212). Caves (1987) and Elwood (1987) offer reviews of the research in the area.

Several scholars from strategic management have addressed this question as well. Their interests are typically whether value creation differs by type of acquisition made and its relatedness. In general, the results here are mixed. Bettis (1981) found that related diversifiers outperformed unrelated diversifiers. Palepu (1985) found that related diversifiers performed better than unrelated diversifiers. Lubatkin (1987) found that related mergers did not create more value than unrelated mergers. Michel and Shaked (1984) found that when firms diversify into unrelated areas their performance is better than those with businesses that are related. Bettis and Mahajan (1985) found that related diversification aids in achieving a favorable balance between risk and return.

5. See Manne (1965) for the seminal article on the market for corporate control. Schleifer and Vishny (1988) suggests that managers can entrench themselves by investing in projects, facilities, and other companies that complement their unique personal skills and abilities. A question does remain whether takeovers for purposes of efficiency in the market for corporate control are the result of internal management failure. Abuse of power by management is a matter of judgment and abuse becomes a vague criterion. To be sure, abuse does occur in some circumstances. But in many situations where the firm's stock price is depressed, more noble managerial motives may be present. In particular, a management team may sincerely believe that their approach, which may require more patience than the shareholders have, is best for the firm in the long term.

6. Note that the price of the acquiring firm's shares does not increase unless the market believes that the negotiated transaction price allows the acquiring firm to retain some of the expected synergy benefits.

7. See Salter and Weinhold (1979, pp. 41–42) for an excellent description of this.

8. The following vignette from a recent conference on corporate restructuring highlights the limited relevance of the financial assets perspective for acquisitions. Gregg Jarrell, at the time chief economist at the United States Securities and Exchange Commission, recounted some congressional testimony in which he argued for the need to allow acquisitions to continue without governmental restrictions. He said that he argued for the macroeconomic benefits of acquisitions to society and suggested that in the long run we are all better off when assets are redistributed to more productive uses. Jarrell said, "A senator looked down over the top of his spectacles at me and said, 'Son, there are no senators here from the state of Macroeconomics' " (Jarrell, 1986).

   We suggest that just as there are no senators from the state called "Macroeconomics," there are no managers from the firm of Macroeconomics, Inc.

9. The importance of understanding how value is created is recognized by many finance scholars. For example, Bradley, Desai, and Kim (1983) suggest that acquisitions via tender offers are attempts by bidding firms to exploit potential synergies.

10. The stakeholder perspective is well presented by Freeman (1984). Also see Summer (1980, Chapter 1) for a discussion of the variety of pressures general managers must balance in their decision making. Andrews (1970) discusses the responsibilities that general managers have to diverse constituencies.

    Donaldson and Lorsch (1983, p. 7) found that in contrast to the view that maximization of shareholder wealth is the primary goal of managers, "their primary goal is the survival of the corporation in which they have invested so much of themselves psychologically and professionally. Therefore they are committed, first and foremost, to the enhancement of *corporate* wealth which includes not only the firm's financial assets reflected on the balance sheet but also its important human assets and its competitive positions in the various markets in which it operates."

11. See Dickson (1990, p. 6).

12. For a broad comparison of how the legal, regulatory, and cultural context of the market for corporate control differs across EEC countries, see Armstrong (1988). A full discussion of how Dutch corporate law formally embodies a stakeholder's perspective, holding managers responsible to broad "corporate interests" (in Dutch *het vennootschappelijke belang*) can be found in Fromm and Haspeslagh (1986).

13. Among transactions were ICI's acquisition of Fiberite, BP's acquisition of Hitco, and BASF's acquisition of Celanese's advanced materials businesses. For a discussion of the industry, see the case "EHC and the Advanced Materials Business," written by Sarah Williams under the supervision of Professor Yves Doz and Associate Professor Philippe Haspeslagh, INSEAD, 1990.

14. See Haspeslagh and Jemison (1987) for an earlier discussion of the distinction between value capture and value creation.

15. Penrose's seminal work (1959) first raised the conception of the firm as a combination of capabilities embodied in an administrative framework. Recently other researchers have stressed more explicitly the importance of capabilities underlying such competitive advantage. Among the scholars developing a capabilities-based view from an analytical perspective are Wernerfeldt (1984), Barney (1986), Jemison (1988a,b), and Dierickx and Cool (1989), and from an administrative perspective: Lenz (1980), Haspeslagh (1983), Bartlett and Ghoshal (1989), Doz (1988), Hamel and Prahalad (1989, 1990).

    Porter (1985) encouraged a focus on the importance of competitive advantages as the basis for performance. Christensen and Fahey (1986) see two types of competitive advantages, one that increases demand for a firm's products and services and one that constrains supply. Demand-enhancing competitive advantages are the characteristics of a firm, its products, or services that cause them to be preferred over those of competitors. Competitive advantages that constrain supply do so by limiting market entry or expansion by a competitor.

Implicit in the writing of Pascale and Athos (1981) and Peters and Waterman (1982) was the presence of organizational and organizing capabilities that allow firms to be more effective competitors.

16. See Andrews (1970) and Selznick (1957) for a discussion of distinctive competence.

17. See Ghemawat (1988) and Dierickx and Cool (1989) for a discussion of sustainable competitive advantage.

18. See Jemison (1988b) for a discussion of how capabilities contribute to competitive advantage and how acquisitions can add capabilities to a firm. See Prahalad and Hamel (1990) for an initial exposition of the concept of care competencies.

19. This concept has been explored by strategic management scholars in light of the concept of strategic groups. See clinical work on strategic groups by Hunt (1972), their relationship to industrial organization economics by Porter (1980, Chapter 7), empirical work by Cool and Schendel (1988), and an extensive review and critique of the literature and concept by McGee and Thomas (1986).

20. Hamel and Prahalad (1989) provide an excellent discussion of this issue.

21. We are indebted to Yves Doz for this example. For a detailed discussion of Canon's organizational approach, see "Canon, Inc." written by Yoko Ishikura under the supervision of Professor Michael Porter, Boston: HBS Case Services, Harvard Business School no 9384151.

22. See "Hanson, Plc.," written by Dean Stone under the supervision of Associate Professor Philippe Haspeslagh, INSEAD, 1990. The importance of these value-capturing benefits does not take away from the fact that Hanson Trust actively pursues value creation in the units they retain, mainly through operating efficiencies that the company seeks through the imposition of tight controls and the provision of strong performance-oriented incentives.

23. There is some disagreement over the influence of tax benefits as an acquisition motive. In a study of 318 mergers and acquisitions between 1968 and 1983, Auerbach and Reihus (1987) found tax benefits to be significant enough to influence the merger decision in 20 percent of the situations they studied. In contrast, Jarrell, Brickley, and Netter (1988) argue that much of the takeover activity in the past twenty years has not been tax-motivated. Gilson, Scholes, and Wolfson (1988) explore the broad range of ways that tax policies and their alternatives can affect the market for corporate control.

24. The impact of restructuring transactions on the value of bondholders' claims on the firm has been the subject of a variety of empirical studies.

Most of these have suggested that corporate restructuring does not significantly harm bondholders. See Dennis and McConnell (1986) for a study of mergers, and Hite and Owers (1983) and Schipper and Smith (1983) for studies of spin-offs. Kim, McConnell, and Greenwood (1977) did show evidence of significant bondholder losses in their study of captive finance subsidiaries. Taggart (1988), in a survey of junk bond financing, argues that while there have been individual cases of significant losses to bondholders, "transferring wealth from bondholders is [not] a primary motivation for issuing junk bonds."

25. There is no shortage of typologies to distinguish among acquisitions from a strategic perspective. Many of these typologies are broad categorizations based on how an acquisition relates to other businesses of the firm, such as Kitching's (1967) often-used distinction between horizontal mergers, vertical integration, market-relatedness, technology-relatedness, and unrelated acquisitions. Others clarify the motives that inspire them, such as Salter and Weinhold (1979), who distinguish between defensive and offensive acquisitions.

26. Panzar and Willig (1977) presented one of the earliest formulations of economies of scope. See also Panzar (1981).

27. See Chatterjee (1986) for an extensive discussion of synergy in acquisitions.

28. In an earlier publication, we used the term "automatic benefits" for the latter category. See Haspeslagh (1986).

29. See Scherer (1970, pp. 267–295) for an excellent summary of the arguments about the relationships among industry concentration (market power) and industry and firm returns. Results on the extent of diversification and market power are mixed. Backaitis, Balakrishnan, and Harrigan (1984) found that firms pursuing related diversification had greater market power, while Montgomery (1985) did not find that market power led to profitability increases associated with diversification.

30. Although the capital asset pricing model implies that diversification does not create value per se, the use of the resulting greater operating stability in countercyclical or otherwise strategic investment behavior may lead to value creation.

31. For a detailed description, see "Esselte-Dymo (A)(B)(C)" INSEAD case written by Andy Kodjamirian under the supervision of Associate Professor Philippe Haspeslagh and Professor Dominique Heau (INSEAD, 1984).

32. The difficulties of transferring context-based knowledge or skills (also known as "tacit knowledge") have been explored by a variety of scholars. Polyani (1962, p. 49) pointed out that "the aim of a skillful performance is achieved by the observance of a set of rules which are not known as such to the person following them." Arrow (1974) suggested that organizations use codes to convey information efficiently and that there are costs to

changing the codes. Nelson and Winter (1982, pp. 81–82) observed that "much operational knowledge remains tacit because it cannot be articulated fast enough, because it is impossible to articulate all that is necessary to a successful performance, and because language cannot simultaneously serve to describe relationships and characterize the things related." From another perspective, Coase (1937) pointed out that information is not costless and Williamson (1975) argued that the use of information is difficult because of its impactedness. Teece (1980) suggests that internal organization may be preferred over markets in generating scope economies from embedded know-how. Itami (1987) refers to such skills as invisible assets. Lippman and Rumelt (1982) discuss how the difficulty in imitating an asset can enable a firm to earn abnormal returns in a competitive marketplace. Barney (1986) discusses how certain inimitable assets like a firm's culture or history are sources of strategic advantage.

33. See the "Note on the Building Society Industry in Great Britain," Teaching Note S-BP-247N, by Associate Professor David B. Jemison, Stanford, CA: Graduate School of Business, Stanford University.

34. The issue of relatedness is central to the study of diversification in general and to acquisitions in particular. Wrigley's (1970) four categories of single product, dominant product, related product, and unrelated product were expanded by Rumelt (1974) to include nine categories within the original four groups. See Rumelt (1974, pp. 11–32) for an excellent discussion. Salter and Weinhold (1979, pp. 61–62) classified acquisitions in two broad categories, related and unrelated, with further subcategories of related-complementary and related-supplementary. Chandler (1962, p. 70) suggests ". . . that it is related effort that should be coordinated and not [merely] 'like things'." Singh and Montgomery (1987) suggest that relatedness is multifaceted with the target firm being valued by different other firms. Haspeslagh and Jemison (1987) suggest that in acquisitions value-creation activities come not from relatedness but from interdependence.

Although Rumelt's early categorizations refer to corporate-level relatedness, much of the strategic management literature on acquisitions has applied these categories to examine business-level relatedness, focusing on the linkage between an acquisition and the acquirer's existing businesses.

Another stream of research has focused on corporate-level relatedness and the overlap between business from a general management perspective. Normann (1976) used the notion of a company's "territory" as the niche in the environment in which the company's "business idea" is operative. Miles (1982) brings in the notion of a firm's domain, which may be conceptualized in terms of the services rendered, the population served, and the technology employed (Levine and White, 1961; Thompson, 1967). Haspeslagh (1985) has discussed the concept of a core competence domain and a business domain as one of the key elements of corporate strategy in a diversified firm. Bettis and Prahalad (1986) also emphasize the importance of general management. They examine relatedness with respect to the dominant logic, which they define as "a world view or conceptualization of the business and the administrative tools to accomplish goals and make decisions in the business" (p. 491). It is this corporate-level perspective that underpins the research design of this study (see Appendix A).

35. Readers familiar with Miles (1982) may see our notion of domain strengthening as encompassing both Miles's domain defense and offense. Miles's domain creation is analogous to our domain exploring. Abell (1980) contends that defining the business is the most important strategic question that general managers face. He proposes a framework for business definition in terms of customer groups served, customer functions served, and technologies utilized.

36. Industry restructuring can be triggered by a variety of factors including:

- *Deregulation,* which removes historically artificial barriers to entry, exit, or competition. For example, the gradual decline of regulatory barriers in the global financial services industry is encouraging consolidation through acquisitions.
- *Technological change* has the same effects, because it can affect minimum scale economies, such as the introduction of digital switching in telecommunications, radial technology in tires, etc.
- *Globalization* through customer need or cost-driven factors. For example, in the automotive paint business the globalization of automotive companies and increasing R&D costs are driving paint suppliers to seek global presence and scale.
- *Competitor initiative,* which may set the industry off on a road to consolidation without strong external triggers. The KMPG merger, for example, has triggered another round of consolidation among the large accounting firms that are already opening worldwide.

37. See "Charles Wang and his thundering nerds," *Forbes,* July 11, 1988, 118–124.

38. See Mullins (1982), Bettis (1983), and Peavy (1984) for a discussion of this issue.

39. See Salter and Weinhold (1979, pp. 161–171) for a discussion of this case. See also "CIBA-Geigy (A)(B)." Boston, MA: HBS Case Services, Harvard Business School), (9-375-246), (9-375-247).

40. See Haspeslagh (1986b) and Haspeslagh and Jemison (1987).

41. The work of Dierickx and Cool (1989) offers insight into these choices between internal development and capability, platform, or position acquisitions. They provide an important theoretical treatment of a firm's competitive position conceptualized as "stocks" of assets in place at a particular

time (analogous to the capabilities in our terminology). Changes in the level of these stocks, which are a function of the "flows" from managerial investment decisions, are necessarily gradual. While acquisitions offer the opportunity to increase the flow of new asset stocks into the firm, the result of the combination of some of these flows may not be time compressible. Acquisitions can be a quick solution to some firms' competitive problems. But, the logic of acquiring additional asset stocks or capabilities to help a firm catch up with its competitors must address important practical questions of the compatibility of these new stocks.

Chapter 3
Understanding the Acquisition Decision-Making Process

1. See "Francoplast (A)(B)(C)(D)" written by Alison Farquhar, under the supervision of Associate Professor Philippe Haspeslagh, INSEAD/CEDEP 1987.
2. See Mintzberg (1987) for an interesting discussion of the relationship between strategy development and implementation.
3. Appendix C covers in detail the range of issues to consider when evaluating an acquisition candidate. See also Salter and Weinhold (1979) for strategic considerations and Rappaport (1986) for a review of financial valuation techniques.
4. Appendix A discusses the sample from which this was drawn.
5. Andrews (1970) suggests that the history of a firm is an important determinant of its strategy. Allen (1979) discusses this issue in divisionalized firms. His theory about predictors of success in reorganizations emphasizes a company's previous history as a strong predictor of changes in organizational structure. In the framework of a longitudinal study, a company's history is operationalized as the company's operational context in previous periods. The operational context comprises product market diversity, diversification, size, debt exposure, and profitability. In the context of multinational management the importance of a firm's history in shaping its individual response to common challenges is stressed by Bartlett and Ghoshal (1989). They see a company's "administrative heritage" as shaped by "its configuration of assets and capabilities built up over the decades; its distribution of managerial responsibilities and influence which cannot be shifted quickly; and an ongoing set of relationships that endure long after any structural change" (p. 19).
6. See Cyert and March (1963) for a discussion of sequential attention to goals and problemistic search.
7. There is a substantial body of research on the usefulness of multiple perspectives in decision making. For example, Janis (1972) introduced the

problems of Groupthink. Other researchers have explored a variety of techniques. For example, Van de Ven and Delbecq (1971) developed the nominal group technique. Mitroff has argued for a dialectical approach to decision making, while Cosier (1978) and Schwenk and Cosier (1980) argue that a devil's advocate approach may offer richer and more effective insights. Our arguments are not intended to downgrade the importance of differing opinions during decision making. Instead, we point out that unless a common purpose is agreed upon, problems will arise during implementation.

8. The selective use of information by participants at different levels and with different roles in the decision-making process has been explored by a variety of scholars. See, in particular, Carter (1971), Cyert and March (1963), and Mechanic (1964).

9. For a pragmatic discussion of valuation issues, see Bing (1980).

10. Appendix C discusses how to link strategic and financial evaluation in acquisitions.

11. This phenomenon, referred to as the "winner's curse," was first identified by Capen, Clapp, and Campbell (1971) in their study of bidding processes for oil leases. Salter and Weinhold (1979, p. 117) suggest that "investors will have different perceptions of an asset's present value."

12. Berkshire Hathaway 1982 Annual Report, p. 5.

13. There is a rich literature on the lack of conformity between organizational decision-making processes and typical economic expectations of rationality. See, for example, Braybrooke and Lindblom (1970), Cyert and March (1963), Lindblom (1959), Quinn (1980), and Simon (1976) for a detailed consideration of rational, economic perspectives on decision making.

14. Bower (1970), in a richly documented study of several capital investment projects inside a large diversified firm, provided the seminal insights into these stages.

15. Bower (1970) observed how the definition of investment projects at the functional initiating levels and the process of building commitment by general managers in the middle were largely shaped by the *organizational context* in which these managers worked. Burgelman (1983), in a study of internal venturing activities, added insights into how the *strategic context* also interacts with what he describes as autonomous strategic behavior by middle managers. Haspeslagh (1983), in a concurrent study of the portfolio planning process of two large diversified companies, as well as a survey of planning practices, described how corporate influence over project initiation and commitment operates in a *strategic,* an *organizational,* and a *cultural context,* as top managers engage in intentionally symbolic behavior. The limited role of corporate strategy implicit in Bower's work can be explained by its time frame, because a more explicit corporate

strategic context was developed after strategic planning practices were introduced in the late seventies.

16. Bower (1972) describes the "life" of a number of capital investment projects and corporate management's indirect influence over their focus, size, and timing.

17. The problemistic search and sequential attention to goals are discussed in Cyert and March (1963). In addition, Cohen, March, and Olsen (1972) suggest that firm decision making can be likened to a garbage can, with problems and solutions often randomly intersecting.

18. For example, among the twenty-one U.S. companies with a market value over $250 million that were the object of a hostile bid in 1989, only one stayed independent, whereas fourteen were taken over by the initial bidder and six by a second bidder. Source: Morgan Stanley.

19. Staw, Sandelands, and Dutton (1981) provide an interesting theoretical model, which can be employed on both managing and researching individual, group, and organizational behavior under stressful conditions, such as those of the acquisition process. They suggest the existence of what they call the "threat-rigidity effect," which manifests itself in centralization of authority, reliance on prior knowledge, reduction in information-processing capabilities, and a reduction of information flows.

20. These factors combine to materially change the perception of risk by the acquisition decision maker. Risk is inherent in all managerial decisions and the scholarly work exploring it is prodigious. Von Neumann and Morgenstern (1947) is the seminal work on the systematic study of risk in the context of economic behavior. Kahneman and Tversky (1979), in their exposition of prospect theory as well as their studies of framing effects (Kahneman, Slovic, and Tversky, 1982), have provided a substantial impetus for research and understanding by showing how the ways in which decisions are framed can affect the decision process and their outcomes. In the broader context of international politics, the work of Schelling (1960) and Allison (1971) shows how two parties' decisions are affected by their consideration of the risks involved. MacCrimmon and Wehrung (1986) provide an excellent and comprehensive treatment of risk and managerial decision making. Ruefli (1990) provides a review and critique of the conception of research on risk-return relationships.

The relative benefits managers expect from acquisitions can affect how acquisitions are treated in the decision-making process. The work on framing effects by Kahneman and Tversky (1979) and the research on threat evaluation by Jackson and Dutton (1988) suggest that acquisition opportunities that are expected to have more positive benefits are framed differently and are subject to different decision-making behavior than acquisition opportunities expected to produce less positive benefits. This situation is often exacerbated by the tendency of decision makers to be overly confident in their judgments or to overestimate or underestimate the risks involved. See also Bazerman (1986).

21. Firms set higher hurdle rates even though such company-specific risk should not, according to modern financial theory, affect the cost of capital used to discount the projected cash flows of the organization. See Van Horne (1977).

Chapter 4
Problems in Acquisition Decision Making

1. For excellent expositions of these prescriptions, see Salter and Weinhold (1979), Rappaport (1986), Mace and Montgomery (1962), and Leighton and Tod (1967).

2. It would not be exaggerating to say that the extent of the corporate due process is often inversely proportional to the size of the deal and the level in the organizational hierarchy of the acquisition's champion: small divisional acquisitions seemed invariably to be subject to a heavy multilevel process of scrutiny, whereas major corporate acquisitions were often committed to largely on the basis of the CEO's personal judgment.

3. Jemison and Sitkin (1986a) provided the initial exposition of these phenomena and the process perspective on acquisitions.

4. A number of problems arise when different groups are involved in decision making. For example, Dearborn and Simon (1958) showed how the functional experience or departmental orientation of senior managers may lead them to redefine the problems to fit familiar types of analyses over unfamiliar types. Moreover, as Allison (1971) and March (1962) have shown, the functional focus of the activities of the largest or most powerful subgroup may dominate the decision-making process.

    The net result of these isolated analyses is a less comprehensive decision that does not consider equally either the available information or the information relevant to the particular acquisition decision. See Fredrickson and Mitchell (1984) and Fredrickson and Iaquinto (1989) for studies of the comprehensiveness of decision processes under varying circumstances.

5. Momentum in decision making has been studied by a variety of scholars. See Staw (1981) and Staw and Ross (1978, 1987) for a discussion of escalating commitment to a course of action. Duhaime and Schwenk (1985) and Langer (1975) discuss how an illusion of control can lead managers to evaluate acquisition candidates less thoroughly. The work of Janis (1972, 1988) and Janis and Mann (1977) provides excellent treatments of how group decision-making processes under stress can have dysfunctional consequences.

6. K. H. Miller, Merrill Lynch director of mergers and acquisitions, as quoted in the *New York Times,* July 3, 1984, p. 37.

7. For excellent discussions of the structure and functioning of investment banks and the investment banking industry, see Eccles and Crane (1988) and Hayes, Spence, and Marks (1983).

8. Rohatyn (1984).

9. "Fiat Still Seeks a Partner," *The International Herald Tribune,* October 15, 1985, p. 7.

10. See "A Lecon de Fusion du Professeur Barnevik," *Fortune (France),* No. 21, December 1989, 81–83.

11. Decision-making behavior in ambiguous situations has been explored by a variety of scholars. In situations where decision makers faced similarly ambiguous contexts, researchers have pointed out the tendency of decision makers to become hypervigilant and focus on familiar practices, information that is easily assimilated, and minutiae that are familiar and easily controlled. See Allison (1971) and George (1980). Other research has found that ambiguous information can polarize preexisting attitudes (Lord, Ross, and Lepper, 1979), which in acquisition situations would lead the parties farther from agreement.

12. "Basquet Case: Anatomy of a Spanish Merger," *The Economist,* January 19, 1990, p. 76.

13. Levin (1989) gives an excellent account of the General Motors acquisition of Electronic Data Systems. For a discussion of the issues around transfer pricing agreements between GM and EDS, see pp. 208–210.

14. See Haspeslagh (1990) for a discussion of differences in resource allocation style across companies.

15. Notwithstanding the conceptual similarity of the investment definition and commitment-building process discussed in Chapter 3, each of these four firms had a very different style with respect to resource allocation decisions. These differences in style had clear consequences for the extent to which acquisition decisions posed problems. The small-sample observations that follow, though supported by more partial observations in a wider range of firms, and by the face validity imputed by the reactions of many managers to these ideas, clearly warrant corroboration in a wider sample. Such a study on the nature and impact of corporate-level decision-making styles across a sample of different national origins is in progress by one of the authors.

   The nature of such corporate-level styles clearly incorporates elements that derive from what Bartlett and Ghoshal (1989) call company-specific administrative heritage. Where Bartlett and Ghoshal (1989) describe the role of administrative heritage in a multinational context, observations in a diversified firm context can be seen in Goold and Campbell (1987).

   At the same time corporate-level decision making is conditioned by national culture. The cultural relativity of management theories based only on samples of firms in the United States is being increasingly questioned after having been the province of some isolated voices such as Hall (1959), Hofstede (1980a,b) and Laurent (1983). The powerful influences on a firm's organization and decision making that reside in national history is discussed in Chandler's (1986) comparison of capitalism in the United States, Germany, Japan, and Great Britain. The impact on decision making of cross-cultural differences in personality characteristics is summarized in Hofstede (1980a) and detailed in Hofstede (1980b). The impact of other aspects of national context, such as the nature of capital markets and (managerial) labor markets, warrants separate attention.

16. For a broad discussion of the pervasiveness of national cultures on business practice, see Chandler's (1990a) comparison of the development of major firms in the U.K., the U.S., and Germany. For a discussion of the influence of national cultures on individual decision making in the context of large multinationals, see Hofstede (1980) and Inzerilli and Laurent (1983).

17. See Hayes and Abernathy (1980) for a discussion of the implications of short-term decision making. In a controversial book published only in Japanese, Morita and Ishihara (1989) criticize the lack of long-term perspective among segments of the American economy under the title "America Looks 10 Minutes Ahead; Japan Looks 10 Years."

   Some scholars in the United States have put forward arguments that an important difference may lie in the ways in which managers are compensated. Rao (1990) writes of the "horizon problem" where "although a firm may have an indefinite life, the manager's claim on the firm is restricted to his tenure with the firm. Managers will therefore prefer investing in projects that have near-term payoffs even though they may not be as good for the firm as other projects with more distant payoffs on which he has no claims. This problem gets even more serious when the firm provides managers with incentives to increase short-term profits" (p. 26).

18. See Donaldson and Lorsch (1983) for a discussion of the goals that managers have for their firms. Also see Abegglen and Stalk (1985) for an excellent discussion of the structure and decision-making styles of Japanese firms. Hayes and Abernathy (1980) and Hayes (1985) provide an excellent critique of the decision-making approaches found in many American firms.

19. The importance of middle-level general managers and their championing role in decision making has been discussed in a variety of contexts. See Bower (1970), Uyterhoeven (1972), Peters and Waterman (1982), Jemison (1985), Burgelman and Sayles (1985).

20. For a discussion of the role of the strategic planning process as a substitute for direct substantive involvement in specific decisions, see Lorange (1980), Haspeslagh (1983), Chakravarthy and Lorange (1990).

21. The literature on strategic decision-making processes has studied analytical and political dimensions of decision making. An essential conclusion of

this literature is that decision-making processes are multidimensional phenomena, and different models are useful for better understanding under different circumstances. March (1962) and Cyert and March (1963) are classic pieces studying the political dimension in decision making. The political influence in decision making at the individual level is addressed by Shukla (1982) and Tushman and Romanelli (1983). Two interesting studies dealing with the political influence of middle-level managers on decision making are Kelley (1976) and Schillit (1987). Several aspects of the analytical dimension in decision making are studied in Allison (1971), March (1978), Fredrickson (1985), and Mintzberg (1978). Finally, for studies integrating the political and analytical dimensions of decision making, see Allison (1971), Pettigrew (1977), and Mintzberg, Raisinghani, and Theoret (1976). Bower's (1970) work provides a model that integrates the relationship between the two aspects. He maintains that cognitive perceptions are central in the definition of investment projects and that political processes are central in developing a commitment to them. See Bower and Doz (1979) for a summary of the arguments of this stream of research.

22. The concept of a firm's administrative heritage is developed and elaborated by Bartlett and Ghoshal (1989).

Chapter 5
Managing Acquisition Decision Making

1. For an initial discussion of the choices involved in developing an acquisition decision making approach, see Haspeslagh (1990).

2. See Appendix A for a description of the sample of companies we studied.

3. See Chapter 9 in Salter and Weinhold (1979) for an excellent discussion of how to consider and use search and screening systems.

4. See Lorange (1980), Haspeslagh (1983), and Chakravarthy and Lorange (1990) for a discussion of corporate strategic planning functions. See Hayes and Abernathy (1980) and Hayes (1985) for a discussion of excesses that strategic planning can bring upon firms.

5. For a detailed discussion of the role of corporate planning staffs, see Lorange (1980) and Haspeslagh (1983).

6. While our discussion of ICI's acquisition team approach is based on our own interviews and observations, the general strategic change process in ICI has been well documented. Pink (1988), a member of ICI's planning staff, describes the role of planning in this process, and Pettigrew (1985) discusses the role of internal organizational development staffs. Farquhar, Evans, and Tawaday (1989) discuss the leadership at ICI of John Harvey-Jones, whose own book on leadership provides fascinating reading (see Harvey-Jones, 1988).

7. Nees (1981) describes the initiation of divestitures as a more corporate-level phenomenon. Bhagat, Schleifer, and Vishny (1989) discuss how hostile takeovers are typically followed by substantial divestitures, Duhaime and Grant (1984) studied the impetus for divestment decisions. See Scherer (1986) for an in-depth discussion of the divestiture phenomenon in light of fifteen case studies.

8. See Levitt and March (1988) and Huber (1991) for excellent reviews of the organizational learning literature. Miles (1981) discusses how firms learn from diversification.

9. An inside account of BP's post-project appraisal approach is described in Gulliver (1987).

10. Appendix C identifies question areas that can be used when screening acquisition candidates.

11. March and Olsen (1976) discuss "superstitious learning" in which individuals "learn" from an apparent environmental response to some action or organizational behavior. But, because the responses are not coupled with consequences in the environment, the learning is entirely coincidental; yet it often becomes embedded in organizational routines.

12. Thompson (1967) notes that the informal organization focuses the researcher's attention on "variables which are not included in any of the rational models—sentiments, cliques, social control via informal norms, status and status striving, and so on" (p. 175). Some of the most important streams of research in informal organizations are presented by the institutionalist school (Meyer and Rowan, 1977, Feldman and March, 1981, and Weick, 1979); the social construction school (Berger and Luckman, 1967, Thompson, 1980); and the enactment school (Weick, 1979).

13. Bernard Schwartz, as quoted in Jemison and Sitkin (1986b, p. 111).

Chapter 6
Understanding the Integration Process

1. See Jemison (1988b) for a detailed discussion of the forces involved in the strategic capability transfer process.

2. See Teece (1980) and Nelson and Winter (1982), especially Chapter 4, "Skills," for an excellent discussion of embedded skills and routines.

3. See Polyani (1962), Nelson and Winter (1982, pp. 81–82), Teece (1980), and footnote 31 from Chapter 2 of this book.

4. See Beman (1981).

5. Financial economists, on the other hand, argue strenuously that firms should not accumulate organizational slack. Jensen's (1987) arguments about free cash flow reflect this perspective directly.

6. Organizational slack is an important concept in strategic management and organization theory. First referred to by Cyert and March (1963, p. 36), it refers to "[the disparity] between the resources available to the organization and the payments required to maintaining the coalition." Pfeffer (1981) discusses the importance of slack resources and incremental slack resources as a source of power in organizations. See Bourgeois (1981) for an excellent review of the concept. Other scholars who have explored conceptions of slack include Child (1972), and Cohen, March, and Olsen (1972).

7. See "Green Giant: The new course that makes it attractive to Pillsbury," *Business Week,* October 2, 1978, pp. 66–67; "It's Good Logic, But is it Good Business?" *Forbes,* November 13, 1978, pp. 138–140; "Pillsbury's Ambitious Plans to Use Green Giant," *Business Week,* February 5, 1979, pp. 87–88; "Pillsbury: Growth Could Suffer as Burger King Profits Shrink," *Business Week,* June 7, 1982, pp. 118–120.

8. Jemison and Sitkin (1986a) discuss the ways in which acquiring companies misapply their own management systems in acquired firms.

9. Laurent and Bartholomé (1987, p. 23) found that senior managers "paid more attention to how the task may affect the relationship while subordinates tend to pay more attention to the impact of the context of the task on the relationship."

Chapter 7
Problems in Acquisition Integration

1. See Jemison (1988a) and (1988b) for a discussion of the grounded theory of acquisition integration on which this chapter is based.

2. See Kotter (1982) for a discussion of how "specific" general management skills really are. Gabarro's (1985) study of seventeen managerial transitions offers rich detail on the ways in which an understanding of context can be helpful to new managers. See also note 1, Chapter 10.

3. The destruction of psychic value, which has received wide attention as a source of problems, is commonly attributed to a clash of organizational cultures. We do not view it this way, however, because our research suggests that viewing this phenomenon merely as a culture clash is too general a view, one that fails to offer insights into the real elements of the problems. The impact of differing organizational cultures on acquisitions is a popular topic among organizational behavior scholars. See, in particular, Nahavandi and Malekzadeh (1988), Buono, Bowditch, and Lewis (1988), Marks and Mirvis (1985), McCann and Gilkey (1988), and Walter (1985). Schweiger and Walsh (1990) provide an excellent review of this literature.

4. See Geertz (1973) for a discussion of emerging ideologies.

5. Reasons why an individual joins and contributes to an organization have been well explored both theoretically and empirically. See especially Bar-

nard (1938), Simon (1976), Emerson (1964), and Roethlisberger and Dixon (1939).

6. The issue of leadership and the development of organizational purpose is at the heart of many authors' arguments about the primary responsibilities of senior executives and general managers. Barnard (1938, p. 87) suggested that "the inculcation of belief in the real existence of a common purpose is an essential executive function." Selznick (1957, p. 17) writes of the responsibility of leaders to institutionalize or ". . . *infuse* [their organizations] *with value* beyond the technical requirements of the task at hand." Zucker (1983) writes about organizations as institutions. Burns (1978, p. 19) suggests that "the crucial variable, again, is *purpose.* [italics in original] . . . the genius of leadership lies in the manner in which leaders see and act on their own and their followers' values and motivations."

   Leavitt (1986) characterizes the direction-setting role of leaders as path finding, as opposed to problem solving or implementing, and suggests that organizations neglect path finding to their peril.

7. Barnard (1938) suggests that employees operate within a "zone of indifference." This is a zone within which they will accept differences in the ways they are treated by the organization.

8. *Financial Times,* February 12, 1987, page 13.

Chapter 8
Understanding Different Integration Approaches

1. See, for example, Kitching (1967) and Bastien and Van de Ven (1986) on size, Chatterjee (1986) on synergies, and Nahavandi and Malekzadeh (1988) on corporate culture.

2. See Haspeslagh and Farquhar (1987) for a discussion of the grounded contingency theory of acquisition integration on which this chapter is based.

3. Interdependence is a long-standing and much-examined construct in the organizational theory literature. Scholars have concentrated on either interorganizational interdependence (e.g., Levine and White, 1961) or intraorganizational interdependence (Thompson, 1967). Acquisitions involve elements of both because the acquired firm may have disappeared only as a legal entity.

   Most typologies of interdependence tend to be operational in nature, rather than oriented to strategic forms of interdependence (Thompson, 1967; Victor and Blackburn, 1987). Even such popular distinctions as Thompson's typology of pooled, sequential, and reciprocal interdependence seem limited to applicability in the tangible resource-sharing aspect of acquisitions. Levine and White's (1961) concept of exchange of what they call "critical elements" corresponds better to our notion of strategic capability transfer. At the same time, their conceptualization assumes a bilateral willingness to exchange, an aspect that, as we pointed out, cannot be taken for granted in acquisitions.

Although many categorizations for interdependence have been proposed, we found them not directly applicable in the context of acquisition integration issues, hence the distinctions we developed between resource sharing, functional skill transfer, general management skill transfer, and automatic benefits (Haspeslagh, 1986; Haspeslagh and Jemison, 1987).

4. The flow can also be in the other direction. Nevertheless, the acquired company managers are overwhelmingly on the receiving end. We will later argue that the ability to maintain a bidirectionality in interactions and changes is an important element in integration.

5. In our research we have classified acquisitions according to their "density of interdependence," ranging from those where the strategic task implied resource sharing across multiple functions (the greatest density) to those that primarily relied on automatic benefits of joint ownership (the least density). See Appendix A for a classification method of our sample of acquisitions on this dimension.

6. The study of organizational boundaries has a rich literature. That organizations have boundaries is acknowledged, but operationally the concept has been difficult to define. Starbuck (1965) points out this problem when he compares a boundary to a cloud. From a distance the cloud can easily be distinguished from the surrounding air. But on close examination one sees only a group of water droplets in a randomly arranged pattern.

Thompson (1967) suggests that organizations establish boundary-spanning units to manage the environmental transactions necessary for success. A number of scholars have addressed different boundary-spanning roles (Adams, 1976; Aiken and Hage, 1972; Aldrich and Herker, 1977; Jemison, 1981b; Katz and Kahn, 1966; Keller and Holland, 1975; Leifer and Delbecq, 1978; Miles, 1976; Tushman and Scanlan, 1981).

Scholars interested in organizational culture argue that multiple organizational cultures are often present in a firm and that seeing them as subcultures is a more fruitful way of envisioning the issues associated with cultural combinations. Martin and Meyerson (1988) and Martin and Siehl (1983) discuss the prevalence of multiple cultures or countercultures in organizations.

7. *New York Times,* December 6, 1988, p. 23.

8. Schweiger and Walsh (1990) offer an excellent review and critique of this organizational behavior and culture literature relating to acquisitions. See also Marks and Mirvis (1985), Sales and Mirvis (1985), Walter (1985), and Nahavandi and Malekzadeh (1988).

9. Elsewhere we have called this the "functionality" of the autonomy need. See Haspeslagh and Farquhar (1987).

10. Elsewhere we have called this the "specificity" of the autonomy need. See Haspeslagh and Farquhar (1987).

11. See Appendix A for the method by which our sample of acquisitions was classified on this dimension.

12. Metaphors can be powerful vehicles to frame in a succinct phrase the purpose of an acquisition. Unfortunately, many managers tend to use metaphors that represent war, sexual conquest, or marriage when describing an acquisition to their organizations. This can be especially dysfunctional if the purpose is more subtle or complex than a metaphor of war, rape, or marriage would portray. Some other metaphors we have seen in use include transplantation, adoption, and making an alloy, each of which conjures up different connotations for the managers.

13. See Appendix C for a discussion of how to analyze in detail the interdependence and autonomy needs of an acquisition opportunity.

14. In such a case, as Shanley pointed out after reviewing an earlier draft of this chapter, in our typology "corrective" or "disciplinary" might be better terms for this cell. Nevertheless, one could argue that such improvements are not strategic in that presumably other firms, or the firms themselves, could make the same changes. If the market for corporate control is efficient, the benefits spotted by one should be competed away if others are equally capable of realizing those benefits.

15. In one sense these ideas parallel the well-established concepts of differentiation and integration (Lawrence and Lorsch, 1967), which were developed as the way organizations can deal with environmental contingencies and can be traced to Ashby's (1956) law of requisite variety. The emphasis here is on intrafirm differentiation, and the preservation of subcultures in order to retain a diversity of difficult-to-combine capabilities. See the discussion of subcultures in note 6 above.

16. Kitching (1974) in a study of ninety acquisitions by American firms in Europe concluded that two-thirds of the "high flyers" (returns above 20 percent) were reported as successful, in comparison with 44 percent of the "dogs" (returns under 5 percent), and 50 percent of the "average" performers. Hofer (1980), in a wide-ranging discussion of turnarounds, makes a distinction between strategic turnarounds and operating turnarounds.

17. There are, of course, also acquisitions in which the acquiring company has the weaker management and the acquired organization ends up gradually occupying the senior positions in the acquirer.

18. Research on the impact of relative acquisition size on performance is as yet inconclusive. The research of Fowler and Schmidt (1989) and Newbold, Stray, and Wilson (1976) found no significant relationships between acquisition size and performance. Kusewitt (1985), on the other hand, found a significant relationship and suggested that the difference in size between

acquirer and acquired should not be large. See also Kitching's findings on the importance of relative size (1967, 1974).

19. Kitching (1974) discusses the importance of market share.

20. Whereas Kitching's (1974) findings on relative size suggest that the larger the relative size, the greater the odds of success, Bastien and Van de Ven (1986) consider relative size as a proxy for relative power. In this conception greater relative size makes it more difficult for the acquiring company to impose its strategic preferences. Shanley (1987), in a sample of fifty-one acquisitions, formally tested the hypothesis that relative size would be associated with the prevalence of post-acquisition change activities, but found this not to be the case.

21. See Jemison and Sitkin (1986a) and Bastien and Van de Ven (1986).

22. Greiner (1972) offers an excellent way to think of the stages of evolution of a firm and how management challenges change as it evolves.

Chapter 9
Integration Approaches and Integration Process Problems

1. See Selznick (1957) and Leavitt (1986) for a discussion of the importance of institutional leadership in general, and Jemison (1986, 1988) for a treatment of institutional leadership in acquisition integration.

2. For the initial exposition, see Haspeslagh and Farquhar (1987).

3. The power of framing effects is the product of an important stream of research. See Tversky and Kahneman (1979), and Kahneman, Slovic, and Tversky (1982).

4. For an empirical study showing how little the actual benefits of acquisitions relate to the expected benefits, see Chakrabarti and Souder (1987).

5. The sample was structured to include in each company acquisitions that were clearly successful or unsuccessful on three indicators: performance relative to the justification, performance relative to the industry, and perceived performance by noninvolved corporate staff members (internal audit or strategic planning).

6. The planned integration approach was determined by excerpting organizational integration intentions and arguments from the documents related to the acquisition justification, with particular emphasis on planned interdependencies and considerations of autonomy. Interdependence was examined in terms of resource sharing, functional skill transfer, general management improvements, and automatic benefits. Autonomy needs were examined in terms of functionality and specificity of culture differences. See Appendix A for an overview of the methods used.

7. The de facto integration mode was determined by examining the actual interdependencies that had been managed, and the degree to which the

acquired unit, or parts thereof, had been left autonomous. Both retroactive analysis over time and a snapshot at the time of the research were made. Data gathered from documents and interviews were analyzed on the basis of the distinctions discussed in the preceding footnote. See Appendix A for an overview of the methods used.

8. For each acquisition, two or three researchers examined the needs for integration and autonomy which in their judgment and with the benefit of hindsight were called for. These individual views were reconciled to reach a consensus judgment, scored based on the distinctions outlined in note 7 above. While the resulting judgment remains subjective and imprecise, our sample of extremes allowed us to feel comfortable with our judgments.

9. See the "EHC Ventures and the Advanced Materials Business" case written by Sarah Williams under the supervision of Professor Yves Doz and Associate Professor Philippe Haspeslagh, INSEAD, 1990.

Chapter 10
Integration: The Initial Steps

1. See "ICI: the Beatrice Acquisition," written by Alison Farquhar under the supervision of Associate Professor Philippe Haspeslagh, INSEAD/CEDEP, 1990.

2. The idea that general management is more industry specific than often envisaged has been emphasized by a variety of scholars. Chandler (1990a, p. 138), for example, in describing the problems with extensive diversifications notes that "too many managers made the mistake of listening to academics who told them that management was a general skill." Beyond being industry specific, a general manager's experience is also to some extent firm-specific and strategic-task-specific. Kotter's (1982) research, for example, suggests that a manager's effectiveness is firm or industry dependent because of the need to use networks to accomplish their responsibilities. Other scholars also have taken the position that managerial profiles fit unique strategic tasks. Turnaround management (Hofer, 1980), for example, and entrepreneurial business development (Miles and Snow, 1978) are seen to require specific profiles.

3. The impact of the misapplication of management systems in acquisitions is discussed in Jemison and Sitkin (1986a).

Chapter 11
Creating Value in Absorption Acquisitions

1. See "Electrolux: The Acquisition and Integration of Zanussi" case written by Lauren Andersen, Nicola De Sanctis, Benjaminio Finzi, and Jacopo Franzan, under the supervision of Associate Professors Sumantra Ghoshal and Philippe Haspeslagh, INSEAD, 1989.

2. See *Fortune* (France), December 1989, and note 10, Chapter 4.

3. This grid is similar to the one used by The MAC Group.

4. See "Esselte-Dymo (A)(B)(C)" case series written by Andy Kodjamirian under the supervision of Associate Professor Philippe Haspeslagh and Professor Dominique Heau, INSEAD, 1984.

5. For an excellent discussion of the diffusion of learning and innovation in multinationals, see Bartlett and Ghoshal (1987, 1989, pp. 115–134).

Chapter 12
Creating Value in Preservation Acquisitions

1. The preservation acquisitions discussed here imply a permanent need for differentiation from the current business domain(s). In such acquisitions the underlying preservation tension may ease over time only if the corporate level itself becomes less domain-specific.

2. As we discussed in Chapter 8, in some cases, acquisitions motivated by domain strengthening or domain extension may be integrated in a preservation mode because of external obstacles requiring the maintenance of an arm's-length relationship, or because the strategic logic gives preference to internal competition over internal coordination. In such cases the next two challenges do not apply.

3. See "BP Nutrition (A1)(A2)(B) and (C)" written by Research Assistants Roselle Bruce-Jardine and Christopher Taubmann under the supervision of Associate Professor Philippe Haspeslagh, INSEAD/CEDEP, 1990.

4. For a discussion of the motives and strategies of oil companies with respect to diversification, see Teece (1980) and Armour and Teece (1978).

5. The dilemma parallels that of new ventures divisions and their relationship to the core businesses. See Fast (1979) and Burgelman and Sayles (1985).

6. See Burgelman and Sayles (1985) for a discussion of championing in internal corporate ventures.

7. Part of this aspect of the research was carried out in collaboration with Professor Yves Doz. See the "EMC and the Advanced Composites Business" case, written by Sarah Williams under the supervision of Professor Yves Doz and Associate Professor Philippe Haspeslagh.

8. See Eisenhardt (1989c) and Bourgeois and Eisenhardt (1988) for a discussion of managing in rapidly changing environments.

9. Normann (1976) sees part of top management's statesmanship role as keeping a balance in the companies' growth culture. This balance comes about through the protection of business ideas that embody new values: "In many successful companies we have found it possible to identify at the highest level power centers that represent ideas and values suitable to different stages in the development of a line of business. One group of

actors commonly upholds values concerned with learning while another upholds values concerned with stability or exploitation" (p. 252).

Chapter 13
Creating Value in Symbiotic Acquisitions

1. For an extensive description, see "ICI: the Beatrice Acquisition," written by Alison Farquhar under the supervision of Associate Professor Philippe Haspeslagh, INSEAD/CEDEP 1988.
2. See Goffman (1952) for the classic treatment of adjusting to a new reality.
3. See Allen (1977).

Chapter 14
Managing Acquisition Strategies

1. Porter (1987) studied the acquisition and divestiture experience of thirty-three firms from 1950 to 1986. His conclusion that firms' diversification strategies had failed was based on whether acquired units had been divested or shut down (failure) or kept in the firm (success). We do not advocate blind acquisition and then divestment of firms. Using the presence or absence of divestment as a proxy for acquisition performance, however, fails to consider that acquisitive firms might be divesting because the nature of the strategic renewal in which they were involved necessitated both acquisition and divestment of capabilities and because of the learning and evolution of the corporate strategy that take place after an acquisition.

2. For an overview of acquisition context in EEC countries, see Armstrong (1988). King in Fairburn and Kay (1989) provides an overview of the U.K. context, and Edwards and Fisher (1990) discuss the acquisition context of the German financial system. Rydén (1972) provides a discussion of mergers in the Swedish context. For a comparison between France, Germany, and the U.K., see also Franks and Mayer (1990).

3. For detailed discussion of the design of strategic planning models, strategic planning systems, and the management of the corporate/business planning process, see Lorange and Vancil (1977), Naylor (1979), Lorange (1980), Haspeslagh (1982, 1983), Chakravarthy and Lorange (1990).

4. For a discussion of corporate strategy in a diversified firm, see Haspeslagh (1985). Apart from an attempt to formulate a concept of corporate strategy in multibusiness firms by Hanna (1968), later authors often equate corporate strategy with different issues, including portfolio strategy (e.g., Lorange 1980), the clarification of "driving forces" (Tregoe and Zimmerman, 1980), or the type of diversification strategy being pursued (Rumelt,

1974). Berg (1984), discussing corporate strategy as an organizing concept, suggested that the concept should address not only portfolio allocation priorities, but also distinctive competence, long-term financial goals, degree of risk, and the range of product diversification. Porter (1985) reemphasized the notion of "horizontal" strategy. Haspeslagh (1985) emphasizes explicit consideration of five interrelated corporate strategy components: (1) the nature of corporate objectives, (2) a conceptualization of the corporate domain of activities in both product-market and, more importantly, capability terms, (3) a clarification of how the corporate level will add value through a combination of operating discipline, a portfolio strategy, and a horizontal strategy, (4) the nature of the renewal strategy, (5) a clarification of the corporate organizational approach consistent with this strategy.

5. Andrews (1971) noted the instability of the traditional strategy framework to deal with the complexity of strategy formulation in complex firms as follows: "The strategic dilemma for a conglomerate world enterprise is one that may not have a satisfactory solution," a position discussed extensively in Bower and Doz (1977). The process school originating in Bower (1970), which asserts that corporate influence over the strategy formation process is shaped through the purposeful manipulation of administrative context, provides a partial, but incomplete, answer. If business strategy is shaped by organizational context, what is the source of the corporate strategy or vision that guides the design of organizational context (Haspeslagh, 1985)?

6. Hamel and Prahalad (1989) and Selznick (1959) provide excellent discussions of the vital role of stable guidance from the top.

7. Ultimately, of course, the economic value of a diversified firm is a function of the extent to which it can increase the value of the cash flows of the underlying businesses or decrease their variation, minus the costs it incurs in coordination (Salter and Weinhold, 1979; Montgomery and Singh, 1984). Although correct, such a definition of value creation is not particularly useful as a guide to managers in practice. Focusing on these three different ways in which diversified companies can influence the cash flow and risk patterns of their underlying operations derives its operational value from the fact that it corresponds not only with distinct ways of creating economic value, but also with organizational design variables (Haspeslagh, 1985).

8. For a supporting rationale for value creation through internal resource allocation based on a more informed but narrow set of internal options, see Williamson (1975). Supporting rationales for operating discipline as a source of efficiency are found in the development of information economics (Williamson, 1975), principal-agent theory (Holmström, 1979), and transaction cost analysis (Williamson, 1980). Ironically, at the same time that economists have developed rationales for this form of value creation, busi-

ness researchers and practitioners have started to question the long-term viability of management approaches based on "squeezing out" profits.

9. Supporting rationales for value creation through a horizontal strategy of capability transfer are to be found in the economies of scope arguments of Panzar and Willig (1981), and Teece (1980), as well as the "organizational routine" arguments embedded in the evolutionary economics of Nelson and Winter (1982). Rumelt (1984) has refined the argument further, pointing to the "irreduceable uncertainty" surrounding the creation of new production functions (new capabilities in our language). Difficult-to-imitate capabilities are thus the most secure sources of competitive advantage. See Barney (1986) and Dierickx and Cool (1989).

10. Jensen (1989) suggests that the entire governance structure of modern corporations is inappropriate. He suggests a shift to LBOs with owner-managers as the predominant managerial genre to ensure closer coordination of managerial interests with owners' interests.

11. See Haspeslagh (1982, 1983) and Hamermesh (1986) for a discussion of the practical implementation of portfolio planning approaches.

12. See Lorange (1980) and Haspeslagh (1982, 1983).

13. Many companies are trying to adopt a "value-based planning" approach, which reinforces the view that corporate strategy is merely the sum of a number of business unit strategies. In this approach the contribution of each unit's strategy to the overall stock market valuation of the company is measured by projecting cash flow scenarios for each business unit and discounting them at a business-specific cost of capital. The implicit prescription is to invest in the growth of businesses that earn a positive spread above their cost of capital and divest or reduce commitment to the others. Despite its theoretical soundness from the perspective of the individual business units, this approach in practice increases neglect of the shared capabilities across businesses and negates the time horizon required for the nurturing of new capabilities.

14. Whereas many authors have examined SBU definition and strategic segmentation issues from an analytical perspective (Abell, 1980), empirical studies have pointed to the administrative incorporation of the SBU concept as the most difficult issue in practice (Haspeslagh 1982, 1983, pp. 302–339; Hamermesh, 1986).

15. Hamel and Prahalad (1990) and Doz (1986b) are endeavoring to come to grips with this issue.

16. Though there is a vast literature on both acquisitions and joint ventures, few authors have focused on the differences and complementarity among different forms of renewal. Hennart (1988) and Kogut (1988) have addressed the issue of joint ventures versus contractual arrangements. Balakrishnan and Koza (1989a) have focused on the theoretical arguments that may underlie joint venture arrangements as opposed to both acquisi-

tions and contractual arrangements. Borys and Jemison (1989) examined the conceptual and operational similarity among different types of alternative organizational agreements, including acquisitions, joint ventures, technology-sharing agreements, etc. Siehl and Jones (1989) surveyed managers on how they saw the trade-offs among different modes. Doz (1990) has explored the conditions under which the market for acquisitions breaks down and "soft" restructuring is preferred.

17. Chandler (1990a).

Chapter 15
Epilogue: Beyond Acquisitive Development

1. See Haspeslagh and Ghoshal (1990).

2. This pattern parallels the pattern of early internalization described in the multinational companies' literature, whereby, after a first export and licensing phase, companies develop internationally through a series of acquisitions that remain loosely coordinated under the umbrella of an incipient international division (see Martinez and Jarillo, 1989, for an overview of the history of research in multinational management from 1953 to 1988).

3. In other words, the composition and functions at the corporate level resemble those of conglomerates, but the implications of organizing this way on substantive decision making by the corporate level are different. For a discussion of the corporate role in conglomerates, see Berg (1971). For a discussion of the different roles of the corporate center, see Goold and Campbell (1987).

4. This description is based on a case written by Avis and Ghoshal, "Saatchi and Saatchi Plc," INSEAD/CEDEP, 1989.

5. For more detail on Valmet's acquisitive development see "Note on the Paper and Paper Machinery Industries" and "Valmet Paper Machinery," written by Heidi Mattila under the supervision of Associate Professor Philippe Haspeslagh, INSEAD/CEDEP, 1990.

6. Cost competitiveness, adaptation, and flexibility, as well as ability to learn and innovate are emerging as the three poles around which multinational companies must be able to compete. Whereas some of the literature on multinational companies' management stressed the ability to reap global scale benefits through coordination (Levitt, 1983; Hout, et al., 1982), other authors have stressed the ability to stay adaptive and flexible (Kogut, 1985b), and more importantly, to combine these two qualities (Doz, 1976; Prahalad, 1976; Doz, 1979; Bartlett, 1979; Doz, Bartlett, and Prahalad, 1981; Porter, 1986, 1987). Recently attention has been paid to the more long-term needs for coordination to result in learning and renewal (Nonaka, 1987; Ghoshal, 1987; Bartlett and Ghoshal, 1989).

7. Because the trade-offs among strategic requirements are necessarily sit-

uational, it is not strategy formulation, but the shaping of an appropriate decision-making environment that is the major challenge. See Prahalad and Doz (1987) for a discussion of this challenge. Several authors have pointed to the shortcomings of simple organizational approaches in shaping the administrative requirements for a global product organization (see Davidson and Haspeslagh, 1982; Bartlett, 1983). Building on their earlier work, Doz and Prahalad (1987) summarize the role and tools of top management in shaping corporate influence to deal with both local adaptation and global integration. Bartlett and Ghoshal (1989) reexamine the same complexities, with more attention to the need for innovation and learning. As a result, the transnational approach to coordination they describe emphasizes the allocation of differentiated coordination responsibility to individuals in the subsidiaries themselves, networked across the organization, within the glue of a common culture.

8. Each of these developments in isolation have been discussed in the literature (see further), but their combined impact has not, although their implications have not escaped managers such as Hans Werthén and Leif Johansson of Electrolux.

9. See Levitt's provocative *Harvard Business Review* article (1983), p. 92, where he first raised the issue of the globalization of markets.

10. For an overview of the marketing literature in this area, see Douglas and Wind (1987). For a discussion from a broader strategic management perspective, see Doz (1986), and Doz and Prahalad (1987).

11. For a discussion of the relation between market evolution and segmentation, see Kotler (1988, p. 371), who notes "as the market's growth slows, the market splits into finer and finer segments, and a condition of high market fragmentation occurs," a condition which, Kotler argues, goes on until a new attribute emerges that has cogent market appeal and may prompt consolidation.

12. Douglas and Wind (1987) emphasize the constraints to standardization but also discuss the existence of global market segments, primarily in industrial markets. This is the trend of which Levitt (1983) wrote. Others, e.g., Killough (1978), are more bullish on global markets, arguing "after all, this is increasingly just one global market. Trends in distribution, in communication and in levels and types of basic buying interests make this so. Maybe we should use the word 'transnational' to describe any product or service offered outside the home country." Broad-based empirical research into the local versus global nature of segments is still to be done.

13. For a review see Martinez and Jarillo (1989).

14. See the work of Doz (1976), Bartlett (1983), Doz and Prahalad (1987), Bartlett and Ghoshal (1989), and Kogut (1985a, 1985b).

15. The network concept has been developed in several lines of research (see Lorenzoni, Grandi, and Boari, 1989). One relates to networks of external

firms and involves an examination of the factors that promote a change from market to network (Williamson, 1975; Thorelli, 1986), or an examination of the strength of the interfirm linkages and their impact on the nature of knowledge transfer (Granovetter, 1985). Another relates to the network of internal units and involves an examination of the factors that promote a shift from hierarchy to network. An older line of research has examined the concept of networks at the level of individuals in organizations and attempts to research and model the structure of such networks (McAlister and Fisher, 1978; Burt, 1982; Tichy, 1981; Fombrun, 1982). Both the research and practice of multinational management have recently paid more attention to this network concept at different levels. Loose networks of firms in Silicon Valley, or the Prato region in Italy, the interfirm cooperation among Japanese companies, and the more formal networking activities of firms like Genentech in biotechnology or Benetton in textiles have spawned empirical research (Lorenzoni, 1983, 1988; Imai, Nonaka, and Takeuchi, 1985; Hakansson, 1987). A rich description and conceptualization of multinationals as networks as well as an argument for the efficiency of organizing coordination in a decentralized network form rather than from the center is found in the work of Bartlett and Ghoshal (1987, 1989).

16. For a discussion of the conditions for making a network approach productive, see Bartlett and Ghoshal (1989).

17. For a discussion of perception lags in the context of multinationals, see Prahalad and Doz (1987, pp. 218–224).

18. For a discussion of the need for these qualities, see Bartlett and Ghoshal (1989), who see herein a major difference between classic multinational companies and the "transnational" ideal they put forward. As they describe them: "The transnational organization is built up in a much more gradual and differentiated way [than the classic matrix organization]." Ironically, its design complexity and subtlety facilitate greater clarity and simplicity in the management processes it defines. Rather than assign joint responsibility for everything, as the classic matrix structure suggests, top management in the transnational retains the clarity of line authority but pays a great deal of attention to the allocation of responsibilities.

Appendix A
Research Method

1. Such a small heterogeneous sample is inappropriate for deductive, theory-testing research in which the goal of sampling is representing the distribution of variables in the population. But when the goal is inductive theory building, the researcher should "choose cases such as extreme situations and polar types in which the process is transparently observable" (Pettigrew, forthcoming, p. 42). This approach to sampling in theory-building

research permits the researcher to develop a more robust theory that will have "fundamental uniformities of the greatest scope" (Glaser and Strauss, 1967, p. 58).

2. In all, 1,127 pages of internal memos and documents were freely provided. In addition, 134 pages were provided in a "bootleg" fashion. For example, one manager made an appointment out of the office at a hotel to deliver internal analytical documents, hand-drawn organization charts, and copies of internal memos pertaining to the merger.

3. Within the broad category of diversified industrial firms (Berg, 1971), different classifications of corporate approach to diversity have been proposed, notably Rumelt's (1974) distinction among dominant firms, related constrained firms, and related linked firms. While these categorizations are based on analytical linkages among the companies' businesses, the dimension of interest here is their impact on decision making at the corporate level, in particular, whether the corporate-level decision makers, systems, and approaches are steeped in the logic of a single (original) core business, or whether the diversification of the firm has been accompanied by a clear distinction between a corporate level and operating units that represent self-contained domains.

4. See Appendix B for an overview of this research.

5. See Rumelt (1974) for the classification scheme.

6. For a description of the company by other researchers and by its own managers, see Pettigrew (1985), Pink (1988), and John Harvey-Jones (1988).

7. The identity of this firm has been disguised.

8. These categories were taken from our earlier work. See Haspeslagh (1986) and Haspeslagh and Jemison (1987). Existing categorizations from the rich interdependence literature were not selected because discussions of the construct in the organization theory literature have concentrated on either interorganizational interdependence (Levine and White, 1961) or intraorganizational interdependence (Thompson, 1967). Acquisitions uniquely involve elements of both, as the acquired firm may have disappeared only as a legal entity. Most typologies of interdependence tend to be operational in nature, rather than oriented to strategic forms of interdependence (Thompson, 1967; Victor and Blackburn, 1987). Even such popular distinctions as Thompson's typology of pooled, sequential, and reciprocal interdependence seem limited to applicability in the tangible resource-sharing aspect of acquisitions. Levine and White's (1961) concept of exchange of what they call "critical elements," corresponds better to our notion of strategic capability transfer. At the same time, their conceptualization assumes bilateral willingness to exchange, an aspect which, we pointed out, cannot be taken for granted in acquisitions.

9. See Borys and Jemison (1989).

Appendix B
Prior Research on Mergers and Acquisitions

1. The financial economics research on this issue is summarized well in Jensen and Ruback (1983). Their results suggest that shareholders of acquiring firms do not benefit or benefit only marginally, while shareholders of acquired firms enjoy substantial abnormal returns to their holdings. Jarrell, Brickley, and Netter (1988) explored similar questions about the value-creating aspects of acquisitions made in the United States from 1980 to 1987 and come to the same conclusions as Jensen and Ruback.

2. Brealey and Myers (1988) and Weston and Copeland (1987) offer full discussions of the capital asset pricing model, and Mullins (1982) provides an overview. The seminal papers in CAPM and a detailed treatment of the model and its assumptions are found in Markowitz (1952), Sharpe (1964), Lintner (1965), and Fama (1968). Jensen (1972) provides a compendium of the most important earlier papers.

3. The work of Lindblom (1959), Mintzberg (1973), Wrapp (1967), and Quinn (1980), provide provocative discussions and support for the idea that strategy making is an incremental, evolutionary process.

4. Simon (1976) offers the classic treatment of non-value–maximizing behavior on the part of decision makers; see also Cyert and March (1963).

Appendix C
Assessing An Acquisition's Attractiveness

1. For a guide to financial evaluation, and in particular to the discounted cash flow method, see Rappaport (1986) and Copeland et al. (1990).

2. We wish to thank the French industrial company that supported an earlier company-specific version that was made from this questionnaire.

3. For a comprehensive approach to industry and competitive analysis, see Porter (1980, 1985).

4. For approaches on assessing international risk, see de la Torre and Neckar (1988). Other articles on assessing international risk include Barrett (1987), Loth (1986), Belcsak (1987), and Melvin and Schlagenhauf (1985). Porter (1990) provides a comprehensive treatment of the reasons why particular national economies may be relatively more or less competitive.

5. For more information on cost analysis, see Horngren (1982).

6. The following books provide helpful approaches for both ratio analysis and financial valuation: Harrington and Wilson (1989); Brealey and Myers (1988); Van Horne (1977); Foster (1986).

7. Be sure to consult your legal counsel on matters of concern to you.

References

ABEGGLEN, J. C., and G. STALK. (1985). *Kaisha.* New York: Basic Books.

ABELL, D. F. (1980). *Defining the Business: The Starting Point of Strategic Planning.* Englewood Cliffs, NJ: Prentice-Hall.

Acquisition Strategy in Europe. (1987). Collection Business International Research Report. Geneva, Switzerland: Business International S.S.

ADAMS, J. S. (1976). "Structure and Dynamics of Behavior in Organizational Boundary Roles." In *The Handbook of Industrial and Organizational Psychology,* edited by M. D. Dunette, 1175–1199. Chicago: Rand McNally.

AIKEN, M., and J. HAGE. (1972). "Organizational Permeability, Boundary Spanners, and Organizational Structure." Paper presented at the American Sociological Association meeting, New Orleans.

AKERLOFF, G. A. (1970). "The Market for 'Lemons': Qualitative Uncertainty and the Market Mechanism." *Quarterly Journal of Economics* 84:488–500.

ALDRICH, H., and D. HERKER. (1977). "Boundary Spanning Roles and Organization Structure." *Academy of Management Review* 2:217–230.

ALLEN, S. (1979). "Understanding Reorganization of Divisionalized Companies." *Academy of Management Journal* 22:641–671.

ALLEN, T. (1977). *Managing the Flow of Technology.* Cambridge: MIT Press.

ALLISON, G. T. (1971). *Essence of Decision.* Boston: Little, Brown.

ANDREWS, K. R. (1970). *The Concept of Corporate Strategy.* Homewood, IL: Dow Jones–Irwin.

ANSOFF, H. I., R. J. BRANDENBURG, F. E. PORTNER, and H. R. RADOSEVICH. (1971). *Acquisitive Behavior of U.S. Manufacturing Firms 1946–65.* Nashville, TN: Vanderbilt University Press.

ANSOFF, I. (1975). *Corporate Strategy.* New York: McGraw-Hill.

ARGYRIS, C., and D. A. SCHON. (1974). *Theory in Practice: Increasing Professional Effectiveness.* San Francisco: Jossey-Bass.

ARMOUR, H. O., and D. J. TEECE. (1978). "Organizational Structure and Economic Performance: A Test of the Multidivisional Hypothesis." *Bell Journal of Economics* (Spring):106–122.

371

ARMSTRONG, T., under the supervision of D. Neven and P. Haspeslagh. (1988). "Note on the Harmonisation of European Takeover and Merger Regulation." INSEAD.

ARROW, K. (1974). *The Limits of Organization.* New York: Norton.

ASHBY, W. R. (1956). *An Introduction to Cybernetics.* London: Chapman and Hall.

ASQUITH, P. R., F. BRUNER, and D. W. MULLINS. (1983). "The Gains to Bidding Firms from Mergers." *Journal of Financial Economics* 11:51–72.

AUERBACH, A. J., and D. REISHUS. (1987). "Taxes and the Merger Decision." In *Takeovers and Contests for Corporate Control,* edited by J. Coffee and L. Lowenstein, 157–187. Oxford: Oxford University Press.

AXELROD, R. (1980). *The Evolution of Cooperation.* New York: Basic Books.

BACKAITIS, N. T., R. BALAKRISHNAN, and K. R. HARRIGAN. (1984). "The Dimensions of Diversification Posture, Market Power, and Performance: The Continuing Debate." Working Paper, Columbia University Business School.

BALAKRISHNAN, S., and M. KOZA. (1989a). "Information Asymmetry, Adverse Selection and Joint Ventures: Theory and Evidence." Working Paper No. 90/32/SM, INSEAD.

BALAKRISHNAN, S., and M. KOZA. (1989b). "Organizational Costs and a Theory of Joint Ventures." Working Paper No. 89/54, INSEAD.

BARNARD, C. I. (1938). *Functions of the Executive.* Cambridge: Harvard University Press.

BARNEY, J. B. (1986a). "Organizational Culture: Can It Be a Source of Sustained Competitive Advantage?" *Academy of Management Review* 11:656–665.

BARNEY, J. B. (1986b). "Strategic Factor Markets: Expectations, Luck, and Business Strategy." *Management Science* 42:1231–1241.

BARNEY, J. B. (1988). "Returns to Bidding Firms in Mergers and Acquisitions: Reconsidering the Relatedness Hypothesis." *Strategic Management Journal* 9:71–78.

BARRETT, M. (1987). "The Euromoney Country Risk Ratings." *Euromoney* 3 (September):353–357.

BARTLETT, C. A. (1979). *Multinational Structural Evolution: The Changing Decision Environment in International Divisions.* Doctoral dissertation. Boston: Harvard Business School.

BARTLETT, C. A. (1983). "MNCs Get Off the Merry Go Round." *Harvard Business Review* (March–April):138–146.

BARTLETT, C. A., Y. L. DOZ, and C. K. PRAHALAD. (1981). "Global Competitive Pressures vs. Host Country Demands: Managing Tensions in Multinational Corporations." *California Management Review* 23 (Spring):63–74.

BARTLETT, C., and S. GHOSHAL. (1987). "Managing Across Borders: New Organizational Responses." *Sloan Management Review* 29 (Fall): 43–53.

BARTLETT, C., and S. GHOSHAL. (1989). *Managing Across Borders.* Boston: Harvard University Press.

BASTIEN, D. T. (1987). "Common Patterns of Behavior and Communication in Corporate Mergers and Acquisitions." *Human Resource Management* (26):17–33.

BASTIEN, D. T., and A. H. VAN DE VEN. (1986). "Managerial and Organizational Dynamics of Mergers and Acquisitions." Discussion Paper No. 46, Strategic Management Research Center, University of Minnesota.

BAZERMAN, M. (1986). *Judgement in Managerial Decision-Making.* New York: John Wiley.

BELCSAK, H. P. (1987). "A Treasurer's Guide to Country Risk." *Cashflow Magazine* 8 (September):40.

BELL, R. (1982). *Surviving the 10 Ordeals of the Takeover."* New York: AMA-COM.

BEMAN, J. (1981). "Exxon's Costly Mistake." *Fortune,* November 21, 53–56.

BENTHAM, J. (1931). *The Theory of Legislation.* London: Kegan, Paul, Trench, Trubner, & Co. Ltd.

BERG, N. (1971). "Corporate Role in Diversified Companies." ICCH 9-371-533, Graduate School of Business Administration, Harvard University.

BERGER, P. L., and T. LUCKMANN. (1967). *The Social Construction of Reality: A Treatise in the Sociology of Knowledge.* Garden City, NY: Doubleday.

BERLE, A. A., and G. C. MEANS. (1932). *The Modern Corporation and Private Property.* New York: Macmillan.

BERMAN, R. J., and M. R. WADE. (1981). "The Planned Approach to Acquisitions." In *Handbook of Mergers, Acquisitions, and Buyouts,* edited by S. J. Lee and R. D. Colman. Englewood Cliffs, NJ: Prentice-Hall.

BETTIS, R. A. (1981). "Performance Differences in Related and Unrelated Diversified Firms." *Strategic Management Journal* 2:379–394.

BETTIS, R. A. (1983). "Modern Financial Theory, Corporate Strategy, and Public Policy: Three Conundrums." *Academy of Management Review* 8:406–415.

BETTIS, R. A., and W. K. HALL. (1982). "Diversification Strategy, Accounting Determined Risk, and Accounting Determined Return." *Academy of Management Journal* 45(2):254–264.

BETTIS, R. A., and V. MAHAJAN. (1985). "Risk/Return Performance of Diversified Firms." *Management Science* 31:785–799.

BHAGAT, S. A., A. SHLEIFER, and R. W. VISHNY. (1989). "The Aftermath of Hostile Takeovers." Working Paper No. 276, Center for Research in Security Prices, University of Chicago.

BING, G. (1980). *Corporate Acquisitions.* Chicago: Gulf Publishing Co.

BLAKE, R. R., and J. S. MOUTON. (1984). *Solving Costly Organizational Conflicts: Achieving Intergroup Trust, Cooperation and Teamwork.* San Francisco: Jossey-Bass.

BORYS, B., and D. B. JEMISON. (1989). "Hybrid Arrangements as Strategic Alliances: Theoretical Issues in Organizational Combinations." *Academy of Management Review* 14:234–249.

BOURGEOIS, L. J. (1981). "On the Measurement of Organizational Slack." *Academy of Management Review* 6:29–39.

BOURGEOIS, L. J., and K. EISENHARDT. (1988). "Strategic Decision Processes in High Velocity Environments: Four Cases in the Microcomputer Industry." *Management Science* 34:816–835.

BOWER, J. L. (1970). *Managing the Resource Allocation Process: A Study of Corporate Planning and Investment.* Boston: Division of Research, Graduate School of Business Administration, Harvard University.

BOWER, J. L., and Y. L. DOZ. (1979). "Strategic Process Research." In *Strategic Management,* edited by D. Schendel and C. Hofer. Boston: Little, Brown.

BRADLEY, J. W., and D. H. KORN. (1981). "The Changing Role of Acquisitions." *The Journal of Business Strategy* 2:30–42. [In part an adaptation and summary, by permission of the publisher, of selected material in the authors' full-length study, *Acquisition and Corporate Development: A Contemporary Perspective for the Manager,* Lexington, MA: Lexington Books, 1981.]

BRADLEY, M., A. DESAI, and E. H. KIM. (1983). "The Rationale Behind Interfirm Tender Offers: Information or Synergy." *Journal of Financial Economics* 11:182–206.

BRAYBROOKE, D., and C. E. LINDBLOM. (1970). *A Strategy of Decision: Policy Evaluation as a Social Process.* New York: Free Press.

BREALEY, R., and S. MYERS. (1988). *Principles of Corporate Finance* 3d ed., Chapter 33. New York: McGraw-Hill.

BROWN, C., and J. L. MEDOFF. (1988). "The Impact of Firm Acquisitions on Labor." In *Takeovers: Causes and Consequences,* edited by A. J. Auerbach, 9–31. Chicago: University of Chicago Press.

BROWN, L. D. (1983). *Managing Conflict at Organizational Interfaces.* Reading, MA: Addison-Wesley Publishing Co.

BROWN, S. J., and J. B. WARNER. (1980). "Measuring Security Price Performance." *Journal of Financial Economics* 8:205–258.

BRUNER, R. F., and L. S. PAINE. (1988). "Management Buyouts and Managerial Ethics." *California Management Review* (30):89–106.

BUFFET, W. (1982). Chairman's letter in *Annual Report to Stockholders 1982,* p. 5. Berkshire Hathaway Corporation.

BUONO, A. F., and J. L. BOWDITCH. (1989). *The Human Side of Mergers and Acquisitions: Managing Collisions Between People and Organizations.* San Francisco: Jossey-Bass.

BUONO, A. F., J. L. BOWDITCH, and J. W. LEWIS, III. (1988). "The Cultural Dynamics of Transformation: The Case of a Bank Merger." In *Corporate Transformation: Revitalizing Organizations for a Competitive World,* edited by R. Kilmann, T. Covin, & Associates, 497–522. San Francisco: Jossey-Bass.

BURGELMAN, R. A. (1983). "A Process Model of Corporate Venturing in the Diversified Major Firm." *Administrative Science Quarterly* 17:223–244.

BURGELMAN, R. A. (1984). "On the Interplay of Process and Content in Internal Corporate Ventures: Action and Cognition in Strategy-Making." *Academy of Management Proceedings:* 2–6.

BURGELMAN, R. A., and L. SAYLES. (1985). *Inside Corporate Innovation.* New York: Free Press.

BURNS, J. M. (1978). *Leadership.* New York: Harper and Row.

BURT, R. S. (1982). *Toward a Structural Theory of Action: Models of Social Structure, Perception and Action.* New York: Academic Press.

CAPEN, E. C., R. V. CLAPP, and W. M. CAMPBELL. (1971). "Competitive Bidding in High-Risk Situations." *Journal of Petroleum Technology* 23(June):641–653.

CARTER, E. E. (1971). "The Behavioral Theory of the Firm and Top Level Corporate Decisions." *Administrative Science Quarterly* 16:413–428.

CAVES, R. E. (1987). "Effect of Mergers and Acquisitions on the Economy: An Industrial Organization Perspective." In *The Merger Boom,* edited by L. E. Browne and E. S. Rosengren, 149–168. Boston: Federal Reserve Bank of Boston.

CHAKRABARTI, A. K., and W. S. SOUDER. (1987). "Technology, Innovation and Performance in Corporate Mergers: A Managerial Evaluation." *Technovation* 6:103–114.

CHAKRAVARTHY, B. S., and P. LORANGE. (1990). *Managing the Strategy Process.* New York: Prentice-Hall.

CHANDLER, A. D. (1962). *Strategy and Structure: Chapters in the History of the American Industrial Enterprise.* Cambridge: MIT Press.

CHANDLER, A. D. (1986). "The Evolution of Modern Global Competition." In *Competition in Global Industries,* edited by M. E. Porter, 405–448. Boston: Harvard Business School Press.

CHANDLER, A. D. (1990a). "The Enduring Logic of Industrial Success," *Harvard Business Review* (March–April):130–140.

CHANDLER, A. D. (1990b). *Scale and Scope.* Cambridge: Harvard University Press.

CHATTERJEE, S. (1986). "Types of Synergy and Economic Value: The Impact of Acquisitions on Merging and Rival Firms." *Strategic Management Journal* 7:119–140.

CHILD, J. (1972). "Organization Structure, Environment and Performance: The Role of Strategic Choice." *Sociology* 6:1–22.

CHRISTENSEN, H. K., and L. FAHEY. (1986). "Resources, Distinctive Competence, and Competitive Advantage." Paper presented at the annual meeting of the Academy of Management, Chicago.

CHRISTENSEN, H. K., and C. A. MONTGOMERY. (1981). "Corporate Economic Performance: Diversification Strategy Versus Market Structure." *Strategic Management Journal* 2:327–343.

CHRISTENSON, C. R. (1972). "The Power of Negative Thinking," Working Paper, Graduate School of Business Administration, Harvard University.

COASE, R. (1937). "The Nature of the Firm." *Econometrica* 4:386–405.

COHEN, M. D., and J. G. MARCH. (1974). *Leadership and Ambiguity.* Boston: Harvard Business School Press.

COHEN, M. D., J. G. MARCH, and P. P. OLSEN. (1972). "A Garbage Can Model of Organizational Choice." *Administrative Science Quarterly* 17(1):1–25.

COOKE, T. E., IN ASSOCIATION WITH ARTHUR YOUNG. (1988). *International Mergers and Acquisitions.* Oxford: Blackwell.

COOL, K., and D. E. SCHENDEL. (1988). "Performance Differences Among Strategic Group Members." *Strategic Management Journal* 11:207–223.

COPELAND, T., T. KOLLER, and J. MURRIN. (1990). *Valuation: Measuring and Managing the Value of Companies.* New York: John Wiley & Sons.

COSIER, R. A. (1978). "The Effects of Three Potential Aids for Making Strategic Decisions on Prediction Accuracy." *Organizational Behavior and Human Performance* 22:295–306.

CYERT, R. M., and J. G. MARCH. (1963). *A Behavioral Theory of the Firm.* Englewood Cliffs, NJ: Prentice-Hall.

DAFT, R. L., and K. E. WEICK. (1984). Toward a Model of Organizations as Interpretive Systems." *Academy of Management Review* 9:284–295.

DAVIDSON, W. H., and P. C. HASPESLAGH. (1982). "Shaping a Global Product Organization." *Harvard Business Review* (July–August):125–132.

DAVIS, M. (1971). "That's Interesting! Toward a Phenomenology of Sociology and a Sociology of Phenomenology." *Philosophy of the Social Sciences* 4:309–344.

DEAKIN, E. B., and W. W. MAHER. (1987). *Cost Accounting,* 2d ed. Homewood, IL: Dow Jones–Irwin.

DEARBORN, D. C., and H. A. SIMON. (1958). "Selective Perceptions: A Note on the Departmental Identifications of Executives." *Sociometry* 21:140–144.

DE LA TORRE, J., and D. H. NECKAR. (1988). "Forecasting Political Risk for International Operations." *International Forecasting Journal* 4:221–241.

DENNIS, D. K., and J. J. McCONNELL. (1986). "Corporate Mergers and Security Returns." *Journal of Financial Economics* 16:143–187.

DE NOBLE, A. F. (1984). "An Analysis of the Association Between an Acquiring Firm's Corporate and Business Level Strategies and Its Resulting Cost-Merger Managerial Decisions." Working Paper, San Diego State University.

DEVINE, I. (1984). "Organizational Adaptation to Crisis Conditions and Effects on Organization Members." Academy of Management *Proceedings:* 163–167.

DICKSON, M. (1990). "A Little Local Difficulty." *Financial Times,* April 28, 6.

DIERICKX, I., and K. COOL. (1989). "Asset Stock Accumulation and the Sustainability of Competitive Advantage." *Management Science* 35:1504–1511.

DODD, P. (1976). "Corporate Takeovers and the Australian Equity Market." *Australian Journal of Management* 1:15–35.

DONALDSON, G., and J. W. LORSCH. (1983). *Decision Making at the Top.* New York: Basic Books.

DOUGLAS, S. P., and Y. WIND. (1987). "The Myth of Globalization." *Columbia Journal of World Business* 22 (Winter):19–29.

DOZ, Y. (1976). *National Policies and Multinational Management.* Doctoral dissertation. Boston: Harvard Business School.

DOZ, Y. L. (1979). *Government Control and Multinational Management: Power Systems and Telecommunication Equipment.* New York: Praeger Special Studies.

DOZ, Y. (1986a). "Government Policies and Global Industries." In *Competition in Global Industries,* edited by M. E. Porter, 225–266. Boston: Harvard Business School Press.

DOZ, Y. L. (1986b). *Strategic Management in Multinational Companies.* Oxford: Pergamon Press.

DOZ, Y., C. A. BARTLETT, and C. K. PRAHALAD. (1981). "Global Competitive Pressures and Host Country Demands: Managing Tensions in MNCs." *California Management Review* 23 (Spring):63–74.

DOZ, Y. L., and C. K. PRAHALAD. (1987). *The Multinational Mission: Balancing Local Demands and Global Vision.* New York: Free Press.

DUHAIME, I. M., and J. H. GRANT. (1984). "Factors Influencing Divestment Decision Making: Evidence from a Field Study." *Strategic Management Journal* 5:301–318.

DUHAIME, I. M., and C.R. SCHWENK. (1985). "Conjectures on Cognitive Simplification in Acquisition and Divestment Decision Making." *Academy of Management Review* 10:287–295.

DUTTON, J. E., and S. E. JACKSON. (1987). "Categorizing Strategic Issues:

Links to Organizational Action." *Academy of Management Review* 12:76–90.

Eccles, R. G., and D. B. Crane. (1988). *Doing Deals: Investment Banks at Work*. Boston: Harvard Business School Press.

Eckbo, B. E. (1986). "Mergers and the Market for Corporate Control: The Canadian Evidence." *Canadian Journal of Economics* 19(May):236–260.

Eckbo, B. E., and H. Langohr. (1985). "Disclosure Regulations and Determinants of Takeover Premiums." Unpublished paper, University of British Columbia and INSEAD.

Eckbo, B. E., and H. Langohr. (Forthcoming). "Takeover Premiums, Disclosure Regulations, and the Market for Corporate Control: A Comparative Analysis of Public Tender Offers, Controlling Block Trades and Minority Buyouts in France." *Journal of Financial Economics*.

Eisenhardt, K. (1989a). "Agency Theory: An Assessment and Review." *Strategic Management Review* 14:57–74.

Eisenhardt, K. E. (1989b). "Building Theory from Case Studies." *Academy of Management Review* 14:532–550.

Eisenhardt, K. (1989c). "Making Fast Strategic Decisions in High-Velocity Environments." *Academy of Management Journal* 32:543–576.

Elgers, P. T., and J. J. Clark. (1980). "Merger Types and Stockholder Returns: Additional Evidence." *Financial Management* 9:66–72.

Elwood, J. W. (1987). "The Effects of Mergers and Acquisitions on the Governance of the Modern Corporation." In *Handbook of Modern Finance*, edited by D. E. Logue, 29B1–29B69. Boston: Warren, Gorham, and Lamont.

Emerson, R. M. (1964). "Power-Dependence Relations." *American Sociological Review* 27:31–41.

Erni, P. (1979). *The Basel Marriage: History of the Ciba-Geigy Merger*. Zurich: Publications Department, Neue Zürcher Zeitung.

Evans, P., Y. Doz, and A. Laurent. (1989). *Human Resource Management in International Firms*. London: Macmillan.

Fairburn, J. A., and J. A. Kay, eds. (1989). *Mergers and Merger Policy*. New York: Oxford University Press.

Fama, E. F. (1968). "Risk, Return, and Equilibrium—Some Clarifying Comments." *Journal of Finance* 23:29–40.

Fama, E. F. (1980). "Agency Problems and the Theory of the Firm." *Journal of Political Economy* (88),288–307.

Fama, E. F., and M. C. Jensen. (1983a). "Agency Problems and Residual Claims." *Journal of Law and Economics* 26:327–349.

Fama, E. F., and M. C. Jensen. (1983b). "Separation of Ownership and Control." *Journal of Law and Economics* 26:301–325.

Farquhar, A., P. Evans, and Tawaday. (1989). "Lessons from Practice in Managing Organizational Change." In *Human Resource Management in Interna-*

tional Firms, edited by P. Evans, Y. Doz, and A. Laurent, 33–55. London: Macmillan.

FAST, N. D. (1979). *The Rise and Fall of Corporate New Venture Divisions.* Ann Arbor: VMI Research Press.

FELDMAN, M. S., and J. M. MARCH. (1981). "Information in Organizations as Signal and Symbol." *Administrative Science Quarterly* 26:171–186.

FINKELSTEIN, S. (1986). "The Acquisition Integration Process." Working Paper, Graduate School of Business, Columbia University.

FOMBRUN, C. J. (1983). "Attributions of Power Across a Social Network." *Human Relations* 36:493–507.

FOSTER, G. (1986). *Financial Statement Analysis,* 2d ed. Englewood Cliffs, NJ: Prentice-Hall.

FOWLER, K. L., and D. R. SCHMIDT. (1989). "Determinants of Tender Offer Post-Acquisition Financial Performance." *Strategic Management Journal* (10):339–350.

FRANKS, J., J. BROYLES, and M. HECHT. (1977). "An Industry Study of the Profitability of Mergers in the United Kingdom." *Journal of Finance* 32 (December):1513–1525.

FRANKS, J., and C. MAYER. (1990). "Capital Markets and Corporate Control: A Comparison of France, Germany, and the UK." *Economic Policy* (10): 1–43.

FREDRICKSON, J. W. (1983). "Strategic Process Research: Questions and Recommendations." *Academy of Management Review* 8:565–575.

FREDRICKSON, J. W. (1985). "Effects of Decision Motive and Organizational Performance Level on Strategic Decision Processes." *Academy of Management Journal* 28:821–843.

FREDRICKSON, J. W., and A. I. IAQUINTO. (1989). "Inertia and Creeping Rationality in Strategic Decision Processes." *Academy of Management Journal* 32:516–542.

FREDRICKSON, J. W., and T. R. MITCHELL. (1984). "Strategic Decision Processes: Comprehensiveness and Performance in an Industry with an Unstable Environment." *Academy of Management Journal* 27:399–423.

FREEMAN, R. E. (1984). *Strategic Management: A Stakeholder Approach.* Boston: Pitman.

FROMM, D., and P. HASPESLAGH. (1987). "The Dutch View of Hostile Takeovers." *Acquisitions Monthly* (September):51–52.

GABARRO, J. J. (1985). "When a New Manager Takes Charge." *Harvard Business Review* (May–June):110–123.

GAGNON, J. M., P. BREHAIN, C. BROQUET, and F. GUERRA. (1982). "Stock Market Behaviour of Merging Firms: The Belgian Experience." *European Economic Review* 17 (February):187–211.

GEERTZ, C. (1973). *The Interpretation of Culture.* New York: Basic Books.

GEORGE, A. L. (1980). *Presidential Decisionmaking in Foreign Policy: The Effective Use of Information and Advice.* Boulder, CO: Westview.

GHEMEWAT, P. (1988). "Sustainable Advantage." *Harvard Business Review* (September–October):53–58.

GHOSHAL, S. (1987). "Global Strategy: An Organizing Framework." *Strategic Management Journal* 8 (September–October):425–440.

GILSON, R. J., M. S. SCHOLES, and M. A. WOLFSON. (1988). "Taxation and the Dynamics of Corporate Control: The Uncertain Case for Tax-Motivated Acquisitions." In *Knights, Raiders, and Targets: The Impact of Hostile Takeovers,* edited by J. C. Coffee, L. Lowenstein, and S. Rose-Ackerman, 271–299. New York: Oxford University Press.

GLASER, B. J., and A. L. STRAUSS. (1967). *The Discovery of Grounded Theory.* Chicago: Aldine.

GOFFMAN, E. (1952). "On Cooling the Mark Out: Some Aspects of Adaptation to Failure." *Psychiatry* 15:451–463.

GOLBE, D. L., and L. J. WHITE. (1978a). "Green Giant: The New Course That Makes It Attractive to Pillsbury." *Business Week,* October 2, 66–67.

———. (1978b). "It's Good Logic, But Is It Good Business?" *Forbes,* November 13, 138–140.

———. (1979). "Pillsbury's Ambitious Plans to Use Green Giant." *Business Week,* February 5, 87–88.

———. (1982). "Pillsbury: Growth Could Suffer as Burger King Profits Shrink." *Business Week,* June 7, 118–120.

———. (1988). "A Time Series Analysis of Mergers and Acquisitions in the U.S. Economy." In *Takeovers: Causes and Consequences,* edited by A. J. Auerbach, 265–302. Chicago: University of Chicago Press.

GOOLD, M., and A. CAMPBELL. (1987). *Strategies and Styles: The Role of the Centre in Managing Diversified Corporations.* London: Basil Blackwell.

GORT, M. (1962). *Diversification and Integration in American Industry.* Princeton: Princeton University Press.

GRANOVETTER, M. (1985). "Economics Action and Social Structure: The Problem of Embeddedness." *American Journal of Sociology* 91:481–510.

GRAVES, D. (1981). "Individual Reactions to a Merger of Two Small Firms of Brokers in the Reinsurance Industry: A Total Population Survey." *Journal of Management Studies* (18):89–113.

GREINER, L. (1972). "Evolution and Revolution as Organizations Grow." *Harvard Business Review* (July–August):37–46.

GULLIVER, F. R. (1987). "Postproject Appraisals Pay." *Harvard Business Review* (March–April):128–132.

GUPTA, A. K., and V. GOVINDARAJAN. (1984). "Business Unit Strategy, Managerial Characteristics and Business Unit Effectiveness at Strategy Implementation." *Academy of Management Journal* 27:25–41.

GUTH, W. D., and I. C. MACMILLAN. (1986). "Strategy Implementation vs. Middle Management Self Interest." *Strategic Management Journal* 7:313–327.

HAKANSSON, H., ED. (1987). *Industrial Technological Development—A Network Approach.* London: Croom Helm, Methuen.

HALL, B. H. (1988). "The Effects of Takeover Activity on Corporate Research and Development." In *Takeovers: Causes and Consequences,* edited by A. J. Auerbach, 69–96. Chicago: University of Chicago Press.

HALL, E. T. (1959). *The Silent Language.* New York: Fawcett.

HAMBRICK, D. C., and P. MASON. (1984). "Upper Echelons: The Organization as a Reflection of Its Top Managers." *Academy of Management Review* 2:193–206.

HAMEL, G., and C. K. PRAHALAD. (1989). "Strategic Intent." *Harvard Business Review* (May–June):63–76.

HAMEL, G., and C. K. PRAHALAD. (1990). "The Core Competence of the Corporation." *Harvard Business Review* (May–June):79–91.

HAMERMESH, R. G. (1986). *Making Strategy Work: How Senior Managers Produce Results.* New York: Wiley.

HANNA, R. (1968). "The Concept of Strategy in Multi-Industry Companies." Doctoral dissertation. Boston: Harvard Business School.

HARRIGAN, K. R. (1985). *Strategic Flexibility: A Management Guide for Changing Times.* Lexington, MA: Lexington Books.

HARRINGTON, D. R., and B. D. WILSON. (1989). *Corporate Financial Analysis,* 3d ed. Homewood, IL: Irwin.

HARVEY-JONES, J. (1988). *Making It Happen.* London: Penguin.

HASPESLAGH, P. (1982). "Portfolio Planning: Uses and Limits." *Harvard Business Review* (January–February):58–73.

HASPESLAGH, P. C. (1983). "Portfolio Planning Approaches and the Strategic Management Process in Diversified Industrial Companies." Doctoral dissertation. Boston: Harvard Business School.

HASPESLAGH, P. (1985). "Toward a Concept of Corporate Strategy for the Diversified Firm." Research Paper No. 816, Graduate School of Business, Stanford University.

HASPESLAGH, P. C. (1986a). "Conceptualizing the Strategic Process in Diversified Firms: The Role and Nature of the Corporate Influence Process." Working Paper No. 86/09, INSEAD.

HASPESLAGH, P. C. (1986b). "Making Acquisitions Work." *Acquisitions Monthly:*14–16.

HASPESLAGH, P. C. (1990). "Acquisitions as Resource Allocation Decisions: A Multinational Perspective." Working Paper, INSEAD.

HASPESLAGH P. C., and N. BERG. (1979). "Diversification and Mergers: Some Trends and Results." Working Paper No. 79-2, Graduate School of Business Administration, Harvard University.

HASPESLAGH, P., and A. FARQUHAR. (1987). "The Acquisition Integration Process: A Contingent Framework." Paper presented at the Seventh Annual International Conference of the Strategic Management Society, Boston, October 14–17.

HASPESLAGH, P. C., and D. B. JEMISON. (1987). "Acquisitions: Myth and Reality." *Sloan Management Review* (Winter):53–58.

HASPESLAGH, P. C., and S. GHOSHAL. (1990). "The Challenge of Strategic Assembly." Paper presented at the Strategic Management Society Conference, Stockholm, 24–28 September 1990.

HAYES, R. H. (1979). "The Human Side of Acquisitions." *Management Review* 68 (November):41–46.

HAYES, R. H. (1985). "Strategic Planning—Forward in Reverse?" *Harvard Business Review* (November–December):111–119.

HAYES, R. H., and W. J. ABERNATHY. (1980). "Managing our Way to Economic Decline." *Harvard Business Review* (July–August):67–77.

HAYES, S. L., III, A. M. SPENCE, and D. V. P. MARKS. (1983). *Competition in the Investment Banking Industry.* Boston: Harvard University Press.

HEDLUND, G. (1986). "The Hypermodern MNC: A Heterarchy?" *Human Resource Management* (Spring):9–35.

HENNART, J. F. (1988). "A Transaction Cost Approach of Equity Joint Ventures." *Strategic Management Journal* (9):361–374.

HIRSCH, M., and J. A. Y. ANDREWS. (1983). "Ambushes, Shootouts and Knights of the Roundtable: The Language of Corporate Takeovers." In *Organizational Symbolism,* edited by L. R. Pondy, P. J. Frost, G. Morgan, and T. C. Dandridge, 145–155. Greenwich, CT: Jai Press.

HIRSCH, P. M. (1987). *Pack Your Own Parachute.* Reading, MA: Addison-Wesley.

HITE, G. L., and J. E. OWERS. (1983). "Security Price Reactions Around Corporate Spin-Off Announcements." *Journal of Financial Economics* 12:409–436.

HOFER, C. (1980). "Turnaround Strategies." *Journal of Business Strategy* 1:19–31.

HOFSTEDE, G. H. (1980a). *Culture's Consequences: International Differences in Work-Related Values.* Beverly Hills: Sage Publications.

HOFSTEDE, G. (1980b). "Motivation, Leadership and Organization: Do American Theories Apply Abroad?" *Organizational Dynamics* (Summer):42–64.

HOLMSTRÖM, B. (1979). "Moral Hazard and Observability." *Bell Journal of Economics* 10:74–91.

HORNGREN, C. T. (1982). *Cost Accounting: A Managerial Emphasis,* 5th ed. Englewood Cliffs, NJ: Prentice-Hall.

HOUT, T., M. E. PORTER, and E. RUDDEN. (1982). "How Global Companies Win Out." *Harvard Business Review* (September–October):98–108.

HOWELL, R. A. (1970). "Plan Now to Integrate Your Acquisitions." *Harvard Business Review* (November–December):66–76.

HUBER, G. P. (1984). "The Nature and Design of Post-Industrial Organizations." *Management Science* 30:928–951.

HUBER, G. P. (1991). "Organizational Learning: An Examination of the Contributing Processes and the Literatures." *Organization Science* 2:46–51.

HUNT, M. (1972). "Competition in the Home Appliance Industry 1960–70." Ph.D. diss., Harvard University.

HUSSON, B. (1986). "The Wealth Effect of Corporate Takeovers. An Empirical Investigation of a French Sample of Cash Tender Offers, Exchange Tender Offers and Controlling Block Trades." *Cahier de Recherche du Centre HEC-ISA,* Jouy-en-Josas, France.

HUSSON, B. (1987). "La Prise de Controle des Entreprises." Paris: Presses Universitaires de France.

IMAI, K., I. NONAKA, and H. TAKEUCHI. (1985). "Managing the New Product Development: How Japanese Companies Learn and Unlearn." In *The Uneasy Alliance: Managing the Productivity Technology Dilemma,* edited by K. B. Clark, R. H. Hayes, and C. Lorenz, 337–375. Cambridge: Harvard Business School Press.

INZERILLI, G., and A. LAURENT. (1983). "Managerial Views of Organization Structure in France and the USA." *International Studies of Management and Organization* 13(1–2):97–118.

ITAMI, H. (with T. ROEHE). (1987). *Mobilizing Invisible Assets.* Cambridge: Harvard University Press.

IVANCEVICH, J. M., D. M. SCHWEIGER, and F. R. POWER. (1987). "Strategies for Managing Human Resources During Mergers and Acquisitions." *Human Resource Planning* 10:19–35.

JACKSON, S. E., and J. E. DUTTON. (1988). "Discerning Threats and Opportunities." *Administrative Science Quarterly* 33:370–387.

JACQUEMIN, A. P., and C. H. BERRY. (1979). "Entropy Measure of Diversification and Corporate Growth." *Journal of Industrial Economics* 27:359–369.

JANIS, I. (1972). *Victims of Groupthink.* Boston: Houghton Mifflin.

JANIS, I. (1982). "Decision Making Under Stress." In *Handbook on Stress: Theoretical and Clinical Aspects,* edited by L. Goldberg and S. Breznitz. New York: Free Press.

JANIS, I. (1988). *Crucial Decisions.* New York: Free Press.

JANIS, I., and L. MANN. (1977). *Decision Making: A Psychological Analysis of Conflict, Choice, and Commitment.* New York: Free Press.

JARRELL, G. A. Comment at conference, sponsored by the Karl Eller Center at the University of Arizona, entitled "Corporate Restructuring Through Mergers, Acquisitions, and Leveraged Buyouts," December 1986.

JARRELL, G. A., J. A. BRICKLEY, and J. M. NETTER. (1988). "The Market for Corporate Control: The Empirical Evidence Since 1980." *Journal of Economic Perspectives* (2):21–48.

JEMISON, D. B. (1981a). "The Importance of an Integrative Approach to Strategic Management Research." *Academy of Management Review* 6:601–608.

JEMISON, D. B. (1981b). "Organizational Versus Environmental Sources of Influence in Strategic Decision Making." *Strategic Management Journal* 2:77–89.

JEMISON, D. B. (1985). "The Role of the Division General Manager in Corporate Strategic Management." In *Advances in Strategic Management,* edited by R. Lamb and P. Shrivastava, 163–179. Greenwich, CT: Jai Press.

JEMISON, D. B. (1986). "Strategic Capability Transfer in Acquisition Integration." Research Paper series no. 913, Graduate School of Business, Stanford University.

JEMISON, D. B. (1988a). "Process Constraints on Strategic Capability Transfer in Acquisitions Integration." Working Paper 88/89 5-1, Graduate School of Business, University of Texas, Austin.

JEMISON, D. B. (1988b). "Value Creation and Acquisition Integration: The Role of Strategic Capability Transfer." In *Corporate Restructuring Through Mergers, Acquisitions, and Leveraged Buyouts,* edited by G. Liebcap, 191–218. Greenwich, CT: Jai Press.

JEMISON, D. B., and S. B. SITKIN. (1984). "Hidden Barriers to Acquisition Success." Working Paper 775, Graduate School of Business, Stanford University.

JEMISON, D. B., and S. B. SITKIN. (1986a). "Corporate Acquisitions: A Process Perspective." *Academy of Management Review,* 11(1):145–163.

JEMISON, D. B., and S. B. SITKIN. (1986b). "Acquisition: The Process Can Be a Problem." *Harvard Business Review* (March–April):64:107–116.

JENSEN, M. C. (1972). *Studies in the Theory of Capital Markets.* New York: Praeger.

JENSEN, M. C. (1983). "Organization Theory and Methodology." *The Accounting Review* 58(April):319–345.

JENSEN, M. C. (1984). "Takeovers: Folklore and Science." *Harvard Business Review* (November–December):109–121.

JENSEN, M. C. (1987). "The Free Cash Flow Theory of Takeovers: A Financial Perspective on Mergers and Acquisitions and the Economy." In *The Merger*

Boom, edited by L. E. Browne and E. S. Rosengren, 102–143. Boston: Federal Reserve Bank of Boston.

JENSEN, M. C., and R. S. RUBACK. (1983). "The Market for Corporate Control: The Scientific Evidence." *Journal of Financial Economics* 11:5–50.

JICK, T. (1979). "Process and Impacts of a Merger: Individual and Organizational Perspectives." Doctoral dissertation. Ithaca: Cornell University.

KAHNEMAN, D., P. SLOVIC, and A. TVERSKY. (1982). *Judgment Under Uncertainty: Heuristics and Biases.* Cambridge: Cambridge University Press.

KAHNEMAN, D., and A. TVERSKY. (1979). "Prospect Theory: An Analysis of Decision Under Risk." *Econometrica* 47:263–291.

KATZ, D., and R. L. KAHN. (1966). *The Social Psychology of Organizations.* New York: John Wiley.

KELLER, R. T., and W. E. HOLLAND. (1975). "Boundary Spanning Roles in a Research and Development Organization: An Empirical Investigation." *Academy of Management Journal* 18:388–393.

KELLEY, G. (1976). "Seducing the Elites: The Politics of Decision Making and Innovation in Organizational Networks." *Academy of Management Review* 1:66–74.

KIESLER, C. A., and R. MATHOG. (1971). "Resistance to Influence as a Function of Number of Prior Consonant Acts." In *The Psychology of Commitment,* edited by C. Kiesler, 66–74. New York: Academic Press.

KILLOUGH, J. (1978). "Improving Payoffs from Transnational Advertising." *Harvard Business Review* 56 (July–August):102–110.

KIM, E. H., J. J. MCCONNELL, and P. GREENWOOD. (1977). "Capital Structure Rearrangement and Me-First Rules in an Efficient Capital Market." *Journal of Finance* 32:789–810.

KIM, W. C. (1989). "Developing A Global Diversification Measure." *Management Science* 35:375–387.

KIM, W. C., P. HWANG, and W. P. BURGERS. (1989). "Global Diversification Strategy and Corporate Profit Performance." *Strategic Management Journal* 10:45–57.

KIMBERLY, J. R. (1979). "Issues in the Creation of Organizations: Initiation, Innovation, and Institutionalization." *Academy of Management Journal* 22:437–457.

KIMBERLY, J. R. (1984). *New Futures: The Challenges of Managing Corporate Transitions.* Homewood, IL: Dow Jones–Irwin.

KITCHING, J. (1967). "Why Do Mergers Miscarry?" *Harvard Business Review* (November–December):84–101.

KITCHING, J. (1974). "Winning and Losing with European Acquisitions." *Harvard Business Review* (March–April):124–136.

KOGUT, B. (1985a). "Designing Global Strategies: Comparative and Competitive Value Added Choices." *Sloan Management Review* 26 (Summer):15–28.

Kogut, B. (1985b). "Designing Global Strategies: Profiting from Operating Flexibility." *Sloan Management Review* (Fall):27–38.

Kogut, B. (1988). "Joint Ventures: Theoretical and Empirical Perspectives." *Strategic Management Journal* 9:319–322.

Kotler, P. (1988). *Marketing Management: Analysis, Planning, Implementation and Control,* 6th ed. Englewood Cliffs, NJ: Prentice-Hall.

Kotter, J. (1982). *The General Managers.* New York: Free Press.

Kusewitt, J. B. (1985). "An Exploratory Study of Strategic Acquisition Factors Relating to Performance." *Strategic Management Journal* 6:151–169.

Lamoreaux, N. R. (1985). *The Great Merger Movement in American Business.* Cambridge: Cambridge University Press.

Langer, E. J. (1975). "The Illusion of Control." *Journal of Personality and Social Psychology* 32:311–328.

Laurent, A. (1983). "The Cultural Diversity of Western Conceptions of Management. *International Studies of Management and Organization* 13(1–2):75–96.

Laurent, A., and F. Bartolomé. (1987). "Managers' Cognitive Maps for Upward and Downward Relationships." Working Paper No. 87/17, INSEAD.

Lawrence, P. R., and D. S. Dyer. (1983). *Renewing American Industry.* New York: Free Press.

Lawrence, P. R., and J. Lorsch. (1967). *Organization and Environment.* Boston: Division of Research, Graduate School of Business Administration, Harvard University.

Leavitt, H. J. (1986). *Corporate Pathfinders: Building Visions and Values Into Organizations.* Homewood, IL: Dow Jones–Irwin.

Lehn, K., and A. B. Poulsen. (1988). "Leveraged Buyouts: Wealth Created or Wealth Redistributed?" In *Public Policy Toward Corporate Takeovers,* edited by L. M. Weidenbaum and K. Chilton, 46–62. New Brunswick, NJ: Transaction Publishers.

Leifer, R., and A. Delbecq. (1978). "Organizational/Environmental Interchange: A Model of Boundary Spanning Activity." *Academy of Management Review* 3:40–50.

Leighton, C. M., and G. R. Tod. (1969). "After the Acquisition: Continuing Challenge." *Harvard Business Review* (March–April):90–102.

Lenz, R. T. (1980). "Strategic Capability: A Concept and Framework for Analysis." *Academy of Management Review* 5(2):225–234.

Levin, D. (1989). *Irreconcilable Differences.* Boston: Little, Brown.

Levine, S., and P. E. White. (1961). "Exchange as a Conceptual Framework for the Study of Interorganizational Relationships." *Administrative Science Quarterly* 5:583–601.

LEVINSON, H. (1970). "A Psychologist Diagnoses Merger Failures." *Harvard Business Review* (March–April): 139–147.

LEVITT, B., and J. G. MARCH. (1988). "Organizational Learning." *Annual Review of Sociology* 14:319–340.

LEVITT, T. (1983). "The Globalization of Markets." *Harvard Business Review* (May–June): 92–102.

LINDBLOM, C. E. (1959). "The Science of Muddling Through." *Public Administration Review* (Spring) 19:79–88.

LINDGREN, U. (1982a). *Foreign Acquisitions: Management of the Integration Process.* Stockholm: Business School Press.

LINDGREN, U. (1982b). Foreign Acquisitions: Management of the Integration Process (Appendix). IIB/EFI.

LINTNER, J. (1965). "The Valuation of Risk Assets and the Selection of Risky Investments in Stock Portfolios and Capital Budgets." *Review of Economics and Statistics* 47:13–37.

LIPPMAN, S. A., AND R. P. RUMELT. (1982). "Uncertain Imitability: An Analysis of Interfirm Differences in Efficiency Under Competition." *Bell Journal of Economics* 13:418–438.

LORANGE, P. (1980). *Corporate Planning: An Executive Viewpoint.* Englewood Cliffs, NJ: Prentice-Hall.

LORANGE, P., and R. F. VANCIL. (1977). *Strategic Planning Systems.* Englewood Cliffs, NJ: Prentice-Hall.

LORD, C. G., L. ROSS, and M. R. LEPPER. (1979). "Biased Assimilation and Attitude Polarization: The Effects of Prior Theories on Subsequently Considered Evidence." *Journal of Personality and Social Psychology* 37:2098–2109.

LORENZONI, G., A. GRANDI, AND C. BOARI. (1989). "Organizational Networks: Three Basic Patterns." *University of Bologna Working Paper.* Originally published in Italian as: Boari, C., A. Grandi, and G. Lorenzoni. (1989). "Le Organizazioni a rete: tre concetti di base." *Economia e Politica Industriale* 64.

LOTH, R. B. (1988). "How to Evaluate Country Risk." *Credit and Financial Management* 88(6):27.

LOUIS, M. (1986). "Organizations as Culture-Bearing Milieus." In *Organizational Symbolism,* edited by L. R. Pondy, P. J. Frost, G. Morgan, and T. Dandridge, 39–54. Greenwich, CT: Jai Press.

LUBATKIN, M. (1983). "Mergers and the Performance of the Acquiring Firm." *Academy of Management Review* 8:218–225.

LUBATKIN, M. (1987). "Merger Strategies and Stockholder Value." *Strategic Management Journal* 8:39–53.

LUBATKIN, M., and H. M. O'NEILL. (1987). "Merger Strategies and Capital Market Risk." *Academy of Management Journal* (4):665–664.

Lynch, H. H. (1971). "Financial Performance of Conglomerates." Working Paper, Division of Research, Harvard Business School, Boston.

MacCrimmon, K. R., and D. H. Wehrung. (1986). *Taking Risks: The Management of Uncertainty.* New York: Free Press

Mace, M. L., and G. Montgomery. (1962). *Management Problems of Corporate Acquisitions.* Cambridge: Harvard University Press.

Magenheim, E. B., and D. C. Mueller. (1988). "Are Acquiring-Firm Shareholders Better Off after an Acquisition?" In *Knights, Raiders, and Targets: The Impact of Hostile Takeovers,* edited by J. C. Coffee, L. Lowenstein, and S. Rose-Ackerman, 171–193. New York: Oxford University Press.

Malatesta, P. H. (1983). "The Wealth Effect of Merger Activity and the Objective Functions of Merging Firms." *Journal of Financial Economics* 11:155–181.

Manne, H. G. (1965). "Mergers and the Market for Corporate Control." *Journal of Political Economy* 73–74:110–120.

March, J. (1962). "The Business Firm as a Political Coalition." *Journal of Politics* 24:662–678.

March, J. G. (1978). "Bounded Rationality, Ambiguity, and the Engineering of Choice." *Bell Journal of Economics* 9:587–608.

March, J., and J. Olsen. (1976). *Ambiguity and Choice in Organizations.* Bergen (Norway): Universitetsforlaget.

March, J. S., and Z. Shapira. (1987). "Managerial Perspectives on Risk and Risk Taking." *Management Science* 33:1404–1418.

Markides, C. (1990). *Corporate Refocusing and Economic Performance.* Doctoral dissertation. Boston: Harvard Business School.

Markowitz, H. (1952). "Portfolio Selection." *Journal of Finance* 7:77–91.

Marks, M. L. (1982). "Merging Human Resources: A Review of Current Research." *Mergers and Acquisitions* (17):38–44.

Marks, M. L., and P. Mirvis. (1985). "Merger Syndrome: Stress and Uncertainty." *Mergers and Acquisitions* (Summer):50–55.

Martin, J., and D. Meyerson. (1988). "Organizational Cultures and the Denial, Channeling, and Acknowledgement of Ambiguity." In *Managing Ambiguity and Change,* edited by L. R. Pondy, R. J. Boland, and H. Thomas, 93–126. Chichester: John Wiley.

Martin, J., and C. Siehl. (1983). "Organizational Cultures and the Counterculture: An Uneasy Symbiosis." *Organizational Dynamics* (Autumn):52–64.

Martinez, J. I., and J. C. Jarillo. (1989). "The Evolution of Research on Coordination Mechanisms in Multinational Corporations." *Journal of International Business Studies* 20 (Fall):489–514.

McCallister, L., and C. S. Fisher. (1978). "A Procedure for Surveying Personal Networks." *Sociological Methods and Research* 20(2):131–148.

McCann, J. E., and R. Gilkey. (1988). *Joining Forces*. New York: Prentice-Hall.

McCaskey, M. B. (1982). *The Executive Challenge: Managing Change and Ambiguity*. Boston: Pitman.

McGee, J., and H. Thomas. (1986). "Strategic Groups: Theory, Research, and Taxonomy." *Strategic Management Journal* 7:141–161.

Mechanic, D. (1964). "Sources of Power of Lower Participants in Complex Organizations." In *New Perspectives in Organizational Research*, ed. W. W. Cooper, H. J. Leavitt, and M. W. Shelly, 136–150. New York: John Wiley.

Melvin, M., and D. Schlagenhauf. (1985). "A Country Risk Index: Econometric Formulation and an Application to Mexico." *Economic Inquiry* 23:601.

Meyer, J. W., and B. Rowan. (1977). "Institutionalized Organizations: Formal Structure as Myth and Ceremony." *American Journal of Sociology* 83:340–363.

Michel, A., and I. Shaked. (1984). "Does Business Diversification Affect Performance?" *Financial Management* 13(4):18–25.

Miles, M. B. (1979). "Qualitative Data as an Attractive Nuisance." *Administrative Science Quarterly* 24:590–601.

Miles, M. B., and A. M. Huberman. (1984). *Qualitative Data Analysis: A Sourcebook of New Methods*. Beverly Hills, CA: Sage Publications.

Miles, R. E., and C. C. Snow. (1978). *Organizational Strategy, Structure and Process*. New York: McGraw-Hill.

Miles, R. H. (1976). "Role Requirements as Sources of Organizational Stress." *Journal of Applied Psychology* 61:172–179.

Miles, R. H. (1980). "Findings and Implications of Organizational Life Cycle Research: A Commencement." In *The Organizational Life Cycle*, ed. J. R. Kimberly, R. H. Miles, and assoc., 430–450. San Francisco: Jossey-Bass.

Miles, R. H. (1981). "Learning From Diversifying." Harvard Business School Note 9-481-060.

Miles R. H., in collaboration with Kim S. Cameron. (1982). *"Coffin Nails and Corporate Strategies."* Englewood Cliffs, NJ: Prentice-Hall.

Miller, K. H. Quoted in the *New York Times,* July 3, 1984, p. 37.

Mintzberg, H. (1973). *The Nature of Managerial Work*. New York: Harper & Row.

Mintzberg, H. (1978). "Patterns in Strategy Formation." *Management Science* 24:934–948.

Mintzberg, H. (1979). "An Emerging Strategy of Direct Research." *Administrative Science Quarterly* 24:519–712.

Mintzberg, H. (1987). "Crafting Strategy." *Harvard Business Review* (July–August):66–75.

Mintzberg, H., D. Raisinghani, and A. Theoret. (1976). "The Structure of

Unstructured Decision Processes." *Administrative Science Quarterly* 21:246–275.

MITROFF, I., and J. R. EMSHOFF. (1979). "On Strategic Assumption-making: A Dialectical Approach to Policy and Planning." *Academy of Management Review* 4:1–12.

MONTGOMERY, C. A. (1982). "The Measurement of Firm Diversification: Some New Empirical Evidence." *Academy of Management Journal* 25:299–307.

MONTGOMERY, C. A. (1985). "Product Market Diversification and Market Power." *Academy of Management Journal* 5:181–191.

MØRCK, R., A. SHLEIFER, and R. W. VISHNY. (1988). "Characteristics of Targets of Hostile and Friendly Takeovers." In *Takeovers: Causes and Consequences,* edited by A. J. Auerbach, 101–129. Chicago: University of Chicago Press.

MORITA, A., and S. ISHIHARA. (1989). *"The Japan That Can Say No."* Kobunsha: Kappa-Holmes. English translation by United States Department of Defense.

MUELLER, D. C. (1969). "A Theory of Conglomerate Mergers." *Quarterly Journal of Economics* 83:643–659.

MUELLER, D. C., ed. (1980). *The Determinants and Effects of Mergers.* Cambridge, MA: Oelgeschlager, Gunn and Hain.

MULLINS, D. W., JR. (1982). "Does the Capital Asset Pricing Model Work?" *Harvard Business Review* (January–February):104–114.

MURPHY, K. J. (1985). "Corporate Performance and Managerial Remuneration: An Empirical Analysis." *Journal of Accounting and Economics* (7):11–42.

NAHAVANDI, A., and A. R. MALEKZADEH. (1988). "Acculturation in Mergers and Acquisitions." *Academy of Management Review* 13:79–90.

NAPIER, N. K., G. SIMMONS, and K. STRATTON. (1989). "Communication During a Merger: Experience of Two Banks." *Human Resource Planning* (12):105–122.

NAYLOR, T. H. (1979). *Corporate Planning Models.* Reading, MA: Addison-Wesley.

NEES, D. (1981). "Increase Your Divestment Effectiveness." *Strategic Management Journal* 2:119–130.

NELSON, R. R., and S. G. WINTER. (1982). *An Evolutionary Theory of Economic Change.* Cambridge: Harvard University Press.

NEUSTADT, R. E. (1976). *Presidential Power: The Politics of Leadership with Reflections on Johnson and Nixon.* New York: John Wiley.

NEWBOLD, G. D., S. J. STRAY,, and K. W. WILSON. (1976). "Shareholders' Interests and Acquisition Activity." *Accounting and Business Research* 23:201–213.

NONAKA, I. (1985). "The Essence of Failure: What can Management Learn from the Manner of Organization of Japanese Military Forces in the Pacific War?" *Management Japan* 18 (Autumn):21–27.

NONAKA, I. (1987). "Managing the Firm as an Information Creation Process." Institute of Business Research, Hitotsubashi University.

NORMANN, R. (1977). *Management for Growth*. New York: John Wiley.

O'REILLY, C. A. (1982). "Variations in Decision Makers' Use of Information Sources: The Impact of Quality and Accessibility of Information." *Academy of Management Journal* 25:756–771.

ORGAN, D. W. (1971). "Linking Pins Between Organizations and Environment." *Business Horizons* (December):73–80.

PALEPU, K. (1985). "Diversification Strategy, Profit Performance, and the Entropy Measure." *Strategic Management Journal* 6:239–255.

PANZAR, J. C., and R. D. WILLIG. (1977). "Economies of Scale and Economies of Scope in Multi-Output Production." *Quarterly Journal of Economics* 91:481–493.

PANZAR, J. C., and R. D. WILLIG. (1981). "Economies of Scope." *American Economic Review* 71:268–272.

PASCALE, R. T., and A. ATHOS. (1981). *The Art of Japanese Management*. New York: Warner Books.

PEAVY, J. W., III. (1984). "Modern Financial Theory, Corporate Strategy, and Public Policy: Another Perspective." *Academy of Management Review* 9:152–157.

PENROSE, E. (1959). *The Theory of the Growth of the Firm*. London: Basil Blackwell.

PETERS, T. J., and R. H. WATERMAN, JR. (1982). *In Search of Excellence*. New York: Basic Books.

PETTIGREW, A. M. (1977). "Strategy Formulation as a Political Process." *International Studies of Management and Organization* 7:78–87.

PETTIGREW, A. M. (1979). "On Studying Organizational Cultures." *Administrative Science Quarterly* 24:570–581.

PETTIGREW, A. M. (1985). *The Awakening Giant: Continuity and Change in ICI*. Oxford: Basil Blackwell Ltd.

PETTIGREW, A. (Forthcoming). "Longitudinal Field Research on Change: Theory and Practice." *Organization Science*.

PFEFFER, J. (1981). *Power in Organizations*. Marshfield, MA: Pitman Publishing.

PICINI, R. (1970). "Mergers, Diversification and the Growth of Large Firms 1948–1965." *St. John's Law Review* (Spring):44.

PINK, A. I. (1988). "Strategic Leadership Through Corporate Planning at ICI." *Long Range Planning* 21:18–25.

POLANYI, M. (1958). *Personal Knowledge: Towards a Post-Critical Philosophy.* Chicago: University of Chicago Press.

PORTER, M. E. (1980). *Competitive Strategy.* New York: Free Press.

PORTER, M. E. (1985). *Competitive Advantage.* New York: Free Press.

PORTER, M. E. (1986). *Competition in Global Industries.* Cambridge: Harvard Business School Press.

PORTER, M. E. (1987). "From Competitive Advantage to Competitive Strategy." *Harvard Business Review* (May–June):43–59.

PORTER, M. E. (1990). *The Competitive Advantage of Nations.* New York: Free Press.

PRAEGER, F. A. (1976). "A Framework for Evaluating Mergers." In *Modern Developments in Financial Management,* edited by S. C. Myers. Hinsdale, IL: Dryden Press.

PRAHALAD, C. K. (1976). *The Strategic Process in a Multinational Corporation.* Doctoral dissertation. Boston: Harvard Business School.

PRAHALAD, C. K., and R. A. BETTIS. (1986). "The Dominant Logic: A New Linkage Between Diversity and Performance." *Strategic Management Journal* 7:485–501.

PRAHALAD, C. K., and Y. DOZ. (1987). *The Multinational Mission: Balancing Local Demands and Global Vision.* New York: Free Press.

PRAHALAD, C. K., and G. HAMEL. (1989). "Strategic Intent." *Harvard Business Review* (May–June):63–76.

PRITCHETT, P. (1985). *After the Merger: Managing the Shockwaves.* Homewood, IL: Dow Jones–Irwin.

PRITCHETT, P. (1987). *Making Mergers Work: A Guide to Managing Mergers and Acquisitions.* Homewood, IL: Dow Jones–Irwin.

QUINN, J. B. (1980). *Strategies for Change: Logical Incrementalism.* Homewood, IL: Richard D. Irwin.

RAMANUJAM, V., and P. VARADARAJAN. (1989). "Research on Corporate Diversification: A Synthesis." *Strategic Management Journal* 10:523–551.

RAO, R. K. S. *Financial Management Concepts and Applications,* 2d ed. New York: Macmillan.

RAPPAPORT, A. (1986). *Creating Shareholder Value: The New Standard for Business Performance.* New York: Free Press.

RAVENSCRAFT, D. J., and F. M. SCHERER. (1987). *Mergers, Sell-offs, and Economic Efficiency.* Washington, DC: Brookings Institution.

ROETHLISBERGER, F. J. (1977). *The Elusive Phenomenon.* Cambridge: Harvard University Press.

ROETHLISBERGER, F. J., and W. J. DICKSON. (1939). *Management and the Worker.* Cambridge: Harvard University Press.

ROHATYN, FELIX. Quoted in *Time*, May 24, 1984, p. 47.

ROLL, R. (1986). "The Hubris Hypothesis of Corporate Takeovers." *Journal of Business* 59:197–216.

RUEFLI, T. (1990). "Risk and Return: Paradox Lost." *Management Science* 36:368–380.

RUGMAN, A. M. (1979). *International Diversification and the Multinational Enterprise*. Lexington, MA: Heath.

RUMELT, R. P. (1974). *Strategy, Structure, and Economic Performance*. Boston: Division of Research, Graduate School of Business Administration, Harvard University.

RUMELT, R. P. (1982). "Diversification Strategy and Profitability." *Strategic Management Journal* (3):359–369.

RYDÉN, B. (1972). *Mergers in Swedish Industry*. Stockholm: Almqvist & Wiksell.

SABATIER, P. (1978). "The Acquisition and Utilization of Technical Information by Administrative Agencies." *Administrative Science Quarterly* 19:411–421.

SALES, A., and P. H. MIRVIS. (1985). "When Cultures Collide: Issues in Acquisitions." In *New Futures: The Challenge of Managing Corporate Transitions*, edited by J. R. Kimberly and R. E. Quinn, 107–133. Homewood, IL: Dow Jones–Irwin.

SALTER, M. S., and W. S. WEINHOLD. (1978). "Diversification via Acquisition: Creating Value." *Harvard Business Review* (July–August):166–176.

SALTER, M. S., and W. S. WEINHOLD. (1979). *Diversification Through Acquisition*. New York: Free Press.

SCHELLING, T. C. (1960). *The Strategy of Conflict*. Cambridge: Harvard University Press.

SCHENDEL, D. E., and C. E. HOFER. (1979). *Strategic Management*. Boston: Little, Brown.

SCHERER, F. M. (1970). *Industrial Market Structure and Economic Performance*. Chicago: Rand McNally.

SCHERER, F. M. (1986). "Mergers, Sell-Offs and Managerial Behavior." In *The Economics of Strategic Planning*, edited by L. G. Thomas, 143–170. Lexington, MA: Lexington Books.

SCHERER, F. M. (1988). "Corporate Takeovers: The Efficiency Arguments." *Journal of Economic Perspectives* 2:69–82.

SCHILIT, W. K. (1987). "An Examination of the Influence of Middle-Level Managers in Formulating and Implementing Strategic Decisions." *Journal of Management Studies* 24:271–294.

SCHIPPER, K., and A. SMITH. (1983). "Effects of Recontracting on Shareholder

Wealth: The Case of Voluntary Spin-Offs." *Journal of Financial Economics* 12:437–467.

SCHIPPER, K., and R. THOMPSON. (1983). "Evidence on the Capitalized Value of Merger Activity for Acquiring Firms." *Journal of Financial Economics* 11:85–119.

SCHNEIDER, S. C., and DUNBAR, R. L. M. (1987). "Takeover Attempts: What Does the Language Tell Us?" Unpublished manuscript, INSEAD.

SCHWEIGER, D. M., and A. S. DENISI. (1987). "The Effects of Communication with Employees Following a Merger: A Longitudinal Field Experiment." Paper presented at the annual meeting of the Academy of Management, New Orleans.

SCHWEIGER, D., and J. WALSH. (1990). "Mergers and Acquisitions: An Interdisciplinary View." In *Research in Personnel and Human Resource Management*, edited by K. M. Rowland and G. R. Ferris, 41–107. Greenwich, CT: Jai Press.

SCHWENK C., and R. COSIER. (1980). "Effects of the Expert, Devil's Advocate, and Dialectical Inquiry Methods on Prediction Performance." *Organizational Behavior and Human Performance* 26:409–423.

SEARBY, F. W. (1969). "Control Post Merger Change." *Harvard Business Review* (September–October):4–12.

SELZNICK, P. (1957). *Leadership in Administration.* Evanston, IL: Row, Peterson.

SETH, A. (1990). "Value Creation in Acquisitions: A Re-examination of Performance Issues." *Strategic Management Journal* 11:99–115.

SHANLEY, M. (1987). "Post Acquisition Management Approaches: An Exploratory Study." Doctoral diss., Wharton School, University of Pennsylvania.

SHARPE, W. F. (1964). "Capital Assets Prices: A Theory of Market Equilibrium Under Conditions of Risk." *Journal of Finance* 19:425–442.

SHELTON, L. M. (1988). "Strategic Business Fits and Corporate Acquisition: Empirical Evidence." *Strategic Management Journal* (9):279–288.

SHIRLEY, R. C. (1973). "Analysis of Employee and Physician Attitudes Toward Hospital Mergers." *Academy of Management Journal* (16):465–480.

SHIRLEY, R. C. (1977). "The Human Side of Merger Planning." *Long Range Planning* 10:35–39.

SHLEIFER, A., AND L. H. SUMMERS. (1988). "Break of Trust in Hostile Takeovers." In *Corporate Takeovers: Causes and Consequences,* edited by A. J. Auerbach, 333–356. Chicago: University of Chicago Press.

SHLEIFER, A., and R. W. VISHNY. (1988a). "Management Buyouts as a Response to Market Pressure." In *Mergers and Acquisitions,* edited by A. J. Auerbach, 87–102. Chicago: University of Chicago Press.

SHLEIFER, A., and R. W. VISHNY. (1988b). "Managerial Entrenchment." Working Paper, University of Chicago.

SHLEIFER, A., and R. W. VISHNY. (1988c). "Value Maximization and the Acquisition Process." *Journal of Economic Perspectives* 2:7–20.

SHUKLA, R. K. (1982). "Influence of Power Bases in Organizational Decision Making: A Contingency Model." *Decision Sciences* 13:450–470.

SIEHL, C., G. LEDFORD, R. SILVERMAN, and P. FAY. (1988). "Preventing Culture Clashes From Botching a Merger." *Acquisitions Monthly* (March–April):51–57.

SIEHL, C., D. SMITH, and A. OMURA. (1990). "After the Merger: Should Executives Stay or Go?" *Academy of Management Executive* 4:50–60.

SIMON, H. (1976). *Administrative Behavior,* 3d ed. New York: Free Press.

SIMON, H. A. (1987). "Making Management Decisions: The Role of Intuition and Emotion." *Academy of Management Executive* 1:57–64.

SINETAR, M. (1981). "Mergers, Morale and Productivity." *Personnel Journal* (November):863–867.

SINGH, H., and C. A. MONTGOMERY. (1987). "Corporate Acquisition Strategies and Economic Performance." *Strategic Management Journal* 8:377–386.

SITKIN, S., and M. BOEHM. (1984). "Structural Relations in Organizations: On the Relationship Between Behavior, Beliefs and Formal Structure." Working Paper, Stanford University, Graduate School of Business.

SLATER, R. (1987). *The Titans of Takeover.* New York: Prentice-Hall.

SLUTSKER, G. (1988). "Charles Wang and His Thundering Nerds." *Forbes,* July 11, 118–124.

SOUDER, W. S., and A. K. CHAKRABARTI. (1984). "Acquisitions: Do They Really Work Out?" *Interfaces* 14 (July–August):41–47.

STARBUCK, W. H. (1965). "Organizational Growth and Development." In *Handbook of Organizations,* edited by J. G. March, 451–533. Chicago, IL: Rand McNally College Publishing Company.

STAW, B. M. (1976). "Knee-Deep in the Big Muddy: A Study of Escalating Commitment to a Chosen Course of Action." *Organizational Behavior and Human Performance* 16:27–44.

STAW, B. M. (1981). "The Escalation of Commitment to a Course of Action." *Academy of Management Review* 6:577–587.

STAW, B. M., and J. ROSS. (1978). "Commitment to a Policy Decision: A Multi-theoretical Perspective." *Administrative Science Quarterly* 23:40–64.

STAW, B. M., and J. ROSS. (1987). "Knowing When to Pull the Plug." *Harvard Business Review* (March–April):68–74.

STAW, B. M., L. E. SANDELANDS, and J. E. DUTTON (1981). "Threat-Rigidity Effects in Organizational Behavior: A Multilevel Analysis." *Administrative Science Quarterly* 26:501–524.

STIGLER, G. (1950). "Monopoly and Oligopoly by Merger." *American Economic Review* (May):23–24.

STINCHCOMBE, A. (1965). "Social Structure and Organizations." In *Handbook of Organizations,* edited by J. G. March, 142–193. Chicago: Rand McNally.

STOBAUGH, R. B., M. A. AMSALEM, and L. T. WELLS. (1984). *Technology Crossing Borders: The Choice, Transfer, and Management of International Flows.* Boston: Harvard Business School Press.

SUMMER, C. E. (1980). *Strategic Behavior in Business and Government.* Boston: Little, Brown.

SUTTON, R. I. (1983). "Managing Organizational Death." *Human Resource Management* (22):391–412.

TAGGART, R. A., JR. (1988). "The Growth of the 'Junk' Bond Market and Its Role in Financing Takeovers." In *Mergers and Acquisitions,* edited by A. J. Auerbach, 5–24. Chicago: University of Chicago Press.

TEECE, D. (1980). "Economies of Scope and the Scope of the Enterprise." *Journal of Economic Behavior and Organization* 1:223–247.

TEECE, D. (1982). "Towards an Economic Theory of the Multiproduct Firm." *Journal of Economic Behavior and Organization* 3:38–63.

TEHRANIAN, H., and J. F. WAEGLIAN. (1985). "Market Reaction to Short Term Executive Compensation Plan Adoption." *Journal of Accounting and Economics* 7:131–144.

THOMPSON, J. D. (1967). *Organizations in Action.* New York: McGraw-Hill.

THOMPSON, K. (1980). "Organizations as Constructions of Social Reality." In *Control and Ideology in Organizations,* edited by G. Salaman and K. Thompson, 216–236. Cambridge: MIT Press.

THORELLI, H. B. (1986). "Networks: Between Markets and Hierarchies." *Strategic Management Journal* 7:37–51.

TICHY, N. M. (1981). "Networks in Organization." In *Handbook of Organizational Design,* edited by P. C. Nystrom and W. H. Starbuck, vol. 2:225–249. New York: Oxford University Press.

TICHY, N. M., AND D. O. ULRICH. (1984). "The Leadership Challenge—A Call for the Transformational Leader." *Sloan Management Review* 3:59–68.

TREGOE, B. B., and J. W. ZIMMERMANN. (1980). *Top Management Strategy: What It Is and How to Make it Work.* New York: Simon and Schuster.

TUSHMAN, M. L., and R. KATZ. (1980). "External Communication and Project Performance: An Investigation into the Role of Gatekeepers." *Management of Science* 26:1071–1085.

TUSHMAN, M. L., and E. ROMANELLI. (1983). "Uncertainty, Social Location and Influence in Decision Making: A Sociometric Analysis." *Management Science* 29:12–23.

TUSHMAN, M. L., and T. J. SCANLAN. (1981). "Boundary Spanning Individuals:

Their Role in Information Transfer and Their Antecedents." *Academy of Management Journal* 24:289–305.

Tversky, A., and D. Kahneman. (1979). "The Framing of Divisions and the Rationality of Choice." *Science* 211:453–458.

Uyterhoeven, H. E. R. (1972). "General Managers in the Middle." *Harvard Business Review* (March–April):75–85.

Van de Ven, A. H., and A. L. Delbecq. (1974). "The Effectiveness of Nominal, Delphi, and Interacting Group Decision-Making Processes." *Academy of Management Journal* 17:605–621.

Van Horne, J. C. (1977). *Financial Management and Policy*, 4th ed. Englewood Cliffs, NJ: Prentice-Hall.

Victor, B., and R. S. Blackburn. (1987). "Interdependence: An Alternative Conceptualization." *Academy of Management Review* 12:486–498.

von Neumann, J., and O. Morgenstern. (1947). *Theory of Games and Economic Behavior*. Princeton: Princeton University Press.

Wallace, A. (1988). "A Bruising Battle Over Bonds." *New York Times*. November, 27, p. 51.

Walsh, J. P. (1988). "Top Management Turnover Following Mergers and Acquisitions." *Strategic Management Journal* 9:173–183.

Walter, G. A. (1985). "Culture Collisions in Mergers and Acquisitions." In *Organizational Culture*, edited by P. J. Frost, L. F. Moore, M. R. Louis, and C. C. Lundberg, 301–314. Beverly Hills: Sage Publications.

Weick, K. E. (1979). *The Social Psychology of Organizing*, 2d ed. Reading, MA: Addison-Wesley.

Wernerfeldt, B. (1984). "A Resource-based View of the Firm." *Strategic Management Journal* 5:171–180.

Weston, J. F., and T. E. Copeland. (1986). *Managerial Finance*, 8th ed. Hinsdale, IL: Dryden Press, CBS Publishing Japan, Ltd.

Wicker, A. W., and C. E. Kauma. (1974). "Effects of a Merger of a Small and Large Organization on Members' Behaviors and Experiences." *Journal of Applied Psychology* 59:24–30.

Williamson, O. E. (1975). *Markets and Hierarchies: Analysis and Antitrust Implications*. New York: Free Press.

Williamson, O. E. (1979). "Transaction Cost Economics: The Governance of Contractual Relations." *Journal of Law and Economics* 22:233–261.

Wolf, B. N. (1975). "Size and Profitability Among U.S. Manufacturing Firms: Multi-National versus Primarily Domestic Firms." *Journal of Economics and Business* (28):15–22.

Wolf, B. N. (1977). "Industrial Diversification and Internationalization: Some Empirical Evidence." *Journal of Industrial Economics* (26):177–191.

WRAPP, H. E. (1967). "Good Managers Don't Make Policy Decisions." *Harvard Business Review* (September–October):91–99.

WRIGLEY, L. (1970): "Divisional Autonomy and Diversification." Doctoral dissertation. Boston: Harvard Business School.

YIN, R. K. (1984). *Case Study Research: Design and Methods.* Beverly Hills: Sage Publications.

ZUCKER, L. G. (1983). "Organizations as Institutions." *Research in the Sociology of Organizations* 2:1–47.

Author Index

399

Subject Index